T0369432

On Wings of Change

A Return to the Unconquered Hearts

by

Ruby H Happel-Holtz

Order this book online at www.trafford.com
or email orders@trafford.com

Most Trafford titles are also available at major online book retailers.

Printed in Victoria, BC, Canada.

ISBN: 978-1-4251-7847-5 (sc)
ISBN: 978-1-4251-7848-2 (hc)
ISBN: 978-1-4251-7849-9 (eb)

Our mission is to efficiently provide the world's finest, most comprehensive book publishing service, enabling every author to experience success. To find out how to publish your book, your way, and have it available worldwide, visit us online at www.trafford.com

Trafford rev. 11/03/09

Trafford PUBLISHING® **www.trafford.com**

North America & international
toll-free: 1 888 232 4444 (USA & Canada)
phone: 250 383 6864 • fax: 812 355 4082

I owe many people my gratitude and thanks but first and foremost i must thank the creator for giving me what talent i have, and the ability to tell my people's story.

My thanks and appreciation goes first to my husband, Charles E. Holtz for his interest and belief in this endeavor. I also thank him for his patience, his help, and the freedom to pursue my work.

My many, many thanks must go to my many friends, and especially to my Indian brother and sister, Alan Roebuck and Nina Weller-Roebuck. It is their faith and work that has helped me to finally finish this sequel. Also, I must thank Jean Adams and the Amargosa Library for all thier help, and in suplying some of the tools that i needed to successfully work at my own speed.

I must not forget to thank my many, many readers who have continuously asked for this sequel to the original book "The Unconquered Hearts."

Last but certainly not least, I must thank my family for their undaunted spirits and their perserverence in upholding the Blackfeet and Cherokee ways, as taught to us by our Grandmothers and Grandfathers.

A

My dedication to My Readers

I shall seek knowledge when my mind no longer has the words,

I shall offer my spirit to my work when words fail me,

I shall humble my soul before the Great Mystery, and,

I shall call upon my Grandmothers and Grandfathers to educate me

In this endeavor, to seek knowledge of their way of life, as known only to them

Ruby H. Happel-Holtz
(Whispering Winds White feather)

PREFACE I

THE BLACKFEET

THE BLACKFEET INDIANS OF THE NORTHWESTERN PLAINS IN THE UNITED STATES AND CANADA WERE KNOWN AS THE DOMINEERING MILITARY POWER ON THE PLAINS.

Feared by the neighboring tribes and enemies of white trappers, they were a nomadic people whose basic food and clothing resources was the buffalo. The Blackfeet and other tribes were reduced to poverty and starvation, by the reckless extermination of them by Indians and whites alike.

The Blackfeet were and are self-reliant forward looking people who through travels to other tribes as far south as Texas, readily borrowed and adapted customs which could help them in their daily lives. Even some of the white's ways were found acceptable, but they stubbornly held on to their traditional culture.

For centuries the Blackfeet have been known to white men by separate names. They are Pikuni, or Piegan, pronounced 'pagan', the Kainah, or Blood, and the Sisika.

The late noted author, Clark Wissler, who had lived amongst them and studied the Native American wrote, "The Blackfeet Indians were on the Plains a long time before the discovery of

America." They were introduced to the horse by the Shoshonis in the 1730's which they would later refer to as "elk dog", and also obtained their first guns from these Indians.

Some people believe that the Blackfeet migrated from the Eastern part of the United States and Canada, but they strongly deny that their forefathers crossed over the Bering Strait from another country. They strongly believe that they have always existed in North America.

Blackfeet men on the average were tall (5'11" to over 6ft), well proportioned, muscular with manly features and intelligent countenances. Their eyes were large, black and piercing, noses full and straight, teeth white and regular, hair long, straight and black. Their faces were smooth and became that way from the plucking of hair from their faces beginning at a very early age.

Blackfeet women were known for their extremely attractive features, and quick wit. They bore their bodies regally and wore their hair long and loose. In later years the mature married woman would braid or twist their hair, crossing it in back of their head, or coil it into buns and place it behind their ears. This style of hair denoted that the woman was married and not available.

The Blackfeet's main source of food and other supplies was the great buffalo that roamed the Northwestern Plains in huge herds. Their hides furnished the covering of their home, the tepee. The Blackfeet almost always decorated tepees on the outside and some also decorated their home on the inside, on a lining. This lining further helped keep the cold out in the long hard winters. Their favorite symbols were the buffalo, the mighty eagle, bears and other animals and birds. The bases of the tepee were often decorated in large circles and squares. Some would be decorated with many stars, the moon and other symbols depicting Mother Earth, randomly done. In order to paint ones tepee one must get permission from the Sharman or the Chief of their clan to do so. This was usually done by a talented male, but sometimes a woman was given this privilege.

The Blackfeet tribes of Montana had many Chiefs. Two of these were the Civil Chief and the War Chief. Both of these Chiefs had limited authority and remained a Chief only by the consent, and the will of the people. The "Head Chief" of the Blackfoot extended his wealth to his followers who were less fortunate. This generosity was a must to maintain his position of honor.

The Blackfeet traditions were upheld in the strictest sense:

First cousins could not marry,

Pregnancy in women before marriage was disgraceful,

Fidelity, and honesty were a must,

Arguments or other disputes were settled by the men's societies,

Murder or theft was not common, but if it did happen these deeds were also taken care of by the men's societies.

Little boys were taught by their grandfathers, fathers, and uncles. Little girls were taught by their grandmothers, mothers, and aunts. Death of a loved one in one's tepee resulted in the women slashing their legs and cutting off their hair, and began a long mourning period, visiting their loved one's burial site every day, and singing mournful songs.

Little boys and girls were taught to sit on a horse usually by the time they were five or six years of age. By the age of ten, little boys were instructed in keeping the family's horse herd, taking them to pasture, and to water every morning, and repeating this every night.

The Blackfeet were astute, providing for their families. Many women rode with their men on these long hunts, cleaning and cutting up the meats, and preparing the hides.

The Blackfeet were not the stoic Indian as pictured in the movies, but were fun loving people who enjoyed stories, practical jokes, horse racing, and other sports. They like to gamble on the horse races and other games, eagerly waging their bets. Traditional raids were mostly for horses and for young warriors to seek out and show their courage; the "counting of the coup."

The Blackfeet took great pride in their horsemanship, and later in their ranches. Their most prized possessions were their families, and in earlier days they would fight to the death to protect their women and children.

The discovery of gold on their lands soon brought the European whites (long knives), and their diseases with them. Smallpox nearly wiped out the Blackfeet, and did destroy other tribes. As the whites began arriving in Blackfeet country the Blackfeet were very curious. This curiosity frightened the whites and combat would ensue. The whites had been brain washed to think that all Indians were savages and only a dead Indian was a good Indian. The miners that came into their country were sometimes despicable men, and never tried to make friends or tried to understand them. The winters were harsh and food was not plentiful for these boisterous men, and many of these men survived because the Indians gave them their food. Little Dog of the Piegans befriended these whites, and kept many of them from starving. It is said that he met his death, because of his friendliness, at the hands of his own people.

Photo lot 25/Plains/Blackfoot/INV 02823800; no neg. #

The last Head Chief, White Calf of the Piegans, was the father of many children. Possible the most famous of these children was Two Guns, who accompanied his father on several trips to Washington. Two Guns would later become a successful rancher in Cut Bank, Montana. His younger brother, No Guns, was my Great Great Grandfather. He was a great hunter and counted many coups as a young man because he was fearless. He hated war, and he hated the infiltration of the many whites who with the help of the U.S. Government were taking more and more of their hunting lands. Most of all he hated that his father ceded more and more of their land to the government, pushing them farther and farther onto the worst lands that would become their Reserve.

The thought of being kept on a reservation was just more than he could tolerate, so he finally broke with his father's clan. Many of the young and old braves were in sympathy with No Guns, and made him their new Chief, and renamed him White Feather. They chose this name because he always wore one feather in his beautiful black hair. White Feather was not only a fearless hunter, but a very tall handsome man. He was also much lighter in skin than his siblings, and had been trained in the missionary schools that his father White Calf, had allowed on the lands.

After the riff with his father, and being chosen by his followers as their Chief, White Feather knew that he needed the guidance of the Great Spirit. He chose his beautiful Rocky Mountains to seek his vision for his people. This vision would lead him to search for a boyhood friend and his brother in the camp of the Sioux. He would ultimately be caught up in the struggle of the Indians against the 7th Calvary.

White Feather White Calf was a valiant soul, always ready to help everyone who needed it. He was a loving husband and father, a great and generous Chief, but above all, he was an Unconquered Heart, whose last thought in life was for his family's survival.

Their path to freedom is chronicled in the book entitled "The Unconquered Hearts" by this Author.

PREFACE II

IRELAND

A little bit of the struggle in Ireland must be included as part of the Preface, as well as the removal of the Indians of the East and Southeastern part of the United States, and more specifically, the Cherokees. The main reason for this is to address the paternal side of the Author's family heritage. The Author's maternal side, the Blackfoot Indians of Montana was well covered in the original book "The Unconquered Hearts." Only a thumbnail sketch will be included here in the sequel.

First, let's look at the Irish.

The trouble between Ireland and Britain began as early as the 1160's and 1170's when the Normans first arrived in that country. They arrived with the intention of making feudal domains and impose an alien ruling class upon the indigenous population. This was much the same as to what happened between the Europeans and Indians here in America.

The Normans, with the Tudor and Stuart Plantations, the imbalance of the advantaged, and the disadvantaged obtained by the Irish, resulted from the Act of the Union in 1800. This left huge gaps (probably for all time), of how the Irish feel about the British involvement in their county. Even though there has been turmoil in the country of Ireland, one thought to keep in mind is "The Irish have never been conquered, regardless of all the fighting." The Normans took over the Irish land and the Irish Princes moved away, while lesser Chieftans simply drove their cattle into the woods and hills. They lived side by side – Normans cultivating lower grounds and the Irish keeping land 600 ft. above sea level, especially in the rough high country of the west. They lived there as they had lived, taking their cattle to the higher mountains in the summer and setting up camps called "booleys" in the open air. Irish kings dined out of doors, sitting at trestle tables with their servants. This lack of class distinction horrified the Normans.

Edward I, succeeded his father Henry VII in 1272, and proceeded to milk the country of the Irish and the Normans dry, in order to build castles. Edward wanted to retain his magnificent style of court which would required huge sums of money. He sent John Wogan to Ireland to raise both men and money. He would also send 3200 men to the Scottish Wars in 1296, and again in 1300, and 1301 to fight.

This plundering of men and resources would cease under Edward II's rule, but the Irish and the Scott's together moved against Edward II. In 1317, Edward and his brother Bruce fell upon the Irish and burned their crops, drove off their cattle to show their authority, and then turned their anger on the manors, leaving misery and starvation behind them. Finally realizing that Ireland was almost gone, the English government provided funds, turning Ireland from an asset to a liability. The Scotts then defeated and killed Edward II, causing the carnage of Ireland to begin.

The English Lords and Anglo Clerics said to the Nation, "It is no more of a sin to kill an Irishman or woman, than to kill a dog", according to a man whose name was Kilkenney.

Also it was said that an attack on the native race was to preserve cultural identity and loyalty to their conquerors. It would also prevent them from being assimilated, or being swamped by a far more numerous people. It was also to help children among the Irish, especially to sponsor children for baptism. The English were not to keep minstrels, poets, storytellers, etc. or sell them food, horses, or armor in time of war. People of English decent who took on any Irish ways were referred to as "English Degenerates."

Early Ireland had women priests in the Irish Catholic Church, but these women were soon banned from their positions. After 1720, Catholic Priests were finally allowed by the ruling of the Protestants, which had heretofore been banned, were again allowed to hold positions. The Catholic Priests had to register with the government, and with that, they became known as the 3rd religious group.

Protestants of the Ascendancy belonged to the Established Church of Ireland, but the descendants were called Presbyterians. They could not be part of politics or local government. They had no vote, and could not belong to a Corporation. After the Pearl Laws, they were much worse off in many ways than the Catholic priests. The priests suffered less humiliation, though often persecuted, while the Presbyterians were not. Presbyterians were seen as a threat to the Protestants who were mostly Scotts, and were mostly tough people who had come to Ireland for the opportunities they could find. They saw an advantage to acquiring cheap farms, and businesses, so not all shops in Londonberry and Belfast, were kept by the Presbyterians.

Then there were the Coiters which were the very poor Catholics who were seeking out a pitiful living on rented small parcels of land from the Protestants. These people were perhaps the most trampled on by the British. Elite or not, the Black Death (Plague) made no distinction of class and killed 40% of the English, and left the early Irish full of it, but surviving. This left 60% of the entire Nation to the Irish.

Henry VIII became a "Protestant of the POPE" along with Martin Luther in Germany, which had been begun by Jan Jus

(Bohemia) in 1517. They called for more teachings of the bible, and less interference by the priests, between man and God. The church had accused them of being heretics and burned them at the stake.

After reading "The Obedience of Christian Man", Henry VIII adopted the book and unwillingly led his country into Protestantism. He also adopted Thomas Crammer who favored his "Annulment" to Catherine, and made him the Archbishop of Canterbury.

In 1608 – 09 the Government of England, though frightened of it, implemented and published the Articles of Plantation which removed most Irish to specially designated areas, (not unlike the Native Americans to Reservations), leaving 500,000 acres of good cultivating land, which was about 1/4 of the whole to be taken as plantations.

English and Scottish land undertakers and senior grantees each received 2000 acres, and were to build a castle with a brawn or fortified enclosure. Servitors or the army were to receive 1400 acres with which to build a brick or stone house. Another category; the deserving Irish were to have 1000 acres each.

Undertakers and servitors had to take an oath of Supremacy and were therefore Protestants. They were not to take Irish tenants, but to clear off the land and bring in planters, preferably Scotts. However, the Scotts, nor the English, showed an eagerness to settle amongst the wild and dangerous Irish. The greedy Undertakers chose to ignore the Article of Plantation and proceeded to grab the land of the Irish tenants.

In 1696 England became so jealous of Ireland they forbid direct import of goods from America to Ireland. They decreed that imported goods had to enter and leave from a British port, causing the goods to be prohibitively expensive.

Next the English attacked the Irish woolen industry, even though it was tiny in comparison to England's. The English manufacturers had grown too jealous and wanted it taxed out of existence.

The Boston Tea Party had a big influence on England because the Irish Catholics and Protestants understood the "taxation without representation." England soon took note of the unrest and gave easing of fishing rights, navigation rights, relief for Catholics, and removed the sacramental test to Presbyterians.

Most important, however, was to allow the Irish to raise a Protestant Militia, with a newly formed militia of 80,000 by the year 1779. Then England had to allow the Irish to trade in goods, such as woolens, and to charge duty and trade freely with any country. It was at this time they too won their freedom in a triumphant speech given by Henry Gratten.

The great potato and other famines, however, would send droves and droves of the Irish people to seek refuge in the new country of America. Entering at the port of New York, most stayed in that area until the Great Land Rush. The land rush gave many an Irishman and his family, a fresh start in the new country.

Like many other people the great new frontier of the West beckoned the Irish and the Scotts, and intermarriage with the Native Americans. They could easily identify with the Indians and their struggles with the U.S. Government; for they had suffered much of the same under English rule.

PREFACE III

THE BEGINNING OF THE END; CHEROKEES AND OTHER TRIBES REMOVAL

First it was the Creeks of Georgia and Alabama in 1813. In the month of the summer moon the removal of the Creeks from their land began. They were forced out of their homes and lands by the Americans, under orders from the government of President Monroe and General Andrew Jackson. By 1819, Cherokee Chief Tahlonteskee and his followers under General William Clark's order, gathered Osage Chiefs, living in the vicinity of the Arkansas River, and supplied them with goods. The Osages were to share their country with a small band of Cherokees. To make this happen, the Osages were supplied with an abundance of whiskey, shiny new pots and pans, knives and other goods to make this deal palatable. Under this influence, the Osages signed away what would become most of Arkansas and a large portion of Missouri.

Tahlonteskee was thrilled with the new land filled with prairie chickens, buffalo herds, hackberries, golden eagles and catfish. The evening star Nahquisi hung low in the night sky as the coyotes howled. It was a good country he argued to himself as he gazed on the long grasses and blossoming clover fields. There seemed to be plenty of food, he thought, as he gazed upon the elk herds, jackrabbits, prairie dogs and numerous other animals that roamed there. The Osages; however, were soon regretting the bargain they had made with General Clark, for everywhere one looked, the white hunters were coming into to the grasslands beginning their wholesale extermination of their animals. The balance of the Cherokee Nation; however, stubbornly clung to their Appalachian villages. The Osages also grew more and more restless with the white hunters and the Cherokees. Their Chief Pawkuska (White Hair), started raiding the Cherokee villages, stealing and sometimes murdering the Cherokee families. On a trip to Prairie du Chien on the Mississippi to get their customary government presents, (which were really bribes for peace), they found them to be unusually meager. This incensed the Osages, but they were even more aggravated on their return home when vengeance seeking Cherokees shot nine or ten of their party. Only Clement and Tellai escaped. The two tribes of Osages and Cherokees were vastly different. The Cherokees lived in well built houses and had very productive farms. The Osages were horsemen who wandered the Plains in resplendent head dresses of feathers, and like other Plains Indians, the buffalo supplied their every need.

Major William Lovely had a proposition for the Osages that the Federal Government would pay all fines they had incurred on raids of the Cherokee villages, if they would cede all the country that lay between the Cherokees and the Verdigris River, and bordered on the south by the Arkansas River.

The government became overly enthused to think they had at last a plan that would rid the Cherokees left in the East. They were treated by the commission, of which one was Andrew Jackson. Jackson, or "Old Hickory" was a hero of the small farmers and trades people. He immediately started rounding up all the Cherokees he could find at Calhoun, Tennessee. The

Indians there were shocked at his demands, "GIVE UP ALL THEIR LAND EAST OF THE MISSISSIPPI". The Cherokees swore they would not give up their homes but Jackson found two half-breeds whom he could corrupt. Grandly they signed a treaty and Jackson quickly forwarded it to Washington. Since the signers were from the Arkansas country, they had nothing to lose. Jackson was proud of his accomplishment even though he knew it did not represent the Cherokee Nation. He advised the government, "We were compelled to promise to John D. Chisholm the sum of one thousand dollars to stop his mouth and obtain his consent; ... without this we could not have gotten the national relinquishment. In the course of the conference we were obliged to promise the chiefs from Arkansas one hundred dollars each, for their expenses, in coming here, and to three other influential chiefs the sum of one hundred dollars." It was 1813 and the Moon of the Running Sap.

Out of the Shawnees in Ohio came Tecumtha urging American Indians to declare for the British, who were at war with the United States. He urged them to push out the rude settlers who thought they were the only Americans that mattered. He called on the Shawnee Beavers, the O'Potawatomis, the Miami Panthers, the Ottawa Foxes, the Miami Lynexes, the Kickapoo Beavers, and the Winnebago Wolves, to lift up their hatchets, knives and rifles against their foe; "for they are weak". He wanted to drive all the whites back across the "Stinking Lake". His brother Tenskwatawe shouted and ordered his red brothers to rise up against the white man from over the water, and then they could deal with the British.

The oratories of vengeance dividing tribes into hostile factions of moderate and fanatics now were more bitter than the Southern Creeks (so called by the whites). This name was given to them because most of the sub-tribes that comprised these nations lived on rivers and streams, and owned sprawling fertile lands in Georgia and Alabama, and belonged traditionally to the Creeks. Since many Creek women had married white traders with names like Weatherford, McGillivary, Farquharson and McIntosh, keeping their peach orchards and livestock was like the air they breathed.

All these people were horrified at the white invaders that were killing the game off, not only for food, but for fur too. Some of the Creeks were fatalists for they had been pushed back from the Atlantic, so they sort of said, "what will be, will be".

Some of the Creeks who were not fatalists were not so inclined, and gave the young Creek Braves red sticks to dance with, and were told the red sticks would protect them. As they danced and stomped their feet, they prophesied miracles, and soon after in a rapid succession came a comet, a meteor shower, and then a mild earthquake. The hot headed warriors believed all that Tecumtha had said. Luimbi Chali, and Red Eagle had misgivings that the red sticks were invulnerable, and wondered why the whites and the Indians couldn't all live together.

Red Eagle was born Bill Weatherford with a Creek mother whose maiden name was Tait, but Red Eagle belonged to the Creeks. He made a well-worn path through the forests to Pensacola, and to Mabila on the Natchez River (called Mobile by the French). Red Eagle admired the efficiency of the white civilization, and found the Religion and Dancing Lake excessive. He believed the invincibility of the ones who carried the red sticks, grotesque.

Andrew Jackson was known to the Creeks as Jacksa Chule Harjo (Jackson old and fierce). Neighboring Choctaws called him the devil.

On July 26th, Colonel Caller's party was joined by more rag-tagged Creeks ready if the command came from a mixed blood Creek, who was in charge, gave it. His name was Devon Badley, who had been educated in Philadelphia. On July 27th, a hot and sticky day as only the south can be, Peter McQueen's Creeks were returning from Pensacola with bright cloth for the women, metal fishing hooks, hunting knives, and British cookware that had replaced Creek pottery. Just before noon McQueen's party stopped at Burnt Corn Creek to eat the game they had caught. The Americans fell upon them. Screeching and yelling they forced the Indians to plunge into the nearby river. The Americans then turned their horse packs loose and plundered the wares that had been purchased for Panton Leslie and Company. They then headed down the Alabama River, with only a few of the Indians pursuing them. The militiamen were so greedy for the wares and seeing no other pursuers, thought they were victorious. The remaining Creek Indians disappeared into a nearby swamp, only to reappear brandishing their guns and ran into a tall cluster of reeds and began shooting the whites. The whites were still standing in an open field but soon disappeared into the saw palmettos thickets, leaving their Colonel Caller behind. He was found 15 days later nearly starved to death.

The Indians having won this battle soon began chanting and drumming throughout the Creek towns of Houhklewaula, Sawanogee, Mooklausa, Woccocaw, Fooschatshge, Eufaula, and Hookeholoodee, throughout the warm summer nights, leaving fear in the hearts and minds of the whites.

A mile east of Alabama, on cypress studded Lake Tensaw, the settlers under Samuel Mims erected a stockade with portholes in the fence. They put up gates off the east and west side, and erected a blockhouse in the Southwest corner. The settlers did not wait for it to be finished before they began pouring in with their featherbeds, spinning wheels, cookware, dogs and dried meat. Generally there was a lack of concern for anything except space inside the stockade. Major Daniel Beasley arrived to take charge and found a general malaise with the 553 people jostling each other around. He immediately ordered two more blockhouses be built for the huge mixture of civilians, whites, half-bloods, officers, recruits, black slaves, and many bedraggled women. It was a very hot and steamy climate in this swamp country with stealthy alligators slithering silently through the dark waters looking for anything edible. In this steaming, over crowded situation, the stockades soon became racked with much sickness. Malaria and dysentery being much in evidence, with cholera soon to follow.

Orders were received by Peter McQueen, the leader at Pensacola, from the Spanish and the British, to "Fight the Americans." Chief Red Eagle pondered the message that all would be well if the fight proved too much for them. As always Red Eagle wore two Eagle feathers in his long black hair. His father was a white Georgian but his mother was a mixture of Creek, French and Scottish. He himself had chosen his Creek identity, in opposition to his brother, John Weatherford, who considered himself white. Red Eagle's half brother, David Tait was a red stick dancer. His sister and her sons were in the war party too, unlike her husband who had run away.

Inside the fort on August 29th two young blacks were ordered to mind cattle in a nearby field. But shortly after passing through the gate, they ran back frightened to death, stuttering that they had seen twenty four Indians in War Paint. The officers rode out but saw no evidence of the enemy. At sunset the blacks were dragged back to Ft. Mims and severally beaten until their backs were striped with blood. The owner of the blacks would not hear of his slaves being beaten for lying, so he was ordered by Major Beasley to leave the fort by 10:00 on the next morning. By this time the two beaten slaves had been sent out to tend the cattle, and again they saw a large group of Indians in the forest. They decided not to go back to the fort with their swollen backs, so they fled to a distant settlement. The slave owner was tied to the stockade in the hot sun and waited to be beaten himself. He was laughed at and ridiculed by card playing people and children, while the sick unnoticed, moaned for help.

Outside the fort Red Eagle and 1000 Red Sticks waited in the enclosed swamps, painted with legs of yellow and faces of black. They were ready for war! At noon at the sound of the fort's bell call to the soldiers for lunch, they swooped down on the fort with a massive whoop. The gate was wide open and the Red Sticks felled Beasley, leaving him to crawl behind the gate and die. Red Eagle tried to hold his warriors back to no avail. He roared at them for caution, "you are not invisible!" They did not listen but rushed on, killing soldiers, settlers, blacks, women and children, with their guns and tomahawks. Outside the fort Indian prophets danced while the others set fire to the main buildings and sheds. A Spaniard knelt and crossed himself, while Samuel Mills screamed, "Oh, God I'm a dead man!" A black slave offered up a white child to save himself, but to no avail.

The stench of Fort Mims was stifling as the Indians collected what booty they could carry, and stepped silently back into the forest as the cotton gin lit up the sky, with it's smoke and flames. The Red Stick's warriors slept through it all in their small camp, but Red Eagle did not. He woke his warriors early in the fogged-in morning and ordered them to bury the Fort Mims dead. Obeying their leader, they went quietly about laying them between rows of potatoes and covering them with loose dirt from the breast of Alabama, and leaves of the potatoes. All of this took place while their Indian brothers moaned from their pain and begged to be returned to their homes. Some never made it past Burnt Creek before they collapsed.

One Red Stick warrior named Sanota hid in the forest with a white woman he had rescued from Fort Mims. She had befriended him earlier, so when he saw her and her children trying to escape the fire that was raging through the fort, her would-be assassin shielded her from the warriors, saying he wanted the family for slaves. Weeks, which faded into moths, he hunted for game for the little family until they were strong enough to be taken to another white settlement. Sanota then faded back into the forest wilderness from which he had come, to join his brother warriors.

Early in September in Nashville, Tennessee, Andrew Jackson (Jacksa Chula Harjo) lay on his death bed. He not only had a bleeding wound from dueling, but his left shoulder had been shattered by a bullet with another embedded in the upper bone of his left arm. Doctors in frock coats huddled over him, sure the end was near. When Jackson rasped, "I'll keep my arms," all the doctors but one were shocked that he had understood their decision to amputate.

On September 12th he was still alive and convalescing on his own veranda of the Hermitage Plantation. This was where he received the news of the massacre by the Red Sticks, led by Red Eagle. He was horrified and demanded, "By the Eternal these people must be saved," meaning the whites. He was sitting up and roaring to the men of his regiment, "The health of your general is restored. He will command in person." He then called for his horse and swung his tall frame upon it, hell bent on riding against Red Eagle and the Red Sticks in their Moon of the Roasting Ears.

Politicians in Washington had ridiculed Jackson as a rough backwoodsman. Uncouth and wearing his hair long, tied in a queue, which hung down his back. They did acknowledge he was better at dealing with the rebellious Indians more than any one else. Out of Winchester, Virginia came another "rough backwoodsman" who prepared his regiment to march against the Creeks; his name was David Crockett.

Choctaw Chief Pushonataha joined the Creeks to fight, even though they were traditional enemies. Jackson then sent his subordinate, John Coffee, to destroy the nearby Creek town of Talluesahatachie. Coffee's force rushed at the doors of the town and killed every warrior, but noted that all the warriors fought with savage fury and met their deaths with honor. In all, 186 warriors were killed and then the soldiers turned their weapons on the women and children until the earth was bathed in their blood from the shooting and slashing. It was noted by one soldier that one "Injun Squaw" had as many as twenty balls blown through her. Davy Crockett noted, "We shot them down like dogs. Not one warrior escaped."

One of the houses had 45 people inside when Coffee's men torched it. He then stood and laughed as the air was filled with screams from the trapped Indians inside. The next day the white soldiers spent the day "eating potatoes from the house's cellars, stewed in the oil of the Indians that had burned in the house the day before." Who, I might add, were the savages?

Jackson continued on with the carnage, taking down the town of Talladego. His draftees were disgruntled at the savagery and tried mutiny, but Jackson held them at bay. As he thundered, "I'll shoot the first man who makes a move to leave." That ended all signs of the mutiny from his troops.

The Red Sticks from eight towns gathered in Artussee, on the east bank of the Calebee Creek, a sacred place known as "Beloved Ground" to the Red Sticks. Here they thought the magic sticks and the Dance of the Lake would protect them. They had no idea a bizarre turn of events of 400 friendly Indians, mostly Choctaws and some Creeks, who opposed the Red Sticks swelled Jackson's ranks under the care of a Jewish trader named Abraham Mordacai. "A queer fellow" among the Creeks, trading in the delicacy of hickory nut oil, relished by the French. This trade swelled Mordacai's riches, but his amorous pursuit of a Red Stick's wife left him with a terrible thrashing and his trading post leveled to a heap of ashes.

Recognizing Mordacai and their Creek brothers, who had burned their town of Artussee under Jackson, burned 200 Creek Indians alive, leveled all 400 buildings at Ft. Mims, Red Eagle led his warriors to the town of Euachati, the most sacred town of all. Jackson's troops swarmed around them leaving the Creeks to evacuate the wives and children to the safety of the swamps. Only when Jackson's troops failed to understand their Commander's order was this possible.

Red Eagle was held at bay, but was too fast for them when he leaped upon his gray horse and wildly rode along the banks of the Alabama River. Jackson and his cavalry were in hot pursuit. Red Eagle recognized that he was trapped, but not to be outdone or captured, he rode his horse to a high bluff above the river, and with only a slight hesitation, he and his horse flew into the air, and in slow motion floated down, down into the water below and sank beneath the waves. As incredulous as this was, Jackson's horsemen watched in total amazement. The holy ground of Ecunchate was; however, reduced to smoldering, charred ruins, but Red Eagle survived.

1814 passed with Jackson's troops searching for Red Eagle who was more determined than ever to never, never give up. Indians were pitted against Indians created by Jackson's troops as they went about laying waste to Creek towns. His determination to subjugate every red man in the United States was working. At Horseshoe Bend, Red Eagle gathered his Red Sticks together, and the militant braves from Hillabee Town, Oakshoie, Eugaulshatahee, Cauca, Hickory Ground, Fish Pond Town, and waited for Jackson and his troops. It proved useless. Jackson had been joined by a large regiment of Cherokees from Georgia and the Carolinas. These Indians has been brain washed to believe the Red Sticks were renegade outlaws, and Jackson had promised them rewards for their help and loyalty. The Red Sticks were knifed, shot and drowned in the brown waters of the Alabama. Only ten Red Sticks escaped; Red Eagle was one of them.

Try as he might, Red Eagle could not ready the warriors, for they were demoralized and their faith was gone. The Religion of Dancing Lakes, and Tecumtha's prophecies had failed them all. Red Eagle was alone to muse his position. There was only one thing to do, present himself to Jackson and beg for his remaining people to be saved.

Red Eagle arrived in the evening, after the evening meal, and suddenly accosted Jackson in front of his quarters. He was dressed in buckskin breeches and tattered moccasins, and Jackson was taken aback by the light skinned Indian.

"General Jackson, I am Bill Weatherford, and I've come to explain who I really am." Shaken by the appearance of an Indian, Jackson finally found his voice.

"Come into my quarters." It was a demand. Red Eagle followed Jackson and once inside continued to explain his presence.

"I can oppose you no longer. I have done you much injury, but I should have done you more, but my warriors were killed. I have no request for myself, but I beg you to send for the women and children of this war party that are out in the swamps. That is where they had to be driven without as much as an ear of corn. They have done no harm. Kill me instead if that is what the white people want." Jackson said not a word or answered but offered Red Eagle a glass of brandy as he studied this man whom he had ordered caught and brought in, in chains.

"You have come in on your accord, you are not in my power."

"Save the wives and children of the Creeks, and I will persuade the peace of all the Red Sticks in my Nation to lay down their arms." Red Eagle now begged for mercy. Red Eagle then downed the brandy. Jackson nodded his head as he extended his hand and Red Eagle took it, whiles studying Jackson's craggy features, then bowing, slipped silently away.

Andrew Jackson sat motionless for sometime, realizing he and the Indian had sealed the fate of the American Indian. America was angered against Red Eagle's leadership in the war. He also knew the Indians had to go. They would have to be removed to somewhere on the Western Plains, and so the removal began. Five decades later, on the grasslands and forest, near the Red and Verdigris Rivers, a Choctaw Indian named Allen Wright gave it its name. The Choctaw word 'houma' for red and 'okla' for people, became the Territory of Oklahoma before it was chartered.

ECUNCHATI was a lost land. A lost dream and became the road of horror that later would be known as the "Trail of Tears".

"It all meant nothing but move a little faster, you are too close to me." *Speckled Snake, Cherokee.*

The Creeks had dallied as an Indian State under a shrewd Chief, Alexander MacGillevray in the 1700's. He had promised land hungry Georgians that he would grant them Creek lands on the Oconee if they in turn would permit his tribe to claim all the land south of the Aitancha, but nothing came of it.

Many years later, a dashing, smooth talking William Augustus Bowles declared he was director-general of the Muskogee Creeks, and tried to form his own empire. He did cut a path through the south, ransacking the warehouses of Pontau Leslie & Company. He was captured, escaped and was captured again. He would die in prison lost in his vision of grandeur.

With the election of Thomas Jefferson to the presidency, and the Louisiana Purchase having been made, the place was now in view as to where to put the "red-skinned" savages. The long knives, however, resented moving in Indians to live beside them. "What did those ringed, streaked, spotty and speckled cattle make of the soil?" They do not till it as the Bible said, "Thou Shalt Till The Ground. This alone is human life."

By 1817, James Madison, a planter from Virginia who had once belonged to Powhaton and his allies, was now President. He confided his misgivings of the Indian removal to his friend James Monroe. "Occupancy of the Indians," James argued, "is the principle that the earth belonged to people who could make the most of it, for human use." Madison argued, "If a French peasant wanted to farm could he not be given a stretch on the Arkansas River because no one else was growing any crops there? It was not a comfortable thought for Madison as he saw that America was marching ever faster westward. Would the settlers there forget Red Eagle and Fort Mims.? If these settlers did not want land for themselves, would their children not want land? Then there was the problem of a trans-Mississippi rail west. What about the Indians who already lived there?

Under James Monroe's presidency, the Indian removal turned from a scheme to a policy. Even though he had long bouts with his conscience, by 1818 there were 6,000 Cherokees on the Arkansas.

Traders and other travelers on the frontier marveled at the Cherokee settlements as "they looked like those of white people."

At first, Monroe thought it was absurd to herd Indians onto a corner of the West. Andrew Jackson; however, did not.

So in Monroe's final address to Congress in 1825, he recommended the Removal Act of 1830, and Andrew Jackson made it policy.

Jackson became incensed with the Seminoles when he heard they were flirting with British agents that were lingering on in the Spanish Florida, which soon became embroiled in war. Jackson decided, without any evidence, that the English were plotting with the Indians. It was later proven that only one of the British was trading with them. His name was Alexander Arbuthnot.

The Seminole War was a success as well as the triumph at Horseshoe Bend. As the Cherokees watched the treaty most had opposed, they now saw it had become the law. However, in 1821 a test made in the United States Supreme Court under Justice John Marshall offered his opinion that shocked the Long Knives (whites).

The defense lawyer for the Indians was no other than constitutional lawyer Daniel Webster, helped by Senator Henry Clay. John Marshall said that they all wanted to save the redskins from degradation and extinction. The Reverend Samuel Worcester, Missionary to the Cherokees, challenged Georgia's attempt to extinguish Indian title to land in the States, and won the case before the United States Supreme Court.

By 1820 the Mississippians were impatient to get the Indians out of their state but the Choctaws remained by the graves of their dead. They still worshipped Nanah Waya, tended their land, built stout houses and mills and sent their children to mission schools.

In order to speed up the Choctaws removal, the State granted Choctaws what it called 'citizenship'. Then under this so-called citizenship, the tribal government of the Choctaws was abolished. The penalty being, should anyone that exercised the office of the Chief, minor or head man or other post of power established by tribal statures or customs of the Indians, was liable to prison and heavy fines.

When Chief Moshulatubbee heard of this he was horrified. Then he thought if this is so, then why not run for Congress? Dressed in flowing robes with silver belts and an enormous silver gorget and wielding his leadership wand of eagle feathers and a clay pipe, he campaigned trails in Mississippi. He was followed by a reporter from the national newspaper, Niles Weekly Register. The whites thought him ridiculous and laughed at him, and determined he still had to move with his tribe, for the land the Choctaws were on was matchless, and the whites wanted it.

Chief Moshulatubbee's campaign set off a civil war among the Choctaws as devastating as the one that racked the Creeks. The state threw the Choctaws country open to rivers of whisky, devastating the Indians further. In the fall of 1831 the removal began after the harvest in the old land. The Choctaws looked on their Nanah Way for the last time. Sheriffs and constables descended on them with fraudulent writs of confiscation for their goods, leaving the Choctaws outraged in their tears.

Nearly 4,000 Choctaws left Mississippi in the first wave of the removal. As winter closed in on them, their story of misery and death became the same as that of the Senecas, Delawares and Shawnees before them. One record accounted that there was "Two hundred horses that died on the road; people are dropping like flies; we are still 200 miles from the Red River; and, we have to go slow because so many are sick and dying. The weather is freezing, a heavy sleet has fallen and the old women and young children have no covering on their feet, legs or bodies, except a cotton under dress."

In 1831 and 1832, the wagon train lurched forward through the storms and floods, and soon they were ravaged by cholera, influenza and pneumonia. Doctors in the white settlements would not treat any of the Indians. Over 100 people died in five weeks and the mortality of the Choctaws was one-fifth of their total number.

And so it went, this scene was repeated over and over with more than twenty-two tribes; the Onondages, Senecas, Oneidas, Cayuaga, Osages, Piankishaws, Weas, Shawnees, Kickapoos, Delawares, Miama Eel River Indians, the Illini, Ottawes, Seminoles and on and on.

Senator Benton of Missouri grew alarmed as more and more of the tribes were dumped on them and exclaimed, "The exiles must be shipped farther west."

The U. S. Government used the Treaty of New Echota in 1835 to justify the removal of the Indians. When the early pre-removal Cherokee leaders signed the Treaty, they signed their own death warrants. The Cherokee National Council had already passed a law that called for the death of anyone who agreed to give up tribal land; so most of the 100 signers of the Treaty were soon killed.

The opposition to the further removal was led by Chief John Ross, a mixed blood of Scottish and Indian descent. He was only one-eighth Cherokee. Even with all the opposition, the U. S. Government and Georgia prevailed and used their justification to force all of the 17,000 Cherokees from their Southeast homelands.

Many were rounded up and loaded into boats in the summer of 1838 and sent down the rivers of Tennessee, Ohio, Mississippi and the Arkansas into Indian Country. Many were held in prison camps awaiting their fate. In the summer of 1838 and 1839, 14,000 Indians were marched 1,200 miles through Tennessee, Kentucky, Illinois, Missouri and Arkansas into the rugged Indian Territory.

The Cherokees were considered the most progressive of all the tribes on the Atlantic seaboard, from the very first contact with European explorers. Their culture had developed and thrived at least 1,000 years in the southeastern United States; especially in the Appalachian states of Georgia, North and South Carolina, Tennessee and parts of Kentucky and Alabama. Their culture would remain unchanged until 1710 when they began to trade with the whites. Their culture would change quickly by the expansion of white settlers and the cession of their lands to colonies, in exchange for trade goods. Also, after contact with the whites, they intermarried and shaped government and a society that was the most "civilized" at that time.

In 1788 a treaty with the Cherokees of Georgia and the Carolinas promised Indians "the right to send a deputy of their choice when ever they thought it fit, to Congress." It looked impressive on paper but the Cherokees were not told the clause meant anything other than an Indian Agent to represent them or their interests and to see that they were not cheated by traders.

More and more Cherokee families were being forced off their lands and out of their homes by the U.S. Military without notice and with only the clothes on their backs. Fear struck the hearts of those Cherokees still in their homes for they knew their time was short before they too would be rousted off their well kept farms and houses. On seeing the terrible debacle that was taking place to their neighbors, a few were able to escape to the mountains of North Carolina. My paternal grandmother with her mother, sister, brother and uncle were one of these families. Grandmother, her father and one brother gave themselves up to the military to save their family. They were later killed for trying to escape. They had been told that if they came in their families would be safe and they would be allowed to reunite with them. These were relatives of Tsali.

They were safe with other Cherokee families who were hiding amongst the evergreen laurels, azaleas, rhododendrons and high pine trees. By day they listened to the slow dripping of a spring as it trickled onto a limestone rock. By night, the women dug roots while the men hunted for animals that they could eat. The rich soil of the mountains fed them well but they were starved in their souls, fearing for their lives.

My paternal grandmother with her mother, sister, brother and uncle were one of these families. On seeing what was happening to their neighbors close by, they decided it was the only way they could survive. To be pushed onto the removal to the West unthinkable.

The horrors that the people were having on the western movement were many. Men were taken from their fields, children from play and women from their kitchens and herded into removable camps without the Military bothering to learn who the children's parents were. They were prodded and pushed with bayonets into rivers with their shoes and clothing on. Shivering, and crying for dry clothing was useless for no one seemed to care. Women and children wept while silver pendants were ripped off their necks, knowing all too well that looters were exhuming graves of their loved ones, stripping off jewelry from the exhumed bodies. Cherokees, who had agreed to exchange Cherokee citizenship for U.S. Citizenship, would later emerge as the Eastern Band of Cherokee Indians of Cherokee, North Carolina.

The descendants of the Trail of Tears comprise today's Cherokee Nation of more than 165,000 with membership. However, there are thousands of mixed bloods living all over the United States that are not members. They do not have a Card telling them who they are, such as my Grandmother, my father and I.

An estimated 4,000 Cherokees died from hunger, exposure, cholera, pneumonia and other disease of what they called the "removal" or "THE TRAIL WHERE THEY CRIED". But historians named it "The Trail of Tears."

Not all Cherokees left Georgia either. Many compassionate white families suddenly acquired relatives with deep suntans. Who would question a white man about his Auntie Jane or Cousin Tom who had recently come to live with them?

REMOVAL OF THE BLACKFEET

Painting by Ruby H. Happel-Holtz

"I cannot believe that the United States government will still continue to pursue the lukewarm system of policy, to her relations with the Indians, as has hitherto been adopted, to effect the purpose of removing nation after nation of them from the land of their fathers into the remote wilderness."

John Ross, Cherokee, 1822

"Away back in that time-1492-theres was a man by the name of Columbus, who came from across the great ocean and discovered the country for the white man...What did he find when he first arrived here? Did he find a white man standing on the continent then.....? I stood here first, and Columbus first discovered me."

Chitto Harjo, Creek

"Brother: when you were young, we were strong; we fought by your side; but our arms are now broken. You have grown large; my people have become small...My voice is weak; you can scarcely hear me; it is not the shout of a warrior but the wail of an infant. I have lost it in mourning over the misfortunes of my people. These are their graves, and in those aged pines you hear the ghosts of the departed. Their ashes are here and we have been left to protect them...Here are our dead. Shall we go, and give their bones to the wolves?"

Chief Cobb, Choctaw

"Father-You know it's hard to be hungry, and if you do not know it, we poor Indians know it...We did not think the Big Man would tell us things that were not true."

The Delaware Chiefs to Indian Department

PROLOGUE

"ON WINGS OF CHANGE"

On Wings of Change is the true-life story written in novel form and is the book that this author originally intended to write until she found out her mother was a Blackfoot Indian. A fact she did not learn until she was 59 years of age. Realizing that she knew very little about her family's ancestor's she researched for 15 years before writing her first book. Now she was ready to continue on and write about one courageous woman, her family and the crooks and turns of her immense struggle through life.

This book is a continuation of The Unconquered Hearts and begins in 1894, and ends in 1987. The author takes you back in time to the Civil War, its effect on an Irish immigrant family, The Trail of tears, and the many wonderful times and sad times of her mothers and fathers lives.

This captivating tome illustrates the customs of the Dickerson family, the maturing of a spoiled little girl, her siblings and selfish insistence to have her own way, which led her down a treacherous path to maturity. Growing up Blackfoot in a society of white people was not easy for Etta Mae. She fought it all the way, only to find that her Indian Grandmother's teachings would be the one thing that would see her through her many sorrows and life tragedies.

Deep and sensitive as The Unconquered Hearts, this book lets you have an intimate relationship with its characters.

Ruby H. Happel-Holtz

Author

CHAPTER ONE

RETURN TO SMITH MILLS, THE PREDICTION

June 1894 arrived in Smith Mills, Kentucky like the opening of a beautiful flower; innocent in the early state of its opening. Young colts frolicked in the bright green pasture as their mothers nibbled the tender blades while keeping an eye on their frisky young. The flowers were poking their heads up with perfect blooms and the maple trees were completely covered with fresh new green leaves. The fruit orchard was alive with blooms and the honeybees and hummingbirds were gorging themselves on the nectar. Indeed, spring had sprung in all its glory.

Independent, Rhode Island Red hens that wanted their own baby chicks, was seeking places to hide their eggs and build nests to hatch them. Morning Star and Little White Dove Flying (Dovie), busy as ever had not gotten all the hens wings clipped, and they in turn were flying daily up into the barn loft laying their eggs. Each and every day Dovie would have to climb up the ladder to the loft and hunt the eggs so that they wouldn't get stale. Today this would not be much different.

It was early in the morning and the First Star Farm and Schoolhouse was about to start another full day plowing the fields, working in many gardens, grooming and training the horses and caring for the many children who lived in the scattered cabins around the farm.

Morning Star (Jane La Velle), her daughter Little White Dove Flying, (Dovie or Alice Dean), her children, Clarence and Rosabelle, Ben Dickerson and his two sons, Walter and Otto, were all gathered at the breakfast table. Morning Star said the Oppie to the Creator to thank Him for another day, for all the gifts that He had given them all and for the ones they were to receive. Little did she know the Creator was about to answer that one thing she wanted most. Night after night, day after day, she had asked for happiness for her beloved, Dovie. As a Blackfoot Indian, she believed and knew she was in touch with Dovie's long deceased father, White Feather White Calf. He had appeared to her many times and had said that he would help the dream come true for his one and only daughter.

Dovie had married J.P. Van Bibber from Eldorado, Illinois, who had seemed like the perfect match for her, but time had proven them all wrong. He was a Blackfoot Indian but he was not a good husband, and a worse father. He had been gone this last time since little Rosabelle was just a few months old, under the guise of looking for livestock for the farm. He was in reality, drinking and carousing with women from the brothels up and down the Ohio River.

Houston Van Bibber knowing of his son's long absences and knowing too that his daughter-in-law needed a lot of help on the farm, sent his nephew, Benjamin Dickerson to Smith Mills to help her. Eventually, he had said, he would be able to work at the sawmill he had purchased there. Houston had fallen in love with all the people on the Star Farm and hoped his son J.P. would too. J.P., however, could not be content with the farm he did not own, nor could he accept the responsibility of being a father. It seemed inevitable to Houston now, that his son would return to his old habits and to the life he knew best, that of a philanderer.

J.P. was a totally spoiled young man. He had been given everything he ever wanted by his mother and then his father. He was not proud of his Indian heritage, and hid it. He only admitted to it whenever it was for his betterment. Houston had thought that giving him a job of hunting for and buying livestock and overseeing the sawmill, would give him enough freedom and traveling to placate his appetite for adventure. J.P. had proven him wrong in every way. Nothing, it seemed, could quench his appetite for women and booze.

Morning Star and Little White Dove (Dovie) had pleaded with Houston to find J.P. and let him know that he had been divorced by Dovie, Indian style, but Dovie needed J.P. to get a legal divorce so that the white man's court would make it legal. He did not, however, ascertain the idea much when they first wrote him about the matter. But, this would soon change.

Much later on that beautiful spring day in June, Grandma Morning Star (Jane), was busy in the kitchen preparing the family's dinner while keeping an eye on little Clarence and baby Rosabelle, while Dovie was out doing her evening chores.

Grey Fox, Golden Eagle, Kip MacKenzie and Bull Bear were still working with Many Waters and a high strung filly that they wanted to enter in the races at Henderson. Their women and children were hurriedly preparing the evening meal and finishing their chores, before the men folk came in to eat. Ben and his boys were not any different.

"Walter, you and Otto, water and feed the horses while I check out the hogs and the chicken house. I expect Dovie has already tended to them but I'll see." Ben handed the reins over to Walter and hurried to the hog house. As he passed by the barn he heard a loud cackling from the hens, stopped, listened, and then walked past the barn. On finishing feeding the hogs and walking past the barn again, he heard a loud cackling again which seemed to come from inside the barn. Something must be after the hens he thought; maybe a raccoon had gotten in the barn and was after them! As he rounded the corner of the barn he saw his boys were already on their way to the house so he would just take a quick look inside and join them in a few minutes.

Quiet as a mouse, he slowly climbed the ladder to the hayloft and when he reached the top he saw Dovie lying beside a basket of eggs, daydreaming. She had not heard him come up the ladder, so he softly stole his way to her side, dropping to his knees. She was so startled she set bolt upright and tried to rise to her feet. But, Ben caught her in his arms as she tried to struggle to her feet. The touch of her body sent electric shocks throughout his own and he could not contain his desire for her any longer. He held her tightly against himself and she did not resist him. She placed her arms around him as he drew her face gently upward and kissed her full ripe lips. She returned his kisses and soon their pent-up passion was released and they became as one, professing their undying love for each other. That now by all the laws of their world, they had become betrothed to each other. They relished in their newfound ecstasy for a few more minutes, talking of their future together and how everyone on the farm would take their wonderful news. They said they didn't really care, but Dovie said to Ben, "Mama will be so happy, for she loves you so very much." They picked up the basket of eggs and walked to the house, hand in hand.

Morning Star had begun wondering where the two had gone and was looking out of the window when she saw them come out of the barn holding hands. She thought her mind was deceiving her at first, but then she took another look, and sure enough, they were holding hands and laughing up into each other's faces. Morning Star raised her face to the heavens for White Feather and the Creator had answered her prayers when he had said in her vision, "Our Dovie will be happy with a man who truly cares for her." Morning Star said nothing to the family now gathered at the table in the dining room. She knew she would not have to say a word for they could all see the happiness in their father and mother's faces when Ben and Dovie came in to eat. Morning

Star began humming to herself as she finished carrying in all the dishes of food for their dinner. Walter and Otto looked at 'Grandma Jane' curiously, for they seldom heard her do this anymore, especially since little Rosabelle had been born. They looked at each other and shrugged their shoulders.

"Grandma, can we start eating now; we are starving." Otto said impatiently.

"No, we must wait. I just saw Dovie and Ben coming from the barn. I think you will like to hear what they are going to tell us. Just be patient a little longer." Morning Star smiled at Otto as she placed little Rosabelle in a high chair, and then tied a cloth under Clarence's chin. At that moment, Dovie and Ben entered the door to the dining room aglow with the new love they had found.

"Come in, come in. Sit, the boys are starving. What took you two so long tonight to get your chores done?" Morning Star could hardly contain herself. She wanted to shout the news she was so happy. Dovie and Ben looked at each other and then Dovie looked at her mother for a long moment and knew that her mother already knew her wonderful news, and she was glad.

"Mama, Otto, Walter; Ben and I are going to be married! We love each other and we are going to be married Indian style. We will have our ceremony right away. We have to tell Grey Fox and have him do the ceremony since he is the Chief here." Dovie let the words rush from her mouth as fast as she could. "Be happy for us for I know that we will all be happy as one big family." Dovie's voice quivered a little and the tears of joy now flowed from her eyes.

The two boys Walter and Otto sat too stunned to speak and just looked from their father to Dovie, and then to Grandma Jane. Morning Star could sit no longer and rushed to Ben and Dovie's side and threw her arms around them, speaking prayers of thanks in her native language, as she did so.

"White Feather told me not to worry that this day would come, and now it is here. I cannot even begin to tell each of you how I feel about your coming together. It is the Creator's Plan.

Yes, we must have a ceremony, and Grey Fox will be just as happy to do it as I am."

"Grey Fox will be happy to do what, Mama?" Grey Fox had entered the room just as his mother had spoken these words.

"A wedding ceremony for Ben and Dovie. They have made their commitment to each other, just now, tonight. Ha, Ha, isn't that just grand?"

"Well all I can say is, it is about time you spoke up for my little sister. I was beginning to wonder if you ever would. It seems every one here knew the two of you belonged together before you did." Grey Fox was smiling from ear to ear. He hugged Dovie and shook hands with Ben, and turned to the boys. "Now Dovie can be your real mother, boys." Grey Fox patted each boy's back as he spoke and then gave his mother a big hug. "Just wait until Rose Marie hears this! By golly, I forgot what it was that I came up here for, I'm so excited." Everyone laughed at Grey Fox's remarks.

"Are you our real mother now?" Walter asked finally. Dovie blushed as she looked at Walter and Otto.

"Yes, I am your real mother now, and Clarence's, and Rosabelle's; and I'm so happy to be your real mother." Dovie answered as she hugged each of Ben's sons.

WHITE FEATHER'S PREDICTION

Morning Star wept with sheer joy that she felt for Ben and Dovie as she embraced them. Nothing could possibly please her more than seeing her daughter beaming with stars in her beautiful black eyes, as she now looked at Ben. She could not help but remember the words that White Feather had said to her in a vision. "All will be right with our daughter. You must trust in the Creator. He will make it right for our Little White Dove Flying. Be patient, it will come when the time is right." Morning Star now knew that this was what he had meant, "all will be right." She trembled a little, but spoke with ardor.

"We must do this marriage right in the Creator's eyes. No, don't say a word Ben, Dovie, for I'll do all the planning for a great celebration. First things first, though. Grey Fox, you are our Chief and you will do the blessings, won't you?" Morning Star was so excited she had not noticed what Ben was about to do. As she turned to go, Ben grabbed her and lifted her off her feet and swung her around and around, then gently setting her back down. As he let go of her, he kissed her softly on the cheek. Grey Fox and Dovie looked on in amusement.

"Yes, of course my mother. Nothing could please me more."

"You can bet your bottom dollar we'll have a grand celebration. We can have a dance and invite everyone we know to help us celebrate our new found happiness. Isn't that right, Dovie?" Ben's eyes were sparkling with his happiness as he enveloped Dovie in his arms, as she whispered to him.

"It will have to be an Indian ceremony only, you know." Quick to set things right, Morning Star gently touched Dovie's face as she softly answered her daughter.

"Of course, my daughter, it will be an Indian ceremony, for you are an Indian woman, and Ben is an Indian man. What else would be more appropriate?" Morning Star's big black eyes now shone with the pride and joy that she felt.

"You are right, my daughter. A Blackfoot ceremony it will be. You are an Indian and always will be. Never forget who you are." Morning Star saw a slight frown came across her daughter's brow and hastened to comfort her.

"Dovie, don't fret. Everything will be fine. You and Ben can get the white man's papers as soon as that rascal J.P. gets the legal parting papers. I'll write Houston right away to get it done. Come, you two, let's go down to Grey Fox's and tell all of the others about the celebration and wedding."

Morning Star was having more and more discomfort from the rheumatism in her feet, so Ben went off to hitch up their little black carriage. Dovie climbed into the carriage and Ben handed little Rosabelle to her and then helped Morning Star into the carriage and off they went. The three adults could hardly wait to tell all of the farm's inhabitants their wonderful news, and there was many. After all, it was still the Star Farm and Schoolhouse, and all the children on the farm were still being educated in the little schoolhouse.

Time had produced many additions to each family. Grey Fox and Rose Marie had four and one on the way. Golden Eagle and Annie Lee had two, Kip and Elk Dancing had three, and a nearly grown Many Waters. Bull Bear and Missy had one nearly grown son, a daughter and two of their own. Ben and Dovie had Ben's grown sons Otto and Walter, and Dovie had Clarence and Rosabelle. Rose Marie met them as they stopped the carriage and helped Morning Star out of the buggy and into their little house, before Grey Fox could tell her the news.

"Well, Mother, I can see you are just about to burst with some very important news, right?" Grey Fox had taken one look at Ben and Dovie, smiled at them, and let his mother do the talking, for she was about to burst with excitement.

"Look at Ben and Dovie, Rose Marie. Can you guess what they have done? Just one good look will tell you, I'm sure!" Morning Star was breathless as she let the words tumble from her mouth.

Grey Fox grinned broadly at his mother and gave her a big hug. He then clasped Dovie's hand in Ben's and kissed the top of his sister's head.

"Like I said before, it's about time you two got together. I was beginning to think you would never speak your mind, Ben." Rose Marie looked a little bewildered as she now looked at her two dearest friends.

"What do you mean, 'speak your mind'? What are you talking about?" Dovie could not stand the suspense any longer.

"We are getting married, Rose Marie. Me and Ben, Indian style. We are really getting married and going to have a big, big celebration, Mama says." Dovie's voice was like a very young girl's who had just been asked out for her first date.

"Oh, how wonderful! Grey Fox and I have talked many times about just this. We were afraid you two would never get together. Oh, Dovie, I'm so happy for you. It is just the best news you could tell me." Rose Marie hugged first Dovie and then Ben. Not to be forgotten or left out, Morning Star began dancing in a circle, despite her pain, and chanting, Aye, ya Aye, ya. Dovie and Grey Fox joined their mother and then Ben and Rose Marie joined in. Out of breath, but happy, Morning Star stopped dancing and became somewhat pensive.

"Bring everyone to the house tomorrow night, just before dark. We will get out plans together for the ceremony of the Sacred Eagle. We will feast too, to thank the Creator for bringing this union about."

Morning Star wanted to get back to the house for she knew just what she must do now. She knew that Dovie would be fuming about what she would wear for her wedding to Ben. It had to be very special. She went straight to her room and unlocked the old trunk that sat on the floor of her closet. Gently she removed the blanket that rested on top and carefully unfolded another blanket, exposing a beautiful soft white elk dress splendidly beaded in blue and white seed beads. All around the neckline and sleeve the beading formed flowers, and on the bottom just above the long fringe. Fringe also was sewn down the backs of the sleeves and on the cuffs. It was just as beautiful as ever. Rows and rows of elk's teeth were sewn just above the fringe on the bottom and at the yolk of the dress.

Tears streamed down Morning Star's face as she hugged the dress to her bosom. In her mind's eye she could see White Feather and herself on their wedding day when she had worn this dress that he had made just for their wedding. She could also see him in his wonderful soft antelope tunic and pants, trimmed in the same fringe as her dress. White Feather had been very broad shouldered and handsome. He was lighter of color than most of the men, especially his brothers. He was a proud man, a fierce hunter, a generous leader and a sagacious Chief.

Morning Star was now lost in her thoughts of long ago. Their union had been such a wonderful, happy one, cut all too short by his death, fighting for all Indian's freedom from the hated 7th Calvary at the Battle of the Little Bighorn. This was the name the whites gave the battle, but she called it "The day my heart was cut in half."

Lost in her reverie, she jumped as she heard Dovie calling to her.

"Mama, Mama, where are you?" Dovie had looked in her mother's room but had not seen her sitting on the floor by the closet.

"I'm here, by the closet, Dovie. Come in, I want to show you your wedding dress." There was a note of intrigue in Morning Star's voice and Dovie was curious as to what her mother had just said. What dress did she mean, Dovie wondered.

When Dovie entered the room she now saw her mother sitting in front of an old trunk holding the most beautiful beaded dress she had ever seen.

"Mama, where on earth did you ever find a dress like this? It is so beautiful with all the beading. Where did it come from?" Dovie's eyes were wide with wonder.

"This was my wedding dress when I married your father, White Feather. He had the women of the clan make it for me as a special gift. Now I know why I saved it. I saved if just for you, for your marriage to Ben. Wear it in your father's name. He would be so proud."

Dovie was speechless. Her mother had never shown the dress to her before. Tears now formed in Dovie's eyes as she though of her father and his death, and then of her parent's wedding ceremony.

"I will be proud to wear it, Mama. Ben will be so pleased when he sees me wearing it." Dovie laid the dress on the bed now, and hugged her mother tightly.

"My sweet mother. You are just full of surprises, aren't you, Mama? I wonder just what Grey Fox has in mind for Ben? Even you don't know that, I bet."

Morning Star laughed heartily at Dovie as she answered.

"I can only imagine."

The day arrived for the wedding. Dozens of people, mostly parents of the children who attended school at the Star Schoolhouse gathered around the tepee where the ceremony was to be held. Dovie, Morning Star, Rose Marie, Elk Dancing and Missy all waited inside for Ben to arrive. They had no idea as to what the men were going to do for they had insisted on secrecy.

Suddenly in the distance, drums began their steady beat, and off in the distance rode a proud Grey Fox, in full Chief regalia. He slowly rode his horse, Wasaka, toward the tepee. Following behind him was Benjamin Houston Dickerson, splendidly dressed in a soft buckskin tunic. Fringe hung down from the sleeves and tunic, almost touching the ground. On his head he wore a beaded headband with one white feather attached. His black hair was braided in to fat braids, with rawhide extensions, tied with large glass beads at the ends. Behind him came Kip MacKenzie, with his flute in hand just waiting for the right time for the Blackfeet Wedding song.

Behind them rode Golden Eagle and Bull Bear with their drums beating out the solemn march. A short distance behind them rod Many Waters on the only white horse on the farm, wearing an all white buckskin tunic and pants. In his left hand he carried the sacred Eagle's Wing, and draped over his arm was the prayer blanket on which the intended couple would stand during the ceremony, barefooted. Walter and Otto rode their mounts on either side of Many Waters until they reached the tepee, then dismounted and stood on either side of their father, Ben. The drums picked up their beat as the men dismounted and took their respective places.

Many Waters dismounted and stood before the door of the tepee and sang for the women to come forth in the name of the Creator. Then he jumped into a circle which had been cleared for this purpose. As he danced he held the Sacred Wing above his head and continued dancing the Blackfoot Eagle dance, singing and waving the Wing in meaningful gestures, as Dovie and the women took their places in front of Grey Fox and Ben. The drummers stopped drumming and Many Waters stopped his dancing and walked to Grey Fox and handed him the Sacred Eagle Wing indicating that the ceremony was to begin. Grey Fox looked to the sky and then waving the Wing over Morning Star's head began the sacred words.

"Morning Star White Feather, do you give your blessing to this union between Benjamin Houston Dickerson and Little White Dove Flying?"

"Yes, as her mother, I speak for her father, too. His spirit is with us."

"And I as the Chief of his band, I honor and confirm this union of my sister and good friend and brother of blood." Grey Fox waved the Sacred Eagle Wing over each of their heads as he spoke.

"Now it is time to state your intentions to each other." Grey Fox handed the Sacred Wing first to Dovie. Her hand shook slightly but her voice rang steady and clear as she spoke her vows.

Looking straight into Ben's eyes with all the love she felt she spoke with strength.

"Benjamin Houston Dickerson, I give you my hand, my heart, my life, and with the help of the Eagle, I will give you a long and joyous life." Dovie then handed the Eagle Wing back to Grey Fox. Grey Fox then handed the Eagle Wing to Ben.

"Yes, my Chief, I accept your sister, Little White Dove Flying, as my sits-beside-me-wife. I give her my hand, my heart, my love, my life, and with the help of the Eagle, I will protect her now and forever." As Ben said these words he felt something he had never really felt in his life before. He felt like a true Indian. He was marrying this lovely little Indian woman who meant more to him than his own life. His heart seemed to swell within his chest as he looked deeply into her beautiful eyes. He knew his love for her showed in his eyes, just as hers had when she said her vows to him.

"By my hand and in the eyes of our Creator, you are now as one with each other. You may take her hand and lead her to your tepee. For you are now her husband and she your wife." Grey Fox bowed slightly and smiled. As was tradition the newlyweds stole away into the house into each others arms forever.

It truly was a joyous occasion. The drummer began beating a joyful tempo and the wedding participants began to dance. The guests ate and drank with zest and danced the night away. This wedding would not soon be forgotten.

Ben and Dovie's wedding was talk of the little village of Smith Mills. Neighbors who had attended delighted in gathering at Buchanan's General Store, and relating the event to those who had chosen not to attend.

Many of the closet neighbors were reluctant to associate with "those heathens" in any way. Jake Buchanan was not one of them.

He had watched Grey Fox and Dovie grow to adults and thought of them as the most outstanding young people in that area. They were smart, educated and always polite and ready to help anyone. He admired the way they both could sit a horse, and had seen them race each other with their horses, Wasaka and Bluenose. They had terrible things happen in their young lives, such as the hanging of Jacques La Velle, their protector, and the death of their father, White Feather. Their mother had done an amazing job raising them and keeping all of the many inhabitants together on the Star Farm. She herself was one amazing woman.

Buchanan had always felt much affection for this small Indian woman and all that she had accomplished. What with her Star Schoolhouse for the unwanted Indian and Negro children who were not allowed in the public school. How could he not admire her?

The fact was he would have liked to know her much better since he was now a widower, but he was afraid to approach her. He was too concerned that an approach might end the good relationship they now enjoyed. All he could do was to not let anyone degrade her, or her family, in anyway. He was now furious with one of the men who had gathered around the pot bellied stove, and his remarks.

"Don't ever let me hear you degrading that Indian woman and her children again. You hear, John? They are the best thing that ever happened to this village. You might say they are the Village!" Buchanan spoke sharply as he slammed more wood into the stove.

"Oh, shaw, Jake, don't get your high horse up. We all know you are stuck on that Morning Star. She is real good to look at, and the daughter, well now, there is a real beauty if I ever saw one! Too bad she had to go and get herself hitched up again." John DeKemper laughed as he teased, just to get Buchanan upset.

"Ain't you guys got nothing better to talk about?" Buchanan bristled at the insinuation DeKemper had made. He was angry, but he tried not to let his anger get the best of him. At that moment Grey Fox walked through the door.

"Good day, gentlemen." He spoke to the men but went straight to the sacks of flour and barrels of sugar sitting in front of the little counter. Buchanan walked behind the counter and offered to help him but Grey Fox shook his head.

"No, nothing else today. Seems our women have run out of flour and sugar since the wedding. Oh, Mr. Buchanan, thanks for coming. It meant a lot to all of us. Pay us another visit soon." Grey Fox laid his money on the counter then turned and looked the men over at the stove, and left as quietly as he had come.

"Damn that Indian! He has a way about him that scares the fire out of a body. I bet he'd just as soon scalp us at looks at us!" Hal Darnell exclaimed, with mocking contempt.

"Yah, he struts around like he owns the world! I heard some time ago, back a few years, he shot a couple of men. Course, I guess they deserved it, seeing how they say the men tried to burn down their cabins with them in it. You remember that, Buchanan?" Robert Hargraves asked, as he stood up now and addressed the store owner.

"I remember all right. I remember too that was the night them men hung Jacques La Velle. A hell of a thing they did, but they got theirs in the long run. That Maurer over at the bank also tried to take their farm away too, but that little woman, Morning Star, outsmarted them. Ha, Ha, well I think that's enough reminiscing for today. I got work to do so you all better be getting along." Buchanan took off his apron as he spoke and the men reluctantly shoved back their stools and left the store, grumbling.

Dovie and Ben were extremely happy together. Their whole lives took on a completely different meaning. They did everything together as much as possible. Ben worked the fields and took to taking little Clarence and sometimes Rosabelle with him. He called Clarence "Little Man", and Rosie he nicknamed "Jack", his other little boy. He told Dovie that Rosabelle was going to make a good farmer. She loved the horses and would sit on Ben's lap all day if he would let her, even in the fields as he plowed. Otto and Walter had Clarence with them much of the time, so Rosabelle got most of his attention.

A few months passed and soon Dovie could keep her secret no longer. She had hoped J.P. would get the divorce, but it seemed it was no use trying to write him about it. She didn't really know where he was, or even if he got the letters that they had sent to his father, Houston. This day she had decided she had to tell Ben, but before she could, her mother decided she needed to talk to Dovie about the same matter.

"My daughter, your secret will soon be known by everyone. Don't let that happen, tell Ben today he is going to be a father. He will be so pleased. You cannot wait any longer, it is not good." Morning Star had placed her hand under Dovie's chin looking boldly into her eyes. Dovie knew she was right but still she wished she had that white man's divorce papers.

"I know, Mama. I will tell him. I had hoped J.P. would get those papers I need, so Ben and I can get a legal marriage, but I know I must tell Ben. You're right. I will do it tonight because Ben has noticed that I have put on a little weight." Dovie smiled at her mother as she spoke.

Ben had noticed that Dovie seemed to have gained a little weight, but on her it looked good – mighty good in fact, he thought as they climbed the stairs to go to bed. He patted her backside as she climbed the stairs in front of him and giggled.

"Stop that Ben, you are an old married man now," Dovie giggled again.

"So are you, an old married woman, but you get better looking all the time. I'd marry you all over again." With this statement, he grabbed her around the waist and carried her to their room, kissing and hugging her all the way. Ben closed the door with his knee and placed Dovie on their bed and started kissing her all over. Dovie pushed him away and sat up suddenly, raising her hand motioning for Ben to stop.

"Ben, be serious for a minute. I have something to tell you that's really important." Dovie took a deep breath as if to continue, but did not.

"So, shoot. What secret must you share with me that's more important than my making love to you?"

"I'm going to have your baby!" Dovie held her breath. She hoped Ben's response would be pleasant and that she had not told him too soon.

"What! You are in the family way! How long? Are you sure?" Dovie nodded her head 'yes', and Ben exclaimed joyfully.

"Oh, sweet Jesus, I'm going to be a father again!" Ben threw his arms around Dovie and rocked her back and forth in his arms, not waiting for any answers to the questions he had just asked. Dovie was so relieved, all she could do was giggle and giggle. Finally she broke Ben's arms from around her before she tried to answer his questions.

"Yes, I am really sure. It must have happened that first time, you know, in the hayloft, for I haven't had my time since. I thought you must have noticed I had gained a little weight."

"We are going to have our very own little one; our special love child; that would be due around the first week of March, wouldn't it? Let's go wake up Morning Star and tell her." Dovie had to laugh now before she spoke.

"She knows. In fact, she knew the first month. She said I showed it in my back. She insisted today that I tell you. I had waited, hoping to get those papers from J.P. She was right, for we don't know when we will get them, if ever. Do we?"

"No, and if you hadn't told me now, I would have spanked you when I discovered it." Ben was so excited he pulled back the covers and jumped into bed with his clothes still on.

"Well, Mr. Dickerson, are you sleeping in your clothes? I can't allow that in my bed." Dovie jumped astraddle of Ben and commenced taking his clothes off, ripping some of the buttonholes as she did. They laughed and romped like two children until they were both exhausted, then fell asleep in each others arms.

The next morning Dovie was feeling a little ill, perhaps from all the excitement from the night before, but probably just a case of the morning sickness that she had on several occasions. Ben however, was so worried that he did not go out to work. Grey Fox and the other men thought this highly unusual, so they all came to the house to see if something was wrong with Ben. Ben met them at the back door and bid them to come in and have some coffee and breakfast. He said that he had something he should tell them all. Dovie by now was feeling like herself and hastened to join the men.

"Come over here my wife. It was not me, boys, but Dovie who was feeling ill. You see, we are going to have a baby. Our own baby!" Ben's eyes grew moist and his lips quivered as he spoke, so Dovie spoke up.

"Ben's is right. We are going to have our baby in the spring. Isn't that just too wonderful!" She jumped out of her chair now and ran to her brother's side.

"Yes, Chief, we are making an addition to the clan. You will have to ordain a protector, as our father did for us, won't you?" Dovie, always the tease with her brother, couldn't resist the temptation now. He had to laugh, and the others had to join in.

"Yes, little sister, I guess that would be a good idea. What do you think, brother Ben?"

"I say, give her anything she wants, but I will always be here to look after our children, but just in case, I guess I will have to name a name right now. Is that right?"

"No, Ben; you need to think on this matter, and you will have plenty of time to do so. Congratulations to both of you, I'm pleased." The other men said their congratulations and then took their leave to attend to the work of keeping the farm running in order.

The remaining five months passed quickly without any adverse problems. Morning Star wrote a personal letter to Houston Van Bibber about the impending birth of Ben's and Dovie's baby. What on earth, she had asked, can we do to make sure the baby will have a legal birth certificate. She had also noted that if the baby's birth was attended by a doctor in the Smith Mills area, the gossip would get out the baby was not J.P.'s and therefore, a bastard. She insisted that they, as the grandparents, must do something to correct this, for it would not be fair to the new little one. Maybe you can think of something since you are more knowledgeable of the white man's way than we are. Had he been able to find J.P.? Did he not think that the only way they could protect the baby was for it to be a Van Bibber, since legally, Dovie was still married to J.P.? And she had added, J.P. did come back here not long before Ben and Dovie got together, and he had slept in Dovie's bed.

Houston Van Bibber read the letter with both joy and sadness. What on earth could he do? For sure, J.P. could not be told of the baby's soon arrival, but that would not be hard since he had not heard from him in over seven months. He didn't have a clue as to where to find him, and now he thought it is better that I don't find him until the baby is born. I don't know just what he would do. He thought and thought and then went in to see his doctor in Eldorado. At first, the doctor did not want to do what Houston had insisted on. But after reminding the doctor of several things that he knew about him, the doctor relented.

"Now, I want to get this straight with you, Doc. You will bring a birth certificate with you when I let you know that it is time. Is that right?"

"Yes, yes. I will bring the necessary paper to show that I delivered the child and that the father is J.P. Van Bibber, even if he is not there. You know though, that this would be a good idea to get him there if at all possible. Surely you have some idea where he went?" The Doctor was a little perturbed at Houston, but he really had no alternative but to agree to sign the birth certificate. Houston had seen him dining with a woman of ill repute, and his wife could not find out. Damn him, anyway. He had not thought too much about his indiscretion until now.

Houston wrote his plan to Morning Star, and asked her to explain it all to Ben and Dovie, and told them he would keep trying to find J.P. However, he had decided that it would be better for everyone, and for their plan, if J.P. was kept unaware. He knew his son, and he knew that if he found out the truth, he would never give Dovie a divorce. He knew too, that he would make as much trouble for Dovie and Ben as he could. No, he thought, it is better not to find him before the birth.

The women at the Star Farm were all busy making a complete layette for Dovie's new baby. The ladies sewed little dresses and gowns, shirts and blankets and Missy embroidered them. She was skilled in the French embroidery and was only too happy to add her talents to the little garments. Each day, for at least two hours, the women would gather together and work furiously on the layette, laugh, and talk of rearing children and how lucky Dovie was to have Ben. She would then say, "Well, don't you think he is lucky to have me?" There would then be lots of laughter and other pleasantries passed between all the women.

CHAPTER TWO

THE NEW ARRIVAL & INTRIGUE

THE COLD NORTH WIND HOWLED AROUND THE STAR FARM USHERING IN MARCH, 1895. INSIDE THE LITTLE FARM HOUSE; HOWEVER, IT WAS WARM AND COZY. DOVIE (ALICE DEAN DICKERSON), (LITTLE WHITE DOVE FLYING), HEAVY WITH CHILD, BEGAN HER DAY EARLY AS USUAL.

She was soon to know it would not be just another day for she knew it was time to pack her suitcase and board a train for Eldorado, Illinois. There, she would have her and Ben's child, just as they had all planned it. She straightened up as best she could for Ben and his two boys, Walter and Otto, were all coming through the kitchen door, all covered in snow.

"My, but you three look half frozen with all that snow on you."

"Yes, we are very cold. I guess there is no doubt that March has come in like a lion this year. Right, boys?" Ben's blue eyes twinkled as he spoke to his pregnant wife. He reached to give her a soft pat, as she whispered in his ear.

"I heard the lion roar myself, and also the little one. We must hurry and get to the train as fast as we can. This time Ben looked at his wife with deep concern.

"Are you alright, Dovie?" Ben exclaimed as he took the heavy granite coffee pot that Dovie was carrying.

"Yes, but we must go soon." Dovie spoke with an urgency Ben had not heard before.

"Boys, hurry up with your breakfast, then clear the table and straighten up the house. It's time for me to take Dovie to the train station."

"Please, one of you go see if Grandma Jane (Morning Star) has finished packing the valises." Dovic placed her hand on her stomach, then added, "Tell her to hurry, please."

"Ben, maybe you should go. Mama is suffering terrible these days from her rheumatism. I thought she would be down by now with Clarence and Rosabelle."

"Of course, Dovie, how insensitive of me. We will all go and help Grandma Jane." Ben was quick to his feet, but Otto, always anxious to please, bounded up the stairs two at a time just as Grandma Jane appeared at the top carrying both Clarence and Rosabelle. Otto, the ever obedient son, took both of the children while Walter fetched the valises from the hallway where Grandma had set them. Ben went in to the kitchen just in time to see Dovie clinching her stomach. With one look at Ben's worried face, Dovie laughed and tried to ease her husband's mind.

"I believe it will be later today, Ben, but we must take the next train out. Take these biscuits to the table and have the boys put the rest of the food on the table. We should grab a bit to eat and then be on our way." Ben nodded as his wife kissed him on the cheek to reassure him. Everyone took their place at the table, but all eyes were on Dovie.

Grandma Jane, never at a loss for words, spoke solemnly, "Boys, the little one wants to make an entrance into this world as soon as he can, so we will be off to the train as soon as we can. We have to leave the house and farm in your hands, just like we have discussed when this time came. We will be gone a few weeks. Grey Fox, Rose Marie, and all the others will help you get all the chores done. I've discussed this time with all of them."

Eyeing her daughter, Morning Star spoke to her and Ben almost slyly now.

"I have made my medicine bag ready and I think that we must leave immediately after breakfast. Boys, you will need to keep the fires in the fireplaces going while we are gone. Also, help your Uncle Grey Fox will all of the outdoor work, for it is far too much for him to do by himself."

"Yes, Grandma Jane. We will keep the place just like you and Papa do." The boys said in tandem

Otto spoke softly to Morning Star as he kissed her on the neck, "You all must be very careful with Little Man and baby Rosie. We are going to be mighty lonesome without our family."

Otto spoke in an endearing voice for he had come to love Grandma Jane and Dovie as if they were his real grandparent and mother. This love was genuinely returned.

"Dovie, you are not eating well. You must eat so that you will have the strength you will need for all the work ahead of you."

"I'm just not hungry Mama, but I will try to eat something." Dovie was pensive as she answered her mother.

Ben rose from the table, put on his good coat and walked to the door. Just before he walked out the door he turned to the two ladies sitting at the table, and with great concern, said to them, "Ladies, I will have the carriage hooked up in just a few minutes. Bring a few extra covers, for it has begun snowing again."

Morning Star and Dovie gathered all the clothing, blankets, food and other supplies together and set them at the front door for Ben to pick up and load into the carriage. Dovie was breathless by the time she had carried all the things downstairs. Morning Star had packed the little blankets and clothing that she had made for the new baby several days before, for she had been counting the days that had past since Dovie and Ben had their first union. She had been positive that Dovie had conceived that very first time, and it looked as if she was right. Tomorrow would be exactly nine months to the day.

"Mama, can you make me some of the tea so that we can take some with us?" Dovie asked her mother wistfully.

"Yes, my daughter. I have already prepared my bag with the birthing tea for you, but it might be a good idea to take some hot liquid in the carriage."

The train station was mostly empty so the little group did not have any problem getting passage to Eldorado. Morning Star was doubtful about taking the "Iron Horse" as she called it, but it was the only way to take care of her daughter, so board she did, with her mouth clinched to a fine line of determination. Little Clarence's eyes grew wide when he saw and heard the train. He didn't know whether to be afraid or gleeful that he was boarding this huge monster. Once aboard, he did settle down, sticking close to Ben's side.

As the train pulled out of the station, the snow began to fall more rapidly, and soon it was coming down so hard the countryside was almost invisible from the trains' windows. Dovie shivered, and Ben took her hand in his.

"What is it, Dovie? Are you all right? Are you in pain?"

"No Ben, I am fine. I wish it would stop snowing though. Surely it can't last too long, this weather."

"I sure hope not, Dovie. But remember, a few years back we had our biggest snow and the coldest weather in March." Ben replied hesitantly.

"Come now, my daughter. It can't last too long, for next month is the beginning of spring, and then comes the moon of the flowers and your birthday. The snow will just melt and feed the ground for flowers. Isn't that right, Ben?" Morning Star's voice had trailed off to almost a whisper as she continued. "That was a wonderful night when the Creator sent you to us. Your father, White Feather, was so proud, but we were in such a precarious spot we couldn't do the birthing ceremony right. The military were all around us and we had to stay hidden for they would have killed us all. That was the night your father had to speak to the Creator as to what he was to do to protect his family should something happen to him. That night, the Creator told your Papa to choose a man from each world, and he chose Papa Jacques and Red Fox Tail to be your and Grey Fox's protectors. Your father was a great man; so loving and so kind to his people. He gave his life so that we could get away and be safe. Do you remember, Dovie?"

"Yes, Mama, I remember my father and all his kindness to the people who chose him for their leader. I remember how he played with all the little children and how he taught Grey Fox and me about horses and the rules we were to live by. I still miss him so much. I wish that he could be here to see his grandchildren." Dovie's voice now had tears in it. Morning Star put her hand on Dovie's shoulder and spoke almost in a whisper.

"He is here! He is with us always. He knows your and Grey Fox's children. He is part of them." Morning Star's voice had grown more stern with each word. She spoke for she had seen and felt White Feather's presence every day of her life since his death. He would always be their protector. At just that minute the train jerked, nearly throwing them all from their seats. Dovie began to laugh and then Morning Star joined in for she knew what had crossed Dovie's mind.

"What is it? Why are you two laughing?" Ben queried.

"I would say that White Feather was making it known that he is here with us to help bring in the new baby." Morning Star chuckled.

"You think that White Feather jerked the train?" Ben couldn't believe they thought such a ridiculous a thing.

"Yes, of course, Ben. Who else beside the Creator could cause a train to jerk like that?" Morning Star was now teasing Ben as she did much of the time. He just couldn't understand all of their ways.

As the train chugged along, the snow began to taper off and one could now see the landscape. It was really a frightening sight as they drew nearer to their destination, for it had been snowing much longer here in Illinois than back home in Kentucky. Little

Clarence had awakened and like all little boys, wanted to go for a sleigh ride, for he was getting tired of his train ride.

"Mama, Papa, I want to get off this 'twain'," he cried, and tugged at Ben's sleeve. "Grandma, make this twain stop so I can get off," he begged. Grandma Jane laughed at little Clarence and gave up baby Rose to her mother so that she could take Clarence for a walk to pacify him. Rosie held her arms out to Ben and jabbered over and over.

"Papa, Papa, Mama, Mama. Eat, Eat," with her big brown eyes looking from one to the other, finally settling down on Ben's lap after Dovie gave her a tiny piece of cookie to eat.

The train finally arrived in Eldorado and the passengers from Smith Mills disembarked. The snow was thigh high around the depot. A large black man was shoveling off the walks and platform to make way for the passengers to walk. A lone man was waiting just a few feet from the train and was now walking toward the little family.

"Morning Star, you did come along. I'm so glad to see you; all of you. Dovie, how are you and Ben and the children? You look wonderful!" Houston Van Bibber was ecstatic to see all of them and wanted to let them know it. Ben had sent a telegram before they left Kentucky so that his Uncle could send someone to meet them. Houston wanted to surprise them so he had come by himself. Everyone chimed in together to greet Houston.

"We are all just fine, Uncle." Ben exclaimed. "The snow is much deeper here than at home. Did you have trouble getting here?"

"No, Ben, that's my surprise. Look over there by the street light. See that team pulling the big red sleigh? I bought it especially so that I could take everyone sleigh riding. I didn't expect that it would be the only way I could get you to the farm." Houston said so very proudly and he waved his hand in the direction of the sleigh.

"Wow, Uncle. It is beautiful and big. I bet it will be a lot better riding for you, Dovie, than the train." Ben said as he pulled Dovie in the direction of the sleigh. Houston grabbed little Clarence, hoisted him to his shoulders and headed for the sleigh with Dovie and Morning Star not far behind him. Ben waited at the train until all of their luggage had been placed on the platform and then made his way to the sleigh loaded down. Everyone had found a place to sit in the sleigh, and after placing the luggage in the back, Ben joined his uncle on the front seat beside Clarence.

The sleigh ride was a real treat for all of them but Dovie. She had said nothing but had experienced several pretty sharp pains during the train ride, and now it seemed they were getting more often. She did not; however, let on, but soon her mother knew that it was a good thing they were near their destination for the baby would surely be here tonight, or tomorrow.

"Dovie, you look pretty tired. Just have a seat here by the fire with your mother and children. Remember Eloise, my daughter-in-law? She is making the bedrooms ready for you and will be down in a few minutes to finish up our dinner." Houston gave Dovie a little hug and escorted her to a chair by the fire. Morning Star followed them and found her own chair. She was very tired and knew that Dovie must be too. She would take Dovie upstairs just as soon as she could and take a little bit of food up too so she would not have to come back down for the night. First though, she would put the children to bed and get the things ready for the birthing. She had timed the pain and knew that it could not be much longer before Dovie would go into real labor.

Houston and Ben had gone off toward a shed in back of the house after dinner was over and Dovie had gone upstairs. They wanted to talk out of range of anyone's ears. What about J.P.'s whereabouts, Ben wanted to know. Had he even started the divorce papers? Would he be coming home while they were there? Did he know that Dovie was pregnant? "Just a minute,"

Houston said with candor, "I'll answer all of your questions. First though, has Dovie been well during her pregnancy?"

"Yes, Uncle Houston, she has. We are very happy. I've never been happier in my life. I hate this secrecy about our baby, and what we are doing here to make our baby legal and honorable." Ben said very frustrated.

"I know, my boy, but it is the only way I can possibly think of to make sure that the baby has a legal birth certificate." Houston took a deep breath and continued. "J.P. has been gone a very long time and I am sure that he hasn't done anything about the divorce. The last time he was here he told all of us that he was living in St. Louis with a woman he was going to marry. I reminded him that he was already married and needed to get a legal divorce. He laughed at me and said some more sarcastic things which I'm sure you don't want to hear. Don't fret about it, Ben. I've made all the arrangement with my doctor in Eldorado for the birth certificate, etc. The fact is that I went to his office before picking you up at the station to alert him to come out later today to see Dovie and perhaps the new baby."

"Thank you, Uncle Houston, for all your help. I know that I have to go along with the plan, but it is so hard not to be able to claim one's own child. It is also hard to make Morning Star understand that it is best for the child. You know what the stigma would be with for all it's life in our society? I could not stand to have my child called a bastard and be scorned." Ben almost cried thinking about this one fact.

"Ben, all you have to worry about is Dovie and make sure she is alright. She looked very tired and needs you to be with her. Morning Star is just like always. It would have been nice if she and I could have gotten together, but I understand her reluctance to marry anyone." Houston ended the conversation thoughtfully.

Everyone was sound asleep except Dovie and Morning Star. Dovie's contractions had gotten harder and harder, and now she was wet with sweat. She had tried to keep from waking up Ben, but now she knew she must. It was well after 2:00 a.m. when Morning Star woke Ben.

"Ben, wake up, Dovie needs you to help her. She is having a harder time with this birth, and needs us all." Something in Morning Star's voice frightened Ben and he was filled with fear. Immediately, he was out of bed and dressed.

"What can I do?" he whispered. "Tell me what to do, Morning Star."

"Take this cloth and keep wiping her face. She is sweating much to much. I have to go to the kitchen and boil some more herbs for the birthing tea."

"Dear Creator, give me the strength to help my daughter; and give her the strength to bring this precious child into the world. Keep it safe, Oh Father, give her great strength and keep her from the birthing fever," Morning Star prayed as she hurried from the room.

Ben had been sent from the room when the labor became more intense. Not long after 8:00 a.m., a lusty first cry rang out and a beautiful little girl was born. As Morning Star placed the baby next to Dovie, Ben bent over and kissed his wife with tears of relief and joy sliding off his cheeks.

This scene would be the same many more times, but this would always be the special one; his and Dovie's love-child.

Her name had been picked out for many months. Dovie had decided that if her baby was a girl, it would be named Etta Mae Van Bibber-Dickerson. And so it was!

Morning Star took the baby from her mother, Dovie, and wrapped it in a soft blanket. As she did so, she checked to make sure the baby had all its ten toes and fingers. She could not help but notice how pale the baby's skin was. Maybe she thought something was not quite right, but still she though she is plump and fully developed. In fact, she was large for a newborn. She had a full head of black hair and a lusty cry, so surely she must be fine. Surely, she thought the Creator would not play a trick on Dovie and Ben, after all Dovie had been through with J.P. Van

Bibber. Ben entered the room to see his newborn, and Morning Star laid the baby in his arms and exclaimed with pride, "It's a beautiful little girl, Ben. I've checked her over and she looks perfect. She is a little pale for a newborn, but nothing to worry about. See how she squints her eyes, like she doesn't want to see her new world." Morning Star laughed now at Ben's clumsy grasp on his new child.

"Yes, Grandma Jane, she has a very light complexion, and look at her eyes, they are blue, not brown like her sister Rosabelle." Baby Etta Mae had ceased to cry as her father spoke and patted her little bottom. She had immediately opened her large eyes and looked at her father, and as if to confirm her father's words, she turned her head and stared at her grandmother. Morning Star clasped her hand over her mouth as she uttered her surprise, "They are blue, indeed. She looks almost white! She wants to see her new world. It's not true, you know, that baby's can't see. Some of them can, and this one can. Mark my words; she is something special, as we already know. Don't we, Ben?"

Little White Dove was fast asleep from her strenuous birth. The doctor had wanted to give her some sleeping medicine but Morning Star said no, she had all the medicines she needs. She had the birthing medicine of our tribe. The Doctor did not argue but proceeded to the sitting room where he began to fill out the birth papers as he had promised he would do.

He wrote:

> *Etta Mae Van Bibber born on this day, March 2, 1895, to Alice Dean White Van Bibber, at Eldorado, Illinois, in my presence, and that of Houston Van Bibber, her grandfather and her grandmother, Morning Star White Feather. The birth was also Witnessed by Benjamin Houston Dickerson.*
>
> *Signed: Dr. Claude J. Adams, M.D.*

Ben carried his new daughter in to show the doctor and his Uncle Houston just how alert she really was. Houston peeked at the little face of his newest grandchild. He exclaimed at her plump little body and bright eyes.

"Well, just look at her. Look at her plump little face and body. And look at these eyes. Look, Doc, how alert she is. She is looking around at everyone, even at you." Houston teased, for he knew Doc Adams was not exactly comfortable with the charade he was participating in.

"Yes, yes, she is a fine baby. Healthy as the day is long. Her mother, too, is a strong, healthy woman who is just fine. Just how long is she staying in Eldorado, Houston?"

"I'm not sure, but it will be until whenever her mother thinks she can travel home," Houston responded.

The doctor snapped his medicine bag closed, looked at Houston, and gave out his orders to Houston and Ben.

"Well, I need to see the mother and the baby before they get on the train. Bring them to my office to make sure everyone is doing alright. I'll have the birth certificate by then. I'll be on my way now. Congratulations, Houston. Mr. Dickerson." Doctor Adams shook hands with both men and bowed ever so slightly to Morning Star. "Good health to you, ma'am."

Morning Star only stared back at the doctor, saying nothing.

Morning Star

BACK HOME AGAIN IN OLE' KENTUCKY

Grey Fox, Rose Marie and Many Waters waited impatiently at the Henderson rail station for the arrival of the new baby and its parents. It had been such a long time since Dovie, Ben and Morning Star had left for Illinois, the inhabitants of Star Farm were very anxious for their return.

Finally the train arrived and there they were, home again. Hugs and kisses ensued for everyone. Ben could hardly wait to show off baby Etta Mae. She had grown so much in the previous weeks following her birth, that it was now evident that she looked much like Ben, only much lighter. Her eyes had changed from dark blue to the color of the sky, but her thick, black hair had remained jet black, and straight.

Everyone oohed and ahhed over the baby and she seemed to recognized that she was 'special'; and proceeded to give out her very first smiles to her new acquaintances. This was only the beginning of Etta Mae's ability to beguile her way to the hearts of everyone she met.

Everyone doted on her and she was never allowed to cry for someone would always pick her up and give her anything she wanted.

Morning Star tried to warn Ben and Dovie not to continue to spoil her so much, but her doting parents ignored her warnings.

Little Rosabelle clung to her Papa, more and more, but begged to hold her new sister. Of course being only fifteen months older, this was impossible for quite some time. Ben, recognizing that Rosie must feel left out, took to taking Rosie with him everywhere he went. She went to the fields with him, rode on the horses with him and was with him for any other chore that he had to do.

This left Dovie free to look after Etta Mae, and do her other household chores. As time passed, Rosie insisted more and more that she wanted to take care of her sister and to play with her. By the time Etta Mae was eleven months old and trying to walk, Rosie got her wish. The two little girls did everything together, and this would be the case for the rest of their lives.

By the time Etta was two, she was as tall as Rosie, so when J.P. made a surprise visit he didn't really know which one was the oldest. His only comment about Etta was she surely had inherited a little bit of his Dutch ancestry, referring to her pale skin. He had laughed knowing full well he, and the others knew, he was pure Indian, and so was her mother, Dovie. They also knew that only the name he had adopted was Dutch.

J.P. did; however, notice that Dovie was again with child, and he felt the pangs of jealousy and knew too that he had made a mess of their marriage and allowed his cousin to take his place as husband, and father. He also saw that Dovie and Ben were very happy, something he had not been able to give Dovie. J.P.'s father, Houston, had insisted on accompanying him on this visit, so he had to grin and bear it and not make any trouble. It would be another five years before J.P. would again visit his children on Star Farm.

Little White Dove Flying "Dovie"

CHAPTER THREE

THE DEHAVILAND HOUSE

HOUSTON VAN BIBBER DROVE HIS BLACK CARRIAGE OUT OF ELDORADO AND HEADED SOUTHWEST FOR ST. LOUIS. HE KNEW THAT HE HAD TO DO SOMETHING TO FIND J.P. AND MAKE HIM GET THE DIVORCE THAT HE SHOULD HAVE DONE LONG AGO. HE WAS DETERMINED THAT HE WOULD NOT STOP UNTIL HE FOUND HIS ERRING SON.

The birth of Ben and Dovie's child, vivid in his mind, created utter disgust in the pit of his stomach. What a fool he was to leave his lovely little wife and baby alone shortly after little Rosabelle's birth, never to return. He had enjoyed having Ben and all his family, and especially being able to spend some time with Morning Star. Then there was that darling new baby who would forever be his grandchild; even if Ben was her father, she would carry his name.

Houston thought of many different approaches that he could use with J.P., but fear now gripped his mind as he drew closer and closer to his destination. He searched his mind over and over, just how he could convince him to get a divorce. Maybe, he thought, this new woman would not live with him unless they were married. Surely, he would not entertain marriage without a proper divorce. He had been relieved that J.P. had not come while Dovie was in labor, and of course he could not ever be told that Etta Mae was not his. J.P. could not be told the truth ever for he would cause as much trouble as he possibly could. He might even black mail Ben and Dovie in order to keep the secret.

"Well," Houston said to himself, "he will never learn it from me!" He had been in such deep thought that he had not realized that he was entering a small village just outside St. Louis. He decided to stop when he spied a small, new looking building that had a sign on it that read, SMITTY'S PLACE – DRINKS & GOOD FOOD FOR GOOD FOLKS. Houston realized that he was very hungry and decided to stop. Perhaps, he also thought, J.P. might have stopped here and maybe they can direct me to the hot spots in town. He hated to admit it even to himself, he would probably be found at one of the bawdy houses. The damn fool!

Houston Van Bibber was a tall man with slightly graying hair that gave him a distinguished look. He only had the beginning of a small belly, a straight back, large hands, and his complexion was not as dark as most Indians. His eyes were almost black and piercing. He was a man not to make angry, and he had to fight many men because of his flashing temper, usually brought on by some derogatory insults about Indians. He did not hide his ancestry, nor did he flaunt it to others. He was satisfied to pass as white for he knew he was a Blackfoot brave. He didn't have to talk about it, just look at me in my best buckskin and black boots. He really was handsome in his Pendleton plaid shirt and buckskin jacket. Houston laughed out loud at his thought as he tied his horse and carriage to the hitching post just outside "Smitty's".

Smitty's had the usual heavy haze that most bars have from the men smoking and it was hard for Houston to see. A few seconds passed and the smoke cleared and he could see that the long bar was nearly full. He walked closer and took a seat at the bar. He could also see many men and women seated at small square tables in a large dining area just through the double doors of the saloon. Houston had scanned the bar before taking a seat and saw that it was highly polished and made of a beautiful mahogany wood, inlaid with small squares in front of each stool. The seat he chose was between an elderly gentleman, well dressed, and a balding middle aged man, small in stature, wearing spectacles. Houston mused to himself as to what each of the men did for a living and concluded that the elderly man must be a land baron and the other man an accountant, or bookkeeper. He noticed how that the only other seat at the bar was between two men that seemed to be having a heated discussion about which breed of hogs were the best for getting to the market early. Houston was now pleased with his choice of a seat.

"Good day to you, good man," the elderly gentleman exclaimed to Houston.

"Thank you, sir. It is a good day." Houston returned the welcome, and nodded his acknowledgement to the little man on his right.

"Pour this man a drink, Smitty, and make him feel welcome. I'm John Farthington. Are you a new resident here, or a traveling man?" Houston, not much for bars or strangers, looked from each man to the other, and quietly stated his purpose there.

"My name is Houston Van Bibber, and I am here looking for my son." As he spoke, Houston fished out a small tin type of J.P. and showed it to each of the men. Each man shook his head, except the bartender.

"He looks a lot like you, and yes I have seen him. He comes in here several times a week. Usually with a 'lady'." The bartender stuttered a bit as he said 'lady', and Houston was pretty sure it must be J.P.

"What's your pleasure, sir?" Smitty asked Houston.

"Oh, a jigger of bourbon." Houston seldom drank fire water but he felt obligated now to join in with the other men.

"Mr. Van Bibber, I believe your son rooms at the same boarding house that I do; the Haviland House. If you would like, I can take you there after we finish our drinks."

The bookkeeper was pleased with himself to be able to capture the attention of Houston, who he could readily see was no ordinary drifter.

"Thank you, good man, that would be most kind of you." Houston thought to himself, I wonder what kind of place this Haviland House really is. Would he find yet another woman living with his son? A dreadful distaste filled his mouth, completely erasing the taste of the bourbon. Houston now wished he had ordered a sarsaparilla.

Houston followed the little bookkeeper about a mile closer to the edge of St. Louis before he turned off the main road into a private lane. The lane was narrow and was bordered on each side by large oak trees. The trees were still very barren and through the bare limbs of the trees, Houston could see a large house in the distance. He surmised that this must be the Haviland House. It looked respectable enough, he thought.

As they come closer, Houston could see this was a stately manor surrounded by many out buildings. One of the buildings was a very large stable, surrounded by a white washed board fence with several carriages parked in front of an ornate gate.

The bookkeeper now stopped his carriage and motioned for Houston to do the same. Houston tied his horse to the hitching post and waited for his new acquaintance to approach. As he did; so, he realized he hadn't asked for his name.

"It is very kind of you to help me, but I don't believe I got your name. The little man laughed hardily and then replied.

"My name is Burt Thompson. Let me take you in to see Miss Lilly. I see that she has the vacancy sign out, so I'm sure she has a room you can rent, at least for the night. See over there on the grass under the establishment's name." Burt Thompson pointed to the sign that read "THE HAVILAND HOUSE" and under that "A TASTE OF THE SOUTH".

Houston nodded at Burt as they climbed the two steps to a large veranda and up to the double doors that were a gleaming, highly polished walnut. They entered a great hall gleaming with highly polished hardwood floors. A very large chandelier glistened from the center of the ceiling, reflecting its light onto a mirrored hall tree. Burt took off his coat, hat and gloves and hung them on the hall tree; smoothed his sparse, dark hair, and motioned for Houston to follow suit.

"Miss Lilly will be in the study and she likes for visitors or guests to meet with her in there." Houston nodded and prepared himself to meet 'Miss Lilly'.

Burt knocked lightly on the first set of double doors on the left side of the great hall and pushed open the door. As they entered, a slender woman rose from a highly ornate Queen Anne desk and came toward them, offering her hand in welcome.

"Hello, Burt. Who do we have here?" Miss Lilly spoke distinctly, but in a very soft voice, as her eyes took in every detail of Houston and his clothing.

"Miss Lilly de Haviland. This is Houston Van Bibber. Houston, this is our lovely Miss Lilly de Haviland of East St. Louis." Houston was almost speechless at the beauty of the lady, but finally remembered his manners. He took the lady's outstretched hand, bent slightly, acknowledged her importance and touched the hand lightly to his lips.

He shuddered slightly, but undetectable, then looked up into the most beautiful eyes he had ever seen. They were a soft brown, infringed in lush curly black lashes. He was fascinated, but did look away for a moment to view the rest of this lovely woman. She was slight in form and rather dark of complexion. Her sienna colored hair was pulled straight back off her face, leaving tiny little wisps of curls around her face. A soft pink ribbon that matched the trim on her dress was tied around her soft curls at the nape of her neck.

Lilly smiled at Houston a bright and welcoming smile and asked, "Will you be staying with us awhile, Mr. Van Bibber?"

Houston tried to smile back but found that his lips felt like cardboard, so he cleared his throat and then spoke to this beautiful woman.

"Yes, I would like to stay at least a day or two. Would that be something you could manage?' Houston thought that he sounded a bit stupid, and tried to stop staring at Miss Lilly, but simply could not.

Her eyes were magnetic and Houston felt he never wanted to ever be out of her sight. His feelings for Morning Star had now flown out the window and he wanted to know this woman better. Lilly was aware of the effect she had on Houston, but something was different about him. She wanted to know him better, unlike most of the men that entered the Haviland House.

"Yes, I have a room for you, and you can stay as long as you like. Come with me, I will show you your room." She picked up a ring of keys and motioned for Houston to follow. Burt and Houston followed silently up the winding staircase to the second floor.

"Here, Mr. Van Bibber, is your room. A full bath is at the end of the hall; and as you can see, all toiletries are supplied. Do you have a valise?"

"Yes ma'am. I do, but I left it my carriage." Houston apologized.

"That's fine. My man, Jackson, will fetch it for you. He will also put your horse and carriage away in the barn. Is there anything else that you need? Oh, we serve breakfast at 7:00 a.m. and dinner a 6:00 p.m. If you will not be eating with us, please give the cook notice. Her name is Agnes. The room and the meals are $3.00 a night for one, or $20.00 a week. Your linens are changed every three days and dirty clothes can be given to the maid and she will clean them for you. Her fees are very reasonable." Lilly's voice had taken on a business tone now as she turned back to Houston, waiting for an answer.

"Thank you again. I will be needing the room for at least two nights." Houston handed Lilly $10.00 as he spoke. "I will be taking my meals with you. I'm sure the food will be better here than anywhere else." Houston smiled directly at Lilly as he felt a surge in his heart.

Lilly blushed at his intense stare as she felt drawn to this man. What in the world was the matter with her, she wondered. This man is just one more boarder; but still she said to herself, he is different. What is it?

Burt Thompson had left the two alone and headed for his own room when he saw the charisma that had passed between them. She had never looked at him that way, and he had never seen her look at any other man like that. He wondered had he started something? He had washed up and was now returning to the room where he had left Lilly and Houston. He was bursting with questions, but he did not want to let on that she had looked at Houston as if he was a big, ripe apple.

"Did you ask Lilly about your son?"

"No Burt, I did not. I thought I would wait until dinner and maybe I could look everyone over first." Houston chuckled as he thought of the surprised look on J.P.'s face when they encountered each other. Houston had said that he would not run around after J.P. any more and get him out of trouble. He had said he was done with that kind of thing and J.P. would have to get himself out of all the entanglements that he got himself into from now on. Now here he was, again. He knew that J.P. was sure that his father would not venture as far as St. Louis to spy on him.

"I lit the fire in my room, did you light yours?"

"No I didn't, Burt. That is a good idea to take the chill off the room. To tell you the truth, I didn't even notice I had a fireplace. Is it all laid and ready?"

"Yes, it is all ready for lighting. It is made ready every night. I could see that Miss Lilly impressed you, just like she does everyone who shows up here. So don't feel alone, she beguiles every man that lays eyes on her. She really is something, isn't she?" Burt was mumbling as he finished speaking for he hadn't gotten over the tugs she made on his heart strings every time he looked at her. He knew he had no chance with her, so he kept his respectful distance.

"Do you play cards, Mr. Van Bibber?" Burt asked.

"Very seldom, Never got in the habit." Houston was thoughtful as he answered.

"What kind of work do you do? As I told you, I'm a bookkeeper. I've been at the Koch Brewery for years now. Actually, ever since I finished school. It's the only place I've ever worked. It pays good and allows me to live here. Thc Haviland House is one of the best.

"I can see why. This place is really beautiful. It's so clean and the furnishings are splendid. Just like the owner." Houston blushed a bright red as he uttered the last words.

"Yes, that is right, but you didn't say what you do for a living." Burt would not be deterred from his question.

"I'm a farmer in Eldorado. I raise horses, mainly." Houston rationed his words now. He felt that he should be on guard with this little man. Exactly why, he could not put his finger on.

"I thought as much when I saw your mount and carriage." Burt replied. "But what about your son? What does he do here in St. Louis? Has it been a long time since you saw him?"

Burt was relentless. He felt there was some mystery here and he wanted to know what it was. Why was this man really looking for his son? What kind of trouble was he in?

"My son has been away from home for some time, which is not unusual since he buys livestock for our farm. I need to find him because of a little problem back on the farm which could affect his purchasing more livestock at this time." Houston wondered about Burt's questions, but tried to act nonchalant now for he was not about to give up the real problem. His mind wandered to that precious little baby girl that had just been born to Alice Dean (Dovie), J.P.'s estranged wife.

Divorce Indian style was fine with him, but it just didn't suffice in the real world. J.P. had been gone for almost two years now, and a real divorce had to be gotten as soon as possible to protect the child. He was sure that there would be more children coming so Ben and Alice Dean needed to get married, for all their sakes.

Houston had insisted that the little family stay with him an additional week for the birth had been hard and Alice Dean seemed much too weak to travel such a long distance. He had taken them to the train, bid them goodbye, and assured them that he would get J.P. to get the divorce. He would just have to demand that he do so and go with him to file the papers.

Houston was shaken from his reverie as he watched Burt shuffling his cards.

"We got time for a couple of hands of poker before dinner." Burt said matter of fact, knowing that Van Bibber would not object again.

"Oh, I'm sorry, Burt. I do have a lot on my mind, but yes, I agree. You might have to give me a few pointers. It's been awhile since I've even held a card in my hand. I won't be a good adversary." Houston laughed at his own inefficiency. He was, however, glad to think of something other than his wayward son.

Miss Lilly closed the door to the study and wrote in her guest book, 'Houston Van Bibber, arrived April 2, 1895, paid for two days. (a handsome man, looks Italian)'.

She laid her pen down and sat for sometime staring out the window not even noticing the soft white flakes as they accumulated on the bushes and leafless trees. Just who is this Van Bibber, and what is it that is so intriguing about him, she wondered.

Houston entered the huge dining room with Burt Thompson and waited a few minutes before taking a place at the table. Five men and two women had already seated themselves as Houston and Burt took their seats. Lilly arrived at just this time and seated herself at the head of the table, her customary seat.

She smiled at the diners and returned pleasantries, acknowledging each one.

The diners looked at Houston when introduced, and then returned to their chatter with each other. Houston only nodded to the other guests, said hello to Miss Lilly, and saw that his son was not among the diners. Houston realized that he was hungry and was thankful for the ease with which dinner was served. The food was delicious, the china beautiful, the crystal spotless; and best of all, Miss Lilly was stunning in a forest green velvet gown.

Houston watched every move Lilly made, growing more and more conscious of his own loneliness and needs. His wife had been gone for a very long time. He had tried to be more than a family friend with Morning Star but she rejected any thing more. She always said that White Feather was still with her and she could not find it in her heart to turn him out. Houston never pressed her, satisfied with her friendship.

He felt his heart skip a beat or two as he watched Lilly laughing and teasing the diners. She did not; however, include him in the teasing.

As Houston watched Lilly and the others, he dreaded to have to talk to her about his son. Had he been there? Was the bookkeeper right, or was he just looking for companionship?

Early the next day after breakfast Houston entered the study to speak to Lilly. He had once again fished out the little tin type of J.P. and handed it to her as he asked the important question.

"Has this man been here at your establishment?" Lilly looked at the picture for a long time before she asked Houston.

"Who is this man to you?"

"He is my son and I need to find him. Has he been here, as the little bookkeeper led me to believe?"

"Yes, he was here I believe. You just missed him, Mr. Van Bibber. But he signed his name as J.P. Dickerson. I'm pretty sure that was him." Miss Lilly explained with concern. And then, as if in afterthought, she continued.

"He did say; however, he would be back in a week or so. He even gave me a deposit on his room. Here, look in my register." Lilly looked up at Houston with enthusiasm as she asked.

"Will you stay until he comes back?" It was almost a plea.

"Yes, I guess that would be best." Houston sounded a little defeated. Lilly was grateful for his answer for she wanted to know this man better. She turned to him and did something she never did with her guests.

"Perhaps we could take this time to let me show you a little of St. Louis, and my gardens here. Surely this will be our last snow. It is the fist of April and spring is just around the corner." Lilly laughed nervously as she waited for his answer.

Houston was relieved that she had been the aggressor, for he did not know how to approach such an elegant lady as Miss Lilly. He was sorely afraid of being rejected, after all, he knew that as an Indian, he was looked at by most white people as being inferior. Houston felt both fear and elation as he answered her.

"Yes, Miss Lilly. I would like that very much. Where do we start?" Houston found himself shaking internally now that the ice was broken. Could she really be interested in an Illinois horse farmer he wondered?

"Put on your hat and coat and we will take a turn in the gardens. Sam has cleared the paths and I believe that a few crotons have popped out for us to see. Come, the sun will keep us warm." Lilly giggled now much like a little girl as she donned her own coat and gloves.

The two walked through the gardens with Lilly pointing out this bush and that tree, where the roses were, and much to their surprise and pleasure, a jonquil had popped out amidst the snow. A few robins had braved the weather and now chirped as they passed by the tulip bed, stating that the tulips were almost up too. The redbud bushes had began to open up and their fragrance was heady.

By the time they had finished their tour, they were holding hands and laughing up into each other's faces. They did not notice the chill in the air until Agnes called for them to come in. She had made a cup of hot tea for each of them she said. Elmer and Bessie had seen them holding hands and they were overjoyed.

They had been worried about their mistress for she never seemed to have any friends. Lilly always said she didn't have time to go out much because the house and its guests kept her too busy.

Elmer had put away Houston's horse and carriage. He had taken note that the horse was of good blood and the carriage above average. Agnes and Bessie had also had a good chance to look over the new guest at the dinner table. Agnes sensed that this man was somehow different than the usual run of the male guests. She had also noticed that Miss Lilly was drawn to him much more than just a guest.

The sweet smell of pies baking filled their noses as they entered the kitchen. Agnes was humming to herself and looking very smug. She knew romance was in the air, even if they did not.

"You must be frozen, Miss Lilly. The two of you have been out in the garden for a very long time. Sir, set your self down here. Would you like tea or coffee? I have both." Agnes's face was flush from the heat of the cooking stove. Her husband; however, was putting more wood in the stove from the huge firebox in the corner. He stopped only momentarily to look at Houston and Lilly. He smiled a bit and then returned to his work. As he left, he gave Agnes a wink and a grin. He hoped something could come of this attraction.

Houston said very little, but his eyes said it all. He was about to lose his heart to this lovely woman. He watched intently as Lilly loosened her soft brown hair and let it curl about her face and drop down past her shoulders in soft waves.

Agnes had not seen her do this since her mother and father had left this world. "Now ain't that something of an omen," she thought.

Houston looked at Lilly in awe, now, for he could see that she was not near as old as she had appeared earlier. She must be no more than thirty. He didn't care, if she didn't.

"Thanks, Agnes. That pie was delicious. May I have more of it at dinner?" Houston chided Agnes, and Lilly decided it was the perfect moment to let their plans be known.

"Oh, by the way Agnes, Mr. Van Bibber and I are going into St. Louis tomorrow. Don't wait dinner on us as we are also going to the opera. And yes, for dinner tonight, reserve a place for Mr. Van Bibber next to me. Come now, Houston, I must be getting back to work, for a little while, anyway."

Lilly seemed to be speaking yet to Agnes, but at the same time she was leading Houston out of the kitchen and down the great hall. She pulled the ring of keys out of her pocket and opened the door almost opposite the dining room. Without speaking she pulled Houston inside and promptly slid the lock on the door and sighed a great sigh of relief.

Houston looked about and saw the room was the size of two rooms, with a small partition in the middle, separating a sitting room from what he could tell now was a bedroom beyond. The rooms were breathtakingly beautiful, draped in ivory lace, taffeta and gold. He could barely see a beautifully canopied bed decorated in the same ivory lace and gold. He was almost speechless for he had never seen anything so handsome before.

"Are these your private quarters?" he asked as he took in the splendor of his surroundings.

"Yes they are, Houston! Just so you know, I have never allowed any man in these quarters but you." Lilly's voice quivered a bit as she went on, gazing down at her feet as she spoke. "I feel you are special. I feel drawn to you as I have never been before, to anyone."

With these words Lilly gained a bit of confidence and walked slowly toward Houston and placed her hands on his chest. Her action surprised Houston temporarily, but before he could answer, she looked up into his eyes and continued. "You must feel as I do. I see it in your eyes!"

Houston could barely speak, but he managed to whisper to her.

"Yes Lilly. Yes I do"

Her arms slid around his neck and he gently pulled her body close to his. He held her there for a moment or two before lifting her face up and gently kissing her lips. He felt her body tremor, as did his own. He then released her and led her to the satin covered Chippendale sofa, and still holding her hand, he whispered to her, "I have never known anyone like you before. You are such a fine lady, and yes, I want you with all my heart and being, but I'm so much, much older than you." Houston's voice was so husky Lilly could hardly make out his words, but she did.

"I don't care how old you are! I think I am falling in love with you." Lilly raised her lips to his face and kissed his cheek, then offered her lips to him again.

Their kiss was so powerful Houston had to put some distance between them while he could, so he moved to the other end of the sofa.

"Lilly, Lilly. Let's not go too fast. You don't know anything about me. Not even where I'm from or why I'm here. You must have more information before you decide. Perhaps you have been too long without a lover. Sometimes lust can overpower one's mind. I don't want that to happen to us. If and when we give ourselves to each other, it must be for love and love alone. Help me, please, for I am weak!"

Lilly was stunned!

She had not thought about what could happen if they kept kissing. She was embarrassed at her naivety, but she decided she didn't care. Agnes was right she thought now, she needed to find a man for her life, and she knew she wanted this one.

"So tell me everything you think I need to know, Houston. I must warn you though, nothing you can say will change my mind. If it's just lust, then I need to know that too. I'm thirty one years old and I've never known a man."

Lilly was almost begging him now but Houston knew she had to know who he was for that could change everything. He shuddered at the thought of losing her.

"Go ahead, tell me what I should know." She pouted as she crossed her arms against her chest and waited.

Houston tried to manage a smile, but to no avail. My God, who would have ever thought this lady was a virgin. That alone is enough to send me packing, but no, he thought, I've never had feelings like I have for her.

"Well, first of all, I'm a horse breeder, a cattleman on a farm from Eldorado. I have grown children, but I'm not married. My wife passed on many years ago. My name 'Van Bibber' is an assumed white man's name for I am really a Blackfoot Indian. My parents recently died on the Reservation in Oklahoma."

Lilly gasped as he spoke the word 'Indian', but quickly covered her mouth and stared at Houston in disbelief. Her shock did not go unnoticed, but Houston knew he must not stop now, so he continued.

"You see, my dear Lilly, I may not be who I appear to be, but I'm sincere when I say I care for you. I came to St. Louis looking from my erring son and I have reason to believe he is the man you said would be back in a week."

Houston fished the picture of J.P. out of his coat pocket and handed it to her.

Lilly looked at the picture, but did not take it. Slowly she released her hand from her mouth and laid them on her lap, never taking her eyes off them. What would he think when he found out about J.P.'s trying to court her, she wondered?

Houston said no more for he could see that she was milling in her mind all he had said.

Finally she spoke much to his relief.

"I don't care if you are Indian, Negro, or anything else. But, you are right when you say we should take our time and get to know each other better. Time is not going to change my mind on what I feel for you. I know that I have never felt like this before. Your lips have ignited a fire inside of me and only you can tame it."

Tears had now started running down her soft cheeks onto her waistcoat.

Houston dropped to his knees and cupped her face in his hand and kissed her soft, pink lips, cautiously.

"So be it. We will spend our time together tomorrow and the days ahead, until my son comes back and see how everything goes. You have lit up my life like you can not believe, but I still have one question for you.

You are so beautiful and such a fine lady. I want to hear how you have ended up alone with this house and all the work it takes to keep it running?"

Lilly was about to speak again, but Houston stopped her.

"Shhh, I don't need to hear this now. We can talk later. I must take my leave now, while I still can." He took a deep breath and held Lilly for a few seconds in his arms, kissed her on the cheek and bid her good day.

Houston took his seat next to Lilly's as two new men joined the guests at the dinner table. Neither man was J.P., but Thompson took the empty seat next to Houston and stared at Houston and then at Lilly. Never very curious, Burt now felt there was a little intrigue in the air, so he watched with fascination at the interaction between Lilly and Houston.

Lilly had smiled as she always did as she entered the dining room, but gave no sign of special interest toward Houston. But Burt could feel something different about them.

What was it, he wondered?

Houston had smarted a bit at Lilly's nonchalant attitude toward him, but understood her need for secrecy at this point. He knew though that Agnes knew that something had made Lilly have him placed next to her at the table. Still, her mood toward him was a puzzle, so he could not help but fidget in his chair, as it seemed she was much friendlier toward everyone but him.

Maybe she had changed her mind once she had thought over the fact that he was an Indian. Most people did. It had been evident that this fact had taken her by surprise. She had said it didn't matter, but maybe it really did.

Houston's mind ran this fact over and over like a broken record, and finally, not able to join in the small talk and gossip, he dismissed himself and left the table. He needed a quiet place where he could think.

Houston's sudden departure unnerved Lilly a bit, but she tried not to let her feelings show. Burt had seen her immense displeasure and found this fact even more intriguing.

Lilly, however, had a problem of her own. How would Houston react to J.P.'s intentions toward her?

Would he still feel the same way about her? She felt a terrible uneasiness in the pit of her stomach, but she vowed she would cross that bridge when it happened. For now, she thought, she had mislead all of her guests into believing they were the most important things in her life.

Breakfast was almost over and most of the diners had left before Houston entered the dining room, apologizing vehemently to Agnes.

He could hardly believe his eyes as he took in Lilly's loveliness.

She wore a beautiful woolen dress that fitted her torso softly, but still enhancing every curve of her body. Her hair was softly curled under a matching blue hat that was slightly titled over her left eye. The feathers adorning the hat teasingly fluttered with her every gesture.

As Houston entered, she rose from her chair and sighed a huge sigh of relief before she addressed him.

"Well, didn't you give me a rush? I thought you had changed your mind." She stopped, waited until Agnes left the room, and then continued.

"So, have you changed your mind?" She held her breath waiting for his answer.

"Of course not! I just had trouble deciding what a gentleman would wear here in St. Louis. That is, to the opera, since I have never been before." Houston smiled at Lilly in amusement.

"Really, you have never been to the opera!?" Lilly exclaimed.

"That's right. I'm just a country kind of guy." Houston laughed at Lilly's remark. Lilly; however, was not going to let anything spoil this day for her.

"Well, you look wonderful. You made a good choice. You will be turning all the single girls' heads; and probably some married ones, too. Never fear, though, I saw you first." Lilly chided.

Houston felt better now, for this was a new adventure for him and he was so glad that Lilly still wanted him. At that moment, Agnes bustled back into the room, as if she had not been listening just beyond the door to their conversation.

"Come now, Mr. Van Bibber, Elmer is waiting to take you in Miss Lilly's carriage."

"Yes, Mr. Van Bibber, come along, Elmer is waiting." Lilly teased as she wrapped her arm around Houston's.

Lilly's carriage was a closed-in surrey, draped at the little windows and lushly padded in dark red velvet. On the exterior of the carriage, a large scripted 'H' was painted in gold. Several little birds were painted on the glossy black background ascending toward the roof of the carriage. Definitely a carriage befitting an important and beautiful lady. Houston smiled broadly and nodded his head in agreement. Agnes and Sam watched in disbelief as the couple climbed in, looking at each other affectionately. Miss Lilly had never took a man in her private carriage before to their knowledge. "My, my," Agnes said to Sam. Could this mean what they thought it did?

Lilly and Houston visited the park, the museum, walked by the river and ate at the Lavender and Lace Tea Room. They stopped at a few of the stores where Houston bought Lilly a beautiful cameo and bottle of rose water. Lilly was delighted with the gifts and insisted on wearing the cameo which pleased Houston even more.

Houston did not care much for the opera, but it did give him an idea as to how others spent some of their time. He liked one of the female singers but thought most of the performers voices much to shrill. He did; however, notice that a lot of whispering was going on, and he could tell it was about him and Lilly. She had been right – the hall was ablaze with flirtatious women and men. He was curious now as to who and what Lilly really was, for everyone seemed to know her by name. He really didn't care much, but it did make him feel a little out of place.

As they approached their carriage to drive home, Houston suddenly stopped and turned to Lilly and questioned her.

"Well, how did I do?" Lilly laughed, genuinely, as she answered.

"Just fine! You created a lot of interest amongst the ladies and the men. They are not accustomed to seeing me with a gentleman." Lilly giggled as if she had made a joke and Houston had to laugh with her.

"I must admit, I did hear a lot of whispering." Houston grinned, showing off his even white teeth.

"I also have to admit I didn't really care much for your opera. I suppose I could tolerate it once in awhile, just to please you, Lilly."

"You do please me very much, Houston, and I promise not to drag you off again, without explaining what the opera is all about." Lilly shivered now, for the night had turned very cold.

Houston helped her into the carriage, unfolded the carriage lap-wrap, tucked it in around Lilly's lovely body, then pulled her close to him. Lilly snuggled close and soon the heat from their bodies made them forget they were ever cold. Very little conversation passed between them on the way home for there was no need. They were relishing in each other's presence as only two would-be lovers can. Houston mused on several subjects. He wondered where Elmer had gone while they ate, shopped and were at the opera. How often did Lilly take these sojourns and did she always go alone? He could hardly believe that she had no suitors. She had changed the conversation when he asked her any personal questions. Why, he wondered?

Elmer had now turned the horses into the lane leading to the house. Lilly suddenly sat up when she realized they were near the house and peered out of the little window.

"Oh my goodness! Look, Houston, every lamp in the house must be lit. What ever can be the reason for this at this time of night?" Lilly was now very agitated.

"I'm sure it is nothing. Don't fret. What ever is the problem, we will face it together." Houston patted Lilly's shoulder, but a sudden rush of fear raced up his back.

Houston helped Lilly out of the carriage and up the front steps. As he opened the front door he saw a man crouched down in one of the chairs in the great hall. Lilly saw the figure at the same time and thought the man asleep, but Houston knew the smell of too much liquor.

"Wait here, Lilly." Houston cautioned, "let me see who this is." The man had risen now and was staggering toward them. Houston was immediately shocked.

"Oh my God! It is you! What on earth are you doing here in the hall?" Houston could not believe his eyes. The man staggered again as he lurched forward.

"You ole dirty son-of-a-bitch! What do you think you are doing with my girl?" The drunken man literally screamed at Houston as he pulled a pistol out of his jacket and aimed it first at Houston and then at Lilly.

"I'll kill you both." The gun was wavering around from one hand to the other as he spoke.

"Put the gun down!" Houston demanded but the man laughed crazily and took better aim at Houston. Houston, always quick on his feet, lunged at the man knocking him to the floor, sending the gun sliding across the floor, far from its owner.

"Get up! What the hell do you think you are doing? You are drunk! I said, get up!" Houston was angrily jerking the man up by his collar. Lilly had covered her face with her hands and had backed herself up against the far wall. In an almost inaudible whisper, she spoke. "It's Mr. Dickerson!"

"No, Lilly. This is J.P. Van Bibber, my stupid son, so drunk he doesn't even know what he is doing."

"Your son! Oh my God! Your son?" Lilly screamed and fell to the floor. The loud noises and scuffling brought Agnes and Sam running in from the back of the house. Agnes stopped short when she saw Houston holding J.P. in a very tight clutch. Sam grabbed hold of J.P. and walked him out of the room as Agnes rushed to Lilly's side. Houston picked up the gun before following Sam and J.P. Agnes shook Lilly, for she seemed to be in a daze.

"What just happened, Agnes?" she asked.

"Don't fret child, Mr. Van Bibber took care of that awful drunk man. He showed up here early in the afternoon demanding to know where you were. I had to finally tell him you had gone into town with Henry. Sam finally let him into his room, for he said he had paid for it."

Agnes took a deep breath and continued to comfort a shaken Lilly.

"He came to dinner asking about you and when you would be home. Sam told him he didn't know for sure. He got really mad then and demanded to know who you were with. Hush child, Mr. Van Bibber and Sam took that man away. Let me help you to your quarters."

Lilly did not resist but went quietly sobbing with Agnes. Meanwhile, Houston and Sam were trying to sober J.P. up.

"Sam, get this fool some hot coffee. Maybe it will bring him to his senses." It was a command from Houston, who now plunked J.P. down in one of the straight chairs at the table in the huge kitchen.

"Yes sir, him sorely do need it." Sam answered in a knowing manner shaking his head as he went about heating up the old granite coffee pot.

J.P. started coming around out of the liquor fog he had been in, mumbling in indignation at his father. Finally, after Houston had forced several cups of coffee down him, J.P. found the courage to question his father again.

"Just what in tarnation are you doing here? How did you find this place and what in the hell are you doing taking Lilly out?" J.P.'s words were still slurred, but his arrogance was returning.

"That's not important now. I've been here several days waiting for your return. Drink that coffee and don't give me any more sass." Houston bellowed at his son.

"It IS important. Just what is your relationship to Miss Lilly?" J.P. was becoming more insistent for an answer.

Houston, fully disgusted now, grabbed J.P. by the shoulder and forced him to stand as he belated the questioning.

"How dare you question me! We will discuss this in your room, not here. Sam, show me to his room!."

"Yes sir. Just follow me up the stairs!" Sam had seen many a drunk in his time and was anxious to get J.P. out of the kitchen. He also was very curious. Just what was going to happen between this father and son, and what part was Miss Lilly going to play in it. What had been a day of joyful speculation for him and Agnes had now turned sour.

As the two men entered the great hall, they saw Agnes quietly close the door to Lilly's quarters.

"How is she?" Houston questioned.

"A little shaken yet. I believe she would like to see you Mr. Van Bibber," Agnes said meekly.

"Fine, later perhaps. You might tell her that, Agnes."

"Yah, Agnes, tell her I'll see her later too! J.P. said arrogantly, mimicking his father.

"Shut up! You are going nowhere near her room, or that lady, or for that matter, anyone else's in your condition. You have done enough for tonight!" Houston was strong arming J.P. up the stairs when Sam opened the door to his room.

Houston shoved J.P. inside and slammed the door behind himself. J.P. stumbled and landed across the bed on his stomach but managed to turn over and sit up with his father standing over him.

Houston was a much larger, taller man than J.P. and J.P. seemed to grow smaller as his father stood over him now, full of anger and total disgust.

"Just how many more times will I have to get you out of trouble? What you did tonight was inexcusable. Threatening to kill me is one thing. But Lilly? How stupid. You ask me what my position with her is, well I might ask you the same except you have none. You can't have any position, you are a married man!" Houston's anger now overtook him as he looked into his son's insolent stare.

"I'm married in name only, you know that. I intended to come back here and ask Miss Lilly for her hand." J.P. was practically whining now. He knew full well that anything he said would be lost on his father, but that did not stop him from trying.

"So, did you plan to tell her you are married?" Houston retorted.

"Yes, and that I was getting divorced."

"Good! That's why I came here looking for you. Alice Dean just had your third child this month. Have you no concern for her or your children?" Easy, Houston thought, he must not know exactly when the child was born, or anything about Ben's wanting to marry Dovie.

"Yes. But Ben just moved in and took over. She did not need me for that farm." J.P. whimpered.

"And that was surely a good thing since you took off for parts unknown when little Rosabelle was born, going home again just long enough to plant your seed one more time." Houston bristled, but was choosing his words carefully.

"J.P., I don't want to discuss this anymore tonight. Tomorrow, I am taking you to a barrister and we are getting the divorce. NO more of your promises. Tomorrow it will be done! Do you understand me?"

J.P. saw the disgust on his father's face and knew he was very serious. He also knew that he was guilty of abandoning Dovie and his children, but to himself he said, 'She is better off without me, but I just couldn't divorce her, for I knew that is what they both wanted.'

"Yes, Papa, whatever you say." J.P. soberly said. He knew it was useless to argue with his father. It is probably best to just get it over with, he thought. I will be free to do whatever I wish then. I also could run later on when he is asleep and do nothing, and I could make sure no one will know where I am. It would serve them all to have to stew a little more. Then, the image of Grey Fox came into his mind and he shivered to think of what that Indian might do if he caught him. He would have to do as his father said. As if Houston had read his mind, he turned at the door and uttered a sentence J.P. would never forget and sever any remaining ties he had left with his father.

"Don't even think about running again. I am your father and I will hunt you down to the ends of the earth. You are not going to cause Dovie, Ben, her mother or anyone else on the Star Farm anymore problems. You have caused them all enough pain, especially Dovie and the children. I will destroy you before you destroy yourself and all that you touch. As far as Miss Lilly, you have no chance with her – she is not a stupid woman. I don't believe she ever had any feelings for you, but that is another matter, especially since you are not free to ever speak to her as such. You have ruined any good feelings she might have had, if she had any, for you. Get a good night's sleep, you are going to need it!"

Houston spoke these last words as he closed the door behind him.

Sam had waited in the hall, fearing some kind of trouble, and was relieved when Houston emerged from the room.

"Oh, there you are, right as I need you. Sam, do me a favor, put the outside lock on this door. I don't want him running out again."

"YES SIR! I can do that gladly!" Sam grinned and sighed a big sigh of relief; and so did Houston.

Houston was not looking forward to his conversation with Lilly. What had been the most enjoyable day for many years, had ended in disaster.

Houston straightened up his clothing and turned toward Lilly's room and hesitated before knocking, looking up and down that great hall, making sure no one was watching.

He tapped softly on her door, but no answer came. His heart started racing in his chest. Just as he was about to walk away, Lilly quietly opened the door, and seeing Houston, she quickly opened the door wider and bade him to enter. She promptly burst into tears and Houston looked at her for a moment, for he could see her eyes were very red from crying. She did not wish him to see her swollen eyes, so she covered her face with a small white handkerchief.

"Please don't look at me. I'm so ashamed. You must hate me," she uttered between sobs. I SWEAR Houston, I did not ever encourage your son. I can't believe he called me 'his' girl. I never went out with him and I don't think I treated him any different than my other guests."

Houston crumbled a little with each sob. He knew full well his womanizing son, so he knew what she was saying was true. He had seen the astonishment on her face when she had seen J.P., and then again when he called her 'his' girl. Houston tried to console Lilly, but she pulled away from him and ran to her bed and flung herself upon it. Houston followed, calling to her over and over.

"Lilly, Lilly, my dearest sweet Lilly. Don't fret so. I know my son and I believe you. Come, sit up and let me dry away your tears." Houston's voice was soft and compelling. Lilly slowly raised her head and reached for Houston, almost childlike.

"Now that's better. Let me hold you and let our day be complete. NO one can take away the joy we shared today." Houston was now kissing Lilly's neck as he encompassed her body softly against his own.

Lilly's sobs grew less and less and finally stopped. She could not resist Houston's embraces. She thought 'he is right, I can't let anything change what I feel with this man. I don't care if he is an Indian, or how old he is. I feel so much love for him I cannot let pride stand in our way.'

Houston held Lilly for a long time, kissing her passionately, and then pulled her to her feet and sat her down on the Chippendale sofa.

Lilly looked at him questioningly.

"Now my dear, I must tell you about my son. Sit here, beside me." He patted the sofa and she sat down beside him. She said nothing but felt a little pang of fear as she looked into his eyes now.

"I'm going to be as brief as possible tonight, but I feel you deserve a little of the sordid story of J.P. I'm sad to say he is not a son to be proud of. I came looking for him because he has three children whom he has abandoned. He just can't stop his old habits. It seems he can't keep away from women and liquor. He is married to a fine and beautiful woman of the Blackfeet Nation. She has a fine family in Kentucky now. It seems though, that is not enough for J.P. He prowls the streets of all the towns along the Ohio River, drinking and carousing with loose women, if you know what I mean. I suppose it is his mother's and my fault. Neither of us ever made him take any responsibility for any of the trouble he has gotten into. Believe me when I say he has gotten into a lot of it. His mother, rest her soul, always insisted I had to bail him out of jail or pay for his shenanigans. We gave him too much money to play around with and he hasn't had to work hard for any of it. His brothers have helped me tend the farm and the cattle on it. Enough said about that. I came here to make sure he gets a divorce from his wife that he promised to do a year ago. His little wife has found someone who will take good care of her and the children, and this fine man wants to marry her. So as you can see, he must get this divorce, and by the name of the Creator, I will see that he does it. Perhaps you can steer me to a good barrister." Houston was dead serious and Lilly now understood what had really happened here tonight.

"I'm sorry! I think I can be of help, Houston. My lawyer can take care of this matter, I'm sure." Lilly drew a deep breath and continued. "About J.P. and me, I must confess I did spend a couple nights sitting on the swing with J.P.; however, I did not take his advances seriously and I did NOT let him touch me intimately. He did say that he had some serious questions to ask me when he returned, so perhaps that is why he called me 'his' girl."

"Hush, my dear, you don't have to explain anything to me. I do want you to know I believe you and after I get J.P. taken care of, we will talk about where our lives are headed."

Houston smiled at Lilly and placed his arm around her and pulled her closer to him. He kissed her softly on the lips and then stood to leave.

"I must go now. You need to get some sleep and we will get the directions to the lawyer in the morning. Good night, my dear." Lilly smiled back at Houston, nodded her head, but thought 'why not stay the night with me'.

She smiled even broader now and blushed a deep pink from her own thoughts.

Houston let himself out into the hall and climbed the stairs to his room. Gee whiz he thought, what a night it has been, as the events of the night recrossed his mind. He climbed into the big, comfortable bed and was soon asleep.

A sullen J.P. and a stern Houston entered the offices of Pinkney and Bowes on Main Street in downtown St. Louis. They were greeted by a tall woman of approximately forty years. "Good morning, gentlemen," she said, "can I help you?"

"Yes, ma'am, I believe you can. We are looking for Mr. Bowes. He was referred to us by Miss Lilly de Haviland." Houston answered.

"Oh, yes sir, your names, sir?"

"Houston and J.P. Van Bibber." Houston answered in his most business like manner. J.P. started to speak but the look from his father stopped him cold. One hour later, J.P. and his father held paperwork for the divorce in their hands.

"Just one thing more, Mr. Bowes. My son here doesn't lay claim to anything on the Star Farm from his wife, this is. Do these papers specify that?" Mr. Bowes eyed Houston seriously before he spoke again.

"Well, no they don't, but J.P. is entitled to his share." The barrister advised. "It sounds like their farm is a very productive one, and we can go into that at the settlement." J.P. squirmed in his chair, but said nothing as he scanned Houston's face. After an awkward silence, he decided he would speak.

"No, I don't want anything from Star Farm. I just want my inheritance from my father." Houston glared at J.P. now. They had settled this matter before they had arrived at the barrister's office. Of course, Mr. Bowes had not been privy to this, so it was only natural he would ask this question, Houston thought.

"Now, Mr. Van Bibber, what are you willing to give to your estranged wife and your children?"

"I hadn't given it much thought." J.P. answered sarcastically.

"Never mind, Mr. Bowes, Alice Dean doesn't want anything but her farm and the divorce." Houston retorted, glaring at his son as he spoke. "Mr. Bowes, I'll take care of seeing she gets her share to take care of the children." Houston was almost hostile as he spoke these words. J.P. straightened up in his chair where he had been lounging.

"What do you mean, Pa?" J.P. questioned.

"I mean, I will do what you should do, but I can't trust you to do it." Houston stood now as if to leave, but the attorney motioned him to sit back down.

"Sorry, sir, but we are not quite finished. You see, Mr. Van Bibber, whatever you plan to do for Mrs. Van Bibber, should be included in the divorce papers. Also, there is one more thing I must address, just so you are aware of it. I will file these papers with the court but it will take some time to get this all done. If there is no contest from Mrs. Van Bibber, you should be a free man within six months."

"Six months! It will take that long?" J.P. could not believe it.

"Yes, I'm afraid so. I'll be in touch for both your signatures when the papers are ready to sign." Bowes rose and walked around his desk and shook hands with both J.P. and Houston and bid them a good day.

J.P. and Houston rode in silence as they headed back to The Haviland House. Each had their own thoughts about what they had just done.

J.P. had mixed emotions about the divorce. He had loved Dovie in his own way, but he just couldn't stand all the people on that farm always telling him what to do. He knew they all were constantly judging him and thought of him as an Indian; which he hated. As he thought of his impending freedom, he was glad that his father had made him come to terms about a divorce. He also thought about what Grey Fox might do if he had chosen not to do it, and shivered at the thought.

Houston's thoughts were about Dovie's pleading to help her find J.P. and make him get the divorce. Morning Star too, had begged him to help them. Now he had done his part and he could get on with his life. What about Lilly? Did they have a future together? Surely she would never give up The Haviland House and he couldn't blame her. Could they come to some kind of agreement or was he being a stupid old man who had fallen in love with a girl who could be his own daughter? Time would tell, he thought, but for now, he had to tend to business at hand. As the carriage turned into the little lane, Houston brought it to a halt and turned to his sullen son.

"J.P., I will be getting my valises together and leaving for home in the morning. I want you to return with me. Now hold on a minute until I finish. I know you were really upset last night with me and Lilly, but you were under the influence of that mighty white man's whiskey. I had hoped you would realize you have to limit your drinking by now."

J.P. tried to interrupt his father, but Houston held up his hand for him to wait.

"Just let me finish what I have to say we will not ever mention it again. Don't ever threaten me or Lilly with a gun again. You were wrong in thinking she was interested in you, and even if she had been, you have no right in leading her on. You are not a free man. You can convort with whores and treat them that way, but Miss Lilly is a genteel lady. I believe her when she says she may have flirted with you, but gave you no cause to claim her as your girl. You owe her an apology. Do you understand me?"

Houston spoke with firm determination. Then almost as an afterthought, he continued.

"You will pack your things when you get home and go to your Uncle's in Blytheville and start a new life there. I have spoken to him about this and he is willing to help you."

J.P. had never ever believed his father would practically disown him. He was so astonished at his father's suggestion he go to Arkansas, he could hardly believe what had just been said to him. As usual, his thoughts were only for himself, and in his disbelief, he uttered words that would serve to anger his father further.

"What if I don't want to go to Blytheville? How can you do this? I should have known you might do something like this to punish me. I guess I won't get anything from our farm when you die, either?"

J.P. stopped short, realizing he had gone too far this time. He wished he could take it back, but it was much too late.

Houston rose from his chair, eyed J.P. intently for several minutes, then in his most authoritative voice he spoke directly to J.P.

"You will do as I say this time or you will inherit nothing! Your brothers have done all the work while you have made a total mess of your life, so far. You can change all that if you want to." Houston turned from J.P. and sat silently until they reached The Haviland House. He felt completely drained of all emotion.

Houston seldom drank, but tonight he would have a brandy and think of Lilly. Perhaps, he thought, I should write a letter to Dovie and Ben tomorrow and let them know about the divorce and my intentions for the mill.

Instead, he drank his brandy and fell asleep. He dreamed of Lilly's soft lips and body and the joy he felt when they had been together.

Several months passed before Houston and J.P. received a letter from the barrister Bowes. He said the divorce papers were ready for the couple's signatures, and then they could be made final.

Houston had said that he would take the paper to Dovie when that time arrived. So off to St. Louis and then to Smith Mills. He informed J.P. that he would take the papers to Dovie, but thought it best that he did not accompany him. J.P. acknowledged that he did not want to go to see Dovie, and Houston sighed a huge sigh of relief. He got a letter off to Lilly to tell her he was coming to St. Louis, and would she accompany him to Henderson. He said that they would stay in a hotel in Henderson. He also told J.P. of his intentions and that after they were finished with the barrister, J.P. would be boarding a train to Blytheville where his Uncle Amman would meet him. J.P. could only nod his head in assent, but said nothing.

The moment the train pulled into the St. Louis station, he saw Lilly waiting on the platform. She looked absolutely beautiful in a powder blue gown and matching hat. Houston's heart jumped for joy at the sight of her.

Houston scooped her up in his arms and kissed her passionately. J.P. looked on in disgust, acknowledged Lilly's presence, and walked away. He felt trapped by his father and took no blame for his own actions.

The weather was bright and sunny in St. Louis and Houston and Lilly took full advantage of the two days they had to wait to board the train to Henderson, Kentucky. They strolled in the park where the air was heady from the many flowers and redbud bushes. The white spirea and the first roses were in bloom, and the couple had to stop and admire them.

Houston stopped and plucked a rose bud and put it in Lilly's hand just as a policeman rounded the walkways. He shook his baton stick at Houston but laughed heartily, and went merrily on his way.

The couple talked of many things. Who can watch the boarding house when I am gone? How long will we be away? Houston had answers for all her questions and she finally agreed to go. What convinced her? He said that he wanted her to meet J.P.'s and Dovie's family. He said, "they will all just love you."

Dovie, Ben and Morning Star were waiting at the train station for Houston's arrival with much anticipation. They were, however, shocked to see he was with a beautiful young woman, not much older than Dovie. Introductions were made and Houston could see the women sizing each other up, and for a moment, Houston thought he had made a mistake in bringing Lilly; but as usual, Morning Star made everyone feel comfortable, as only she could.

Dovie too, was her sweet self, holding Etta Mae and Ben was holding little Rosabelle. Lilly thought it's a handsome family that she was now looking at and asked to see the baby better.

"Welcome to Kentucky, and to our home," Morning Star said as she embraced first Houston and then Lilly.

"Thank you kindly, Morning Star, but I think Lilly wishes to stay at the hotel here in Henderson."

"No! You must come to our home. We are friends and family," Morning Star insisted. "Any friend of Houston's is our friend, too!"

Lilly was mesmerized by these two little Indian women and knew she wanted to know them better. Lilly was in a strange new world, for she had never known any Indians before. These women were small and beautiful. Their features were fine, not large like most of the pictures had shown them to be. Their hair was the same shiny black as Houston's and their eyes large and dark brown, except for Ben.

He had the most beautiful blue eyes that she had ever seen. How could this be, she wondered. Lilly watched Ben and Dovie, and one could easily see they were very much in love and devoted to one another. Lilly found herself extremely curious about all of these Indians and agreed to stay at their home without any coercing. Houston was a little puzzled with Lilly's change of heart, but very glad that she had accepted their offer, and his people.

As the carriage neared the farm Lilly was astonished to see a huge tepee sitting atop a small hill, and just beyond it a very large log cabin. Morning Star, always in charge, beamed a big smile at Lilly before she spoke.

"There it is! That's my tepee, given to me by White Feather, my husband. Maybe you would like to see inside, Miss Lilly?" Morning Star said in a question.

"Yes, yes I would. It is beautiful. Did you paint it yourself?" Lilly exclaimed as they drove nearer. "I've only read about tepees but I have never seen a real one." Lilly was even more curious now.

"Yes, I did paint it, inside and out. You will see for yourself." Morning Star looked intently at Lilly and then added, "You must like Indians a little for I can see you are much taken with Houston, and that is good." Lilly laughed heartily as she now looked intently at Morning Star before she answered, thinking 'my, she knows how to get right to the point.'

"Yes, Morning Star, you are right. I am much taken with Houston. I don't know much about Indians, but if they are all like you, then I must say I'm happy to know all of you. I want to learn more and I believe you, Alice Dean, and Ben, are going to help me do that." Lilly ended soberly.

Everyone in the carriage laughed and gave their hearty answer to Lilly's statement.

"You can bet on it," they all answered in unison.

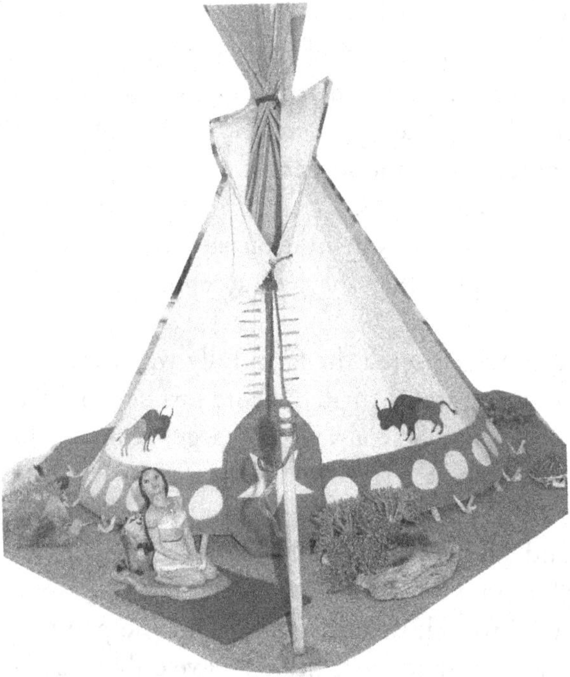

Replica of Morning Star's Teepee

CHAPTER FOUR

GROWING UP BLACKFOOT IN KENTUCKY

ROSIE AND ETTA MAE WERE BOTH EXCITED WITH THEIR NEW SISTER ETHEL'S BIRTH. THEY WERE FASCINATED WITH THE BABY'S TINY HANDS AND FEATURES, BUT THIS FASCINATION SOON WORE OFF FOR ETTA MAE. SHE BECAME EXTREMELY JEALOUS OF ALL THE TIME HER MOTHER SPENT WITH THE BABY. BEN AND DOVIE AGREED THAT THEY WOULD HAVE TO MAKE SURE SHE OVERCAME HER JEALOUSY SO THEY CONTINUED TO GIVE HER EVERYTHING SHE ASKED FOR.

Grandma Jane again warned them to be careful and not give into all her whims. They tried not to favor her, but after all, she was their 'love child', so no matter what or how many children they had, Etta Mae always came first. She always got the new bows for her hair, new shoes, and other clothing first and was allowed to do as much as she pleased. This pampering, however, did not mean that she did not have her own chores, and that she had to learn all the things all of the other children had to learn.

By the time Etta Mae entered the first grade, she, Rosie and her brother Clarence, had three little sisters, Ethel, Frances and Myrtle. From the very beginning, school was not much to Etta Mae's liking. She was so used to being catered to at home; she had a hard time for the teacher showed her very little attention. Try as she did, the teacher failed to come under Etta's spell. That however, was not what sent her home crying on many occasions. It was the bigger kids; relentless with insulting remarks about her and her family, that caused the problem.

On the first day of school, the kids started calling her, fat, because she was plumper than Rosie. Then they made fun of her because she didn't look like her brother and sister. Also, she would not join in the rougher games played on the school grounds, and didn't ever want soil on her clothes. You might say they called her prissy.

When these kinds of insults didn't make her go home crying, the kids took to saying she was nothing but a 'dirty injun kid', an outcast, and that she didn't belong in a white school because Indians were nothing but savages, and stupid. They took up to chanting, "Etta Mae is a dirty little savage who thinks she is white. She must have lied because she is an injun." Etta Mae would run away and hide anywhere she could find, or take off for home. Rosie and Clarence tried to protect her as much as they could.

When they told the teacher about the kids actions, she would just smile and say that, "They didn't mean anything by what they said" This continued throughout the first two grades with Etta Mae spending her recess and lunch-time in the schoolhouse, and only going out to play when the teacher forced her to.

After three years into grade school, the insults turned from teasing to pure insult not only about Etta Mae, Rosie and Clarence, but also about her mother and father. One day Etta Mae and Rosie were playing hopscotch with two other girls, when several big boys grabbed Etta Mae and dragged her behind the schoolhouse. Rosie tried to make them stop but they just laughed at her and said that they were going to see for themselves if she was the same color all over her body. Etta Mae screamed, scratched and kicked at the boys but they were too much for her. They tore her clothes and called her a bastard child, for she was not the same color as her sister. They said she must have had a white father, and that her mother was an Indian slut who would sleep with any white man. Etta Mae covered her ears and screamed and screamed but it seemed the more she struggled the more the boy's appetites whetted. Rosie in the meantime ran to the male teacher to come to her sister's aide. Fortunately, he arrived before the boys had torn off most of Etta's dress. He rightly paddled the boys and tried to clean Etta Mae up, but she was so devastated he finally had Rosie and Clarence take her home with a note of apology to her parents. Etta Mae was almost hysterical by the time she arrived home and refused to go back to school.

Dovie and Ben went to the schoolteacher and tried to make sure that the teasing was stopped, but to no avail. Rosie, Clarence and some of the other children from Star Farm were continually harassed about their Indian blood. Most of the other kids just put up a fight and took care of the problem themselves.

Dovie remembered all too well, what had happened to her and her teacher, Mr. Curtis, and she did not want this repeated, so there was nothing to do but to take Etta Mae out of school and home school her.

Morning Star was only too happy to help teach Etta Mae, and to have her home to help her mother with the younger children. Morning Star was suffering more and more from the aggravating rheumatism. She was not able to do many of the chores she had done in the past. Ben had made her a chair with wheels on it so that she could get around a little bit better, but this did not allow her to do all the cleaning and cooking that she had done before either.

On Etta Mae's tenth birthday little William was born, also very light in color, and with the same blue eyes as his sister and father. He would become nearly as pampered as Etta Mae, and was called "Boss," the rest of his life.

Rosie and Etta Mae had begun to feel overwhelmed with all their little brothers and sisters, and spoke of it to each other often. How, they wondered, could they stop the babies from coming so often? Neither had any idea just how babies got in their mother's tummy, and dared not ask anyone. By this time, Walter had moved away and Otto had followed him to good paying jobs in Indianapolis, Indiana. They would visit their parents as often as they could. Their leaving had made more room in the house, but still all the bedrooms were filled with the ever arrival of a new baby.

On many occasions, the two girls would climb up into an apple tree in the large orchard, and discuss why the Creator was sending so many babies to their house. Then, shortly after one of these talks, Rosie had her twelfth birthday and was visited by Mother Nature with her menses. Rosie was somewhat horrified to learn that the Creator could send her a baby if she got married. Of course, the first thing she did was to tell Etta all that her mother had told her about becoming a woman. The two girls decided at that time that they would never get married because they did not want any babies. Babies, they said to each other, were entirely too much work.

A few moons passed and Etta Mae entered womanhood. The two girls became very aware in the change in their bodies, and how much different they were treated by the inhabitants on the farm. They were young ladies now, Papa would say, and insisted that they now had to ride sidesaddle, with their protesting every inch of the way.

Another big change was that some adult always had to be with them at every function they attended outside their home. Grandma Jane told them that they no longer had to wear their hair in braids, but could curl their long black hair if they wished. Etta Mae delighted in this fact, but Rosie did not much care. She did, however, call on Etta Mae to fuss with her hair, and primp her cheeks with powder and rouge, occasionally. Both girls had perfect complexions and were exactly the same size for years, 4 feet 10 ½ inches. This would change, after a time, for Etta would reach a full 5 feet tall.

Dovie took to making their dresses alike and many people thought they were twins. The girls would giggle at this and shyly look away, as they had been taught to do.

Three years had passed since Boss's birth before little Lela made her appearance. By this time both girls were aware that Papa had more to do with Mama as to how the Creator sent babies. Perched high in their private tree hide-a-way, they discussed this subject a lot. What could they do to help stop babies from coming, they wondered, and decided to ask their older brother Clarence just how this all happened. Clarence could only laugh at his sisters, but did give them a bit of information that both cleared up the subject and awed them at the same time.

"You girls know how we get new colts and calves? Even the hogs do it, the chickens and all the other animals too. The bible calls it begetting." Clarence finished with a shake of his head at his sisters' ignorance, but saw how this information had shocked them, so he added, "It would be best for you to go talk to Grandma Jane, and she will tell you all about creation. It's something you should know." With that, Clarence walked away leaving the girls staring at each other, a bit confused.

Grandma Jane, Myrtle and Rosie shared a bedroom so that night Etta Mae exchanged her bed with Myrtle, and she joined Rosie and Grandma for their enlightenment.

Many things were changing with Etta Mae and Rosie. Rosie, who had worked beside Papa since she was a small child, now found herself working only with her mother, Grandma Jane and Etta, in the house and gardens. Papa no longer called her "Jack", his pet name for her. This made her feel very sad. Papa Ben explained that she was now learning to be a lady and it was not appropriate for him to call her by that nickname.

Clarence was nearly a man and had taken to calling on a young lady by the name of Gertrude Coleman. He was a strong healthy young man who had many of the girls on the Star Farm giving him the eye, but he never seemed interested because they all seemed like his sisters.

All of the children on the farm had been reared together as a tight knit family, so as far as he was concerned, they could not be approached. Ben and Dovie had done their job well in teaching all their children the Blackfoot ways, which forbid first cousins to marry. Grandma Jane the matriarch, made sure all the Indian ways were taught, and kept.

Several of Grey Fox's daughters had married and moved away from the farm. Josie had married Bill Davis and moved to Mt. Vernon, Indiana. Later, she would move near New Harmony. Nakomi married Friemiller, and lived in Mt. Vernon. Winona married William Miller and moved to Bufkin, Indaina. One of Grey Fox's sons changed his name to Robert White, and married a Schmitzer girl. They lived in Point Township, south of Mt. Vernon.

Bull Bear's son Lance was the first to leave the farm. He changed his name to John Lance Stout and bought some land east of Henderson, Kentucky.

Many Waters finally found his mate for life in Golden Eagle's daughter Ramona, and stayed on the farm with their father and mother.

Bull Bear and Martha's little daughter, Starlight, married Kip and Elk Dancing's son Jacques Eagle Feather, set up a cabin adjacent to their parent's home. They would later be known as the Jacques Whites, and would move to a small plot of their own not far from Uniontown, Kentucky.

The Star Farm continued to be productive in livestock and crops, but the horses would always be everyone's most important asset. It seemed Ben, Grey Fox, Golden Eagle, especially Many Waters, had a mystic connection to the horses, and between them they raised and raced many mounts for local and other racetracks.

Ben was an especially proud father of his many children and took great delight in taking his three oldest daughters shopping in Henderson. Etta Mae was always allowed to pick out what she wanted first, and then help her younger sisters. Rosie was not much interested in shopping, but would finally make her choices and then she and Etta Mae would make selections for the family left at home.

On one of these trips, Clarence accompanied his father and sisters on a shopping trip. He shyly asked his sisters to help him pick out a gift for his girl friend, Gertie. Ben was surprised at this for he had thought Clarence's relationship was not serious. Clarence, somewhat reluctant, informed them all he intended to marry Gertie if she would have him. Ben, a little taken back at this revelation could not help but comment.

"That is a surprise indeed, isn't' it girls" Not wishing to lecture but felt he needed to make some comment on the subject continued, "You are mighty young to be getting married, son. If Gertie is interested in marriage then you must have an engagement for at least one year. Gertie is even younger than you are. Have you mentioned any of this to her parents?"

"No, Papa, I wanted to ask Gertie first." Clarence answered hesitantly. Rosie and Etta Mae could hardly contain their delight for they had known Gertie most of their lives. She had attended school at the farm with the other Indian mixed bloods, before they were allowed in the public schools. Ben now studied Clarence in a totally different light. Clarence, it seemed, had become a man right under his nose and he hadn't even noticed.

"Well let's look for a small gift for Gertie, to help break the ice for Clarence. Girls, we can discuss the engagement later. Just wait until your Mama hears that her first born is thinking of getting married.'

Ben chuckled as he led his offspring's toward a small glass case that held some bracelets and necklaces. Rosie and Etta Mae hugged their brother with great affection, as they helped him decide on this gift.

Rosie and Etta Mae could talk of nothing else but the possibility of an engagement party, and queried Clarence constantly about Gertie. Clarence, however, said little to nothing about his intention, for he had lost his nerve for several months, before he gave Gertie the lovely necklace he had picked out for her in Henderson.

Nearly a year later, Gertie's parents gave their consent for the engagement. Ben and Dovie then began making all the arrangements for the great celebration of the gift exchange between the parents Gertie's parents were part Cherokee and like many other of that Nation, had escaped to the mountains rather than be thrown into the removal from their homes.

Rosie and Etta Mae were ecstatic to think they would finally be able to attend a dance with real musicians. They primped their hair and faces, and sewed constantly. Everyone had to have new clothes for this great occasion.

The men taunted Clarence while they made preparations to roast a pig, and the women planned what each one would make for their guests to eat. Who would make the pies, and who would make cakes? Of course, it was understood that only Morning Star could make her delicious sweet beans. As the women worked at their given chores, Morning Star said that she knew that White Feather would be watching as their first grandchild was to become betrothed for a new life. Little did she know that many other big changes were in store for her and the entire family.

NR

CHAPTER FIVE

CHEROKEE, IRISH AND BLACKFOOT MEET

George and Edward Hutchison wandered into the Dickerson's kitchen during their break from the music making and dancing. There they saw Etta Mae and Rosabelle refilling bowls of food for their guests. The two girls turned from their work as the brothers entered the kitchen shyly looking away from the men's stares, but neither one could contain their giggles.

George was mesmerized as Etta Mae finally looked coquettishly at him, and then attempted to move past him into the room filled with the guests. She had never seen him before this dance, but felt him to be the most handsome man she had ever seen. His curly red hair and brilliant blue eyes were hypnotic, and when he reached out and touched her arm, she felt shock waves curse throughout her body. She managed to pass him by, for out of the corner of her eye she saw her mother watching her, and her sister Rosie. This was the very first time that either she or Rosie, had been allowed to participate in one of the neighborhood dances, and only tonight because it was Rosie's birthday. Alice Dean (Dovie) and Benjamin Dickerson knew that their daughters would cause quite a stir with everyone, especially all the eligible young men. Both girls were small, beautiful and extremely well proportioned, for their young ages. They would have to be watched over continuously.

Etta Mae

Rosabelle

George Hutchison II was not easily dissuaded when he saw something he liked. He knew too, he was at least ten to twelve years older than this young girl. He would have to get permission from her parents if he was ever to be allowed to court her, which he sorely desired. As he watched her the rest of the evening, he noticed that she did not seem to have a beau. She danced only with her sister, and brother, and once with her father. He was about to approach her, when she suddenly was whisked off by her Uncle Grey Fox White Feather. George knew Grey Fox, and liked him very much. It was a chance visit to his father's farm down by the river that they had met. He had gone to visit his grandparents, the Jewells. As he watched Etta Mae dancing, he decided that he would be friendly and cordial to Etta, her sister, and her parents, paving the way to be formally introduced by Grey Fox, after the dance was over. Grey Fox was only too glad to give him the introduction he desired and warned George that his sister and brother-in-law might not be too thrilled with his attentions.

George was not easily dissuaded when he saw something he liked, and he definitely liked what he saw in Etta Mae.

As with most families, in that time, marriages for their daughters were arranged by the girl's parents, as to who would be the most suitable for their daughter's welfare. Money was not the main issue of the Dickerson's, but they did want someone they felt could give Etta Mae a comfortable life. George Henry Hutchison II was not their first choice. He had two strikes against him; his parents were Catholic, and he was much older than their Etta Mae was. However, on learning that his mother was one-half Cherokee, and he did own acreage in southern Indiana, he was more acceptable. Also, George was always well dressed, courteous, a perfect gentleman, and not too forward. Ben and Dovie still had their reservations for they could readily see he was fond of fun, and that he would be away from home with his music making. They could also see that Etta Mae was very interested in him and they couldn't say no to her, ever. After much discussion, they decided that they would let George call on Etta Mae, but cautioned him that she was very young and that she could only go places with him in the daytime. He could however, call on her at their home in the evening.

George found this acceptable since he had been waiting a few months for their answer, and would have agreed to most any arrangement. George was also told that Etta Mae could not attend neighborhood dances with him unless they accompanied her. This also was agreeable; in fact, he was glad because he knew that she would be swamped with offers from all the young men that attended.

George Henry, showered Etta Mae with gifts, took her for long buggy rides, taught her to roller skate, had long dinner feasts and met her and her parents at many of the places that he and his brothers played music. Etta Mae reciprocated with loving arms, and sweet wet kisses, stolen in the Dickerson's parlor. George was head-over-heels in love for the first time in his life. He was very cautious because he knew that her parents would send him on his way if they found out. He would admonish Etta Mae to behave and she would just giggle and tease him more. He tried to tell her all about his family, but she said it did not matter who he was, she liked him even if he was part Indian. She also told him that she never told anyone that she was Indian, and wished that he would not mention it to anyone again. George complied.

At one of the neighborhood get-togethers Etta Mae met two of George's younger sisters, Nora and Audibelle. Nora was married to Jim Darnell, the storekeeper at Uniontown, the mining town down river. Audibelle was unmarried and full of fun, acting on any impulse that she would get. Her main interest was to dance every dance, and to do so with every available man she could find. She was a beautiful red head with a zest to have all the fun she could. She was a very accomplished dancer, giving little demonstrations of Irish jigs, and the latest dance in fashion. George would admonish her from time to time, for he was worried that her behavior might be a bad influence with Etta

Mae's parents. Underneath though he was proud of Audibelle, doted on her, and thought her just wonderful. Her flaming red hair was long and very curly, floating about her beautiful face as she laughed, and had a good time no matter where she went. Secretly, Etta Mae was a bit jealous of Audibelle, but Audibelle thought Etta Mae the most beautiful person she had ever seen. She wanted her brother to marry Etta, and would calm down her fun just to suit her brother.

Almost a year had passed since George had started calling on Etta Mae, then everything would suddenly change. Etta Mae was almost eighteen when she met the brothers Meinschein, from St. Phillips, Indiana, at a dance and betrothal party for her brother, Clarence. The guests were playing spin the bottle, and subsequently, urgently on by his mother, William Meinschein was to dance with Etta Mae. William Meinschein, was the middle son of Lena and the long deceased father, Phillip Meinschein. William lived on their farm with his mother and his two brothers. Apparently, that was all anyone seemed to know about them, except that they were somehow related to Gertie, Clarence's fiancé.

Etta Mae was extremely beautiful that night, in her powder blue taffeta dress that matched her eyes, and the ribbons tied in her jet-black hair. She had a small straight nose, high cheekbones and a small soft mouth. Her skin was much lighter than any of her siblings, and one would never guess that she was an Indian maiden, and that was just what she wanted. She had made up her mind that after all the harassment, slurs and insinuations she had suffered at school, she would never tell anyone she was a dirty injun kid, as she had been called. Her ridicule had become so great, that Ben and Dovie had taken her out of the local school at the third grade level and proceeded to teach her at home, as they had so many others.

William Meinschein had noticed Etta Mae upon arriving at the party. He had never seen such a beautiful person. His own mother was large and drab, and very domineering. This night she had noticed Etta Mae too. How could she help it, she was the belle of the ball. She had seen the look on her son's face when he saw Etta Mae, and urged him to ask her to dance. She said it was a game that young people had to play, to get the girl of their choice. She instructed him to be on his best behavior, and to remember all the things he had been told by her. Never wanting to bring any of his mother's wraths down on himself, all he could say was, "Yes, Mama, I remember." The fact that all Etta Mae's family was well to do farmers, and horse breeders, helped Lena Meinschein make her decision as to whom William would dance with. She had spoken to her son about the standing these people had in their community, but that did not matter to him anymore. He was honestly, completely captivated by this lovely young girl, who was now laughing up at him and seemed downright interested in him.

Lena Meinschein watched the dancers and did not miss the mutual attraction that seemed to be passing between her son and young Etta Mae. She smiled to herself; everything was going just as she had planned. She had picked William to come to the dance for he was the most attractive of her three boys, and the least attached to her. He was the one who would give her some grandchildren. As she watched the two young people, she decided that she would just introduce herself to the girl's parents now, while they were watching them dance. She had formed a plan in her mind as to how she would make William do as she wanted him to do, and it seemed that she really hadn't had to give him her help. Lena knew that her oldest son would never leave her – they were much too close. Her youngest son was just becoming a man, and she would see to it that he would never leave her either.

William was very stubborn and different from the other boys and she had never been able to control him as she did his brothers. Lately, he had talked about nothing but girls, and she knew that he was ripe for the plan she had in her mind. The fact was, she had practically suffocated her sons, monitoring their every action; another fact was, she ran the farm with an iron hand and did not intend to let any other woman take her place on the farm or with her two other sons.

Personally, Lena could be a very gracious, an imposing figure. She knew how to beguile a male with ease so she presented herself to Ben as soon as she saw him standing alone. She had no knowledge before she came that these people were Indians, a fact that could not be denied even if they would have wanted to, which they did not. She did not care for any other group of people except Germans, like herself, but this did not deter her plan, in fact, it spurred her on, for she planned to use this against the girl, when the time came. She was quite sure of herself as she swished across the floor in her long black dress and feathered hat, toward Benjamin Dickerson.

"How do you do, Mr. Dickerson, I'm Lena Meinschein, and I see our children are enjoying each other's company." Lena beamed a big smile, trying for a little flirtatious fluttering of her eyes, and then stared boldfaced into Benjamin's eyes, and thought, "Perhaps he's not all Indian, with those sky blue eyes."

Ben was a little startled at this woman's brashness, but answered with as much graciousness as possible, for he had noticed the slightly heavy, large boned woman when she had first entered the house with her boys. He assumed they were some of Clarence's acquaintances or maybe Gertie's.

"Glad to make your acquaintance." Ben scanned the dance floor and saw Etta Mae dancing with a tall, dark stranger, and smiled as he answered.

"Yes, they do in fact, but it's hard to tell with Etta Mae, for she loves to dance." Ben felt awkward now, not able to sense this woman's purpose.

"Perhaps I should introduce you to my wife, Dovie, Etta Mae's mother.' Ben wanted to be rid of this woman, for she had taken hold of his arm quite possessively.

"Yes," Lena answered, "that would be very nice."

Dovie (Alice Dean White Feather Dickerson) had not missed the two young people, obviously enjoying the dance, and neither had she missed that large woman taking hold of Ben's arm. She had bristled, as she watched her husband and the woman approaching her. Alice Dean (Dovie) had a quick temper and was a bit jealous. She could, however, plainly see that Ben was ill at ease with this large woman who was commandeering him across the floor.

Ben unwrapped Lena's arm from his and stuttered slightly of embarrassment, for he could see Dovie's anger rising. The music had stopped momentarily as the red haired musician laid his fiddle down, and was now walking across the floor toward Etta Mae, and the stranger.

George Hutchison II, had felt pangs of jealousy as he watched Etta Mae laughing up at the young man and thoroughly enjoying herself. He and Etta Mae had been seeing each other on a regular basis for the past year, and just the past week at the skating rink she had said she loved him, and he proposed marriage. She had said he would have to get her parents permission, and he said he would after this betrothal party. George had a quick temper and it showed now in his face, and it was all he could to keep from punching the stranger in the face, for he knew what his intentions were, or at least he thought he did.

"This is my dance Etta Mae," he muttered almost inaudibly, as he whisked her away from William Meinschein. Dovie watched this episode, then turned toward her husband.

"This is Mrs. Meinschein, the young man's mother that Etta Mae was just dancing with. She wanted to meet you." Lena sensed Dovie's animosity towards her, and didn't' hesitate to try and take control of the conversation.

"I'm Lena Meinschein, and I have two other boys here tonight. We are distant relatives of your son's fiancé, Gertie. Gertie invited us here tonight, and said that there would be several young women here tonight that are available for marriage, and she knew that my William is looking for a suitable young woman to be his wife.

He seems quite taken with your daughter, the one you call Etta Mae." Dovie never at a loss for words eyed this brash woman, speechless, and looking to Ben for more information. Ben was just as dumbfounded as Dovie, and before either of them could speak, William joined them.

"Here, William, come here and meet the parents of the young woman you were dancing with, Mr. and Mrs. Dickerson." William bowed slightly and touched Dovie's hand to his lips, just as he was instructed to do. William Meinschein towered over Dovie a good foot and a half, and she was fleetingly reminded of someone in the past as she gazed at the tall dark stranger, but who, she wasn't sure.

"I'm very pleased to make your acquaintance, both of you. You have a very lovely daughter and I would like permission to call on her, if she is not spoken for." William delivered the rehearsed words with a believable manner, for he was totally taken with Etta Mae. No matter to him that she was an Indian, as many of the folks here were. She was beautiful and like his mother had said, her parents were very well to do, and educated far better than he was. He hoped that with all his heart she would welcome his intentions.

Dovie's face blushed crimson at the forward words of this stranger, but she finally regained her composure, and looked at the woman, Lena, as she spoke with candor.

"Thank you for your compliments, young man, but this is neither the time, or the place to discuss such an intimate matter. You would, however, be welcome to visit our home at a later time to get better acquainted with our daughter, and her entire family. Now, if you will excuse us, we need to attend to our other guests and make the betrothal announcement." Dovie took Ben's arm and escorted him to the kitchen, much to his relief.

"Well my dear, I have to thank you for rescuing me from that woman," Ben sighed a sigh of relief and gave Dovie a kiss on the cheek.

"And just what did you make of all that conceit?" Dovie asked Ben. "Just who do they think they are – that horse of a woman? At least her son wasn't so forward. I don't think I like her a bit." Dovie pouted now, but cautioned Ben to silence as she saw Gertie and Clarence coming to get them to make the betrothal announcement.

Clarence's younger sisters, Frances, Myrtle, Lela and Ethel, with his young brother Boss, had all gathered on the stairs to hear the announcement and to get their share of cake and other goodies, before being hustled off to bed. It was the first time they had seen so many strangers in their house, and they were all excited about gaining a new sister. Rosabelle and Etta Mae had dressed them all in the newly made clothing just for this occasion, and they now stood on either side of their younger sisters and brother.

Etta Mae wore a pout on her lips from the reprimand from George, as to her actions with William Meinschein. She felt she was innocent of doing anything wrong and stubbornly refused to feel otherwise. It was their first argument and she felt defiant now as she tried to smile as if nothing had happened. She loved George, but thought him too possessive, after all, she told her self, they were not even engaged; he hadn't even spoken to her parents yet, and she knew they thought his religion was too different from theirs in the Creator. They had often spoken of the injustices the Indians had endured from the Jesuits, and Mission priests, in earlier days, and how the local priest had snubbed them because they were Indians. Now as she stood waiting for the wedding announcement, she thought to herself, "I might just give George something to get jealous of." She had seen her parents talking to William Meinscheins mother, and knew he was interested in her.

Etta Mae was Ben and Dovie's 'love-child', and had been spoiled rotten all of her young life. She had always been pampered, having the ribbons for her hair first, her new clothes made first. She never had to work in the tobacco fields like her sister Rosabelle and the younger girls had to do when they became old enough to do the work. Her skin was so light that her mother and father were afraid that she would get too 'hot' from the hot sun. Of course, she would have blistered had she spent long hours hoeing in the fields. Rosabelle, on the other hand, was Papa's helper. From the time she laid eyes on Ben, she had cried for him to hold her, followed him everywhere, when she was just a toddler. As Rosie got older she was the one child that volunteered to 'help Papa', so Ben started calling her "Jack", his fourth boy. Rosabelle looked nothing like a boy, with her enormous cinnamon colored eyes, petite figure and long black hair. She had a dark complexion and had blossomed into a real beauty, in spite of herself. She wasn't much interested in boys, but knew that she would be expected to marry before Etta Mae, since she was older. Benjamin was not Rosie's biological father, but the only father she had ever known. Her real father, J.P. Ban Bibber, had left right after she was born leaving her mother and brother Clarence on their own, until cousin Ben Dickerson came to work in the nearby sawmill. J.P.'s father, who owned it at the time, had sent him there.

Ben rapped sharply on a piece of hard wood until there was silence in the room, and then motioned to Clarence and Gertie standing in the kitchen doorway. He motioned for them to join him and Dovie. With his hands on each of the young people's shoulders, he spoke with pride.

"As all of you know this celebration tonight is to give honor to our "Creator" for bringing these two youngsters together. It is my honor and my wife's, to announce that Clarence, our son, and Gertrude Steinkamp Coleman, will be joined in marriage in the moon of October. Everyone here is invited to the wedding, which will be held right here in this very room." A loud applause rose from the many people gathered together and interrupted Ben.

"Now having said that and making the betrothal known, let there be music for the intended couple to start off the next dance."

Etta Mae had been searching the room for William Meinschein but did not see him anywhere, so she started toward the door to see if she could find him, but her mother caught her by the arm.

"Just where do you think you're going, young lady?" The tone in Alice Dean's voice was enough to stop Etta Mae, but not enough to keep her from her intended task of finding William.

"I just thought I would get a breath of fresh air, Mama." Etta Mae turned all the charm she could muster, on her mother, but Alice Dean saw right through her intentions.

"No! You will not follow that young man outside. We don't know those people."

"But Mama, he was so nice and I like him a lot, I want to talk to him some more. Please let me find him." Etta Mae could normally persuade her mother in just about anything, but this was an entirely different matter. Alice Dean had found herself disliking everything about William, especially his mother.

"You have danced with every young man here tonight, and I think you a bit too flirtatious with that William, who you don't know at all. Papa and I gave consent for them to visit us, if in fact William is interested in knowing you better.

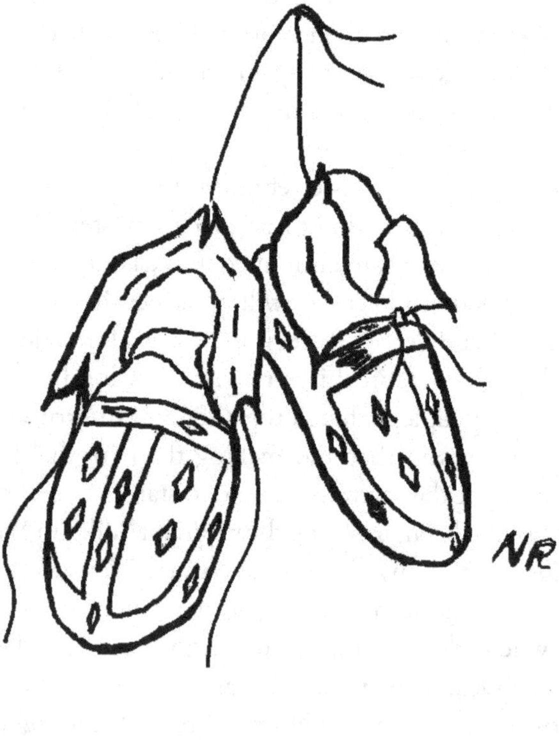

Now come along," Alice Dean's voice and manner told Etta Mae not to try to cajole her mother anymore. Secretly, she was pleased that William had been invited to come back. However, she did not know if she liked the brash act, his mother had displayed on behalf of her son.

"Oh thank you, Mama, Papa, for inviting them back. You know they are relatives of Gertie!" Ben had joined his wife and daughter, and never failing to say what was on his mind, he spoke a little sarcastically now.

"Actually, Etta Mae, William's mother asked to come back. A bit forward, don't you think? Did you take notice of her? She was almost as tall as me, and almost twice as wide. She is a big woman, with a domineering manner. I expect her boys do just as she says." Ben's eyes sparkled with a devilish twinkle, even with his sarcasm. Etta Mae looked at her father in disbelief.

"That huge woman, dressed in black is William's mother?"

"Yes, Etta Mae, and William had two brothers' here also. I guess you must have danced with them too, since, as your mother said, you danced with every available man here and I think even a few who were not available." Ben, never one to admonish his daughters, now thought it best to let her know that he did not approve of her flirting with every man she danced with.

"Oh!" Etta Mae now covered her face with her hands, a little embarrassed, for her Papa never scolded her. Tears welled up in her sky blue eyes and she quickly ran out of the hall where they were standing. Several weeks passed with George and Etta Mae making up, but George had not yet spoken to Etta's parents of his intentions to ask for her hand in marriage. He felt that he had to have more to offer her before he asked, and was busily going about it in his way, to make himself more presentable. Etta Mae didn't care, at least for the present, she found Williams intended visit fascinating, and planned to use it to get George to speak to her parents.

So, who was this George Hutchison and where did he come from? Who was his family? To answer this question, we must go back in time to the 1860's, and the arrival of the Hutchison's in Virginia.

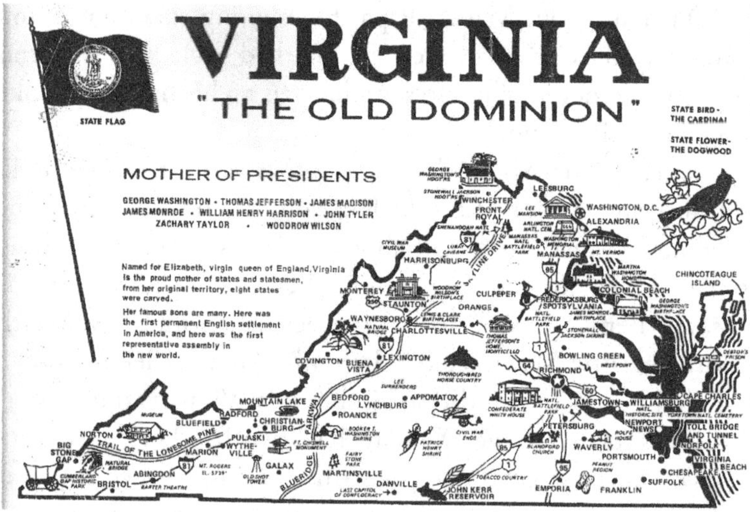

CHAPTER SIX

1863 - ARRIVAL OF THE IRISH

THE BOAT WAS DOCKING FINALLY IN THE HARBOR OF JAMESTOWN, VIRGINIA. IT HAD BEEN A LONG AND ARDUOUS TRIP FROM THE COAST OF IRELAND FOR THE LITTLE IRISH FAMILY, BUT HOPE HAD TUNED INTO REALITY, AND THE BEAUTIFUL GREEN HILLS AND PASTURES WERE A WELCOME SIGHT. JAMES EDWARD HUTCHISON AND HIS WIFE, ERIN ROSE WERE BONE TIRED, BUT THE EXCITEMENT OF A NEW HOME, IN A NEW COUNTRY, FILLED THEM WITH GREAT ANTICIPATION. THERE WERE MANY OTHERS ON THE SHIP FROM IRELAND WHO HAD COME FOR THE SAME REASONS AS THE HUTCHISON'S. THE POTATO FAMINE AND THE GREEDY ENGLISH HAD ALL BUT STARVED THEM TO DEATH. THE MASS OF EAGER FACES NOW GATHERED ON DECK TO GET A GLIMPSE OF THIS NEW COUNTRY.

Most of the men were just like James Edward, trying to escape the tyranny of England and the great famines that had swept across all of Ireland. Like James Edward, they had lost their farms to the lords of England who had over run them. They could not pay the heavy taxes levied on their lands, so their homes, land and livestock were confiscated, leaving them with nothing.

Erin and James now stood peering at the coastline with all the others when they felt their children tugging on their clothes. Sean Michael and Louise Marie were just as excited as their parents to get a glimpse of where they were going to be living from now on. James Edward and Erin Rose smiled at their children and bolstered them up on their shoulders so that they could see.

Erin Rose was heavy with child again and was so thankful that her new child would be born in this new land. The children were very excited to see the green land that now lay in front of their eyes, and exclaimed to their parents that it looked much like where they had come from – County of Cork.

Jamestown was alive with activity for hundreds of people had come to see this ship dock, and look over her passengers. One man in particular, was searching the faces of every passenger, and when he finally saw James Edward, his face broke out into a happy smile. He ran to James Edward and hugged him, and then hugged Erin Rose and each of the children.

"Hello, ole chap, I see that you made it, with nothing for the worse. The Lord be blessed for getting you here all safe and sound. 'Tis a blessing I will never forget." The two men clasped their arms around each other again, and muttered words that were not audible to anyone else's ears.

"Uncle Patrick, this is my wife Erin Rose, and our two little ones. Erin, this is me Uncle Patrick who is responsible for getting us here." James Edward was almost overcome with his gratitude, for the gift his Uncle had given him; a chance to make a better life for his family here in America.

Patrick Michael O'Leary was a self-made man who had thrived in this new country. He had been willing to take the chance with the adventure of coming to the wilds of this new and sometimes hostile land. It had not been easy for him as a young man. He had done everything from farming, as an indentured person, to cleaning the street and horse stables, just to stay alive. One day a gentleman whose horse he was tending to, asked him if he would like to work for him on his large farm. He had said that he had many acres, and many livestock, and was in need of someone who could handle his horses. He had said then that he had been watching him for sometime now, and felt that he was the right person for the job. Patrick O'Leary was only too happy to take the position for he was making meager wages working at the livery stable, and other menial jobs just to keep shelter and food for himself. The gentleman that gave him a chance, was John Henry Bellefleur, a very wealthy man in the State of Virginia. Patrick worked hard at his new job, with his wife, Fiona, who helped in the manor house and they had managed to save a little money. He had, in fact, become the overseer of the Bellefleur Plantation. When they had saved enough, they spoke to John Bellefleur about work for his nephew, James Edward, the son of his deceased sister Maggie O'Leary Hutchison.

Erin Rose caught her breath as they turned onto a white fenced lane. There were trees lining the lane and horses, everywhere. She looked enthralled at the green pastures, and at the beautiful whitewashed buildings shining in the noonday sun. James Edward felt as much in awe as Erin, so much so, he thought he was looking at a little bit of heaven. He could hardly believe his eyes.

"Glory to God, Uncle, you did not begin to explain all of this. It is surely the Garden of Eden. The Blessed Mother, herself, has truly smiled on you and now on all of us. How can I ever repay you for this wonderful new life?" James Edward had sucked in so much air that his chest felt as if it would explode, and he could think of nothing else to do but grab his wife and plant kisses all over her face. Patrick Michael chuckled to himself, as did Erin Rose.

"'Tis a pleasure of mine to help you out, my boy; your dear Mother, Paddy, and me self, made a pact. If I ever could, I would send for you and your family, if you had one. 'Tis my pleasure to give you a helping hand, but I assure you that it will not all be paradise. The work is very hard sometimes, but you will be my right hand man and you will have your own little house for you and your children. I don't mean to be indelicate, but, I can see for myself that you will be a father again very soon." James Edward nodded that he was right and asked the question that he had been pondering since he got off the ship.

"Is this man you work for a kind man, or a bastard like the ones we left in Ireland, The Lords and Ladies who took our farm?" James Edward shivered at the thought of working for one of those scoundrels like the ones he had left behind.

"There are no Lords or Ladies in America; and neither is the man we will both be working for, a scoundrel. He was only too happy when I told him I had a young, hard working nephew that I wanted to bring here to help on his farm. 'Tis a fact that I'm to bring you and your family to the main house, so as he can get acquainted with the likes of you." Patrick had barely gotten the words out of his mouth when they climbed a little hill after turning sharply to the right. There on slightly higher ground, sat the most beautiful two story Georgian house that they had ever seen. It sat majestically in all the eloquence of a beautifully gowned woman, with its gleaming white pillars, manicured lawns, and blooming shrubs surrounding it. James Edward and Erin Rose gasped at the beauty that they now beheld. The carriage had barely come to a stop when the great double doors to the house opened and a man dressed in splendid clothing came to greet them. Following along behind him, was a giant of a light-skinned black man also dressed in a beautiful uniform that matched his masters.

"Good day, good day, my good man. I see that your family did indeed arrive. Won't you all come into the house so that I can be acquainted with all of you? Patrick has spoken highly of you and I can't wait to get to know all of you." As John Prescott Bellefleur spoke, he offered his hand to Erin Rose, and helped her out of the carriage. As she stepped out of the carriage, her bonnet fell back onto her shoulders, revealing her brilliant long, curly, red hair, which now gleamed brightly in the sunshine. Erin Rose was a pretty woman with fine features, but her hair made her even more beautiful. John Bellefleur did not miss her beauty, or her beautiful red hair. For a moment, he hesitated as he took in her beauty, and one could see he was totally taken off guard, but tried not to show it. Both James Edward and Patrick saw the look of appreciation, and then the look of utter frustration on John's face.

John Bellefleur was nervous and he showed it as he escorted Erin Rose into the house, leaving all of the others to gather up the valises and the children. The huge black man looked quizzically at John and Erin Rose, and then retrieved the valises, spoke to the carriage driver and followed the entourage into the house through the great double doors. John Bellefleur still holding Erin Rose's arm, bid them welcome.

"Welcome to my home, I trust you will find it comfortable. I have just this minute decided that you, James Edward, and your lovely family will reside in Bellefleur Manor with me. We can make your little cottage larger for the new addition, that I can see you are about to be blessed with. Neither Patrick nor I realized your family was growing. Right Patrick?"

""Tis sure, sir, Mr. Bellefleur, 'tis most kind of you to offer my niece and nephew to live here in your home, but I assure you they will be quite comfortable in their little cottage." Patrick was a bit embarrassed at the suggestion that the cottage was not adequate for his nephew, for it was much larger and better than anything they had in Ireland.

"No Patrick, I won't hear of it, for I can see Mrs. Hutchison's time is near. Here she will have to do no work and a doctor can attend to her quicker. She will need help during her confinement. The children will need to be looked after, too. I would be honored to have you here, Mrs. Hutchison, at Bellefleur Manor. James Edward I'm sure that you can see that this arrangement would be best for your wife and children, for now." Erin Rose and James just stood in the great hall with shock written all over their faces. Patrick knew there was no use arguing the point any further, for when John Bellefleur made up his mind about something, neither Hell nor high water, would make him change it. Again,

Patrick noticed the quizzical look on John Bellefleur's face as if he was trying to remember something as he looked at Erin Rose.

"Mr. Bellefleur, I don't rightly know what to say, but as your new employee I want to do everything you wish. If it pleases you to have us here, then we accept until our cottage is ready." James Edward felt as if he was dreaming for he had never even been inside such a grand mansion before, let alone live in one. He could only look at Erin Rose as she nodded her head in assent for she was too stunned to speak.

"Come now, come into the dining room, our dinner is waiting. Oh, Harrison, take the valises up to the west wing, and take the children into the kitchen to eat. Ask Bessie to fix their dinner. You will then help them to their rooms." This order did not set well with Erin Rose and she dared to speak her mind.

"Begging your pardon, sir, my children will stay with me. They are in a strange place and will be too frightened to eat if you separate us. I will go with them to the kitchen myself, if they cannot eat with us. They are well behaved though, sir." Erin Rose's voice was that of a protective mother and was filled with a bit of defiance too. Wasn't it enough this man had already made different arrangements for their living quarters? She was not going to let anyone take over her children.

"Oh, Mrs. Hutchison, how insensitive of me, of course, you are right. You can see it has been a long time since little ones were in the manor. I'll just have Bessie bring in more settings." As John Bellefleur spoke, he tugged on a large tasseled piece of gold rope and almost like magic, a sweet faced Negress appeared in the dining room.

"You rang for me, sir?"

"Yes, Bessie, these two youngsters will need plates and silverware. They will be dining with us, and Bessie, I hope you have a 'special' dessert for the master and mistress here!" John chuckled as he spoke.

"Yes sir, Massa, and I'll bring better chairs for the Missy and Master." Bessie's face was all smiles now for she was thrilled to have children in the house again. It had been far too long since she had seen her Massa so happy.

"Mama, why is that man and woman calling us Master and Missy? That's not our names." Sean Michael whispered to his mother as he tugged on her arm to be noticed. His mother had to laugh now, and her laughter filled the room with a light musical sound, that fell as a welcome relief to James Edward. His wife had a fiery temper at times, and he had flinched when she spoke up for the children.

"Tis just a custom, I expect." She looked at her benefactor now for a polite introduction. Mr. Bellefleur, this is Sean Michael, and sir, this is his sister, Louise Marie." Both children now looked more closely at the stranger whose house they were going to live in, and smiled gratefully. They were both very tired and extremely hungry and anxious to eat, but continued to smile saying nothing. At just that moment, a young, slender woman entered the room carrying a high chair in one hand and a little booster in the other. She smiled broadly at all the guests, picked up Louise and planted her in the high chair. She then proceeded to place the booster chair in place and helped Sean Michael to sit on it. Sean thanked his helper and smiled broadly at her; she patted him on the head and started to take her leave. John Bellefleur asked her to wait.

"Mr. and Mrs. Hutchison, this is Marcianne. She will be helping you to look after the children. Marcianne has always lived here. She was born right here in this house. Her mother was a French woman who came here from France, when she was a young girl. She passed on some years ago. I am sure you will find Marcianne a big help, Mrs. Hutchison. She is family. Marcianne these kind people will be living here at the manor until we make their cottage a little larger." Marcianne smiled at Erin Rose and James Edward but said nothing. She had the same look of puzzlement that John Bellefleur had when they had first met. Just at that moment, Bessie came in with bowls of food, followed by Harrison with a silver coffee service. He proceeded to fill all their cups, then turned to the children and set two glasses of milk before them. He then did a strange thing; he kissed each of the children on the top of their head, and silently left the dining room.

It was a delicious meal and a brilliant cap-off for the Hutchison's arrival in America. The happiness they felt that night would only grow and grow, as they became an intricate part of John Bellefleur's family.

Patrick O'Leary left his nephew to return to his own cottage, and his wife Fiona. Patrick could hardly believe what happened with James Edward and his family. He just couldn't understand it, for he had never seen John Bellefleur so taken with anyone. That speech had made about Marcianne being family, was another surprise. He would have to talk this over with Fiona for she was a lot more perceptive then he. Fiona however, was just as bewildered as Patrick was.

"Maybe he is just lonely," Fiona said. "Well maybe," Patrick said "but Fiona, why would he be so taken with James Edward and his family without knowing them better?" It was as if they are his family already. Just think on it. We can count the times we've dined at Bellefleur Manor on our fingers. Well I hope this just means something good for James Edward and his position here, but frankly Fiona, I just don't know what to make of it all." Indeed Patrick and Fiona were very puzzled.

James Edward and Erin Rose thanked John Bellefleur for his hospitality and followed Harrison to their quarters. There were three rooms given to them, two bedrooms and a lovely little sitting room. Harrison had said that there was a nursery right across the hall for the new baby, when the time came.

John Bellefleur had finally excused himself for the evening but not before he instructed them about breakfast. He wished to meet with both of them in the library at about 9:00 a.m. to fill them in on the duties that James Edward would have. He then had bid them a good night and retired to his quarters, somewhere in the huge house.

The next morning, Harrison ushered James Edward and Erin Rose into the huge room where all kinds of books lined shelf after shelf, the likes of which neither James Edward nor Erin Rose had ever seen. John Bellefleur did not miss the interest Erin Rose showed as she looked at the many titles.

"I see you must like books like I do, Mrs. Hutchison," John mused.

"Oh, yes sir, I've never seen so many volumes before. Have you read them all?" Erin Rose asked the master of the house, quite childlike.

"Yes, I believe I have. It has taken me a few years to do so. The fact is, it has taken me most of my life. You may read any or as many of the books as you please. There are even some children's books that your children might like to hear. Why don't you look the titles over, while James Edward and I speak of his duties here?"

"Yes, sir, I would like that." Erin Rose was thrilled for she liked nothing better than to read a good book.

"Now James, let's discuss what I have in mind for you. Patrick has told me what a great rider you are, and how good you are with the horses. I don't know if he told you that we raise and train horses for harness racing here. I'm sure you know what that is. We also have a few mounts we race on the track with riders. Now Patrick did not tell me that you were a small man in stature. So, I've changed my mind about your job here." James Edward was quick to go to his own defense and interrupted Bellefleur.

"Sir, begging your pardon, I may be small but I can out ride or work any horse better than most. I understand how they think, I'll...," Bellefleur smiled at his young employee as he interrupted him now.

"I'm sure that is true and that is why I've decided that you will be our jockey for all occasions. You have the build, the weight; I mean that won't hold them back. How does that sound? Of course, you will be working with your Uncle for he is the best trainer we have ever had here at Bellefleur Manor."

"That sounds wonderful, sir, and I thank you for it. You will not regret it." James Edward was so excited that he felt as if he might leave his body, or it might leap into the air by itself. God had surely smiled on him this day.

"Did you hear that, Erin Rose? Mr. Bellefleur wants me to be his official rider for his race horses!" Erin Rose could hardly believe her ears. She and James decided last night that they did not care what kind of labor they would be doing. Just to be able to live in this beautiful place they would do anything asked of them. Now, James had been offered an unbelievable job, one that he had always wished for. Erin Rose dropped the book she had been looking at and jumped up and down in excitement, then ran and hugged her husband, and gave John the biggest hug he had had in a very, very long time.

"Glory be to the angels in Heaven, we never expected so much. You are truly a wonderful man, John Bellefleur. Such a wonderful man, I expect there may be a little bit of Irish in you!" John blushed from the praise and laughed at Erin Rose's last statement.

"You are right, my dear. But you at best must calm yourself; we don't want that baby born this night." John Bellefleur couldn't remember just how long it had been since he had such a genuine pleasure as he had now with these two people. He dismissed the young couple for now, and said that he would join them shortly down by the first horse barn. He picked up a picture of a young woman who looked much like Erin Rose, kissed it and replaced it on the same spot, which it had been sitting, as a lonely tear cursed down his cheek and his lips trembling. He picked the picture up once more and whispered to it,

"My dear, I've been given a second chance, with a little Irish girl, who looks so much like you with your endearing ways.

Bellefleur Manor was huge in acreage. It's rolling meadows stretched as far as one could see in each direction. The manor house sat on a neatly manicured lawn encased in shrubs and trees. To the one side, a lovely manicured garden of shrubs and a rose garden was shared by a greenhouse where John Bellefleur spent his time when he was not working with his horses or smoking his pipe on the large veranda that graced the entire front of the manor.

There were many barns with horse stables in all of them, and a racing track just beyond the last of the barns. The barns were all painted white, trimmed red on the doors and the frame around the windows. Beyond them was several cottages, one of which was a beehive of activity. Bellefleur had brought in carpenters and masons and they were busy putting on an addition to one of the cottages.

Patrick and Fiona's cottage sat only about four hundred yards away from the last barn and not far from the other cottage in progress. In between the two cottages was a small patch that was for a garden for the two families. Fiona now was waiting to meet Erin Rose to show off her own little house.

Fiona O'Leary was a handsome woman. Plain in her manner of dressing, which tended to accentuate her dark brown hair and blue green eyes. She was much taller than Erin Rose, and slender of hips and bosom. She was quick to laughter and enjoyed the freedom that the Bellefleur Manor afforded her and Patrick. She was also very glad to now have Erin Rose and the children here to keep her company. She had never had any children of her own and she knew that these little ones would help fill a void in her and Patrick's life.

James Edward had taken to his job with much enthusiasm and his Uncle Patrick and Aunt Fiona had taken to him. He and Erin Rose were most anxious to move to their own little cottage. She had said over and over to Fiona that "the house is just grand up there but a bit too roomy for the likes of poor Irish people." Fiona had answered that it was her "nesting" instincts, because she was in the family way.

One fact that neither James Edward or Erin Rose could understand, was why were there so many Negroes living on the plantation. They did not hold with the practice of slavery at all, and in conversation with John Bellefleur one day, Erin Rose had spoken out to say so. John had answered her with a little too much complacency.

"But my dear, they have always lived here, their mama's and papa's too. Where would they go and what would they do to earn their way? Most of these folks have no skills and little book learning. There is much unrest in the country between the North and the South. The subject of slaves is a volatile one. I have thought long and hard on it, and I have made up papers for all my people in case there is a war. Many folks who did live here have left and gone farther north. Some have come back because they just didn't fit in. No my dear, don't you fret about all of this, for I expect you will be glad for their help very soon." John Bellefeur patted Erin Rose on the shoulders as he explained the existence of the many Negroes.

Just about a month had passed when this conversation had taken place when the birth pains started. Erin Rose had been climbing around all day, hanging up fresh curtains that Fiona had made for her. This one; however, was much harder. She gathered her two little ones up, said goodbye to Fiona, and headed for the main house. Her time had come, sooner than she had expected, and she would need the help of a doctor or a mid-wife; whichever John Bellefleur and Marcianne would send for. Aunt Fiona said she would help Marcianne look after the two children while she was confined.

She hurried now as fast as she could, pulling the children with her, stopping only when a contraction hit her. Each one was harder than the last.

Harrison was out by the summer house and saw that something was wrong. Bessie was with him and immediately knew what was happening and heard the urgency in Erin Rose's voice.

"Come help me, my time has come! I need help to my room. Find Mr. Bellefleur and Marcianne so they can send for the doctor, please." Erin Rose's voice trailed off as another contraction hit her, nearly causing her to fall.

"Don't you fret now child. I'll take you to your room and Harrison will find Mr. Bellefleur. Hush, child. Ol'e Bessie done helped many babies to be born, and I'll help with this one too. Lean on me and I'll see to it you don't fall. My, my, it's been a long time since we had a new one in this house." Bessie chuckled in delight as she practically carried Erin Rose to the house.

Much later that night, a loud, lusty cry came from Erin Rose's room, and George Henry Hutchison, the First, was born.

He was a sturdy little boy with a mop of reddish brown hair on his tiny round head. It was hard to tell who was the most excited, the father or his benefactor.

John Bellefleur was completely enthralled when James Edward made the announcement.

"His name will be George Henry to honor our most gracious host, John Henry Bellefeur. Should we have a brandy to celebrate, sir?"

"Yes, by all means. You and Patrick come with me to the kitchen, we will have Harrison make preparations for everyone on the farm to celebrate tomorrow. This is the first child born in this house since my own little Yvonne was born." At that memory, John Bellefleur's eyes clouded over and he left the room before he completely broke down.

Patrick and James Edward looked at each other, but said nothing, until they met Harrison in the kitchen, where they were filled in on who Yvonne was.

The celebration was wonderful. Harrison and James Edward carried Erin Rose downstairs to meet with all the guests from the plantation. The folks on Bellefleur Manor had fallen in love with the kind and beautiful Erin Rose, and now they brought gifts of crocheted booties, sweaters, blankets and little rattlers for the new baby. Their hearts, as well as John Bellefleur's had been revived. It was as if Miss Yvonne had returned to all of them. Even in all the excitement, Erin Rose had seen the tear that had coursed down John's cheek as he held the new baby, so she decided to ask Marcianne about Yvonne; who she was and how she, Marcianne, related to the family. Questions that had been haunting her since the first night they had arrived at this wonderful place.

"Marcianne, just what did Mr. Bellefleur mean when he said you were family?" Erin Rose had become very fond of Marcianne and knew she would not mind the questions.

Marcianne looked at Erin Rose for a long time before she answered.

"I thought you already knew. It is no secret here on Bellefleur Manor, just to the outside world. My mother was John Bellefleur's sister-in-law. She came here from France when his wife, her sister, Emilee, took sick with the 'consumption'. She had no other family, so my mother came to be with her and to help raise their little girl, Mary Yvonne. Yvonne is the young girl in the picture in the library. I've expected that is why my Uncle has been so taken by you. You see, Yvonne had the same beautiful red hair like yours, and in fact, looked much like you."

Marcianne smiled affectionately at Erin Rose.

"What picture are you talking about?" Erin Rose asked a bit surprised.

"The one setting on the little table between Uncle's chair and the window in the library. It was taken just before she was killed."

"Killed! How did that happen?" Erin Rose felt a sharp pain in her heart for John Bellefleur.

"She loved to ride her horse and one day she decided she could ride one of the jumpers, and was doing just great until she rode the horse down by the little stream behind the barns. The horse balked and she was thrown for some distance across the stream and was knocked unconscious. She never regained her senses and died several days later. Uncle John was devastated over her death. They say my Uncle was so devastated over her death that he had the horse killed and refused to have anything to do with the jumpers for years."

"Oh my goodness, what a tragedy." Erin Rose was shocked to silence for a few moments, and was deep in thought when Marcianne began to speak again.

"Now my mother was as devastated over Yvonne's death, as she had practically raised her due to her mother's illness. My mother went into seclusion, not going out for a long, long time. She had no reason for going to the outside world but that left her very lonely. So lonely that she sough solace from the servants here in the house. Uncle John hardly saw anyone either for several years. To this day he has not fully recovered, but your coming has been the best thing that could have happened to him. He dotes on you, you know." Marcianne looked at Erin Rose, now trying to decide if she should go on with her story, or wait until another time. Erin Rose; however, was not completely satisfied, for she knew she had not been told all of the facts.

"So it 'tis a horrible tragedy, but I don't think you have told me the whole story. Something is missing." Marcianne smiled at the ever curious Erin Rose.

"No, that is not the whole story. My mother was very lonely and sought out a light skinned man who worked here in the house. He had befriended, and consoled her over the loss of her sister, and Miss Yvonne. They grew very fond of each other and eventually found they were in love. Uncle John is not a prude and actually approved of the bond they had formed and wanted to get them officially married, but that was out of the question here in Virginia. Marriage was out but pregnancy was not. I was born here in this house and my father still lives here."

"Your father lives here!" Erin Rose's eyes grew large with this incredible statement.

"Yes, Erin Rose, Harrison is my father. My Uncle held a ceremony from the bible and pronounced them married. The shame of not being legally married to my father, as her husband, was finally more than mother could take. One night, she went out of the house and never returned. They say she just walked into the pond and drowned. I was too little to understand just what had happened. Uncle John has always been there for me, just like a father, and never has he ever treated me any different than he would his own daughter." Marcianne's face clouded over in sadness and Erin Rose threw her arms around her new friend to comfort her.

"Oh my poor dear Marcianne, I'm so sorry. I had no idea. You have been so good and kind to me and my family. I'm so sorry for all you have been through."

"Thank you, Erin Rose, but don't be sorry. My mother must have suffered dreadfully and my father has always been there for me too. Uncle John took out formal paper and legally adopted me and sent me to school. He has given me everything he thought I wanted. My name is registered as Marcianne Bellefleur, but you now know the truth. I'm really Marcianne Harrison."

"But Marcianne, don't you have a beau, or go out with any young people?" Erin Rose asked with the sorrow she felt. This lovely young girl needed to be with people her own age.

"Once I had a beau, but he never wanted to take me out anywhere, and when I asked him why, he just said he couldn't. I never saw him after that. Well now you know, and I want you to know you are a bright light in my life as well as James Edward and the children." Erin Rose hugged Marcianne again and kissed her on the cheek.

"Marcianne, I'll always be your friend. You can count on it."

CHAPTER SEVEN

CIVIL WAR

THE ARGUMENT BETWEEN THE NORTH AND THE SOUTH OVER SLAVERY AND THE THREAT OF SUCCESSION BY THE SOUTH FROM THE UNION FINALLY CAME TO A HEAD. JOHN BELLEFLEUR WANTED NOTHING TO DO WITH THE POSITION THAT MANY OF HIS NEIGHBORING VIRGINIANS WERE TAKING. HE HAD LONG AGO GIVEN ALL OF HIS PEOPLE THEIR FREEDOM PAPERS AND BID THEM TO STAY OR GO, WHICH EVER THEY DECIDED. MOST HAD STAYED, BUT MANY NOW WERE PULLED APART AS TO WHAT TO DO. STAY OR GO?

They were treated well and had a place to live and food to eat. Their work was not hard and their master (as they called him), was more like a friend than a boss. They liked their jobs of looking after the horses and tending to the farm animals.

Still, the talk was that they should help their fellow man and his effort to be free. Many of the cabins of Bellefleur had become empty, and little at a time, as some of the families ventured farther north.

The Confederate Army officers, under Colonel Harrington, arrived at Bellefleur one beautiful sunshiny day, just as John and James Edward were about to leave for the town of Centerville,

Virginia, where they would be racing several of Bellefleur's prize horses.

Colonel Harrington and his men entered the tree lined lane leading to the Manor House in great anticipation of their new quarters at such a good place. The gold braid on their jackets and the highly polished swords flashed in the bright sunshine as they rode closer to the house.

They were an imposing bunch and James Edward's flesh crawled as he remembered the British officers almost riding him down as they seized his little farm. He did not; however, show any signs of fear. He had felt secure here at Bellefleur and was determined to stand his ground.

Surely, it would be different here in America.

John Henry had discussed the war with him several times and had gone about giving his people their freedom papers and some of the younger men had left to join the fighting that was no where near Bellefleur.

Nothing much had changed at the plantation, but James Edward felt that ominous feeling in his gut that all was about to change. John Bellefleur walked toward the men as the Colonel dismounted.

"Good morning, Colonel; men." John Henry tipped his hat, "What brings your and your men here to Bellefleur so early in the morning?"

"Good morning, Bellefleur. As you know, our troops need all the help they can get and we know you have many horses here what would aid our cause. Also, we need many other items of food and clothing. But most of all, we need a place to establish a post for orders to be carried out and Bellefleur has been chosen for this purpose." The Colonel's voice was crisp, almost brittle, and smacked of military aggressiveness.

"I'm sure as a patriot of the South, you will be more than glad to help us establish headquarters here for me and my men."

John Bellefleur was astonished at the Colonel's request and had to struggle to maintain his composure. He wanted to yell at the Colonel and order him and his men off his property; but he knew he could not.

'Patience,' he said to himself; and after a short silence, John spoke, choosing his words carefully.

"Headquarters, eh? Well I suppose we can make room for everyone at the Manor, sir."

"These are just a few of the officers and men that will be living in the manor. There will be a whole regiment setting up their tents here. Also, we will be rounding up your people to help keep the men fed and clothed."

The Colonel was now barking out orders rather than requesting.

John Henry bristled for a moment, but added good naturedly as he possibly could.

"Colonel, all the Negro's left on Bellefleur our free people. I don't have any slaves here. I'm sure they will be more than willing to help you though."

"Well, Bellefleur, I only hope so. By the way, just who is this man with you?"

"Sir, he is my herdsman and jockey. He has just come over here from Ireland with his family. This is not his war." The Colonel grimaced and interrupted John.

"I'll give you to understand that it's every man's war that lives in this state. We can discuss this matter later. Right now, we will take count of your stock and people. You will make the manor ready for us to move into, tomorrow."

Colonel Harrington saluted John Bellefleur, mounted his horse and rode off toward the barns, with his men following close behind.

"Well, James Edward, it seems you have swapped one war for another. You don't have to worry; I won't let the Colonel drag you into this mess with the North."

John now wore a grim look of fear on his face; something James Edward had not seen before.

"Sir, don't you think you should go with the Colonel?"

"No! When the military decides what all it wants, I'll be ready for them. I do have some influence in these parts, and it looks as if I'm going to have to use it. Right now, we need to get a move on or we'll miss your first race. I've got a lot of money riding on you and 'Pint of Gold'. Let the Colonel fend for himself for now."

"Yes, sir. You're the boss."

James Edward laughed now; the soldiers were completely out of his mind. He had to win now, John was counting on him, and this new situation with the military was just the thing to get under his skin enough to edge him on.

They came away much richer that they had even imagined. James Edward won three out of his five starts, including the claiming race, for the two year olds. 'Clear Vision' was a black, sleek gelding that had left all the other two year olds many lengths behind. Both men were ecstatic with their wins for a few minutes, as John forgot all about the Colonel and their impending residence at Bellefleur.

Erin Rose had seen the officers enter the barns and several of the cabins, but they did not come near hers. Still, she was a nervous wreck waiting for James Edward to come home.

'What did all this mean?' she wondered.

The soldiers stayed a long time at Uncle Patrick's, who was alone in his cottage. Erin Rose had a tremendous urge to run to the Manor House to see if Fiona knew what was going on. She did not; however.

She decided that it was best to stay hidden in her cottage. Maybe the soldiers would leave and not even know she was around. She had had a very bad experience with the British soldiers and she did not want to face that situation ever again.

She would just wait for James Edward to come home.

Finally, she saw the soldiers leave. She tried to brush her fear aside and breathed a sigh of relief when James Edward arrived a few moments later.

It was almost dark and when he opened their little cottage door, he was still basking in the glory of his wins.

His wonderful day was soon met with the reality that the soldiers had spent most of the day at Bellefleur. He refused, though, to let all of this dash his spirits, and soon had Erin Rose laughing and dancing with him.

They had been at Bellefleur now for a few years, secluded, for the most part. Now, he knew that this situation would change, exactly how, he just didn't know.

He thought to himself, 'I will worry about that tomorrow, but for now, I will take what happiness is due me.'

He had even agreed with John's statement that this was not his war, but as he saw the frightened look on his wife's face, he wondered if she had seen the soldiers.

"What's wrong, Erin Rose? You look like you've seen a ghost."

"There were many soldiers here all day, going in all the buildings. I'm so afraid it's going to be the same as in Ireland."

James Edward spoke the words but really did not totally mean them. Erin Rose sensed he didn't understand the scope of the day's events.

"Don't worry darlin'. Let me tell you how many races I won. You won't believe it. Mr. Bellefleur gave me one whole purse for winning three races. Can you believe that?"

James Edward now really saw just how frightened his wife really was, and fear struck his heart.

"Did those soldiers come here, to this house, Erin Rose?"

"No, but they did go over to Uncle Patrick's and were there for a long time. I've been too scared to leave the house to find out what they wanted over there."

"Surely, Uncle Patrick or Aunt Fiona would have come right over if something was wrong." James Edward had now taken Erin Rose into his arms and kissed her cheek trying to reassure her, but the fact was, he now felt the same fear he had had when he saw the soldiers ride up the lane in the early morning.

Morning finally arrived and James Edward and Erin Rose were awakened by a loud banging on their door. It was Patrick, breathless and unable to speak.

"What is it, Uncle Patrick?" James Edward squinted his eyes toward the sky.

"It's barely light outside." Patrick nodded his head, yes.

"We have been invaded, son. Come see for yourself!" James Edward hurriedly pulled on his pants and joined his Uncle outside.

Hundreds of small tents littered the fields west of their cottages and extended southward to the lower barns. Horses roamed this area at will and soldiers were everywhere. The two men gasped at the sight, as even more soldiers were moving in as they watched.

"Come, lad; we best be getting up to Mr. Bellefleur about all of this commotion and invasion. It seems the war has come to us."

"Yes Uncle. Just let me put Erin Rose's mind at ease." Erin Rose had followed the two men outside and was now standing barefooted in her nightgown, in the dew on the grass. She started to meet her husband, but he stopped her.

"Go back into the house. Go back to bed Erin Rose. It is in the wee hours of the morning. Uncle Patrick and I have to go to one of the barns and then to the main house to see Mr. Bellefleur. Go on, now, go back to bed."

James Edward gave his wife a kiss and walked her back to her bed.

"It is far too early to get up. Stay here until I get back. I won't be gone long." He winked and pinched her on the buttocks and added, "Stay here and keep the bed warm for me. I'll be right back."

Erin Rose laughed at her husband's insinuation, and crawled back under the covers.

The two men ran to the main house, ignoring all the soldiers, but stopped as they entered the fenced-in yard around the Manor.

There was Colonel Harrington and six officers, unloading a large cannon and carrying loads of equipment into the Manor through the front doors. Harrison, Marcianne and Bessie were all protesting the intrusion, but the Colonel was not listening, and rudely called out to them.

"Get out of our way! We have work to do. Your master knows of all of this. By the way, where is he? Not a very good welcome for the people who are going to save all of this for him."

He waved his arm, encompassing the entire plantation.

John Bellefleur had quickly dressed and was now coming into the great hall where the confusion was mounting.

"It's all right, Harrison, I did know the Colonel was coming, I just didn't know it would be so early. Go on about your chores, Marci, Bessie; I'll be in to discuss all this with you in a little while." Puzzled, Marci protested.

"But Uncle." John quickly interrupted.

"Go Marci, and tend to your bed making and cleaning. I'll answer your questions later. Bessie set up the dining table to feed these hungry men. All seven of them!" John Bellefleur barked out the orders as if he was accustomed to ordering people around in a gruff way.

Marci, Bessie and Harrison left the room in complete confusion at John's anger. What on earth had they done to cause it, they wondered.

"What's that, that nigger girl called you? Sounded like 'Uncle', that's what." Colonel Harrington asked, laughing as he said the words, for no self-respecting Southern Gentleman would allow such a thing from a Negress. "Surely I misunderstood her, you couldn't be her uncle now, could you … unless?"

He finished with a knowing smirk. John Bellefleur swallowed hard and looked defiantly into the Colonel's eyes, hating what he knew he knew he must say to spare Marcianne.

"Of course, you misunderstood. She was addressing my man Harrison. Have your men take your paperwork and other necessary equipment into the library just down the hall, through the double doors, there. That room will be best to set up your office. There are several desk type tables you can use. I'll have the main sitting room cleared to further accommodate your needs. Bessie or Marci will come when your meal is ready."

John turned to go and then added an afterthought.

"I must say that I am very surprised that you are back so soon. I did not expect you for a few more days."

Just as he finished a loud bugle call sounded in the distance and John rushed to the nearest window to see all the soldiers and their tents taking over his entire farm. There had not been time for a warning from James Edward or Patrick. John Bellefleur sank into a nearby chair, shocked into silence. His face was ashen and he felt that he would surely be sick.

"Sorry old man, but your place is perfect for our regiment to march from. Not too close or too far from the coastline, or the fighting. The plantation is well hidden from the main roads so as to not attract any attention, and a good distance from Centerville."

The Colonel now fished in a large leather pouch and finally drew out several papers.

"I received these orders from the top to move my troops here, post-hast. As you can see, the orders are for you to supply us with any and all the things we need." The Colonel smugly handed some official looking documents to John Bellefleur. Patrick saw the look of frustration on John's face and asked to help.

"Mr. Bellefleur, can James and me help you in anyway?"

"No, Patrick! Patrick, James, it's my patriotic duty to help the South in any way that I can." John looked over the documents and then handed them back to the Colonel.

"Colonel Harrington, I'll do everything in my power to help the Confederacy, but for right now, could I have a few minutes alone with my men here. Patrick will be the man who will be getting you whatever you need for your men." John said these words as a new fear now gripped him.

"Of course, Bellefleur, take all the time you need, we're not going anywhere." Laughing arrogantly, the Colonel disappeared through the outside doors.

"Come, come with me!" John rose from his chair a bit shaky, and led James and Patrick out of the room and up to his own bedroom.

"Hurry, before someone sees us. We will go up to my private hideaway."

Patrick and James Edward looked at each other in surprise, but did not say a word. They followed him to his room on the second floor, and once inside, John went straight to the far corner of the room, placed a chair there, climbed upon it and pushed hard on the ceiling, and the cornice just below it. To James and Patrick's amazement, part of the ceiling slid down under the molding, revealing a large space with a ladder. John pulled the ladder down into the room and proceeded to climb the ladder.

"Follow me, men, and pull the ladder up when you get inside the room."

The room they entered was small, almost dark with only a small, round window which looked upon the meadows. One could see for miles Patrick noted as he gazed out of it. Now that their eyes had adjusted, they could see that there was a bed and lavatory facilities, a small chest with a tall mirror, a small table and chairs, on which a kerosene lamp sat. As Patrick and James looked about, all they could say was, "Golly." John; however, proceeded to speak in a very low voice.

"I brought you up here just in case any of us, especially the women, need to be hidden. Do not tell anyone about this room, not even your wives. Presently, I have been the only one who knows of it. With all the military here now, and whoever else may come, in the next months, years, we may have to use it for our safety, or the women's" James and Patrick had now taken a seat with Bellefleur at the little table, feeling a fear they had not felt before. Would this war spill over more and more into their lives, they wondered.

"I really don't know just what this war is going to bring all of us, but one thing is for sure, I don't believe it will be very good. Marcianne may be the first that will be in danger. She called me 'Uncle' in front of the Colonel, and he took note of it right away. I explained to him that she was addressing Harrison, but I don't know if he bought it or not. I expect the soldiers will try to take advantage of her, Bessie, and possibly Fiona. I don't believe Erin Rose will be, if she stays out of the main house. Surely, if the battle does not go well and the Northerners come in, we may well all be in great danger, but Marcianne with be in the most. I've heard horrible stories about what happened to women of high color from all military. Should there ever be a time where any of the women here at Bellefleur are in any danger, we can hide them up here. It might be up to you, Patrick, to take care of this. My guess is that I will be expected to take some part in the war. In the meantime, go along doing anything you can to keep these men happy. Do you both understand?"

"Yes sir," James and Patrick answered half-heartedly.

"Another thing; we must have some kind of password to let each other know if we think there is a problem ahead, so we can meet here secretly. Let's see – I know if we need to meet, let's say, "Top of the morning to you' and add the time to meet by saying, 'I'll be back by noon or after supper', or a given time of some kind. Should we have to use this room, I will get food hidden by taking my food in my room. Now, let's go downstairs. I'll go down the front stairs and the two of you take the backstairs. James Edward, take Marcianne with you to your cottage until I come for her. Make some excuse that Erin Rose needs her. Patrick, you come back to the library and by that time I'm sure I will have some order from the Colonel."

John Bellefleur stood now and motioned for the men to climb back down the ladder, put it back in place and shoved the ceiling back in place by the molding. Quickly he changed his clothes to a riding habit and hurried back just in time to be greeted by the Colonel and some of his men.

The Colonel looked at John intently for a few seconds and then spoke with a bit of curiosity. "I see you are ready to ride with me, right? Let's be at it then. Where are your men?"

At that moment Patrick appeared at the library door and called out to the Colonel.

"I'm here, sir, at your service." Patrick smiled broadly at the Colonel in his normal good natured way. "Tis a pleasure to help you, sir."

James Edward led Marcianne to his cottage saying he would explain when they got inside. It was still early in the morning and Erin Rose had done as her husband had instructed, and went back to bed. The opening of the back door and several voices brought her awake. She quickly donned a wrapper over her nightgown and ran to see who was with James Edward.

"What is wrong? Are you alright, Marcianne?" Erin Rose asked curiously as she looked from her husband and then back to Marcianne. James Edward knew he had a very large task before him in order to keep the women from panicking.

"Come; sit with me at the table. Do we have any coffee or tea? Yes of course. Here Marcianne, let me pour you a cup." Erin Rose knew something was up, for she could see the fear in her husband's eyes. Marcianne too, looked as if she had seen a ghost.

"Come Erin, look out the front windows. See, the Southern Troops have invaded Bellefleur, and that is why Mr. Bellefleur wanted to see Uncle Patrick and me so early. The Colonel and his officers have taken over most of the Manor, and Mr. Bellefleur wants Marcianne to stay here with us until he comes for her. He has told the Colonel that you are ailing and need Marcianne's help. Marcianne, tie a scarf or something around your head like the servants wear and if anyone asks who she is, she is just another servant that Mr. Bellefleur has sent down to help you. Do not answer any other thing."

"But why, James Edward? Aren't these the South's soldiers, and are to protect us?" Erin Rose asked innocently.

"Yes, they are the Southern forces, but they are just men too. You are both fine looking women and we all know the stories. Especially Marcianne, you would be the first to be in harms way. The Colonel heard you call Mr. Bellefleur 'Uncle'. John denied it, said you were referring to Harrison."

Marcianne's face was now drained of all color as she, James and Erin watched the soldiers going in and out of every barn, chicken house, hog house and on down to the little cottages where a few of the negro still lived.

James Edward knew his wife and Marcianne were filled with fear, so he tried to act as if everything was just fine.

"Now you two ladies have nothing to fear. Mr. Bellefleur knew these men were coming, and so did I. We just didn't expect them so soon, and certainly not so many of the regulars. Colonel Harrington and his officers will be using the Manor House as their headquarters. I don't exactly know what all the soldier's needs will be, but Mr. Bellefleur is obligated to help the Confederacy. I expect by now he has papers to that effect. Go on with your daily chores, but do not go out of the yard. Watch the children closely and under no circumstances Marcianne, are you or Erin Rose to go to the Manor House, for now. Mr. Bellefleur will give us more directions later. I must be heading back up there, in case Mr. Bellefleur needs me."

James Edward stood now and touched the tiny nose of baby George, stooped and kissed him and quietly left the house, so not to wake the other children.

LIFE WITH THE MILITARY

JAMES EDWARD CAREFULLY STOLE BACK TO THE MANOR HOUSE WONDERING JUST WHAT REALLY WAS GOING TO HAPPEN TO THEM ALL. HE DIDN'T LIKE THE COLONEL, AND HE SURELY DID NOT LIKE BEING SURROUNDED BY ALL THE SOLDIERS. THEY WERE EVERYWHERE IT SEEMED. WOULD HE BE FORCED TO JOIN THE MILITARY? WOULD HIS UNCLE PATRICK? HE SURELY HOPED NOT. IF MR. BELLEFLEUR ASKED HIM THOUGH, HE WOULD HAVE TO DO IT FOR HIS SAKE. SURELY HE THOUGHT UNCLE PATRICK IS TOO OLD TO HAVE TO GO TO FIGHT IN A WAR.

Aunt Fiona saw him come in the back door and ran to meet him. She was very anxious to know what was happening.

"What all is going on, James Edward? The dining room is full of soldiers. Bessie and I have been cooking up everything we can find, and Harrison has been serving the table. Are they going to be here very long?" Fiona was wringing her hands around a kitchen towel and trying to hang on to his arm all at the same time.

"Aunt Fiona, I'm sure that things will take on a more organized way after today." Realizing he was very hungry himself he quipped. "As a matter of fact, I'm starving. Can I get something in the kitchen to eat? I can listen to the conversation in there without anyone knowing I'm listening." James Edward now pinched his Aunt's cheek, and gave her a little hug. She calmed down a bit and assured James Edward there was food for him in the kitchen.

Fiona was well liked at Bellefleur, and soon after their arrival, John Bellefleur put her in charge of all the women who did the cooking and cleaning. At first some of the women thought they did not need anyone to oversee what they were doing, especially the young laundress, but in time everyone came to love her. She had taken Marcianne under her wing and became like a mother to her. She now was quite worried about her. Why had he taken her from the Manor? She would never let Marcianne go into Centerville by herself for fear something or someone would accost her. She still worried about her but now she had Erin Rose, and what a Godsend that was. She knew there was no need to worry anymore after the two women had been taunted and called "misfits" by two teenage boys. She smiled to herself now as she remembered that Erin Rose had jumped out of the carriage, grabbed the two boys, unexpectedly, shook them so hard they started crying and yelling for help. Erin Rose got back into the carriage, Marcianne said, like nothing had happened. However, they had not been taunted anymore.

"James Edward, what is going to happen now?" Fiona asked again.

"I don't believe much will change Auntie except for the work involved taking care of the Officers. They are going to be taking their meals here at the manor. I know it will be an added chore for all of you, but maybe it won't last too long. Just keep your distance from the men, and by the way, I took Marcianne down to my cottage, so the men would not accost her. John told Colonel that she was taking care of Erin Rose and the children because my wife was ailing, should the Colonel ask." Fiona made a face at James as she handed him a plate of eggs and potatoes and a fat pork sausage. She placed her hands on her hips and gave her best Irish answer.

"Well, 'tis one thing or another I suppose. As long as I don't have to see the likes of them running all over me house, I'll just be a going about me business. Drink up, so I can pour you some more coffee that you'll be a wanting." Fiona acted folly enough but in her mind she was remembering the soldiers of the Queen, and how they went about killing livestock and raping women. She decided at that moment she would never let a man assault her that way, even if she had to kill him; and that went for Marcianne and Erin Rose too.

The soldiers under Colonel Harrington's orders gathered up hogs, cows, chickens, and slaughtered them to feed the huge amount of soldiers on the plantation and in the field. The field workhorses and mules were rounded up too, hitched to the military supply wagons; and driven toward Richmond. All the residents at Bellefleur were most relieved as most of the soldiers left the plantation, and hoped that they would not return. James Edward knew though that they would be returning from time to time for the duration of the war. He only hoped that he would not have to leave his family and don an army uniform. It was bad enough when John Bellefleur would be gone with the Colonel for weeks at a time. The soldiers left behind manning the regiment, felt that nothing was out of line, and would order everyone around like to the slave masters which some of them were.

On one of these tours John Bellefleur had returned to his plantation very weary and decided to retire to the tiny little study he had set up for himself, on the third floor. He thought that he was safe from interruption and decided to take a quick nap. He was dozing when a loud knock came at the door, which awakened him with a start.

"Bellefleur, my man saw you come in and come up here. Open the door; I need to ask you a question!" The Colonel seemed a bit upset and did not apologize for his intrusion, but pounded on the door.

"Yes, yes, I am in here. What is it?" John shook himself awake wondering what could be so all fired important. He had just left the Colonel not more than forty-five minutes ago.

"Open the door, now!" The Colonel demanded, so John opened the door and bid the Colonel step inside; asking him again, what is it?

"Where is that high yeller gal? We've looked everywhere for that mulatto that was here when we first arrived. Where is she Bellefleur?" John Bellefleur had hoped that Marcianne's absence would not be noticed, but now he knew he had to think fast to protect her.

"Oh, you must be talking about Marci. Well she had to go to one of the cottages to help out with a sick wife. The woman is ill and has three small children to be looked after. The children know Marci best of the servants, so I sent her down there to help out until the woman is able to do her own work. What do you want with her?" John's stomach turned over with fear, but he smiled now at the Colonel.

"To help keep my officers entertained. Her Uncle said she played the harpsichord. My men found her very attractive and I want you to get her back up here to this house. Damn the sick woman, send another darky to tend to her!"

There it was, just what Bellefleur had been afraid of. He shivered now at the thought of what Harrington considered entertainment, besides music. Some how, he had to stall off the Colonel, placate him some other way. Talk; agree with him for now, think of something.

"I can see how you and your men would want Marci, for I myself find her attractive at times, but I have something else I think your men might find exhilarating, until Marci is more available." John pretended an air of excitement he did not feel, but an idea struck him that he thought might just save Marci, for now.

"Ya'll Bellefleur and just what might that be?" Colonel Harrington asked a bit disgruntled.

"A Cock fight! There's a cock fight right close by. You understand I can't say just where it is, but I will lead you there, and it's tonight." John spoke in a low, confidential voice, as if he was involved in a bit of intrigue, for cock fighting was not the most legal thing in Virginia.

"A Cock fight! Well that does sound interesting. You got a cock for that ring?"

"No, but I assure you, you won't be disappointed."

"Well, let's go tell the men. It will make their day, but don't forget, we want that wench, Marci, to serve us and I don't mean food. What time do we need to be ready?" Colonel Harrington was appeased for the moment but he had no idea of letting go of Marci, and John knew it. He would just have to keep the Colonel busy for the next few days and hope for orders for them to leave out again.

"We probably ought to leave within the hour. I'll make sure we have plenty of beverages to drink. A cock fight isn't much fun without a little enrichment." John laughed heartily and winked at the Colonel and left him standing alone in the hallway.

John Bellefleur hurried to the kitchen and after a few words with Bessie and Harrison, Harrison hurried toward the cottage to get James Edward.

"James Edward, Master Bellefleur wants you to get dressed in a hurry in your riding suit, and come to the house. He wants you to accompany him and them officers to a cock fight, and, he has something else he has to tell you! Marci child don't go anywhere near that house. Dem men's up there asking for you. Massa' say you tending to sick Mrs. Hutchison – I'sa got to go now, but stay out of sight child!" Harrison left as quickly as he had come so as not to waste the time he needed to put the liquor and food in baskets for his master to take with him and the officers.

Marcianne and Erin Rose cringed at Harrison's words, "Those men were asking for Marci." Both women knew what that meant. John Bellefleur did not care much for cock fights, but it turned out to be just the trick to take the soldier's minds off Marcianne, or any other young woman on the plantation. John excused himself after the first fight, making sure the men still had plenty to drink, and went to the nearby inn to set up lodging for himself and the officers. He knew they would all be too drunk for the long ride home. James Edward remained with the men and later would help the men on their horses and escort them to the Inn.

They were an unsightly group, but was thoroughly enjoying themselves singing and joking, sometimes insulting each other. The war was the farthest thing from their minds. James Edward mused that soldiers were soldiers regardless of what country they were from; rowdy, rude, boisterous, and looking for a fight. The innkeeper had been grateful when John Bellefleur said he was paying for the nights lodging for the military who had just moved in. He had told the man that they had took over his plantation, saying it was his duty to serve the Confederacy any way they wished. Now that they were arriving drunken and loud, he wasn't as sure that he wanted them or John's money. James Edward tried to assure the innkeeper that he really had control of the Officers and men, but he knew that the task ahead of him would be a difficult one. Once he got the men to their rooms, he was surprised that they fell asleep without any problems.

Colonel Harrington awakened his officers and men early, sought out John and James Edward, and made their way back to Bellefleur Manor. They were met by a military courier with orders for the rest of the battalion to move out quickly, and join the fighting at Richmond. John and James Edward were tremendously relieved to hear this news and could barely wait to inform the rest of the inhabitants of the Manor. John was especially relieved for Marcianne's sake, but he knew she would have to remain in the little hideaway until all the soldiers had taken their leave of Bellefleur. He had mentioned to the Colonel that Marci had runaway sometime in the night and that he had just found out this fact when they had come back from the cock fight.

James Edward made haste to advise Erin Rose, his Uncle and Aunt about the good news. He warned them that it would take some time for all the soldiers to move out with provisions to last them in battle, and warned them to stay as close to their cottages as possible.

It took a total of five days to ready and pull-out the troops. They had to pack provisions in their coffers, break down all the tents, and load all of their weapons and horses, but they did not seem to be in a hurry to leave. Their demands for livestock and other foods was horrendous, leaving Bellefleur almost empty. Colonel Harrington had also cornered John Bellefleur and said that they would be back with a commission for him to join in the fight. John thanked him and said he would be glad to be under his command, but he really did not mean it. He did not want to join in the fight for he thought himself too old to be of much good. The real fact was he was horrified to think he might have to go and bear arms against his fellowman. He knew too, that if he had to go James Edward would surely have to go with him. If the war worsened he also knew that Patrick would have to go regardless of his advanced age. What on earth would the women folks do to get along he pondered. Finally, he came up with a plan in his mind as to what he should do, if such a thing became necessary.

Colonel Harrington, however, was never to return to Bellefleur. This was a fact that all of the residents were eternally grateful for.

Bits and pieces of news of the fighting came to Bellefleur via the many people on the roads. Some were confederate soldiers returning home. Others were just drifters. Soon it was not just a few. Droves and droves of people; ragged, hungry, half clothed and starving soldiers and civilians, dotted the roads of Virginia. The little road past Bellefleur was no different. The residents of Bellefleur doctored, nursed, fed and allowed the wounded to rest. Some who were on foot were given horses to help them on their way home. Finally, after months of carnage, the War between the States was over. The Negroes were freed people, and the real devastation began. The horrors on Bellefleur Manor were just beginning.

The Yankees moved in, and completely took over everything, and everybody living at Bellefleur. First they ran off all the Negroes that were left except Harrison, Bessie and their families. They were kept to take care of the soldiers and their officers. Even though the Negroes had their freedom papers, and wanted to stay in their homes, they were physically herded out onto the road with only the clothing on their backs, weeping and crying to stay. The O'Leary's and the Hutchinson's were forced to move to one cottage, and they were made to serve the Military. John Bellefleur was allowed to remain in the Manor with only his bedroom and the little study allocated to him. He was only allowed to take his meals in the kitchen and was stripped of any help from Harrison. John had feigned illness when the soldiers first arrived unexpectedly, and called for Patrick and James Edward to come to his room. Captain Harkness, who was in charge was very suspicious of John but allowed the two men enough time to come to John's aide. Captain Harkness, however, listened at the door to their conversation. The men were all savvy to the Captain so they chose their words carefully, asking what they could do for John. He had asked the men if they could bring him some of the yellow concoction that their wives used for aching muscles. They said yes, but Fiona might have to make up some, but they would try and get back to him by dark. As they started to leave, the Captain opened the door and told them they had chores to do, and to get at them, but not before James Edward said, "Top of the morning to you Uncle."

Dressed in riding pants and jacket, Marcianne was smuggled into John's room, under the darkness of the night, with the help of Harrison. Once again she had to climb the little ladder and stay in the little hideaway. The Captain had already made known that he intended to have her as his personal maid. He had laughed when he made this statement and acknowledged to his men and all the others there that he expected more than just keeping his clothes cleans and his food served to him. He even went so far as to suggest that a bed would be prepared so that she could sleep in his room.

Erin Rose and Fiona lived in fear of their lives. Fiona had been kept many nights in the kitchen with Bessie, trying to meet the demands of the rude soldiers. Fiona and Patrick lived in constant fear that she would be raped, for the soldiers took the liberty of touching her buttocks and making lewd suggestions to her. She in turn acted as if it was of no concern to her, but inside she trembled constantly. Erin Rose never ventured out of the cottage and only allowed the children outside when their father could be with them. Sometimes a couple of soldiers came to the cottage during the day but Erin Rose would not unlock or open the door. She kept the little ones quiet until the soldiers got tired of knocking, and left.

Captain Harkness, under U.S. Grant was a ruthless man and began watching every move and action John Bellefleur made. John soon knew the time had come for all of the inhabitants left at Bellefleur, to find a way out of the horrors they were living in. He thought on his former plan again and slipped a note to James Edward through Harrison. It read:

My son we three must meet again in secret. Find the way. BHJ.

Patrick and James Edward answered at the bottom:

Tonight before the cock crows.

They showed the note to Harrison and told him what it said. He said that he would be ready. To just come to the kitchen window, the key to John's room would be there.

The three men huddled together and finally had the plan they needed to escape from Bellefleur Manor and Virginia. John had the details worked out, and told them he had a relative in Kentucky where they could stay for a short time, until he could find some other resources. He explained that Kentucky was a neutral state during the war, so that they could be more or less free from the military. John also told them that he had withdrawn all of his funds from the bank in Centerville when the war hit Richmond. He would have enough to buy another place in Kentucky. Patrick, he said, would have to be very careful and so would James Edward. But, they needed to get packed and ready to leave at the first possible chance. He said that the barn closest to their cottage always had two coaches and a couple of wagons stored there and that he hoped that they were still there. Pack only the very essentials for we will need all the room for the ladies and children. Do as much as you possibly can in the dark, so the soldiers will be unaware of your actions. Should you be confronted by any military, tell them you have orders from me to make available the coaches, but you do not know what for. If this happens you will have to be ready to leave immediately.

Patrick and James Edward crept out of the house and steadfastly made their way to the barn, and sure enough, there under the piles of hay were the two carriages and wagons.

The hope now of getting away from underneath the Yankees, spurred the O'Leary's and the Hutchinson's to reassess what had happened here in Virginia. They knew too that not one of them could be left behind. They also knew that they were all survivors and that there was nothing for them to do but move on. Their years here at Bellefleur had been the most wonderful ones of their lives, but move on they would. None of them wanted to leave John behind, but they knew he knew best.

Weeks passed but the day finally came when they knew they could not delay their move any longer. A soldier had come to the cottage while James Edward and Fiona were all working, and Erin Rose was alone. A knock came on the door and Erin Rose tried to stifle the baby from crying but could not. A louder knock came and then the door was pushed open, breaking the lock that had been placed on the door. The soldier grabbed Erin Rose and backed her up against the wall, tearing her clothes as he did so. He was laughing at her astonishment as he began fondling her breasts. She screamed but no one was near to hear her. The two children began crying and tried to help their mother, but the man flung them off. This did, however, give Erin Rose enough time to grab him by the hair as she knocked off his hat and began biting him on the neck and kicking him in the crotch. The man fell to the floor in a faint. Much later Erin Rose came to herself to find the children hiding under the kitchen table, scared out of their wits. The man was still lying on the floor, not moving or making any noises. She was so petrified that she could not even move, except to crawl under the table and with the children. There James Edward would find them, sobbing and holding each other, as well as Little George.

"Come out Erin, children. The man can't hurt you anymore, he's dead. My God! My God!" He exclaimed when he saw that half of Erin Roses' clothes were torn off exposing her breasts. "Oh my darling, did he hurt you bad? Did he try to rape you?"

"Yes," she whispered, "he tried. Is he really dead?" she asked her husband.

"Yes, I'm afraid that he is. Get a cover and we will cover him up until Patrick gets here. I only hope no one comes looking for him." Too stunned to talk, Erin Rose just stared and stared at the soldier. James Edward could see that his wife was so traumatized that he got up and fixed her a cup of hot tea. He took the children to their bedroom telling them to stay there with their little brother until he came back for them. Then he covered the man's body with a quilt. Patrick came home and was met at the door by James Edward. Nervously he relayed what happened and asked Patrick what they should do with the body. Patrick never hesitated with the answer.

"We will hide it under the hay that we took off the carriages. We will finish packing then and slip away in the night. We cannot wait another day. The soldier will be missed and no telling just what they will do to us to try and find him. I must first go back to the Manor and tell John what has happened, and get his help to get Marcianne out of the hiding place and into one of the carriages with Erin Rose and the children. James Edward was to drive the other carriage with Fiona and Sean Michael. Patrick drove one of the wagons piled high with their meager belongings. Each carriage and wagon left, one at a time, silently as a tiger in the night, while the soldiers slept and only one guard was at the main house. They took the little dirt lane that led out into the fields and then onto the little road that let them on their way to Kentucky.

They were gone for three days before their absence was even noticed. Captain Harkness and his men were busy trying to find the missing soldier. They had canvassed the roads and finding some horses missing, they decided that he had run off with them.

Missing people were of little concern to the Captain but the missing horses were another matter. John Bellefleur and Harrison were much relieved at his lack of interest in the O'Leary's and the Hutchison's disappearance, but the Captain made the rest of the people's lives miserable. He said John Bellefleur was at fault that he was missing horses out of the barns. John said nothing in return but did the chores that the Captain had now ordered him to do.

The Captain and his troop's constant needs were nearly working John, Bessie, her two young boys and Harrison nearly to death. It was fetch this, fetch that, get me more to drink, clean our offices and on and on. John had written his cousin Robert Prescott about the little group who would need his help, and said that he would join them just as soon as he could find the chance to escape.

A month passed before John found that chance. A courier came with a notice that Captain Harkness and his men were to meet his General on the nearby James River, for a possible reassignment for some of the men. The Captain left only two men standing guard at Bellefleur. John knew he would have no better chance than this and spoke to Bessie and Harrison to make ready to leave in a hurry that night. John Bellefleur put his other plan into motion, to drug the guards, so that they could make their escape. He invited each one into the house and served them some of his best brandy with a little potion of atropine that had been extracted from the belladonna plant, but not enough to be deadly.

In the wee hours of the morning, John Bellefleur, Harrison, Bessie, her sister and Bessie's two sons, drove out of Bellefleur never to return, without incident. Bessie's sister drove a wagon loaded with all of the escapees' possessions, with their two children and a gangly young man that was a helper in the barns. They tried not to look back on their days at Bellefleur but it was like leaving a member of their family, for all of them had been born on the Bellefleur Plantation.

James Edward and Erin Rose had been given directions and a letter from John Bellefleur, directing his cousin Robert Prescott to help the little group when they arrived at his place, near Louisville, Kentucky. He also said that he would bring his people as soon as he could find a way to escape the Northern soldiers.

The little group drove their horses and carriages as fast as they could manage, but the roads were muddy from the recent rains, and hard to maneuver. Also, there were still many people trying to get back to their homes, soldiers and people that had been displaced. That was good for the little group from Bellefleur. Since there were no Negroes (Marci did not look like most Negroes), with them, they were seen as just more poor people moving their few possessions somewhere else. Food and lodging was the biggest problem for the travelers, for there were few inns and even less food at the inns. Dirty and very tired, they finally found the house of Robert Prescott. The children were immediately put to bed after being fed, and it was not too soon for any of the weary adults. Thankful to be in a house again they were soon fast asleep.

In the meantime John Bellefleur and his entourage made sure that all of the Negroes in his care had their "freed" papers as they climbed aboard the carriage. Once on the road John hid under a blanket until they reached the Kentucky State line and found sanctuary with a black family. They had been stopped many times but since their papers were in good order, the Virginians and the Union soldiers were only too glad to be rid of all the blacks that they could.

After many long weeks all of the residents of Bellefleur were reunited at the Robert Prescott farm. Needless to say, it was a very joyful reunion but flawed by what had happened to the farm during the war. Most of the main house had been burned to the ground, the fields plundered, and the people all had been run off, escaping through the underground tunnel at the Funkhouser Post in Evansville, Indiana. Robert Prescott had remained a neutral side and the renegades had made him suffer for it. He now was most grateful to be able to assist his cousin in any way that he could. He had started the rebuilding of his farm the minute he heard that the folks from Bellefleur Manor needed help. James Edward and Patrick immediately pitched in helping in any way they could. The tobacco fields needed cultivating and they would help with the rebuilding of the burned buildings.

Robert Prescott was totally appreciative to have women in his house again for he had to raise two children now. His Mary Jo has passed on in the past winter from the consumption leaving him the job of raising his children alone. The children were just delighted. They now had children to play with and three wonderful ladies to help take care of them. It truly became one big happy family, but John was growing restless living in his cousin's house. He was anxious to find a place of his own, where all his people could again be on their own. He began to take trips farther south in Kentucky, and on many of the trips he took James Edward with him. During their travels they found that Kentucky was still unpopulated with much of it still in woodland, and some places were just wilderness.

John and James Edward liked traveling around, they liked the adventure of seeing what lay on the other side of the hill as they roamed the countryside.

One of these trips took them into the rolling hills of the southwestern Kentucky. James Edward stopped his horse atop a large hill and breathed in the fresh air. It was cool and crisp, and as he looked about him, he was reminded of his home in dear ole Ireland. The green rolling hills were breath taking and he knew he had found the place he would want to bring his family to. The ground was darker and richer, and he knew it would grow all that he and his family would need to make their living.

As if reading his mind John Bellefleur said hopefully to him, "James Edward, this is where we will come, this will be our new home, for it reminds me of Virginia the first time I saw it." James Edward could only nod in the affirmative for he was overcome with the joy that "Uncle John" (as he now called him), felt the same as he did.

The two men rode on in silence and finally reached a little village where they stopped a young man on foot, and inquired as to the town's name. The young man was none other than the son of one of the town's founders, and proud of it. He was quick to answer the inquiry.

"Why sir, this is Morganfield, the biggest town around these parts." The young man looked intently at James Edward and John, shaking his head in wonderment and disbelief that anyone would not know the name of this town. He tipped his hat at the gentlemen and walked on down the un-cobbled street.

John and James Edward rode their horses on down the dirt street and dismounted in front of a building with a sign reading "Red Dog Saloon." John frowned at his surroundings, but inwardly he was very curious. James Edward was also taking in the town's few buildings, but as he did so, he noticed a big sign further down the street reading "Land for Sale". That, he thought, is where we should be going, but John had surmised that the only rooms for let would surely be above this saloon. He reached out and fondly slapped James Edward on the back and proceeded into the saloon, motioning for James to follow.

It was pretty late in the day now, so of course the usual piano player was pounding out the tunes of the day and the saloon was occupied by just a few men at the bar. Several others were seated at a nearby table playing cards. John stopped just inside the door and took in the atmosphere before seating himself at the bar. James Edward followed his every move, sensing this might not be a friendly bunch, but he was wrong, for the bartender was now extending his hand, in a friendly greeting.

"Howdy strangers, what you best be havin'?" The man's huge mustache wiggled as he spoke causing James Edward to smile broadly.

"Well I'll have some of your famous bourbon, and an ale her for the lad. Don't want to spoil him." John Bellefleur put silver on the bar not knowing if his currency was good here in Kentucky.

"Never saw you boys in these parts before, where you come from?" The bartender spoke as he filled the glass of ale for James Edward.

"Louisville. We heard there was land down here for just the taking. Sure hope so, the hills around here are truly beautiful." John was now fishing for information but the bartender seemed suspicious, and turned toward James Edward.

"What about you? You look like you just got off the boat. Irish, I'd guess, ain't you?" The bartender smirked a little, but before James Edward could answer, John answered for him.

"Yes, by golly, he is Irish. How smart you are, but he came here from Louisville with me. He's been in this country for sometime now, with his family and with me."

"Well by jove, drink up fellers, and welcome to Morganfield. You can call me Jake, Jake West, ya'all that's me name."

"Glad to know you, Jake," John and James Edward said in unison, "I bet you know where we can get a room for the night, right?" John inquired.

"Bet your bottom dollar, I do. Right here, upstairs, we got nice clean rooms for the night or maybe two? You want one or two?" Jake eyed John and James Edward curiously now, and waited for an answer.

"Two, Jake. Maybe a hot bath would be nice. Can you arrange that?" John laid five dollar gold piece on the counter now as he spoke "Will that take care of the rooms and the bath?" Jake West's eyes glistened with joy as he looked at the gold piece on the bar.

"Yes sir, that'll more than take care of it all. Here let me fill your glasses again, and then I'll get Mattie to show you to your rooms." Jake West was overjoyed at the money these men were spending, and he was going to make the most of it.

"When you all want breakfast, just come down and Mattie will oblige you. She's my wife and darn good cook she be. Bet you could use some grub right now?"

"Well Jake perhaps after we take care of our horses and tend to a little business, we will take you up on the 'grub'. Come, son, let's take a look at the rooms." As John finished speaking a woman of about forty years entered the room smiling, with a large ring of keys in her hand. She was rather plump, very fair with straight blondish hair, which was pulled tightly back and coiled into a bun. She was obviously of German descent and had a very thick German accent.

"Yawl, follow me up the stairs," she ordered, and the two men did as they were told. The rooms were fastidiously clean but contained little furniture, with an iron bedstead, a washstand, one chair and small table by the bed with a kerosene lamp on it. Just above it were a couple of hooks to hang the towels and another for coats.

"I get the hot vater ven you ready, you say to Jake." With this statement Mattie disappeared.

The two men were weary from their long ride of the day and decided to rest for awhile before bedding down their horses, so off came their boots. They sat down on John's bed, and without much ado John fell fast asleep, but James Edward was anxious to get things done. He rested beside John for a short time and then tiptoed out of the room, locked the door, and went downstairs. He was about to leave when Jake stopped him.

"You know, son, I clean forgot to ask you your name. Mattie jumped all over me, so would you mind signing them on the book here." Jake shoved a large ledger in front of James Edward and handed him a pen. James Edward looked at Jake for a moment, and then wrote, 'J. Bellefleur and J.E. Hutchison, Louisville, Kentucky'. Jake now smiled and retrieved the pen.

"You know, I didn't rightly think you could write your letters, 'cause you sure don't talk much, Irish." Jake chuckled at himself and James Edward smiled at him slightly, wondering just what the insinuation really was.

James Edward led the horses to the livery stable at the end of the little village and had them bedded down for the night. He walked back to the saloon and had another ale. This time he asked for a ham sandwich and Jake hurried to Mattie to fill his order. James Edward later let himself quietly into John's room, just as he was waking up and greeted him a little surprised.

"Where you been? Didn't you rest any at all?" John rubbed his eyes and yawned.

"Just for a little while. I took the horses to the livery stable and had another pint, as my father would say," James Edward laughed now and his blue eyes sparkled "Oh by the way, I put your saddle bags on the chair over there." The two men washed their faces, combed their hair and went out to see the people who had the "Land for Sale" sign with great hope.

CHAPTER EIGHT

NEW HOPE – PACK UP YOUR WAGONS

THE OLD HOUSE SAT HIGH ON A GRASSY HILL, JOHN WAS REMEMBERING THE GRAND DAYS AND BIG PARTIES OF A TIME LONG GONE. STILL THERE WAS ELEGANCE ABOUT THE HOUSE THAT JOHN BELLEFLEUR COULD FEEL, AND HE KNEW THAT HE COULD RESTORE THE HOUSE TO ITS FORMER ELEGANCE. HE ALSO REALIZED THAT IT WOULD TAKE A HUGE PORTION OF HIS REMAINING FUNDS TO REBUILD AND REFURBISH THE PLACE, BUT HE FELT IT WAS WORTH IT. HIS FAMILY DESERVED IT, HE SAID TO HIMSELF; GEORGE HUTCHISON AND HIS FATHER, JAMES EDWARD, AND HIS BEAUTIFUL MOTHER, ERIN ROSE, MUST HAVE A PLACE OF THEIR OWN. HIS BEAUTIFUL ERIN ROSE HAD TAKEN THE PLACE OF HIS OWN YVONNE, AND SO THEY WOULD INHERIT WHAT THEY HAD HELPED HIM BUILD. GEORGE HENRY A LITTLE OVER EIGHT YEARS OF AGE WAS AS MUCH LIKE HIMSELF, A TRUE HORSEMAN, AS A LAD COULD BE. HE VIEWED HIM AS HIS VERY OWN SON.

James Edward stood as if in a trance watching the puffy clouds moving silently overhead, as he continued to stare at the land surrounding him. He had never dreamed Kentucky could be so beautiful. His thoughts turned as ever to Erin Rose, whom he knew would love this beautiful place with its rolling hills and green pastures as far as one could see. Just beyond the south pasture he could see a little creek where a few horses and cows drank to their satisfaction.

The recent war did not seem to have touched this place as it had so many plantations and the lives of all who had lived at Bellefleur Manor. John Bellefleur was also relishing in the tranquility of the landscape and felt that he had come home. The two men finally turned to each other and John's voice brought James Edward out of his reverie.

"Well James Edward, what do you make of all this beauty?"

"It is a bit of heaven I do believe. So very green and flourishing with the need of someone to love it and to let it find its glory again as to what it can be." James Edward was almost melancholy with his answer.

"I'm glad you feel that way for that is how I feel. This will be our new home. Together we will make it a grand place for you and Erin Rose to raise my grandchildren. Let's go back to town so I can sign the papers and make payment arrangements today, before someone else sees this place is for sale.'

"You mean it? This is going to be ours?" James Edward could hardly believe what John had just said, "Oh how happy Erin Rose will be when she sees it. She will dance you a jig to show you her appreciation, and Uncle Patrick and Aunt Fiona will be just as glad."

"Yes, there will be plenty of room for everyone, but we will all have to work hard now that all the darkies are freed. Erin Rose was right when she told me Mr. Lincoln did the right thing. No human should be slave to another man." John Bellefleur laughed as he recalled the words that Erin Rose had defiantly lashed out at him when he said he couldn't get along without slaves on his plantation.

John and James Edward rode back to the little village of Morganfield and signed all the necessary papers, gave the man a draft to cover the down payment and title search. Then they rode as fast as they could to the home of Robert Prescott, where their family was waiting for them. They could hardly wait to tell them all the good news.

John and James Edward were greeted by an ecstatic Marcianne with her own good news. She flashed her left hand back and forth before their eyes but neither man picked up her signal. Undaunted, she began to speak repeatedly as she gave her Uncle a big hug to welcome him home.

"Look, look Uncle John, look at my hand. I'm going to be marred to Robert! Isn't that just wonderful?" We have already made the arrangements for the Ceremony to take place right here in the house. Fiona and Erin Rose have finished my gown and, and," she exclaimed breathlessly.

"My goodness girl, you must calm down or you won't last long enough to get to the Ceremony," John laughed as he hugged his niece affectionately, and kissed her on the forehead.

"James Edward and I have some good news too, but let us all go inside so we can tell all the others."

"But Uncle, aren't you at least a bit surprised about my marriage?" Marcianne now looked totally puzzled.

"Not at all surprised Marci, but glad for you. I was sure this was going to happen, especially since Robert had told me just how much you meant to him. He also asked me if I would permit the marriage, and I told him yes. By the way, is he home?" Marcianne just stood looking at her Uncle for a moment before she answered.

"You are sneaky, Uncle, but to answer your question; no he is not at home. He is busy making all the arrangements with the priest, and also he said he had to purchase some clothing for the wedding. James Edward, are you just a little surprised?" She asked childlike.

"Yes, my dear Marcianne, 'tis a real thrill to congratulate you. You will make a fine Mrs. Prescott." James Edward tipped his hat and gave Marcianne a slight bow, where upon she giggled and almost pushed him down, a little embarrassed. At just that moment Erin Rose burst from the front door excited to see her husband and benefactor were safe and sound. She flung her arms around her husband and then gave John a big hug. As he turned back to James Edward he threw his arms back around her and lifted her off her feet, kissing her sweet face.

"'tis a joy to see you Erin Rose. How are the wee ones? Well, I hope." Erin Rose did not have to answer, for now all three children ran to meet their father and John. Sean Michael was now 13 and Louise Marie was 11. They had grown into a handsome lad and lovely young girl. George Henry now ran straight to his Poppi John, and John lifted him high in the sky. Hugs and kisses were exchanged all around as the two men were swamped with the excited children. Sean Michael usually void of most displays of affection could not help but show his excitement of seeing the two men he loved most in the world. It had seemed to him they had been gone forever, and he had begun to be worried about when they were going to return.

"Isn't the news of Marcianne's wedding just the best thing? Isn't it just wonderful?" Erin Rose asked excitedly.

"Yes it tis Erin Rose. I expect you will be wanting to go shopping for some finery yourself, for this grand occasion. Well now that can be taken care of, but just wait 'til you hear the grand news that Uncle John has to tell everyone. You are just going to be so thrilled. I believe that Marcianne will be even more thrilled about that too." James Edward grinned now, from ear to ear. He loved taunting the ladies. James Edward's blue eyes twinkled with mischief. "Tell them Uncle."

"Yes, I believe what I have to tell you all will be a big thrill for everyone." John answered knowingly.

"Poppi what is it?" What could be as exciting as a wedding?" Erin Rose bubbled with curiosity that her adopted father had aroused in her.

"Yes, Poppi, tell us, please tell us." The young children pleaded.

"Where are Patrick and Fiona?" Are they in the house? No, then Sean Michael go find them and bring them to the house. What I have to say affects them too." John tousled George Henry's curly red hair, and with his arm around his small shoulders, escorted him and the others into the large Prescott parlor.

Everyone gathered around the large fireplace, including Bessie and Harrison. As John Bellefleur spoke the good news of finding a new home for them all, the excitement rose higher and higher until Erin Rose could stand it no longer.

"You have found us a home of our own, our very own? We're going to have our own place again? What does it look like: Oh, I don't care how it looks; Where, Poppi, where is it?" Erin Rose's cheeks now glistened with tears of joy. She had felt so displaced for so long since leaving Bellefleur Manor, and she knew her Poppi must have felt much worse than she did. She just could not contain herself and ran from one to the other, hugging each and everyone, she was so excited.

"Well family, the farm is about 75 miles from Prescott, and the buildings need a lot of repair, but just wait until you see the green hills surrounding it. We will be close to a friendly little village called Morganfield." John was now beaming from all the excitement he had just created.

"Morganfield, eh, I believe Robert knows that country, Uncle John. I have heard it is beautiful but still pretty rugged for the most part. Is it fit for crops or just for raising animals?" Marcianne now looked at her Uncle seeking more knowledge about this new purchase.

"Yes Marcianne, Patrick, we will have plenty of land for horses and crops. The house is large; it's an old brick federal that I have already set about for some repairs to be made. The war did not reach that area, but it did leave the house mostly empty except for an older couple and one man who tends to the cattle on the farm. Patrick, you and Fiona will have your own quarters in the main house as well as James Edward and Erin Rose. The war may have ripped some families apart, but it has made us one big happy family. And now we are to be blessed with an addition, with Marci getting married. I expect that will also bring in many little ones for all of us to love."

Fiona now looked at Patrick and then addressed John for she could only imagine what was in store for her and Patrick.

"Sir, just how big is this house?"

"Well, Fiona, I believe it has 16 rooms besides the kitchen, and the quarters for cooking and canning in the hot months. We may change some of what is already there when we get everyone installed. Oh, ladies, one of the great features of the house is the large up-stairs-porches. You will just love them I know. There are many gardens around the house that surely need your touch Fiona. Patrick, your work is cut out for you in the barns. I bought all the livestock on the farm, and plan to recreate part of Bellefleur for the new horses." Bessie, Harrison and Marcianne looked back and forth from one to the other, with questions readily recognizable on their faces. Seeing this, John continued.

"Marcianne, I can see you have something on your mind. First, let me congratulate you again on your wedding to Robert. He is a fine man and I know he cares a great deal for you. Just to ease your mind, none of us will be leaving until after your wedding. I have known for sometime this probably would all come about, and I couldn't be happier for you." John now turned his attention to Bessie and Harrison.

"Harrison, you and Bessie will have to make your own decision as to weather you want to stay here with Marci and Robert, or to come with me. We have been together for a long time but if your wish is to stay on with Marcianne, I will understand. I do want you to know that I would sorely miss my old friend, but whatever your decision is now, you can change anytime you wish it, as far as I'm concerned." John Bellefleur took a deep breath now, for his voice had faltered at the thought of Harrison not being with him in their old age.

"Bessie, the same goes for you and your sister. Take your time for there is no rush. Tell your sister what I have told you so she can decide what she wants to do with her family."

"Massa, I don't need any time, wherever you goes, me and mine goes with you. I was born in Bellefleur and you have been so kind to me, and saved our lives from the soldiers. What ever you nee's me for, I will do. Where ever you go, I goes with you." Bessie was near tears as she finished speaking and quickly left the room to find her sister, Pearl, to tell her the good news. Bessie did not like Prescott very much for she had to work in the fields, which was not to her liking. She was glad for the safety it had afforded them, but she had felt like a misfit all these many months. Pearl was elated at the news of a new home for she felt the same as Bessie- out of place.

Harrison said nothing, he couldn't. He was so happy about the new home, but his happiness was dulled by his pain of leaving his beloved daughter. He also knew that the newlyweds would not need the responsibility of looking after him. Harrison was now in his late fifties, and many of the ills of the elderly had set upon him. His joints had stiffened and the manual labor he had been doing had taken its toll on him. He knew his decision could only be to go with one life-long friend he had ever had. He also liked the feeling that he belonged somewhere, something he did not feel here at Prescott. He hated leaving Marcianne, but she would have Robert, and in time her children. They could visit often for it was not that far away.

"Massa, I feel the way Bessie do, I go with you. I been with you since a little boy, and Marci will have Robert to look after her now. Besides, I don't think you can get along without me, in our old age." Harrison laughed now easing the tension in the room, as he put his arms about Marci's shoulders, and looked into her face for approval.

"Patrick, James Edward, we will discuss more about our new home and my plans for it after dinner. Children, help you Poppi upstairs, I need a short rest. Marci, Fiona, Erin Rose, you all can fill me in on the wedding details with the others tomorrow. I'm very happy you made up your mind, Marci, to be Robert's wife. Come children, help Poppi up the stairs." The children all too happy with their chore, now helped John out of his chair and helped him up the winding staircase. James Edward and Erin Rose followed close behind, closing their bedroom door softly behind them.

Marci's wedding was, oh so splendid. Robert Prescott spared no expense for the decorations, food and drink. Every servant and members of all the families were adorned in the very best clothes that could be found. The lawn was set up with tables and chairs and was draped in ribbons and flowers. A white satin altar entwined in ivy and rose buds was made especially for the ceremony. John Bellefleur had dozens of white carnations, roses and green fern sent in also to decorate the altar and the center of every table. Fiona and Erin Rose had worked magic in creating the wedding gown and dresses for themselves. The children of Erin Rose were ring bearers and flower girl. Louise Marie looked much like a little angel in a duplicate of the wedding gown which was made of white satin and lace. Much, much lace created a long train for Marci's wedding gown. Fiona and Erin Rose wore gowns of soft antique rose satin, made in the same style as Marci's wedding dress. They were styled in empire waists with long tight fitted sleeves to the wrist, ending in v-cut scallops extending over the wrist. Buttons which fastened the sleeves, ended just above the elbow in huge puffed sleeves at the shoulder. As was the fashion of the day, a flouncey bustle made of rows of ruffles adorned the back of the dress, set off by a huge bow at the waist. Soft music played throughout the day by a local string band, which strolled the grounds with their music making after the nuptials.

Marcianne insisted that Harrison walk her to the altar much against Robert's wishes. He felt it would taint her, and the wedding. John Bellefleur understood what Robert was trying to do, so he stepped in, and insisted that he was her 'adopted' father and he needed to help walk her down the aisle too. Surely, this would save her from pompous ridicule if they both gave her away. This factor made the local priest very happy for John had taken him in his confidence as to Marcianne's birthright.

After the ceremony, Patrick, James Edward and Sean Michael played happy lilting Irish tunes on their violins so that everyone could dance. Little George Henry sang a beautiful "Oh Danny Boy" in a rich soprano, creating quite a stir amongst the many, many guests that had poured in for miles around.

Prescott Manor had been fully repaired, and this occasion was the first big occasion for pleasure since the terrible war had ended.

The newly married couple slipped silently away during the dancing and festivities for a two-week honeymoon, somewhere in the south - Destination unknown.

PACK UP YOUR WAGONS

WITH THE FESTIVITIES OUT OF THE WAY, IT WAS NOW TIME TO BEGIN THE PACKING FOR THE MOVE TO MORGANFIELD. WAGONS AND CARRIAGES WERE PACKED AND BRIMMING-OVER WITH FEW POSSESSIONS FROM BELLEFLEUR, AND A FEW NEW ONES THEY HAD ACQUIRED SINCE COMING TO PRESCOTT MANOR. JOHN HAD ARRANGED TO BUY A FEW MORE HORSES FROM ROBERT PRESCOTT FOR HIS MOVE, SO JOHN BELLEFLEUR, PATRICK O'LEARY, JAMES EDWARD HUTCHISON, AND YOUNG SEAN MICHAEL ALL RODE THERE RESPECTIVE HORSES WHILE THE REMAINDER OF THE ENTOURAGE RODE IN CARRIAGES. OVERALL, THERE WERE EIGHT ADULTS AND FIVE CHILDREN, EACH HAPPY AND SAD AT THE SAME TIME. LEAVING MARCIANNE HAD WRENCHED ERIN ROSE AND FIONA'S HEARTS, FOR THEY HAD BECOME THE BEST OF FRIENDS, REALLY MORE LIKE SISTERS. ERIN ROSE'S CHILDREN ALL FELT THE PAIN OF THE SEPARATIONS, BUT THE TASTE OF A NEW ADVENTURE HAD SOMEWHAT DULLED THIS PAIN.

James Edward watched the three women as they parted and then pressed them into their carriages, so that they could be on their way.

"Come ladies, everyone is waiting for you. We must be off now, for it's a long way from here." With a quick kiss for Marcianne and a handshake with Robert, James Edward mounted his horse, tipped his hat, and spurred his mount to move out.

John was shaking Robert's hand thanking him for all the help in their time of a great need. Robert assured his cousin that he would be bringing Marci to visit in a couple of months. They shook hands, and the wagons and carriages began the long journey to a new home.

The spring rains started coming on their second day of travel, making the road muddy and slowing their travel down to an early stop at an inn. The passengers were only too glad to get out of their wet clothing and partake of some rich beef soup that was the evening specialty. The innkeeper only had three rooms left so the men took one room, the women another and the boys another. It was the first time for some of the children to sleep in an Inn, and they were having the time of their life.

The sun rose early waking Patrick and James Edward. They in turn woke the other two rooms, rapping loudly on their doors. All the commotion also woke John and Harrison.

Finally, everyone was up and of course, starving. After a breakfast of Kentucky ham and eggs, biscuits and gravy and crispy fried potatoes, the travelers were back on the road. The roads had dried somewhat making their travel a little faster, but it still took four and a half days before they came within sight of their new home.

John Bellefleur turned his horse into the tree-lined lane and bid the others to follow. The lane was long and the trees had already budded out in full, making the house obscure from their eyes, but suddenly there it was, and everyone let out a yell of joy. They had arrived finally, and there it was, just as John and James Edward had described it. A huge red brick with white shuddered windows and doors, sitting on a little hill all covered in green, green grass. It looked like paradise to them all. Erin Rose pulled her carriage to a stop, stood up and yelled loudly enough for all to hear.

"Mercy be! to the angel in Heaven, 'tis a dream I'm a seeing! It's bigger than Bellefleur!"

John and James Edward burst into laughter at their excitement. Fiona was speechless as well as Harrison and Patrick. Cherry trees all in bloom and flowerbeds surrounded the house. In the middle of the circular drive was a bed filled with blooming tulips, daffodils and tiny white flowered bushes, the likes of which none of them had ever seen before.

The fence that surrounded the house and the rest of the farm had been freshly painted in a gleaming white, as well as all of the shutters on the house. One could see the upstairs and downstairs porches were also freshly painted.

The fields around the house seemed even greener, if that was possible, to James Edward. It seemed a miracle had been accomplished since they had last seen the farm. As they got closer to the house they could hear hammering and sawing and many men running about with tools and lumber.

As their horses and carriages came to a stop, an elderly, white haired, bearded man rose slowly from his chair on the porch and made his way down the red brick steps to greet his visitors. John Bellefleur dismounted and offered his hand to the man.

"Good Day sir, I'm John Bellefleur, the new owner. Do you remember me, Mr. Clay?" The elderly man looked perturbed at John.

"Yes, of course, I remember you. I may be old but I still have all of my facilities, young man. I have been expecting you!" Dalton Clay's voice had a slight edge to it.

"Sir, I wasn't sure the property man had gotten in touch with you as yet, I meant no insinuation that you were forgetful," John's voice, mixed with concern and respect, as he tried to make amends "As you can see, I have quite a family with me and I hope you won't be put out too much with our arrival!"

"Oh, shaw, of course not. You are the owner of all of this." Dalton Clay waved his arms about himself as he spoke.

"We are ready to move in to Morganfield, in fact, we have moved most of what we didn't agree on leaving. You will see, we only need to take our valises out now. Let's don't stand out here another minute, I'm sure your women folks are anxious to come inside." Dalton Clay turned now and made his way back up the steps onto the veranda. John had a sigh of relief. He had not really known just what to expect from the past owners, for the real estate man had said they had second thoughts about selling out. Their age won over, however.

"Come everyone, we are to go inside." John addressed his family now with much anticipation. Everyone scrambled out of their carriages as fast as they could manage, with James Edward and Patrick helping the women. Louise Marie, always verbal, could not control herself any longer.

"Mama, are we going to live with that old man?"

"Hush, child! Don't ask questions now. We will find out soon enough." Erin Rose looked at Fiona and rolled her eyes in dismay, but wishing to laugh instead. Fiona smiled back at her knowingly.

They all entered behind the elderly Mr. Clay and found themselves in a large hall, with highly polished wood floors and lovely velvet covered chairs. Mirrors framed in ornate gold frames adorned the walls where a long matching Queen Anne table stood with a beautiful fresh bouquet of roses and spring flowers. Their fragrances permeated the air and took away some of the formality of the room. Standing near the table stood a small elegant dressed woman. As they approached, she held out her hand to the white haired Mr. Clay.

"This is my dear wife, Mr. Bellefleur, folks. Her name is Isabelle, and this is our manservant, Moses. He will help you get your valises and other things upstairs. We will then be ready to leave, but our Hannah will stay on for a few days to help you to settle in and to help prepare food for you all. If you would be so kind, I would appreciate it if you would bring her into our new residence in Morganfield, whenever you are ready that is."

"Of course, of course, Mr. Clay, you are most kind and we are all most appreciative for your help to get us settled." Mr. Clay nodded in approval as Bessie now spoke up, for she could stand it no longer, she wanted to see the kitchen where she felt much more comfortable.

"I will help Hannah, ma'am, sir, if you will just show me the way." Isabelle Clay smiled at Bessie, thankful for her help.

The rest of the group was ushered into a large formal sitting room filled with beautiful upholstered furniture and lacy white curtains on the windows. Draped over the white curtains were rose-colored, velvet draperies, swaged in the middle and held on the sides by huge gold gilded rosettes. Mrs. Clay reached to the side of her chair and pulled on a long gold cord and almost instantaneously, a large black woman beaming with delight, came in carrying a huge silver tray, laden with a silver carafe, tiny cakes and cookies. Bessie could hardly contain herself, but managed to do so as she offered the goodies to everyone.

Isabelle Clay also seemed utterly delighted as she watched everyone select from the silver tray, their choice of sweets. Erin Rose was ever watchful over the children, making sure they did not spill anything on the beautiful furniture. Bessie had taken her and her sister's children to the kitchen with her. Harrison had tried to follow them but John Bellefleur had pressed him back into his chair. Harrison was ill at ease, for he had seen the looks of the Clay's disapproval, as he remained seated beside John accepting his cup of tea just like everyone else. John also noticed the Clay's disapproval and chose to ignore it. This was now his house and he would be damned if anyone would tell him how to live in it.

"When you are finished with your tea, Mr. Bellefleur, I will take you to the outbuildings and introduce you to some of the people who were left here to help you."

"Thank you sir, I think we should be going now so that you and Mrs. Clay can be on your way to Morganfield before it gets any later." As the two men walked from building to building, unlocking and relocking each building's door behind them, John was mystified as to why all the locks, so he had to ask.

"Mr. Clay, I'm unaccustomed to everything being locked. What is your reason?" John wore a frown on his face but Mr. Clay only looked at him with distain.

"Oh, of course, I see you have a different attitude toward your darkies, but you will find they will steal you blind here without the locks," Clay spoke with sarcasm "These Negroes may have been freed, but actually they are just the same as before the war. You know what I mean.'

"You mean there are black folks here that don't have their freed papers?" John was shocked at Clay's words.

"Oh, they have been freed alright, by Lincoln, but they have no where to go. I let them stay on just for there vittles and a place to sleep." Clay cleared his throat and continued, "If I didn't keep everything under lock and key they would make off with anything they wanted and I'd never see them again. You'll see, they are lazy and don't want to work for their food even." John said nothing but thought these people are probably not getting all the food they needed and nothing else. Then as they were walking on, John noticed the many dark faces hiding behind buildings, watching with frightened faces. John knew he would have to gather the many Negroes together and let them know that things would now be different for them.

Moses had hurried to finish loading the Clay's valises into the double-seated carriage and helping him was a slender young black girl of maybe fifteen years of age. Hannah also was helping, crying periodically hugging the young girl, and wringing her hands between sobs. Hannah would speak to the girl and one could tell she was giving the young girl instructions as what to do. The young girl would nod her head in understanding then Hannah and she both cried while hugging each other. John would learn later, the young girl was Hannah's youngest daughter, Cora Lee, who had not wanted to go with Mr. and Mrs. Clay, away from her mother. The Clay's were still steeped in the master and slave syndrome, so they thought that they could continue ordering their servants to leave or go, as they saw fit.

John Henry Bellefleur sighed a big sigh of relief as the Clay's drove away. At that precise moment, he decided the name of the farm would not be known as Clay Manor any longer. He pondered the thought for a few moments and decided it should have an Irish name. He would name it for Erin Rose who had become so important to him. That's it; I'll call it the Rose of Shannon Manor, and get a lovely gate built at the entrance of the main road so that everyone will know this is a different farm now.

Satisfied with his thoughts, John made his way to the second floor to spend his first night in the Rose of Shannon Manor.

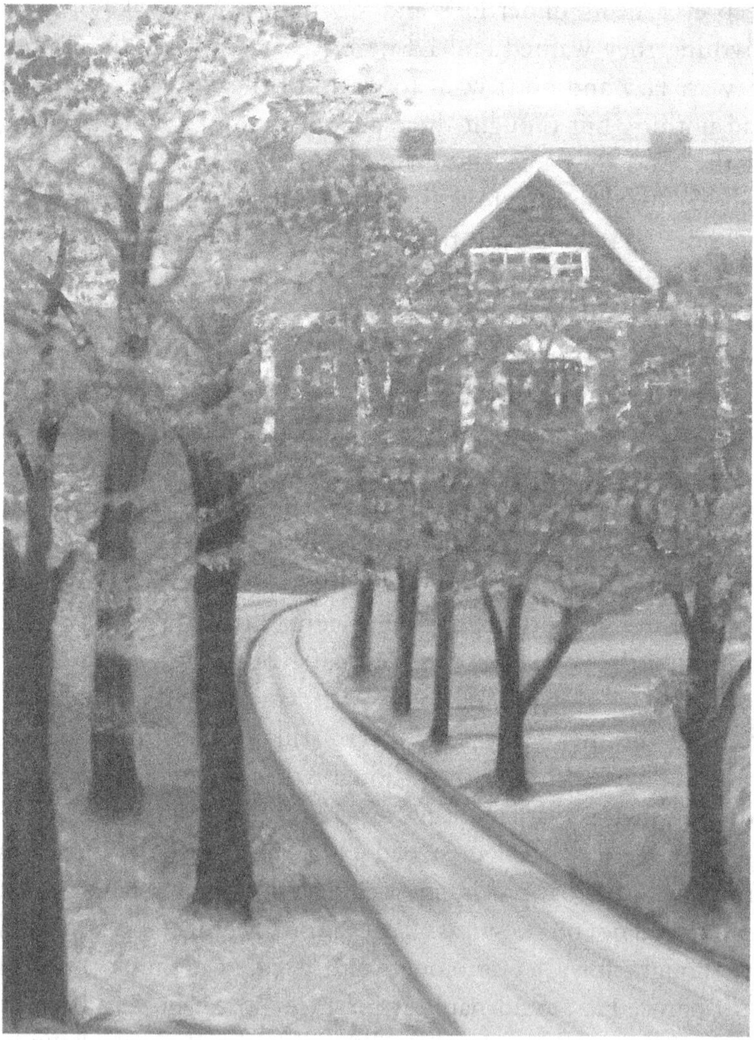

Rose of Shannon Manor

CHAPTER NINE

A NEW DAWNING

The Hutchison's, O'Leary's, John Bellefleur and his people had no trouble settling in their new home. Many changes took place at Rose of Shannon Manor so that the inhabitants felt more at home here in the State of Kentucky. The first big change came when John gathered all the black folks together and told them that they were free to stay or go. If they wished to stay, they would be given their freed papers and paid for their labor, above their food and lodging. The sum would be meager at first, but as the farm grew so would their wages. He introduced them to Harrison, Bessie and her sister and acknowledged that the first job Harrison was to do was to select one of the men to go with him and take the locks off the many buildings. He was to be shown where each family lived, and should their quarters be in need of repair, Harrison would make a note of it.

John introduced James Edward and Patrick, and their families to all of the people. He said that they were his family and should be treated with the utmost respect. He also told all of the people that if they wished to leave and needed train fare, he would pay for it. All they had to do was to give him the address where they were going. John waited to hear who wanted to leave, but no one came forward. He was relieved for he really did need everyone to stay to help put the Manor back in good shape.

Harrison resumed his tasks of running the Manor, Bessie, her sister and their children took on the remaining household chores, with Erin Rose and Fiona overseeing their work. Everyone was happy with their new home and began their work of cleaning, repairing and refurbishing with utter joy of purpose.

The Manor was soon to be noticed in the surrounding countryside, and referred to as the big house out there with all those freed Negroes. The fields were planted in tobacco, corn and lespedeza, but enough acreage was saved for the many pastures that would be needed for horses and cows that were to come in the future.

The children loved their new home and the new freedoms they found there. Each had their chores and did them without resistance. George Henry especially loved all of the animals, but his first love was soon to become hunting with his Poppi Bellefleur.

The years seemed to fly by and soon George Henry had grown into a sturdy young man but his Poppi Bellefleur was not as active as he once had been. John still liked to go hunting every chance he got, and by now had gone farther south for game into the mountains of Tennessee. There he had met a family by the name of Jewell who had befriended him and his fellow hunters, and now he had told James Edward and George Henry he wanted to hunt up his friend to see how he and his family were.

"We will take the river as far south as we can and maybe we will bag a deer or two while we are looking for their cabin. It is hidden very well because, you see, Jean Leone Jewell is married to a Cherokee woman whose family had to flee for their lives. She and her family were one of the families that the government were about to remove to Oklahoma Territory, so they could sell their property to the whites that wanted to settle in Georgia." James Edward listened to John as he remembered the one and only time he had gone with John to Tennessee and met the Jewell's.

"Yes Uncle, I remember the Jewell's. They had several children, I believe. Two girls, I believe. George Henry I expect you might be interested in them, right? If I remember right, they were just your age and pretty too." James Edward teasingly addressed his son now.

"Oh Pa, I don't need to meet any girls in Tennessee, there are plenty right here in Morganfield, but I do want to see that country, Poppi."

"Then it is settled. We will leave in a couple of days, when the rains let up a little." John Bellefleur was now anxious to get his gear together, so he left the other men standing and went off to see what all he would need for the trip. James Edward, somewhat younger than John, vented his concerns to his son about John's ability to make such a long trip now.

"George Henry, I'm not so sure that Poppi ought to make this trip. He is not as agile as he was. This past year had been hard on all of us, but especially for John and Harrison.. The fact is, my bones have been giving me a lot of trouble during all this rain." George Henry looked his father in the eye for a moment before he answered.

"Father, I did not know that you have been ailing. You never said so to me before. Are you not wanting to go? Maybe we can take it a little easier that we usually do. It seems to me that Poppi won't be taking kindly to any suggestion that he not go. Didn't' it seem to you that Poppi was most eager to see his friend again, almost like it was a must?"

"Yes, lad, I did indeed hear that in John's voice. Something that he just wants to do one more time, I believe." James Edward said thoughtfully and George Henry looked at his father as he mused his words.

The rains finally let up and the three men set out on their hunting trip that would take them deep into the woods of Tennessee. They did manage to kill one deer on their way, but the huge river they had to cross before they reached the mountains was swollen out of its banks. Entire areas were still flooded and the river was running swiftly, taking bridges and debris with it.

The bridges that were still standing had been greatly damaged, and proved very dangerous. James Edward cautioned John that they should turn back or find some other way across the big river. John, now finding himself very tired, insisted that they had to cross and that he was sure the bridge would hold them. George Henry volunteered to cross first to test the bridge. He hollered back at his father and Poppi that some of the boards were loose, and they needed to stay to the far right side of the bridge. The two men guided their horses single file across the bridge, James Edward crossing first. Just as John got to the middle of the bridge, his horse veered to the left and stepped on a loose board causing the horse to stumble, throwing John off and down into the rushing waters below. Knocked unconscious, he was carried by the rushing waters down river. George Henry kicked his horse and tried to follow, but by the time he caught up with John, and plunged into the icy water, John had already met his maker. George Henry was horrified that he was not able to save his Poppi. He pondered this over and over, 'why hadn't the bridge given away when he or his father crossed?' Somehow it seemed to him that it had to be his fault. James Edward too felt that they should have been able to prevent this accident. Why hadn't either one of them seen the loose board? They asked themselves over and over. James Edward now remembered he did not think they should have come on this long trip, and he suffered much guilt. From then on, he was never to return to his once jovial self.

The news of John Bellefleur's death reached Morganfield by the time his body arrived at Rose of Shannon Manor. The entire population here were in disbelief. How could their wonderful Poppi be gone? Why had it happened? What would happen to all of them, something none of them had ever given thought to. However, John Bellefleur was a man of great foresight. He knew this day would come and his beloved family would need to be taken care of, so he had laid out, in great detail, his last will and testament. One-half of Rose of Shannon Manor was to go to his only living relative and adopted daughter, Marcianne Prescott.

The remaining one-half was to go to George Henry Hutchison, with the knowledge that all of the Hutchison's, O'Leary's and remaining staff, would be allowed to remain on the estate as long as they lived, or wished to live there. The small farm that John had purchased some time ago down by the Ohio River, was willed to the Jean Leone Jewell's family.

The Attorney finished reading the will, closed his briefcase and reached to shake George Henry's hand, but George Henry was so full of grief at loosing his Poppi he had hardly heard the words that pertained to him. He had spoken little since the accident, keeping to himself, roaming the fields and nearby woods, grieving in silence. He jumped now as the attorney brought him out of his daze.

"Congratulations, George Henry." James Edward and Erin Rose seated on either side of George Henry pressed their hands to his shoulders and shook him slightly into the present.

"George Henry, did you hear what Mr. Green just said?"

"No, sir, I'm sorry. What did you say, father? What did you say Mr. Green?"

"George Henry, Mr. Bellefleur left you half of Rose of Shannon Manor. That would be about two hundred acres, and half of all of the other buildings, house, etc. A goodly sum I might add. I will have a complete listing of everything for you in a few weeks." Barrister Green closed his briefcase and prepared to leave. Each and everyone congratulated George Henry on his good fortune, but he could only mumble in return. His pent up tears began to flow down his cheeks, and he had to escape, so he fled the room.

Erin Rose, seeing her son's grief, followed him. She had been worried about his silence and inability to succumb to his grief. She knew now that he would need someone to talk to when he was ready. Poppi had been the focus of his entire life, since he had been old enough to follow John around, and Erin Rose knew not the words to comfort him.

Marcianne Harrison Prescott, Johns only living relative, was not amazed that her Uncle had given George Henry one-half of his estate, but her husband Robert, was a little taken aback. He said to Marcianne that they would just have to buy George Henry out. In addition, he felt that he would have to take John's place in running the farm and the horse stables. Marci was not at all sure that her Uncle would approve of such a thing. What, she asked would all the family do? Where would they go? He had said that they would have enough money to buy a little farm somewhere else, and that was not his worry, and that he would speak to George Henry about it.

"I can not do that, "George Henry said when Robert made him his offer "I just can't do it. It would be like selling my family out." Still riddled with guilt and grief over his Poppi's death, he could not even conceive Robert's offer and asked that he not speak to him again about selling. "We will all remain here and run the farm as we always have, we will give you half of the proceeds from the sales of the livestock and any grain sold. Maybe one day, in the future, I can buy your half and that would solve everything." Robert Prescott only grunted at this statement. In the end, Marcianne reminded her husband that it was one-half hers, that they did not need to worry about the proceeds from it, nor did she want it if it meant displacing her good friend Erin Rose and her family.

Fall arrived with Barrister Green coming to the Rose of Shannon once more. He had been trying to find this Jean Leone Jewell, but it seemed he was nowhere to be found. James Edward and George Henry said that they could find him if need be. The barrister reminded them that John Bellefleur had willed his place down by the river to Jewell and that he needed to come take title to it. In all the fuss and loss, neither man had been able to get the sad and wonderful news to the Jewell's. Now they agreed that it was their duty to go to the Jewell's home.

Barrister Green left and James Edward discussed as to whether they would be able to find the cabin in the Smoky Mountains by themselves. The forests were very dense this time of the year, but they agreed that they had to go now

CHAPTER TEN

CHEROKEE SORROW AND JOY

In 1830 Winfield Scott and Andrew Jackson, (Jacks Chula Harjo), meaning "Jackson old and fierce" by the Crees, and "The Devil" by the Choctaws, ordered the complete removal to the West of the remaining Cherokees. They were to be led by John Ross, a half-breed, of Scottish and Cherokee blood.

The removal came sudden, and family after family was driven off their rich producing farms. Scores and scores of Cherokees were driven by the military, from their wonderful homes without so much as a suitcase of clothing for them or their children. Some were able to escape by leaving their homes before the military came down on them. They ran to the mountains of North Carolina and hid in caves there. Jean Leone Jewell's wife was one of these people. She, her husband Ksali, their children, her husband's brothers, Little Bear and White Elk, made their escape after seeing the soldiers of the military forcing their neighbors out with bayonets. Ksali and White Elk had almost run into the military men under Winifred Scott. They knew these were treacherous men, who had informed the Cherokee Chiefs that they had to emigrate to the West, so they hid in a nearby pine forest. They watched as their neighbors were beaten into submission, tied up like cattle, and driven from their homes. Frightened beyond all comprehension, they then raced down the road to their home, gathered up Tiana and the children, some clothes and food and raced off toward the mountains for the shelter, knowing that if they were caught, they would be killed as fugitives. They took two horses for the children and supplies and rode as fast as they could toward safety. Once they reached the mountains, the men knew that the horses would have to be hidden away and they would have to continue on foot when they reached high range. Ksali knew that Winfield Scott knew where most of the Cherokees had gone to hide, for he had over-heard him speaking of it, saying that, "they could all be gotten later". Ksali knew that he had to find a different cave to hide his family or they would surely be found.

The time came all too soon for them all to dismount and continue on foot. Thankfully, as they dismounted the moon slipped out from under a dark cloud to show off its bright silvery light. The light was sorely needed and appreciated by the little group of Cherokees, as they clawed their way up the steep slopes of the mountains. Ragged now and barefooted, Nakomi and Little Bear tried to stay with their mother and the baby, Winona, who was strapped to their mother's back on a cradle board. Tiana urged her children on as she struggled to keep up with her husband. Finally, she could climb no longer, for she was exhausted, and the baby had started to whimper. Tiana knew she dared not to call out for her husband, or let the baby cry; for fear that a soldier was nearby. She knew too, that if they were found they would be returned to the removal or killed.

Ksali and White Elk were searching out the best possible place to climb up the steep mountainside when Ksali realized his family was not directly behind him. Fear gripped his very being but he knew he must go back for his family. Ksali whistled the call to communicate with his brother to let him know he had stopped below him. Both Ksali and White Elk were tall and powerful men, but they had known the trip would be very hard for the children and Tiana, so they had promised each other that whatever happened the remaining one would take the family to safety in the mountains.

Ksali found Tiana and his children as well as White Elk's son. He lifted his two little children to sit on his strong shoulders, spoke softly to his wife to rise and follow close behind him. As he lifted his children, he saw their bloody feet and tears of sorrow sprang to his eyes. Their clothing torn almost to shreds from the prickly bushes, tangled azaleas and dense rhododendron, sweet potato vines and sticky thistles they had to fight their way through. White Elk's son's arms and feet were also bleeding, but Ksali knew that they could not stop now so he urged them on up the steep mountainside.

Suddenly, out of nowhere, the outline of a soldier and his gun appeared a few feet from them. With his gun drawn, Ksali knew the soldier was on the hunt for the escapees. Ksali cautioned everyone not to move, or whisper. He then crept silently like a panther up behind the soldier, and plunged his knife deep into his back. The soldier fell without a sound. Still crouching, Ksali crept back to his wife and children, urging them to move on as fast as they could manage while there was some darkness to cover them. He said that they must find the cave on the other side of this peak that White Elk knew about, away from the other escapees. They would be safe there he told them, as he urged them on. Ksali continued to use all of his senses as a lookout for more soldiers for he knew there had to be more. He also knew when they found the dead soldier they would hunt more furiously to find them. The moon had begun to fade just as they found the little cave and White Elk. Tiana and the children were so exhausted that all they could do was to lie down on Mother Earth's bosom and sleep. Somehow, Little Bear was not with the rest of the party, and when he did not show up after what seemed an endless time, Ksali and White Elk became worried; maybe he had hurt himself and was unable to climb the steep slope. The men had thrown off their heavy packs and had tried to rest for a few moments, but the cave had gotten very cold, so they decided they would hunt for wood and start a little fire. Surely, Little Bear would be there when they returned, but he was not. There was nothing to do but try to find him before the soldiers did.

Ksali and White Elk took two different paths back down the mountain to find Little Bear. Ksali wondered how it had happened that Little Bear had not stayed with the others, and then he realized that he had been at the tail end of the procession when they saw the soldier. In his haste to get his family to safety, he had not noticed that Little Bear was not with them. Silently and cautiously, Ksali picked his way back down the steep slope and then suddenly he heard loud angry voices, and froze in his tracks. He placed his head close to the ground to see if he could hear more clearly, and soon knew that there were many men just below in a small clearing in the rock, and then he saw the many soldiers.

The crash of a whip and a scream came from the clearing and the soldiers. Ksali stole silently closer until he could see the horror of the scene before him. Five soldiers had captured Little Bear and bound him to a tree. One of the officers held a bull whip high in the air threatening to strike Little Bear again, as another soldier was kicking him hard in the side.

"Where is your father Ksali?" the officer demanded to know, while forcibly pulling Little Bear's hair and banging his head against the tree which he was tied to.

"I don't know, I only came to hunt." Little Bear cried, and the whip found his bare back again. Blood spurted from the new cut of the whip, but Little Bear continued to repeat he was only hunting.

"You are lying! No one was at your house when we got there. We found your two horses and you will die if you do not tell us what we want to know. Where are they?" The whip found its target again and Little Bear cried out in agony. Ksali flinched each time Little Bear was struck and he knew what he must do. He had to save his young nephew, but how could he save his family too?; Maybe he could make a deal with these white men. He knew he must try something before they killed Little Bear. Ksali said a prayer to his Creator, and then stepped out of the dense grove of trees into the clearing, surprising the soldiers and Little Bear.

"I am here, and what he says is true, only he and I are here to hunt. We rode the horses until it was too difficult for them to climb any further." Two soldiers grabbed Ksali but he flung them off, only to be struck by the butt of a rifle. He was stunned momentarily, but did not fall to the ground. He held up his hands in surrender and spoke.

"I'm a peaceful man. What do you want of me?" He spoke directly to the officer in charge and the officer saw that Ksali was not going to try to get away, so he stopped the men with the whip and the rifle.

"I have orders to bring you, your family and your brother in. You are in contempt of the orders of immigration to the West, given by General Jackson. Our orders came down by Winfield Scott. You are under arrest," The officer said sarcastically, and then ordered his men to tie Little Bear and Ksali together then forced them down the mountain at bayonet point, and threw them into jail.

Ksali was questioned over and again as to where his brother and family were, but Ksali held to the fact he did not know. He said that they were at home when he left, so they must have been captured by the military. He was beaten senseless time and again, and then shot along side his nephew. When Ksali saw that he could do nothing but keep silent to save his family he pleaded for his Creator to lead them to safety. Shot and bleeding, Little Bear and Ksali were left to a horrible bleeding death, but neither man gave up their family's whereabouts.

In the meantime, White Elk had returned to the cave where Tiana and the children were, expecting to find Ksali and Little Bear with them. When he returned empty handed and Ksali and Little Bear did not return, they both sensed something dreadful had happened. They both also knew they would have to leave this cave and look for another place to hide. If Ksali could, he would find them somehow. White Elk took a sharp rock and drew a picture of an eagle flying northeast with several baby eagles following close behind. This was a message for Ksali should he get back to the cave. Devastated but hoping against hope, the little group picked up as much of the packs as they could carry, doused the fire, and made their way toward another refuge. For six days they traveled as fast as they could, leaving much of the Smoky Mountains behind them. Exhausted, they finally decided they had gone far enough to be safe, at least for a while.

The following day White Elk set off to try to find them some fresh meat to eat when he stumbled on a small cabin perched high in a densely wooded area. No one was home, and on looking closer White Elk decided that no one was living in the cabin. It was a wonderful find and he could hardly wait to bring his little family to it. This is the cabin where Jean Leone Jewell would find them a few years later.

Hearing their story of escape and the disappearance of Little Bear and Ksali, Jean Leone soon became a frequent visitor at the little cabin. He had been terribly lonely, trapping animals for their fur, and spending most of his time in the deep forest of the Smokies. He now was overjoyed at the thought of some humans becoming his friends. The children came to adore him and never wanted him to leave. White Elk grew very fond of Jean Leone too, but he was restless and wanted to find out what had happened to his son and brother. One morning very early, he set off down the mountain, never to be seen again by anyone.

Tiana was now alone with her three children, and Jean Leone Jewell. Jean Leone was a handsome Frenchman who had thought that he would never marry, but marry he did. He saw that Tiana needed him as much as he needed her. They eventually were married in a tiny church at the foot of the Great Smoky Mountains. They would have two daughters and one son, Claudette, Alice Marie and Leon. It was this cabin that they had enlarged to take care of the addition to their family which John Bellefleur found, on one of many hunting trips.

John Henry Bellefleur found the little Jewell family to be delightful and could listen for hours on end to the many tales of the Cherokee Indians and their real story of the removal to the West. Tiana and her children were very shy around John Bellefleur, and John understood why. It seemed that she never really ever trusted a white man again. Her children soon came to love to have him visit, for he always lavished them with gifts that they could never have had if not for him. Several times John brought James Edward Hutchison with him to visit, and that is where they were headed with George Henry when he met his demise.

James Edward and George Henry cut their way through the dense foliage of the mountains searching for the hidden cabin of the Jewell's. They hated to have to tell them of John's death, but could hardly wait to tell them about the little farm John had left them. How would they react? They wondered. Would they be glad to have the farm or would they be afraid to leave this well hidden place?

Several hundred yards before they saw the cabin, they saw two pretty, young girls in the distance. They appeared to be gathering some kind of berry, and did not notice the men as they approached, almost silently. Suddenly, just as the men reached the briars where the girls had been picking the berries, they saw the girls quickly gather up their baskets and disappear into the green of the trees.

"Well now, what do you make of that? I thought they were going to let us see them. That must have been Jewell's daughters. It has been several years since I've been up here. Those girls look more like women."

"Yes, father, it seems that girls grow up faster than boys. I looked through my spy glass and what I saw was some very pretty women, if you know what I mean?" George Henry blushed at his own thought. He was at an age that women were of the most importance to him. The girls in and around Morganfield, however, had not sent his emotions into full speed ahead. Now, he thought, these girls looked different and he liked what he saw. He could hardly wait to get acquainted if these were the Jewell's daughters. He said as much to his father. James Edward cautioned him not to be too aggressive. Indian girls, he said, were different.

"You must remember these girls are Cherokees and extremely shy. Their father is French and zealous about his family's safety, so go slowly and be a gentleman."

"Yes, Papa I will not shame you in my behavior," George Henry laughed as he spoke, and the merriment in his eyes spoke a thousand words.

The two men followed the little path the girls had taken and they soon came to a clearing and a high board fence, built much like a stockade. Inside there was a cabin and several other buildings, chickens, two goats and a pigpen. A black haired man and woman were seated at a corn grinder while the two girls they had seen earlier were excitedly talking at the same time to the man and woman.

"Hark! Who goes there?" Jean Leone Jewell had heard their approach even above the girls chattering.

"Tis I, James Edward Hutchison and me son, George. We come seeking Jean Leone Jewell to deliver a message from John Henry Bellefleur." James Edward held his breath, for a moment, as he spied a gun toting Jean Leone Jewell. The gate opened and Jean Leone stood motionless for a moment, then he grasped James Edward in a big bear hug. He acknowledged George Henry's presence and then asked of John Bellefleur.

"You say you have a message from my friend John. He is not with you, I see. Is he ill?" James Edward winced for he knew the news be brought would be hard for this man to handle.

"Mr. Jewell, your friend John, was on his way to visit you during the hard rains, when he met with an accident. He has passed on to meet his maker. I am so sorry to have to deliver this terrible news to you. I know that you loved John very much as we all did, but he is in a better place by far. We do have some wonderful news to tell you though. I think this news will help to make you feel much, much better, Jean Leone." Jean Leone's face filled with astonishment and great sorrow at this news he had just received. His voice trembled with sadness as he answered James Edward.

"I don't think anything can overcome this sad news my friend." Jean Leone burst into a soft sobbing, as the tears began to glisten on his ruddy cheeks.

"I am so sorry for this heartache, but I think our other news will help. Mr. Bellefleur did not forget you, and I'm sure you will never forget him. He had a will and this is what he gave to you. The barrister asked me to get these papers to you, so you can take title to the property John left you. Here, look at this."

"Property? What are you talking about?" Jean Leone now looked completely puzzled, as James Edward handed him the legal papers.

"Jean Leone, John Bellefleur left you and your family a small farm located along the Ohio River. It is located between Morganfield and Smith Mills, Kentucky. The property is mostly woods, but has very good land. It is near one of the best farms in that part of Kentucky, called the Star Farm and Schoolhouse. The people who own that farm are Indians, just like you, ma'am." Tiana looked at James Edward, and then at her husband, in amazement. Jean Leone saw that Tiana was very confused.

"You say Indians own a big farm near this one that you say John left us?" Jean Leone could hardly believe what James Edward had just said.

"Yes, that is true. You will like this place I'm sure. You won't have to hide in these woods anymore… you can move there. My son and I will help you, won't we George Henry?" James Edward had hit on this idea that they could convince this little family to move while they were there to help them. George Henry nodded his assent as he stood just inside the little sitting room. He had not been able to take his eyes off the youngest daughter, and she returned his stare periodically. Her sister was trying to hear all the adults' conversation, but she also was watching what was happening between her sister and this new young man called George.

The young girl who had struck such a fancy with George Henry was Alice Marie Jewell. She was a stunning young woman with her black hair and sparkling dark eyes. Her figure was just beginning to blossom, and the peasant dress partially exposed her small round breasts. The dress was gathered in at the waist by a beautiful hand crocheted scarf where it accented her slender body and tiny waist. She became aware that George was staring at her breasts, and coyly pulled the scarf up around her shoulders, partially blocking the low cut of the neckline. As she did so, she looked way and blushed, but did not run away. She was as fascinated with George Henry as he was with her. He knew in his heart immediately, that this girl was the one he wanted. She was like no other girl he had ever seen. But, what would her father say to his being interested in her? He was suddenly brought back to reality when he heard Jean Leone call to his daughters to come to the table where he was seated.

"Come here, Papa has something for you to hear. Sit here beside me." Jean Leone patted the bench he was sitting on. The girls hurried to their fathers call, but as Alice Marie passed by George Henry, she looked into his eyes and gave him a big smile, showing off her straight even teeth. More important, the smile lit up her eyes, which now looked like stars to George Henry. He had a sudden impulse to grab her and kiss her soundly, but of course, he couldn't.

"Girls, did you hear what James Edward just told me? Look at these papers, they are a deed to a farm near Morganfield, Kentucky. It now belongs to us. We can move out of these mountains, and your mother will not have to hide anymore. We will be legal citizens up there. John always wanted us to move up to his country. Oh, my, my! Bring out the wine, and some glasses, Tiana, we are going to celebrate. Thank you, thank you my friend!" Jean Leone was now dancing all around, hugging his wife and daughters, and shaking his visitors' hand over and over. He was indeed a happy man. His daughters were astonished at their fathers' reactions, for they had never seen him in such a festive mood. He was blowing kisses toward the heavens and uttering words none of them could understand. James Edward and George Henry just had to laugh at him as he pulled Tiana to her feet and whirled her around and around. John Bellefleur had certainly had given this man an enormous gift that he would never forget. As Jean Leone finally started calming down, James Edward thought he needed to put a plan together so that they could help these people move to their new home.

"Jean Leone, if you and your wife would like, George Henry and I will escort you to this property. A nice little house there has some furniture in it, so the ladies will have a place to stay. Or, if you like, you can bunk with us for a few days and then go to the property." James Edward thought he knew what Jean Leone's answer would be, he would do as his benefactor had wished it to be.

"Yes, yes, we will go with you. Tiana, girls, get your things packed. We will pack up everything in wagons and move to Kentucky. We will never have to hide anymore. We are free! We can live and mix with other folks. Hurry now, we will leave tomorrow morning, for I expect we will have a long way to go."

"What on earth will we do with the pigs and chickens, and our goats; we can't leave them behind to starve." Tiana was pleading now with her husband for she did not understand what everything meant just yet.

"Don't fret, Mama, we will take care of all of them. You and the girls get the household goods together. Hurry now, make haste and make food to take along with us. Make food for all of us tonight. Praise the Lord! Ha, ha, ha, my dream is coming true. John I love you, you old scoundrel." Tiana placed her hand on her mouth to stifle a shocked gasp and looked at Jean Leone in distain.

"Jean Leone, you must not speak so of the dead. You must be more respectful," she admonished. Jean Leone's answer was to swoop her off her feet and plant kisses all over her face, while she struggled to get away, totally embarrassed.

The three men and Jean Leone's son repaired two wagons, built a few crates and some chicken coupes to transport the livestock. Tiana, Alice Maric and Claudette killed five chickens, fried them down and put them in a basket with other meats and vegetables for them to eat on the way. Finally, they were ready to leave.

It was a very strange little parade they made as they wound their way through the heavy forest and then over the hills and streams toward a new land and a new home. James Edward and Jean Leone had found an old canvas and had stretched it over the wagon for the women's protection, just in case of rain. Behind this wagon, a milk cow was tied to follow, and behind the other wagon were the chickens and pigs. The two goats were tied together behind that wagon and bellowed most of the way, despite Jean Leone's threat that they would be turned into roasted meat if they did not shut up. George Henry gave Jean Leone his horse so that he could ride on the wagon with Alice Marie and Claudette. Young Philippe Jewell took turns riding in the first wagon and then the other. James Edward took the lead of the procession and sometimes Jean Leone would ride with him. Tiana drove the other wagon most of the time with Jean Leone and Philippe. The trip took five days and nights. Finally, they arrived at the little farm along the Ohio River just as the sun was setting over the water. It was a grand sight to see the joy on all of the Jewell's faces as they entered the little house and claimed it as their home.

The trip had served another big purpose, George Henry knew by the time they reached Kentucky, that he would ask Alice Marie to be his bride.

A SWEET, SWEET MERGER

George Henry Hutchison ushered Alice Marie Jewell, carefully into the grand hall of the Rose of Shannon Manor. He felt a flush of pride a he looked fondly on his intended bride. She was a real beauty, but very shy. She now was nervously holding his arm in awe of her surroundings. She was a little frightened at the impending meeting of George's family. Would they like her, she wondered, and would they treat her as if she was not their equal as many of the people did in that area. She knew that a lot of people here in Kentucky were just like the ones they had left behind in North Carolina and Tennessee. They did not like Indians.

On seeing the frightened look on Alice's face, George Henry hastened to comfort her. "Don't be afraid, Alice Marie, my mother and sister will just love you. How could they help themselves? You know how lovable I think you are." George teased.

"Of course you would say that, but just how many people live in this huge house, George?"

"Let's see. There is my mother and father, Erin Rose, and James Edward, my brother, Sean Michael, his wife, Margaret. We call her Maggie, and their small children, my sister Louise, who is betrothed and my great Aunt Fiona. Now don't you start worrying, my father has been singing your praises ever since we met you that first time, you know at the cabin in the mountains?" George Henry now squeezed Alice's hand to reassure her, as he helped her take off her wrap. Then he removed his coat and hat and hung all the garments on the mirrored hall tree.

Taking a deep breath he knocked softly on the double doors that led to the formal parlor where he knew his family was waiting for them to arrive.

Erin Rose was quick to her feet for she had long anticipated this meeting. At first glance she could now see why her husband and son had voiced such wonderful accolades for this girl. She was indeed beautiful and one could readily see she was somewhat shy. Erin rose liked her demeanor for she hated a forward woman.

"Come in, my dear," Erin Rose extended her hand to Alice, "welcome to our home. It is our honor to have you. Come; sit beside me on the sofa." George Henry smiled at his mother's unabashed forwardness.

"Just a minute, Mama, let Alice meet everyone first. This is of course my father whom you have met, my brother Sean Michael, and my sister Louise Marie." Each person acknowledged their introduction, and smiled graciously as they did so.

"Where is Margaret and Aunt Fiona?" George Henry asked as he looked around the room.

"In the kitchen making sure everything is just right for our dinner!" Erin Rose quipped. "Your Aunt Fiona has been all a tither all day waiting for you to arrive." Erin Rose laughed, putting everyone at ease.

Alice Marie sat down on the sofa beside Erin Rose, smiled at her, then searched George Henry's face for an answer.

"Your Aunt Fiona lives here, too?

"Yes she does, Alice Marie, my Uncle Patrick passed on a few years back, God rest his soul. They are the people who brought my family from Ireland before I was born. Aunt Fiona is like my grandmother.

"I see. Your family is much like mine. It stays together."

"Yes, young lady that tis a fact. Now my dear, I must compliment you on your beautiful dress. Did you sew it yourself?" Erin Rose always quick to notice good workmanship, and could not help but notice Alice's exquisite dress of emerald green taffeta, fashioned in the day's tightly hugging lines from the bosom to the waist, then flowing into a voluminous skirt. Alice's shiny black hair and sparkling dark brown eyes seemed to be trying to out shine the color of her gown. The tiny rows of handmade lace at the sweetheart neckline softened her ample breast that lay just below the ruffles.

"Yes, m'am, I sew all my clothes. My mother taught me and my sister when we were very young." Alice Marie, now sitting with her hands in her lap, shyly smoothed her gown making sure there were no wrinkles in it.

James Edward had been sitting patiently by as the women chatted but decided it was his turn to make Alice welcome.

"It is very good to see you again, Alice Marie. Are your parents well?"

"Thank you sir, my parents are well, and they send you their best wishes, and invite you to take time with them, and you too, Louise, and Sean Michael. They hope we can all be in the best way with each other." Alice blushed a slight pink now feeling shyer than ever before, but managed to say the invitation in a soft but sincere voice.

"Enough of this talk-Alice Marie, if you are to be my sister then lets leave these folks and go check out our dinner. I'm starving, aren't you?" Louise had jumped to her feet and now pulled Alice off the sofa, laughing as she did so.

"Good idea, Louise. Why don't you show Alice around the house?" George Henry was pleased that his sister had broken the stinted questioning.

As the double doors closed behind the two girls, Erin Rose couldn't but exclaim her feelings.

"George Henry, Alice is perhaps the prettiest girl I have ever seen except perhaps, Louise Marie."

"Tis a fact, mother. I told you how pretty she was and how smart too!" James Edward teased.

"Yes you did, but how can a woman trust her husband's judgment of a young girl!" Erin Rose's eyes now flashed with merriment.

"I like her brother. She has a nice way about her. It must be the Indian blood." Sean Michael voiced his opinion, and wondered about the Indian side of his future sister-in-law.

"Yes, Sean. Her Indian ways are a great part of her personality, but please remember that her folks are still a bit cautious about this fact." George cautioned.

"We will honor this son, for I know her family has been through much; having to hide ancestry just to be able to live. Won't we mother?"

"Yes of course! Now say no more, I think she is just right for you George Henry, and we will all do everything to make her feel at home with us. Come all of you, dinner must be ready by now." Erin Rose, took her son's hand, and led him off toward the kitchen of the great manor.

Alice Marie Jewell Hutchison, was a very shy girl, and now she was even more withdrawn here in the Rose of Shannon Manor, for its size was overwhelming to her. This jolly family of her new husband did everything to make her feel as one of them, but her early seclusion in the mountains had made its impact on her and not easily overcome.

The first year of their marriage, Alice would spend many a day between her family and the Hutchison's. On one of these visits, she would meet Greyfox White Feather. This opened a whole new world for Alice, for she found that he was an Indian just like her. Greyfox invited them to visit his farm and meet his Indian wife and family. George Henry also found Greyfox a really likable fellow, and was very pleased that Alice had found a new friend, and especially an Indian family just like her. The two families would visit often and the women on the Star Farm would nurture Alice through her pregnancies.

The first year brought George and Alice their first child, James, named after his grandfather. Then Sophia and Ella arrived. Eighteen months later came Edward, then Nora, and a few years later George Henry the second, would make his entrance. Last but certainly not least came red-haired, vivacious little Audibelle.

The many rooms at the Rose of Shannon were filled with laughter and happiness as the children grew into teens and adults.

The acreage was much and the tobacco fields were plenty. Buildings had to be added to dry the tobacco, and fields of lespedeza, and corn, had to be tilled, and harvested. George Henry and all the folks on Rose of Shannon worked the fields and tended to the many cows, chickens, hogs, and a couple of goats. The most important thing grown on the farm next to the tobacco was the splendid horses that were raised and groomed for racing. James and George Henry would remain the overseers of these horses, for their breeding and training.

Most farmers in that part of Kentucky grew tobacco and a few other crops, but times were proving harder and harder for them to continue to sell their tobacco as they once had. Large tobacco wars and angry mobs began torching barns across the country, burning everything in sight. Ravished farmers would wake up in the middle of the night to see their out buildings, and fields blazing out of control.

The night riders burned warehouses and fields of tobacco of everyone they thought were selling to the monopolies. In the summer of 1909, Rose of Shannon would suffer its first fire.

Silently and ruthlessly the hooded riders swooped down on the Rose of Shannon and set fire to one of the warehouses, burning it completely down. They left a warning sign that informed the inhabitants that this was only a taste of what would come. It read; STOP SELLING TO THE MONOPOLIES, OR ELSE.

George Henry, Sean Michael, and some of their help had run the night riders off before they could torch the fields. Guns in hand they had fired at the riders scaring them away for now, but their loss of drying tobaccos was extensive. For months George Henry and others stood guard to make sure this didn't happen again.

A year passed with no more incidents, so the men on the farm relaxed their vigil. Tobacco prices had become so low that growers were becoming more and more desperate. George Henry and Sean Michael, however, were not one of them. Their tobacco crops had been very productive. They had been able to rebuild their drying barns and warehouses but had no alternative but to sell to their only bidders, the monopoly. Their barns were full and the new crop was ready to harvest, so both brothers felt they could relax for another few weeks. George Henry and Alice Marie decided to take their children to visit their grandparents in Smith Mills. Perhaps too they would be able to visit the Star Farm and its many inhabitants.

Sean Michael and Maggie said they would stay up at the big house and tend to all the chores while they were gone. George Henry II was 17, Audibelle 15, and Edward was almost 20 years of age, and the only children left at home. The older boys and girls had married and left with their spouses. Edward and George Henry II decided to visit their brother James who lived with his wife Mamie, near Mt. Vernon, Indiana. These three Hutchison boys were gifted musically, and would get together as often as they could to make music together. They had decided long ago that they would form a band as soon as George Henry was old enough.

Sean Michael and Maggie were enjoying themselves by the fireplace of the manor, but were suddenly jolted to fear by the crashing sound of a brick being thrown through the front glass window, nearly striking Maggie in the head. They both screamed. Shaken by the sudden intrusion, Sean Michael jumped from his chair and grabbed Maggie in his arms trying to protect her from any more harm. It was then that they both saw the note that was wrapped around the brick. It read: THIS IS YOUR LAST WARNING, TRAITORS MUST PAY.

Needless to say Sean Michael and Maggie were dumbfounded, as well as thoroughly frightened. As they talked over the situation they decided that they had to let George and Alice know what had happened, and agreed to send their son Patrick to fetch them home the next morning. Sean and Maggie mounted the stairs that night weary and frightened as to what might happen next.

Sleep evaded them for most of the night, but finally they both fell into a restless sleep. Alice Marie was also very restless and could not sleep. George Henry awoke to find his wife holding her head and walking up and down the room.

"What's wrong? What are you doing up in the middle of the night?" he questioned. Alice answered as a cold chill raced up her spine. "

"I cannot sleep. I feel cold, shivery."

George Henry felt his wife's brow and found her very warm.

"Alice you are very warm, are you not feeling well?"

"No, my husband, I'm not ill but something is very wrong, terribly wrong, I feel it here, in my heart. We must go home right away, now George! We must go home now! Something is wrong at our home." George Henry looked at his wife for a few moments before he spoke again. He had learned that Alice was able to sense many things he did not understand, but honored her feeling for they were always right.

"Alright, my dear, we will leave first thing, but come back to bed now."

"No, George, you must get up now! We must leave right away, something awful is about to happen. I'll get the children up, and tell Mama and Papa. They will understand." Alice was already dressed and was now leaving the room. "Hurry up," she called, "We must make haste."

Sleepy eyed Audibelle climbed into the buggy beside her mother and father, and off they went toward Morganfield, and home. They drove most of the night, stopping only occasionally. The moon was full and the horses had no difficulty in seeing the silvery path ahead of them. As they finally turned off the main road they saw a huge orange glow in the sky. Driving closer their worst fear was realized. The orange glow was directly over their farm. Driving closer they could see that the tobacco fields were all ablaze, and then as they whipped the horses to a faster pace and came nearer, they could see flames licking out of the windows of Rose of Shannon Manor. They then realized all of the barns were also ablaze. Horror struck their very beings. George Henry finally screamed as he whipped the horses into a fury.

"God, oh God, what ever can we do? Help us oh lord for we are now helpless in this raging inferno." Sensing their imminent danger the horses reared up nearly turning the carriage over.

George Henry and Alice jumped from the carriage as soon as it came to a stop, and joined the line of workers trying to put out the fires in the manor house. Others were at the barns trying to get the frightened animals out of their stalls. Children were screaming, cows were mooing, men were cussing, and the women were crying and moaning. Children were sitting on the lawn in their night clothes crying, scared out of their wits. Neighbors from all over had come to help and the many workers were almost overcome by the smell of burning flesh. Many of the horses would not come out of the barn and were burned alive.

Many hours later most of the fires at the Manor house had been put out leaving it in total ruin. Rose of Shannon was dead. Fiona had been overcome by so much smoke before she was rescued; she passed on as the melee passed before her aged eyes.

Erin Rose and James Edward exhausted and shocked beyond words could only look at the ruins of their beloved home, and weep. A lifetime of love and labor had now gone with the wind.

George Henry and Sean Michael watched in utter horror as the few horses were rescued from the burning barn. Thunder and lightening began as if the Gods were angry, and just as sudden the rain came down in torrents, putting out the remaining fires in the fields and other buildings.

Alice Marie and Maggie found George and Sean sitting on some bales of hay with their heads in their hands, sobbing over the great loss that was theirs. Alice placed her hands on their shoulders to comfort them, but Maggie could only join in their tears.

Hush, hush, wipe away your tears, not all is lost. The Creator sent the rain and saved some of our crops and livestock. We must thank Him for that. All of our children are safe and we can be thankful for that. Come back to the house with us, we must comfort your mother and father. Their loss is greater than ours. They need us all now for they are in their declining years, but have the knowledge we will need. Come George, Sean, Maggie, come, we must keep our family together." Alice's voice was calm even though she felt the pain they all felt. George Henry looked at his beautiful wife and took strength from her. He wiped the tears from his eyes and helped his brother to his feet.

"Alice is right Sean, we have our families all safe and Mama and Papa need us. Come; let's go find them and the children."

The smell of charred wood was thick in all their nostrils as they set about cleaning the old house. Each one had his or her own thoughts as to what they would all have to do to make the old house come alive once more. The windows were gone, and the fire had destroyed much of the interior wood. The furnishings for the most part had escaped the fury of the fire, and now looked mighty inviting to the weary families as they gathered together, thankful for what was left; God had saved their home.

Edward and George Henry II returned home a few days after the fire and could not believe their eyes as they saw the charred ruins of the fields and buildings. George Henry (my father) told me that he and my Uncle Ed were paralyzed with fear for their parents and grandparents. They slid off their horses and ran into the house to find their loved ones. Alice Marie had seen her sons riding fast toward the house and ran to meet them, yelling to them in her relief that they were alright.

"Boys, boys you have come home early, saints be praised," she exclaimed with joy in her voice. Both boys thrilled to see that their mother was just fine, grabbed her and planted kisses all over her face.

"Papa, is he alright, and Grandma and Grandpa? Is everyone okay?"

"Yes, we are fine," Alice answered weakly.

"What on earth happened here? Did everyone get out safely? Uncle Sean and Aunt Maggie, where are they? Oh my

God why did this have to happen?" Breathlessly, the boys ended there questioning. They had been gone a week only to return to devastation.

"We are all just fine, Uncle Sean did suffer some burns but he is just fine, all except Aunt Fiona. She got too much smoke in her lungs and passed from this earth. Grandma and Grandpa were able to get her out but they too suffered from the smoke. We laid Fiona to rest in the little fenced in area over there" Alice hesitated for a moment, then finished answering their question.

"How did the fires get started?" Edward asked.

"It had to be the night riders that did this; no one knows who they are. A brick was thrown through the window with a warning, but the fires were set soon after everyone went to bed. I'm so sorry to have to tell you but we lost many of the horses. The heat was just too much to save them all, and they were too scared to come out of the barn themselves. That is how Sean got burned. He was trying to get them all out of the barn." Alice's face was now covered in tears as she continued.

"Sean and Maggie grabbed their children out of their beds and helped to put out the fires in the house. We came home to see everything on fire. I had an omen that something terrible was going to happen, so we rushed home. Your father is working down by the old warehouse. He will be glad you came home early, and so am I."

Both boys stood glued to the ground while listening to their mother's account of the blazing inferno they encountered when they arrived home. They felt utterly helpless. They gave their mother a hug, then took off to find their father and uncle. They had to make sure they were okay.

Sean Michael had not been as lucky as his wife Maggie and the children. He had suffered many, many burns on his arms and face His hair had been singed badly and looked much like a burnt pile of wire. His nose was blistered and his eyebrows were gone. He was hardly recognizable. Both men, however, were thrilled to see the two boys as their help was sorely needed.

Neighboring farms began to place watchdogs and guards around their properties in a desperate attempt to ward off any disasters such as the Rose of Shannon had seen. Local law enforcement added deputies trying to find the arsonists, to no avail. However, this would be the last big fire set in that part of Kentucky, to the tobacco farmers.

The Rose of Shannon Manor would never be completely restored and six years later it would take another victim. At the onset of the great influenza epidemic, Alice Marie, would fall ill and die. George Henry II would be twenty three years of age and his father's only helper on the farm, except for Sean Michael. Brother Ed had married Emmy Morlock and moved to southern Indiana. Signs of the great depression were forming all over Kentucky. More and more farms were abandoned and many of the nearby mines were now closed. People were moving into the cities looking for work and soon remove these few jobs to be had there.

The death of Alice Marie had nearly undone George Henry, but his co-owner of the farm, Marcianne Bellefleur Prescott came to his aide. Now in her early sixties, she arrived in one of the new touring cars. She had heard of the fire disaster but did not respond because of her very sick and frail husband. Alice Marie's passing could not be ignored.

George Henry and Sean Michael were very glad to see Marcianne for they had been giving a lot of thought to the problems they were having trying to eke out a living for all of the inhabitants. Maybe she can give us some help, they contemplated.

"What a wonderful surprise to see you here, Marcianne, it has been far too long since we had a visit from you. How is Robert? Is he doing better these days?" George Henry asked.

"Not too well, I'm afraid. I think he has given up hope of ever getting any better." Marcianne hesitated for a few moments before continuing.

"What about yourself, George Henry? I know the trauma that you have been through. What do you plan to do now that Alice is gone?"

"I don't rightly know. I feel lost without Alice. She was what kept me going here in all the turmoil. I just don't know how we will be able to carry on in light of these hard times." George Henry answered in despair.

"Well, maybe I have an answer for you. You have been a wonderful partner, and I have been repaid many times over, so I give you this offer. I will buy your one-half ownership at a fair price. That is if you will stay on and rebuild the barns. The old house though must be completely torn down. It is far too dangerous to be occupied any longer. The timbers were damaged badly in the big fire. With this done, I believe I can sell the whole farm to a man I know, who raises horses. What do you think about that? Marcianne felt saddened that the old place had to go, but she knew it was not a safe place to live. George Henry thought for a long time before answering.

"Thank you Marcianne, for this consideration, for I'm sure you know it's like parting with one of my family, to sell my part of Rose of Shannon. Sure Poppi Bellefleur, long gone now, would understand what we must do. I will take your offer for I can hardly bare to be here without my darling, Alice Marie. Young George and Audibelle are fine young people, and a great comfort, but they are anxious to be on their own, someday. What about, Sean Michael? Where will he go with his family?" Marcianne frowned thoughtfully before she answered.

"That is a question. For the time being say nothing about me selling out to anyone. Sean and his family can continue to live here as always. When I'm able to sell, maybe he can stay on with the new owners. I'll try to make that part of any deal I make. I'm sure any new owner will be glad to have someone who is familiar with the running of the farm." Marcianne sighed deeply before she continued. "Now that we have settled on the sale, let's find everyone and have a celebration. Alice Marie would like that. We must get our spirits lifted, and what better way than to toast her life here on the Rose. Come, my friend, let's find all of the others." Maricanne rose and took George Henry's arm, entwined it in hers, and led him out of the old library with its smoked covered walls. They found Sean, Maggie, George II and Audibelle in the great dining room. This was the only room in the house that had not been touched by the fire.

Parting from the Rose of Shannon was almost more than any of the Hutchison's could do; but part they must. Amidst the packing and turmoil of moving, many tears were shed by both the Sean Michaels, and the George Henry's families, and their goodbyes were only temporary, for they knew they would be frequent visitors in each others homes.

George Henry, with the help of his children, George II and Audibelle, found a small farm between Morganfield and Uniontown. It was no match for the Rose of Shannon but had fertile land, a nice frame house, and many outbuildings. The barn was huge and contained six very nice horse stalls. The house had two stories, four rooms downstairs, and four bedrooms upstairs, and the floors were all parquet hardwood which thrilled Audibelle. She said that it gave the house a little of the opulence of the Rose of Shannon. The Hutchison's were happy just to have their own home again with their father, even though they all missed their mother, Alice Marie, terribly.

George II set about fixing any and everything that had a loose board, or needed a nail or screw. Audibelle cleaned and sewed and worked wonders with the little bit of furniture they had been able to salvage, while their father scoured the countryside for livestock.

Edward and James visited often with their families, and always ended their visit with the three boys making music for everyone. They began to seriously think about putting a band together. All three of the boys played several instruments, with George II playing the most. His favorite, however, was the violin. Not long after their first engagement in Kentucky, they began receiving requests for weekly engagements all over Kentucky and Indiana. Audibelle had a lovely voice and a gift for dancing, so she joined her brothers at most of their engagements for a little extra entertainment. Years later George Jr. would meet the one and only woman he would ever love at one of these engagements.

The following years for the inhabitants of the Rose of Shannon were hard ones. With very little of the tobacco left in the fields, and in the warehouses, the Hutchinson's barely eked out a living. Erin Rose and James Edward never fully recovered from the disaster passed on in the same year within days of each other.

CHAPTER ELEVEN

TEMPTATION AND BETRAYAL

A few months had passed after Clarence's betrothal party before the mail carrier delivered a formal blue envelope, addressed to Ben and Alice Dean Dickerson. Curious as always, Etta Mae and Rosie, could hardly wait for Papa to get home, so Mama would open it. She and Rosie were both very excited about the letter's contents, for Rosie had been seeing one of the Farmer boys, and Ethel had been seeing the other. Rosie had told Etta Mae that Sam was going to ask Papa if he could marry her, but she somehow knew the letter wasn't from the Farmers. They would never send a letter in the mail for that would be something too formal for them.

Finally Ben returned home from Henderson, with his wagon loaded down with all sorts of things. Greyfox White Feather had gone with him, and now stood watching as Etta Mae, and Rosie came flying out of the house to greet them. He wondered what on earth had his two nieces in such a tizzy. He had to laugh for he thought Ben was in for it. He loved these girls like his very own and had helped to raise them both, in traditional Blackfoot style.

He watched now as they bodily dragged Ben toward the house with Ben struggling to free himself of their grasps.

"What in tarnation has gotten into you girls? Is something wrong with your mother, or you Boss?" Ben loved his daughters and humored them in most things, but he just didn't understand what all the fuss could be about, for they both were talking at once.

"I, God, girls, calm down. What is it you say?"

"Papa, Papa, a very important looking letter came while you were gone, and Mama wouldn't open it 'til you got home. Hurry! It's got to be real important. Just wait 'til you see the blue envelope it came in!" Rosie and Etta Mae tried to explain at the same time.

"Well just let go of me, I can walk myself. I can't see how a letter could be so all tarnation important."

Dovie was waiting at the door just as curious and excited as the two girls. She just couldn't imagine what it could be about. She handed the blue envelope to Ben and he raised his eyebrows as he looked it over, turning it over and over. The letter was addressed to Mr. & Mrs. Benjamin Dickerson, in a fancy handwriting.

"Open it Papa, please open it." Etta Mae beseeched her father. Ben slowly took a little letter opener from the ebony table, and carefully ripped open the envelope, and withdrew a sheet of blue paper that matched the envelope. The sheet of blue paper was encased in a fine white tissue, and made the message seem even more impressive to the girls. Ben looked at the message a few moments, and then began to read aloud.

"Dear Mr. and Mrs. Dickerson,

This is my formal request to visit your home on September 5th, year of 1912, so that my son and I can get better acquainted with you, and your daughters. We will arrive at approximately 3:00 p.m. should this be an inconvenient time, please advise as to when we could pay you, and your family a visit. Please answer immediately. Thanking you again for the enjoyable time at your son's engagement celebration.

We await your answer with anticipation, and with our best regards,

Lena and William Meinschein
St. Phillips, Indiana

"Well, my fine young nieces, just what have you been up to, to get such a proposal?" Greyfox had entered right behind the girls and Ben, for curiosity was one of his few vices, and he knew one of these days soon, he would be culling out would-be-suitors for his little Josie and Nakomi.

No one said anything but they all stared at the blue stationary, and the writing on it, in amazement. Dovie spoke first with a bit of satisfaction.

"Well at least they have some class after all, but a formal request to visit is a total surprise, isn't it Ben?" Ben nodded his head, and shuffled his feet around before he spoke.

Yes, it sure does not seem like something that brash woman could, or would write. I'm more than dumbfounded, but I guess I will have to answer it, or you will Dovie, your writing is much better than mine." Dovie frowned at Ben for a moment.

"You are right, it does not seem like that woman could write in such a penmanship. Greyfox you should have heard this horse of a woman, asking for her son to start courting Etta Mae. She was loud and downright rude." Greyfox answered with a chuckle.

"Well, Papa, Mama, are you going to answer? Are you going to let William come and see me?" Etta Mae asked impatiently.

"Yes, of course Etta Mae, we will answer the letter, I just don't know what to say, I really did not like that woman. There is something very different about her." Dovie did not quite know what it really was that upset her except her brashness and boldness, but she knew Ben felt the same way.

"When did all this happen?" Greyfox asked curiously.

"At the announcement of Clarence's betrothal in October" Dovie answered her brother, still in disbelief.

"But Mama, Papa, I really like William. I don't care about his mother." Etta Mae pouted.

"Now Etta Mae, don't be hasty. What about George? I thought you were quite taken with him, and we do know who he is. He's a real gentleman, not loud and boisterous." Ben scanned his daughter's face and did not like the flightiness he now detected in his beloved Etta Mae.

"Oh, shush! Papa, George is too slow to make his intentions known to you. Maybe this will give him something to think about." The words passed Etta Mae's mouth so quickly she didn't even realize what she was saying.

"Etta Mae! This is not a game to play with a man's feelings. I won't have you teasing these men, just to make them jealous of one another. It's not proper" Ben was angered at his daughter's words but decided after a minute or two, that maybe that would bring George to speak of his intentions. He liked that red headed Irishman, since he had gotten to know him better, and had felt he would make a good and decent husband. He and Alice Dean (Dovie), had decided that should he ask for Etta Mae's hand in marriage, they would grant him his wish. They had decided to grant him his wish for George was all she had talked about for months. How much fun they had, going skating, and dancing, and best of all he was not a drinker and he never mentioned anything about her being an Indian, or his being Catholic.

"If your Mother agrees, we will invite them to come on the 5th. What do you say Alice Dean?" Etta Mae waited impatiently for Papa never, hardly ever, called her mother Alice Dean, unless it was something really serious.

"Perhaps we should honor their request since they sent such a formal request-William must be a serious young man"

"Oh, thank you Mama, Papa! Rosie, I want you to be present with me all the time, they did request daughters." Etta Mae was elated and secretly she thought, "I'll show George he isn't my only suitor."

George would call on Etta Mae, three times in the next month but Etta Mae did not tell him about William Meinschein's impending visit with his mother. Each time George came she hoped it would be to ask her parents for her hand in marriage, but he had not spoken to her parents, so she decided not to bring up William either. George told Etta Mae he was going to southern Indiana to see his brother Ed, and his family. He did not tell her about his intentions while there. The fact was he was going to finalize his purchase of a few more acres of land, and to start the building of a small house for them to live in, once they were married. When he had this done he was going to buy her a ring and get her parents permission for their marriage. He would have something to offer her parents for their permission, as was their tradition, the exchange of gifts.

George Henry Hutchinson II was a jovial man, who loved fun, and the best of all music, but he was a man of few words, except in song. This fact about himself, would be regretted the rest of his life. Etta Mae was the love of his life, and realizing she was so much younger than himself, he gave her the freedom to enjoy herself as she wished, never realizing what too much freedom for Etta Mae might mean to her; his lack of real affection, and his delay in asking for her hand in marriage was like an insult to her already wounded pride.

The morning of September 5th, the Star Farm was busy getting everything ready for the expected Meinscheins. Every person and horse had been groomed and re-groomed. The house dusted, and re-dusted; the best dishes were laid out in the dining room, and pots of delicious food were ready for the dinner. Etta Mae and Rosabelle had tied ribbons in their shiny black hair, to match their new dresses. Etta Mae was not a bit nervous, but her Papa and Mama were. They were the ones who had the encounter with Lena Meinschein, and were not sure if they really wanted her son to court their daughter. They would have to wait and see.

The Meinscheins arrived at precisely 3:00 P.M. Just as they had said they would, in a fine carriage they had hired at the Smithie's in Henderson. Lena Meinschein had spent the past six weeks getting William educated by the best teachers in Evansville, Indiana, in speech and social graces. Lena and William had spent the entire morning buying chocolates, perfume and delicately embroidered handkerchiefs. They had even found some beautiful tortoise shell combs for the ladies of the Dickerson house. They had bought special tobacco, hand rolled cigars and special blended bourbon for the men. Lena had said to William that she wanted to show those "Indians" the Meinscheins had class too. Lena had even bought special clothing for herself, and William, and had her hair dressed in a salon, something she had not done in twenty-five years. She knew she was no beauty, but with the new clothes and hair dressing, she felt she was at least a bit handsome.

William was an innocent, and had no idea as to what his mother was really up to, for all he could think of was the beautiful little girl he had danced so merrily with. His anticipation had mounted as his mother put him through all the social graces she felt he needed, before they made their visit to the Dickerson's farm.

On their trip from the hotel in Henderson, Lena Meinschein had tried to explain what she had planned for their visit.

"William, I saw how taken you were with Etta Mae Dickerson, and all I've done in the past six weeks is so that you will be a suitable suitor for her. You will use everything you've been taught to persuade her parents, and Etta Mae, that she can't live without you. You will not talk about anything on the farm, I'll tell them what I want them to know. You will agree to everything I tell them. Do you understand me?"

"Yes, Mama, do you really think she will marry me?" William asked timidly.

"Yes! We may have to make several visits but this one is the most important. I intend to have some grandchildren, and you are my only hope and she should be just like a brood mare."

Lena laughed boisterously, and William smarted at his mother's insinuations, but he feared his mother so much he knew there was no use in protesting. He also knew she was not fond of Indians, and had been completely surprised at all the trouble she had gone to, to try and persuade the Dickerson's to allow him to court their daughter. The Meinscheins arrived in a flourish of anticipation at the farm and was immediately greeted by Benjamin Dickerson.

"Good afternoon, Mrs. Meinschein, William. Do come in, the ladies are waiting inside." Ben could hardly get out his greeting for his surprise in the change in Lena Meinschein was almost unbelievable. She only vaguely resembled the woman of six weeks ago. The young man too, seemed to have made a metamorphosis in his appearance, and manners.

"Thank you sir, if you can assist my mother, I will just gather up the packages we have for you." William smiled broadly at Ben, now, as he went around the carriage, and handed his mothers arm over to Ben.

Dovie, Etta Mae and Rosie watched as Ben ushered the guests into the large, comfortable sitting room, where a few weeks ago, had been filled only with dancers, and musicians. Now all the furniture and rugs had been set for the guests, and Lena Meinschein was duly impressed. She had not missed the large barn and other buildings on the farm. In fact envy had consumed her, and she hadn't even seen the birthing barn or the training track down by the woods, or for that matter, all the many cabins that were down below the hill.

Introductions were made with William touching each of the ladies hands with his lips, and a slight bow. Chocolates were presented to the ladies, as well as the dainty handkerchiefs and toilet water. Etta Mae and Rosie were slightly embarrassed, but Dovie graciously accepted the gifts understanding that they had far more meaning than the girls could understand.

The afternoon and dinner went very well with Ben and Dovie relaxing somewhat. Lena suggested to William that he might take the girls for a ride, along with some of the smaller children, if they wished. Frances and Myrtle were delighted. William complied immediately as any gentleman would. The younger children were sent out to play, so the adults could talk alone. Lena could hardly wait but finally mustered up the patience that was needed before she approached the real reason for the visit. She had heard all sorts of stories about how long it took to make talk with Indians, how they had to take gifts, and not to be too aggressive in what her plans were for her son. So, she waited for a little time before speaking again as William and the Dickerson children took their leave.

"Mr. and Mrs. Dickerson it has been our pleasure today to meet with you, and I must compliment you on your fine home and family; it is one of the best that I have seen. As you know, my William is very much interested in calling on your daughter, Etta Mae. She is a fine looking woman, and it would be our honor if you would give your consent for William to call on her again – by himself. Of course, I know that you would want the two young people to be accompanied by someone in my absence." Lena purred, and took a deep breath, for she was unaccustomed to having to play the role of a genteel lady.

"Yes, we are fully aware of your son's interest in our Etta Mae." Ben cleared his throat and Dovie took up the conversation.

"As Ben said, we are aware that William is interested in Etta Mae, but we do not know how she feels about his courting her. She has many suitors, one in particular that she if very fond of." Lena bristled a bit as she answered.

"You mean the musician, George Hutchison?" Lena just had to let them know she was aware of much more than they could possibly know. She had done her research well. Ben was totally surprised at Lena's answer.

"Well yes, as a matter of fact, you are right. Mr. Hutchison is an honorable man that we know quite well, and are sure his intentions are honorable. We do not know much about you and your family, Mrs. Meinschein, Ben spoke quickly before Dovie got the chance, for he had seen a strange look cross her face. He too was a little taken aback that this woman knew far more about them than he was comfortable with.

"Of course, you would want to know more about me and my family – our financial standing to say the least. Well let's start with our farm. We have three hundred acres, all of which would be tillable soil if we desired; however, at the present we have a dairy herd, pigs, and chickens, grow our own corn and wheat. Our land is some of the best in or around St. Phillips. St. Phillips is a small place about fifteen miles southwest of Evansville, and about the same distance northwest of Mt. Vernon, Indiana. I have three sons none of them are married, that help me run the farm, and from time to time we hire extra help as we need it. My deceased husband Philip was a frugal man and left us very well off. We have a large home, a summer kitchen- and a wash house, plus many other buildings on our place. It is very comfortable, if I must say so myself. My husband was reared Catholic, but we were not. Does this help you to know who we are?" Lena finished the elaboration of her standing with a cunning smile, as she noted the looks on Ben and Dovie's faces; especially this Indian woman, for she could see she was somewhat impressed, but surprised at her answer.

"Yes, Mrs. Meinschein, you sound quite prosperous, but let's wait and see how Etta Mae feels after she has spent some time with your son, today. We would like to show you around our farm if you would like." Dovie looked at Ben as she spoke, again finding that strangeness in the pit of her stomach.

"Yes, I would like that."

"Then come, let's start with the training track Dovie, Mrs. Meinschein." Ben was only too glad to get out of this stifled atmosphere, here in his own house. Besides, he couldn't wait to show off their farm, livestock, and especially the horses.

Ben harnessed two horses to the buggy and drove toward the house to meet the ladies. He noticed that Dovie looked happier that she had all day, and reached out and patted her on the shoulder. As he did so, he also saw that pout of her mouth take over, and he knew she was thinking what he was thinking. "We'll show her that we aren't just poor Indians, as her tone had implied."

Ben drove directly to the race track and brood mares barn, and as they neared the track, Lena could better see the size of this Star Farm. She could not begin to understand it all. There were cabins and gardens, all around, and when they got out to go into the barn, by the track, they were met by a tall handsome man with the same long black hair as Dovie's, Ben's Etta Mae's and Rosie's. Then another young man appeared on the scene. She was very confused and a bit frightened for these men were moving toward her. Sensing Lena's confusion, Ben began introductions.

"Mrs. Meinschein, this is Greyfox, Dovie's brother and our nephew, Many Waters. The two men in the corral are Golden Eagle and Bull Bear, with their sons." Lena stifled a would be cry, regained her composure as she tried lamely to greet the men now standing before her.

"I see how do you do?" She uttered to the men, totally intimidated. She felt frightened, and blurted out her fear.

"Is everyone on this farm here, Indians?" she asked in amazement, but wished somehow that she could have taken the words back as soon as they left her mouth. Ben eyed Lena's face intently before he spoke again.

"Yes, for the most part. At least in their hearts everyone her are Indians." Ben answered, now a little amused at Lena's apparent amazement at his answer.

"Just how many people live here, I mean are people living in all these cabins?" Lena looked from one face to the other, as she questioned Ben.

"That's right, Mrs. Meinschein. Every one of the cabins are occupied by our kinsmen, and their families. Only a few of our people have left our farm, but most have chosen to stay and raise their families here, where they find no ridicule." Dovie answered Lena Meinschein's questions now, for she saw Rose Marie and Annie Lee approaching with several small children with their flaming red hair flying in the slight breeze that had now started to blow across the meadows.

Lena Meinschein felt even more uncomfortable, and intimidated. She had no idea what to say or how to act. She could plainly see the women approaching were white women, but the children were obviously of Indian Heritage.

"Hello ladies. How are the twins today? Come to us, we have someone we want you to meet." Dovie called out with honest pleasure at the sight of them. "Annie Lee, Rose Marie, this is Mrs. Meinschein, the young man's mother that Etta Mae and Rosie are out riding with. Mrs. Meinschein this is my sister, Rose Marie, and her mother Annie Lee." Dovie practically cooed as she gathered the children together with a loving embrace.

"And these are Annie Lee's grandchildren."

At just that moment a very, very dark little boy ran out of the nearby barn, stopping only to climb the white board fence around the corral, yelling at the men in the corral on horseback.

Lena Meinschein gasped at the sight of the dark child. They even have Negroes living here, she thought, and an intense look of disapproval flashed across her face. Bad enough these people are Indian, but Negroes too. How disgusting! She managed to clear the look of disgust from her face, but not before everyone present saw it. Ben, the ever diplomat, decided to explain.

"The young boy there on the fence, belongs to our brother Bull Bear, the large man in the ring. He's a Blackfoot from Canada, and a fine, fine man. He has lived with us all since before Dovie was born." Ben grimaced at his own words as he now stopped short in his explanation. Why he was trying to explain anything to this woman, he wondered.

"Oh, I see. Mr. Bull Bear himself is quite dark, but handsome." Lena Meinschein said lamely because she had seen the look of disgust on both the Dickerson's faces. Dovie had even flinched at Lena's words and the strange feeling of foreboding, passed through her body again. Annie Lee's quick wit had not dimmed with time, and now saved them from further embarrassment.

"I'm glad to make your acquaintance, Mrs. Meinschein; I saw Etta Mae and Rosie driving around with a handsome young man, I have yet to meet them. Forgive me, but I don't believe I caught his name." Annie Lee knew this kind of woman to be dull, self-centered, and a controlling woman, who thought no one but Germans were of any worth. She would have to warn Dovie and Ben, for they were not too wise with the white man's world, even though they had been living here in Kentucky most of Dovie's young life.

"Yes m'am, I'm glad to meet you, Annie Lee, and your last name is?" Lena asked pompously.

"Annie Lee Golden Eagle. My husband is Bull Bears brother." Annie Lee turned now to Dovie.

"Please excuse us Dovie, Ben, we must get on with our chores. Come Rose Marie, children." Annie Lee took each child by the hand and walked away with dignity, not looking back.

Ben and Dovie watched Annie Lee's departure for a moment, not quite knowing what to say, for Annie Lee was always very social with everyone. Dovie finally called out to the men in the corral, waved her hand, gathered her skirts and climbed back into the buggy.

"Ben dear, help Mrs. Meinschein up, and let's finish our rounds of the farm." Dovie had not missed the indignation in Annie Lee's voice and neither had Ben. Just what to say or do, neither one knew, so they let it pass.

Ben drove the carriage down to the river, then to the sawmill, back to the main barn by the house and then to the front door. As they did so they saw the young people coming up the lane from the main road. Etta Mae's parents sighed in relief as they watched the happy young people approaching.

William was, of course, the first to jump out and offer his hand to Etta Mae, and then to Rose, laughing all the time for he felt he had made the best conquest of his life. He had fallen head over heels in love with the farm and its surroundings, as well as Etta Mae. She had even let him put his arm around her while they were walking down by the river. She had said she liked him and wanted him to call on her again, soon. He had told her she made him feel giddy and happier that he had ever been in his life. He held her arm tightly now as they approached her parents.

Mr. and Mrs. Dickerson, Etta Mae and I would like your permission for me to call again in two weeks on a Sunday." William waited with betted breath, for he knew that his mother could be very aggressive with people, and he knew too, this would not work with these people.

"This is your desire, Etta Mae?" Ben asked surprised by the young man's aggressiveness.

"Yes, Papa, Mama, I would like that very much."

"Then permission is granted. We will see you all on two Sundays from now." Lena Meinschein only smiled at her son now, for his performance was well done, and she had accomplished her goal. She would not accompany her son in two weeks; no need, she thought, my plan is in motion and I won't be needed until his visit to finish off my plan.

Two days later George Hutchinson came calling. Dressed in his best suit of clothes, as always, he looked the gentleman he was, and was known all around to be. Etta Mae was thrilled to see him, and they spent the better part of the day walking and talking, and then George had dinner with the family. He played games with the younger children, played his mouth organ, danced an Irish jig for everyone's entertainment, for he loved all the people on this farm, and found they returned his affection. His intentions had been to tell the Dickerson's about his little farm and the new house he was building for Etta Mae, but somehow he just couldn't get out the words. Later he thought, when it is near completion, and I can show it to Etta Mae's father. Then Rosie spoke of William's visit. Rosie did not like what Etta Mae was doing and tried to tell her she would end up being sorry, but Etta Mae had just laughed at her. Somehow she had to let George know, so she spoke up.

"It's a shame you didn't come here a few days ago, George, you could have had the privilege of meeting Etta Mae's new beau." Rosie only looked at George for she knew better than to look at Etta Mae, or their parents.

"Rosie! That was uncalled for!" Ben spoke, angered by what he thought was nothing more than jealously, for after all, Rosie was older and should be the first one to marry.

"No, that's okay, Papa." Etta Mae was actually thrilled that Rosie has spoken of William's visit. Maybe, she thought this will get George to finally speak up, but George's Irish temper and pride would not let him say anymore.

Ben hastened to smooth things over but George now felt played the fool and stood up to go. Etta Mae tried to rescue the situation but George was not having it. Etta Mae followed him out of the house, trying to explain herself, and finally he stopped to answer her pleas.

"So it was only William Meinschein. He doesn't count with you. What kind of a fool do you think I am? When you make up your mind whether it's him or me, let me know!"

"Please George, don't go away angry at me. I only said he could come because you haven't spoken to Papa yet." Etta Mae was now near tears, but George was so angry he couldn't hear anything she said. All he could think was, 'all that work for her, and she's courting another man.' Maybe his brothers Ed and Jim were right, maybe she was too young for him. Too young to know her own mind, they had said. Well she could just have that German bastard, but his heart was so full of pain and disbelief, he just couldn't believe it. As he drove away, he decided he would find out just whom he was up against for he could not believe that he had really lost Etta Mae, after he now remembered her words.

"Etta Mae," they said, "its best George found out now before he heard it from someone else. He has a right to know. We tried to tell you not to play games with George, but if he loves you he will think it over and come to his senses."

"No, he won't come back. He said I had to choose, but he hasn't even asked you, Papa.

Maybe he never really wanted to marry me." Etta Mae became even more hysterical, so Dovie took her into the kitchen, bathed her face in cool water, and made her drink some of Ben's toddy of honey, lemon, ginger and brandy. Soon Etta Mae had calmed down and went to her room to sleep. Ben talked to Rosie about what she had done, but he did not feel that she wasn't right.

"Rosabelle, it was not kind of you to tell George about William, you know that don't you?"

"Yes, Papa, but it could have been worse if I hadn't said something. You know Etta Mae is just stringing both of them along. She likes that sort of thing. She told me she wanted to make George jealous. Well she sure did a good job of that. I've never seen him so angry." Rosie's words rang true in Ben's ears, but he, like Etta Mae, couldn't understand why George had not asked for her hand in marriage. Ben could only shake his head, for now it seemed he wasn't ready to make a commitment to marriage, so maybe it was a good thing there was William.

By the time George had reached the ferry in Uniontown, his temper had cooled. His thoughts kept going back to the one statement he could remember. "I only did it to make you jealous so you would ask Papa if you could marry me." He wondered, did she really mean it, or were they just some more words? Well, he thought, I'm going to find out all I can about these Meinscheins, that no one seems to know much about, and he did.

Every dance he and his brothers played for, he would ask everyone if they knew the Meinscheins. He had no luck at all at first. Then he began hearing a few rumors then was asked why he was inquiring about the Meinscheins.

"Just curious, I guess. They don't seem to mix much with their neighbors, do they?" George was speaking to the local grocery man, Jake Gerber.

"It's kind of funny you asked me about them," Jake said, "I have a dairy farm not too far from St. Phillips and I am friends with the owner of the general store there, in the Weinzappels. Just this past week he mentioned to me that that woman was in his store, and a strange thing happened," I asked him what he meant and he said, "well, she lives way out on that hill with her three sons, and she never lets them out of her sight, especially the oldest one. You would think they were married, if you didn't know that they were mother and son." Weinzappel paused, and look sheepishly at George.

Intrigued, George asked him, "How's that?" and he answered with, "it's hard to put into words, exactly, but once I saw the son with my very own eyes, feeling his mom's breasts and kissing her on the lips. They kind of whispered something to each other, and then laughed. I was just coming out of the back room, so they didn't know that I saw them." George was pretty shocked at Weinzappel's words, but didn't let on.

He just said, "Well, you can never tell what goes on in the world these days, can you?"

George's flesh crawled at Gerber's story, but having seen Lena Meinschein, he felt she would be capable of anything. Now he was worried about Etta Mae's link with the family. What kind of a mess was she getting herself into? He wondered. Her mother and father were pretty naïve where the world was concerned, and they were so fond of their daughter, they would agree to anything she wanted. With this bit of information he would somehow need to go to the Dickerson's and give them the information he had, so that they could do their own investigation. His pride was so wounded, he needed all the courage he could muster to go speak his mind and tell Etta Mae's parents his intentions of marriage to their daughter. He knew he had waited much too long, so he decided to get the ring and go to Smith Mills. This, he thought, would solidify his intentions.

William Meinschein returned two weeks after his mother and he had the first visit to the Dickerson farm, just as he said he would, and every week after that. Etta Mae was thrilled to see him for she had heard nothing from George and this only made her anger at him fester. She had gotten over her anger at Rosie and they were best of friends again. She, William, Sam Farmer, (Rosie's beau), and sometimes their sister Ethel, would all go to Morganfield. Soon this would become normal and the three couples were a constant. Sam's brother, Harry, would become Ethel's steady beau; they would all go skating or dancing and just have a marvelous time. Etta Mae seemed to have forgotten all about George on the surface, but many nights she could have been heard sobbing herself to sleep, if she and Rosie had shared rooms, but they didn't. Each of the older girls shared a room with one or more of their younger sisters.

On one particular visit the three couples went dancing on the Island Queen excursion boat, which took them down river to Paducah, Kentucky and back. It was Williams treat and made a big impression on Etta Mae's mind. On this visit William bought Etta Mae a lovely ring, made of sapphires and aquamarines which were her birthstones. William had told her the ring was a token of his love for her, and her acceptance would bind them together as being a pledge to each other to be engaged. He said that he would ask her parents for her hand in marriage if she would accept the ring. Etta Mae was overwhelmed with the ring and did accept it, for it was very beautiful. When they docked at the ferry she showed it off to her sisters, and later they went to Ben and Dovie to tell them of their intentions.

"Marriage, Etta Mae! Do you know what you are doing?' Ben and Dovie had not seen this coming at all; the announcement caught them completely off guard and left them weak and breathless. So much so, they had to sit down on the sofa to try and absorb what William was saying.

"Yes, Mr. and Mrs. Dickerson, we want to be married and right away while the weather is still a bit warm. I'm staying over and my mother will join me at the hotel tomorrow. She says she has a big surprise for us." William was all aglow with his new found love, and it showed.

"My God in Heaven, this is all so sudden! You have only known each other a few months. You are very young William, as is Etta Mae. How do you intend to support my daughter?" Ben's shock turned to concern now.

"Well, sir, my family is very well to do. After we are married for a few months we will go back and help mother run the farm. My mother has arranged for us to live in my grandparent's house in Evansville, for a few months. It is a lovely old house, on Wabash Avenue. I'm sure Etta Mae will love it. It has many bedrooms, and a nursery, and," William stopped after he mentioned nursery, for he realized he had said more than his mother had told him to say. He blushed a deep red and Ben thought it was from embarrassment about the word "nursery" and what it implied.

Etta Mae was as excited as William. She had heard all the words about a lovely old mansion, but, that had little effect on her. Moving to Evansville was a dream-come-true. A big city, she was going to be living in a big city, where no one would ever know she was an Indian. She knew that her light skin and her father's blue eyes would never give her up. She hated being referred to as one of "those Indian girls" from Smith Mills. She vowed to herself she would never tell a soul; she would never tell her children, no matter what and she would forbid her family from telling them too.

Dovie had remained too stunned to speak. She could only look at her precious daughter and wonder if it could be true. She would be so far way from home, something that had never occurred to her before. She knew Etta Mae was head strong and when she made up her mind about something, nothing could change it. Was this one of these times? Finally she managed to rise and embrace her daughter.

"Etta Mae, you are so young, can't you wait 'till the moon of the flowers comes? Evansville is so far away. You don't know anyone there. What will you do all by yourself?" Dovie couldn't keep the tears from running down her cheeks, she was so distressed.

"Mama, don't fret so. It's what I want. I'll be living in a fine house in a big city, and I'll have plenty to do, besides, I'll be with William. It's what I want Mama, Papa, please say yes." Etta Mae was pleading now with her parents to give her away.

"I can't give you my answer tonight, young man. I think you should take your leave, for the night, and we will see you and your mother, tomorrow." Ben was a bit curt, so William did not hesitate to take his leave. Etta Mae followed him to his carriage. There they entwined themselves in a lusty embrace. Etta Mae smothered William with unabashed kisses and let her body be pulled tightly against the lustful William.

Ben watched for a second and then called Dovie's attention to their daughter's behavior. They looked at each other and their decision was made – they knew their daughter would get what she wanted one way or another.

Lena Meinschein arrived at the farm with William the next day with Lena's 'surprise'. It was all part of her plan. She had booked passage to New Orleans on the Delta Queen for Etta Mae and William's honeymoon. Etta Mae squealed with delight for this had been another dream she had had – to sail for days and days to New Orleans. Like her Mama had once done. She had heard and read so much about the city; the couple would have to be married at once, she said, in order to take advantage of the trip. Her plan she told Ben and Dovie, was for all of them to go into Henderson to the Justice of the Peace, then on to Evansville to show everyone where the newlyweds would reside after the honeymoon.

Dovie found Lena Meinschein's engineering of an immediate wedding very distasteful, to say the least. Ben felt revulsion toward the woman who had maneuvered her son, and now his daughter, into this sudden marriage. His distrust mounted but Etta Mae ws determined to get what she wanted.

"Papa, Mama, I never wanted a big wedding with all the fuss and work it would cause you. This would be so much better. William and I will have lots of time to get acquainted better while we're on our honeymoon, time to plan our life together." Lena smirked, for little did Etta Mae know, she had already planned everything to the last detail.

"No, this is all much too sudden a turn of events; I must make a few changes to your plan Mrs. Meinschein. While your generosity for the trip to New Orleans shows your good faith, we must be assured that Etta Mae will have a suitable home. I suggest you show us the house in Evansville, then if everything is as you say, we can then go with these children to get their marriage license and then to the Justice to marry them." Ben had become suspicious as the suddenness of Lena's insistence for the marriage to be immediately, but he did not want her to see his fear.

"The fact is Mrs. Meinschein, Mrs. Dickerson and I have our wedding gift that we will give them after we see the house." Dovie nodded her assent now, for she could see that Lena Meinschein's eyes had narrowed with displeasure from all of these changes. She had not anticipated such a request, but William was almost gleeful at the thought of a fine gift from Etta Mae's parents, so it was now his turn to convince his mother to be a little relenting.

"Mama, I think that is a fine idea for Etta Mae and Mr. and Mrs. Dickerson to see where she is going to live with me. Etta Mae is right. We have a long time on the boat to get better acquainted. Mother, you must understand that the parents of a girl would be much more worried about their daughter, than a mother would be for her son." Lena Meinschein could have strangled William for such a statement, but she also knew she had gotten herself trapped. So, she did the only thing she could do; she agreed, and thought that, actually this might be better in the long run. She only hoped the people she had hired to redecorate the old house would have it at least half way done. She had given them a few more weeks to have everything completed, so she just didn't know what she would find.

"Well, if that's the case, we had all best be on our way to Henderson and let you get your packing done Etta Mae. We will meet you at the hotel and complete your plans. Say your goodbyes, William, we must be going." With this order, Lena walked out of the house a little frustrated. Maybe the Dickerson's would change their minds once they saw the house. She could only hope not, if her William was ever going to get any part of this farm for himself. She could see that the Dickerson's doted on Etta Mae, and with her firmly with child, they would give her anything she asked for.

Etta Mae ran up the stairs calling to her sister Rosie.

"Rosie, Rosie did you hear that? I'm going to Evansville to see where William and I are going to live. Did you hear me, Rosie?"

Rosabelle Dickerson was not easily excited, and this was something she did not feel good about. Not at all. She had misgivings about William and his family. Etta Mae would never take the bossing around that she knew she was bound to get from William's mother. She also felt that Etta Mae was only thinking about the trip to New Orleans, and the house in Evansville, not what marriage to William would be like.

"Yes, Etta, I heard you. You actually are going to marry William? What about George? Just last month you were pinning around because he hadn't talked to Papa. I can't believe you would choose William, he is so dominated by his mother that it wouldn't surprise me if she went on the honeymoon with you."

Rosie sort of chuckled, but she meant every word she had spoken.

"Oh, Rosie, surely she wouldn't do that. I just won't go if she does. Once we're married, I'll be the one to tell William what to do." Etta pouted.

"Don't be so sure of that. I don't like it one bit. Neither Mama or Papa really want you to marry that German boy, and that IS what he is – a boy. Even Sam says he's not even dry behind his ears yet. He probably won't know what he is supposed to do with a wife, but I'm sure his mother will tell him."

"Oh my goodness Rosie, what are you implying. Well I don't care what anyone thinks, I'm doing it, so just help me get my things together for tonight, and tomorrow. I think Papa will insist on some kind of ceremony beside the Justice of the Peace, in his office. I'll need all my things packed for the honeymoon. Oh, Ethel, help Rosie get my things together. Oh, goodness, I wanted you girls to stand up with me, and Uncle Greyfox, and oh my, how will I ever get everything together. I don't have a special dress, and this isn't the way I planned to be married."

Etta Mae had become rattled just thinking of everything she had to do, and seemed not to be able to do anything. Rosie and Ethel gave her hugs and told her to just calm down, they would take care of everything. Ethel said she thought it the most romantic thing she had ever heard of, and wished it was she and Harry that were getting married.

"Etta, calm down, Mama has been preparing for this for a long time now. She has a whole trousseau made for you, and me. Here, just look in this trunk." Rosie had been helping her mother as well as her other sister with sewing, and had indeed put together a lovely trousseau. Etta just stared and stared at the mountains of satin and lace now exposed for her eyes to see. She was completely overcome, that she had not even realized she had helped her mother embroider the linens, make some of the lace that now decorated other garments in the trunk. Etta Mae sank to the floor as she cried out.

"Mama, Mama, Mama, what on earth will I do without Mama?"

Etta Mae was overcome by what her mother had done for her as her beautiful blue eyes now glistened with tears of sadness. How could she bare to leave her Mama and Papa and all the rest of her family? Her doubts were smashed by her father's voice.

"Etta Mae, we must hurry so we can get to Henderson before dark. You won't need to take a lot of thing. Your Mama wants to take you shopping too, so hurry it up, up there." All three girls giggled at their father's excited voice as they threw things into a black valise and kissed their sister goodbye, for now.

Etta Mae wiped away her tears and walked bravely down the stairs where her Mama and Papa waited. She looked at each of them for a long moment before she spoke what was on her mind.

"Mama, Papa, I have but one request. If I must be married by a Justice, I want it done in our house, here with my family; other wise, I don't want to do it at all, not like William's mother wants it to be." Ben and Dovie smiled at their daughter, for she had just said the very words they had wanted to hear.

"Your wish fills our hearts with pride and joy and it will be done your way, or no way at all, right mother?" Ben said Dovie nodded, and the proud parents ushered their daughter out the door and onto the waiting carriage where Greyfox White Feather held the reins for them. Etta Mae gave her Uncle a hug and a big kiss, and he returned the gesture, for he loved this darling little girl, the first born of his sister with Benjamin Dickerson.

It was quite late when the Dickerson's joined the Meinscheins in the hotel dining room. William rose to seat Etta Mae and Ben seated Dovie. Not much conversation was held since Lena had ordered ahead for the Dickersons. Much to Etta's surprise, for his mother made her very nervous. William could see she was ill at ease, so he paid Etta as much attention as he possibly could. During dessert, Ben decided it was the right time to break the news about Etta's refusal to be married in the Justice of the Peace's Office, but wanted it held in her home with her family.

"Mrs. Meinschein, William; I'm going to the Justice's Office first thing in the morning to make the necessary arrangements for Etta Mae to be married in our home." Ben hesitated as Lena nearly choked on her mouth full of food, and William looked as if he was going to be sick. He knew his mother would be furious at this change in her plans.

"I don't believe it is too much to ask for Etta Mae definitely said that is the only way it can be – the marriage." Etta Mae did not look up, but continued to busily eating her dessert. She was torn about the marriage, and wished that she had not consented, but the lure of living in Evansville, and a trip to New Orleans outweighed that decision. Dovie watched Lena's every move now, and saw her struggle not to start yelling at Etta Mae, or Ben, or even at her. William followed Etta Mae's effort in keeping his eyes lowered, but Dovie saw him shiver, and then his hands start trembling. Dovie had not realized before this, just how frightened he was of his mother. Ben also saw the trembling and knew he needed to try and set him at ease, somehow.

"Lena, I realize this is quite a change in your plans, but I can't see that any harm will be done. William will come with me to the Justice, and then we will all go to see the house where the young people will reside. William will then come back to the farm for the wedding, and of course, you too. You of course will have to decide if you need to go home first, or just wait and come to see them off, on the Delta Queen. In the meantime I will handle the tickets and anything else that might come up." Ben stood now, and stood over Lena. She was in such a state of shock at the words Ben had spoken, she could hardly rise from her chair. Ben the ever gentlemen, gave Lena his arm to assist her.

"Here, let me help you Lena. It is my hope that you will not blame William for any of these changes, for it is no way any of his doing. William, I'll have your room changed to the one next to mine, so that we can get started early in the morning. The ladies can get ready then, for our trip to Evansville. Come, let's all turn in now. Oh, William I'll come with you so I can help you move your things. Etta Mae will go with her mother." Ben's statement left no room for anyone to contest his wishes. His matter of fact manner did not lend for any refusal from anyone. Ben and Dovie could not help but see the look of hatred on Lena's face.

Lena Meinschein was so angry she could not speak, but left herself be propelled by Ben to her room, all the time thinking to herself, "Damn this Indian bastard and his family. I'll get even with them for this insulting attitude toward me. After all, she thought, I'll have control over your daughter, once they return from New Orleans, and I'll show you how much revenge I can make your daughter pay for."

The trip to Evansville proved to be everything Lena and William had promised it would be. The old family home on Wabash Avenue was one of many old mansions on the street. The Meinschein home was an elegant red brick structure of three stories. The front of the house was rounded off with lovely white pillars supporting the roof of the porch. The back of the house served as the servant quarters which were disconnected from the main house, by a covered porch. Both of these structures were covered with ivy as well as the back and side of the manor. The rounded front porch was encased by bush after bush of hydrangeas which were now beginning to bloom. Several tall oak trees sat on the well manicured lawn, with a brick walkway leading to doors on each side of the porch. One led into the kitchen, and another into an informal sitting room. The rounded room in front was huge, and was splendidly furnished in lovely, upholstered, antique furniture. One wall was paneled in gold gilded mirrors and a grand piano and two winged back chairs. On the opposite wall was a satin covered chaise lounge sofa, which was encased at each end with round tables, and a pair of Tiffany lamps.

In front of the large window, which was draped in wine velvet, was a handsome vase filled with dozens of red roses and baby breath. At the opposite end of the room was a huge carved mahogany mantle. Above the mantle was a large portrait of a very austere, but handsome, man in a military uniform.

Etta Mae caught her breath at the elegance of this lovely parlor, for she had never dreamed of having such a sumptuous home. As she drew in her breath, she now felt that her decision to marry William was a good one.

William was just as surprised as Etta Mae at the changes that had taken place in his grandparent's home. It seemed that his mother and the workers had done wonders in refurbishing the old place. He had not been in the old house since he was very young, but he knew his mother had spent a fortune on the house's refurbishment, and for the trip to New Orleans. He also knew that his mother never gave away anything without a price. He decided to put all of this out of his mind for he saw the joy that had taken over Etta Mae's face. The ominous feelings that he had, were wiped away as he remembered how Etta's father had taken over and helped him with his mother the night before. He also decided he didn't care if his mother showed up for his wedding ceremony or not; thc fact was he hoped she would not, and he got his wish.

Lena Meinschein did not come back to the farm, for the wedding, she was just too angry at her soon to be in-laws. "The nerve of those savages to think they can get away with insulting me, she thought. They will soon learn, their precious daughter would soon be in her charge. She would show them a thing or two!"

Lena did come early to the docks so that she would be there when the wedding party showed up. Her patience was about to fail her when she got her first glimpse of the wedding present from the Dickerson's.

Lena's first glimpse told her this had to be someone other than Etta Mae and William, but on second look she saw it truly was William and his bride. They were in the most beautiful black leather and silver carriage she had ever seen, and it was now coming down to the Delta Queen. It was drawn by two sleek, black, high stepping geldings, and she had to admit that she had never seen anything more beautiful. The harness was studded in silver to match the silver eagles on each side of the carriage. The seats were padded thick, in the same black leather as the carriage, and even the floor was covered in leather. Ben had spared no expense when he had the best local buggy shop make this carriage. He had thought that it would be for Etta Mae and George.

Etta Mae was a vision of loveliness in her powder blue suit with its slightly trailing long skirt. On her shiny black hair, which was coiffed in soft braids and crossed on the back of her head, she wore a hat fashioned of the same material as her dress. A silk faille hat boasted several fluffy feathers that blew softly in the breeze. Driving the carriage was Etta's Uncle Greyfox, and her Aunt Rose Marie. Her dress was just as stunning as Etta Mae's. Seated beside Etta Mae was her sister Rosabelle in her matching suit of a soft peach. She looked adorable. Dovie was abloom in her dusty rose outfit and Ben Dickerson never looked more handsome in his black suit of a fine material. Greyfox was the only one who wore any resemblance of native clothing. He had a soft buckskin tunic and pants that was beaded and fringed almost to the excess.

Lena Meinschein wondered just how these people had managed to get all of these clothes and the carriage together in such a short time. She could not help but think as she looked at Ben and his family, just how handsome they really were. Still she thought, they are all just Indians and a step away from being savages. The people at the Delta Queen now gawked first at Greyfox, and then at all the people disembarking from the carriage. One could readily see that the man in the Indian suit was just a lackey for the young people in the magnificent carriage, until Etta Mae hugged her Uncle. He in turn gave her a kiss and a big hug. The crowd gasped at this extraordinary display of affection in public. Lena winced, for this definitely said that he was more than the driver of the carriage.

Lena kept her eyes lowered and did not address Greyfox or Rose Marie, but nodded to Rosabelle, and offered her hand to Dovie. She gave William a quick peck on the cheek, and whispered something in Etta Mae's ear, which would not be revealed until many months later.

CHAPTER TWELVE

HONEYMOON HOUSE OF HORRORS

Ben, Dovie, Rosabelle, Rose Marie, and Greyfox all watched as the little streamer glided away from the docks, and entered the main stream of the Ohio River. Dovie and Rosabelle had tears in their eyes and Ben wore a look of deep concern. He still was not happy about this marriage. Dovie had, however, convinced him that the marriage seemed like a good thing for Etta Mae. She would have her own lovely home with plenty of room for her children. William seemed like a good boy, especially when he was away from his mother. Neither of them had any idea that Lena Meinschein had cooked up this charade. She had been afraid that Etta Mae would not consent to the marriage, and certainly not her parents without thinking tiiat the couple would be living in Evansville. She laughed to herself as she thought about what she had done to make the marriage happen.

The first night of their trip William had restrained himself in his desire to make love to Etta Mae. He knew she was a virgin and his mother had cautioned him to be understanding and patient because a woman's first time could be painful. She had even given him some tips on what to do if this was the case.

William and his brothers had laughingly discussed his "breaking in" of Etta Mae. Much to William's surprise Etta Mae made no complaint and seemed to enjoy their love making as much as he did. Etta Mae, however, felt no emotion for William, so she just closed her eyes and tried to enjoy her husband's appetite. Her mother had said that the emotion of love and caring for each other would grow as time passed.

The honeymoon trip to New Orleans had been everything that Etta Mae and William had been told it would be. They took long walks and romped in their hotel room like two spoiled children, which they were. Etta Mae had decided that she had everything she could possibly want and was a bit sad to leave the town, but leave they must. She felt free and wonderful looking forward to living in that beautiful house in Evansville. William, however, seemed uptight and a bit sullen for he knew not what his mother held in store for him and Etta Mae.

The steamer docked and the newlyweds were met by the hired man, Hansen, who said he had a letter for William from his mother and that he should read it right away. The newlyweds looked at each other and wondered what on earth could his mother want on their first night home? William nervously unsealed the letter and began to read his mother's handwriting. As he read his face became redder, flushed with anger. Etta Mae watched as he read but could not stand the suspense any longer when William did not speak about the letter's content.

"What does she want? What does the letter say?" William did not answer right away for he could not believe what his mother had written. He knew Etta Mae was not going to receive the news and the changes they were going to have to make, very soon. William folded the letter and jammed it in his pocket wondering just what was Etta going to do when he told her what the letter said.

"William, answer me or let me read the letter. What does it say?" Etta Mae was becoming furious with William's secretive attitude. William could only feel that for his mother now as he realized she had lied to him too. She had never had any intention for him to live in his grand parent's home. She had spent all that money on the house just so she could make Etta Mae and her parents consent to their marriage. She had intended to sell the house all along. Damn her anyway! What will Etta Mae do when I tell her? He knew she would be so angry with him; would she leave him? He could barely speak he was so angry, but tried to not let it show as he meekly answered his new wife.

"It just says that we are to come out to the farm right away, and that the house on Wabash had been sold." William could not look at Etta Mae now, all he could do was wait for her anger to boil over, and it did.

"What on earth are you saying?! Etta screamed. "We are not going to live in Evansville as you promised! Tell me it isn't true! Are you saying we have to drive miles and miles out to St. Phillips now? I won't do it! I tell you, I won't do it! No! Take your hands of me, let me go! I'll just go back to my home in Smith Mills! My Papa will never allow this to happen! Your mother lied to us and to my family! Papa will never let your mother treat us this way," Etta Mae collapsed into tears and frustration. What on earth could she do she wondered, after all she was married to William now.

William was stunned at the thought of Etta Mae going back to her parents, for he knew that his mother might do just about anything she could think of to him, if this happened. He had to take control of this situation as much as he disliked what his mother had done to him.

"Get a hold of yourself, Etta Mae. Stop these hysterics. You will go to the farm with me. You are my wife now and you will do as I say. Hansen, we will drop you off at the house and then we will be on our way." William knew he didn't really have a choice but to obey his mother's wishes for he had no other income to take care of himself, and now he had a wife to provide for.

With tears running down her cheeks and sobbing, Etta Mae climbed into the buggy, devastated. As the horses left Evansville behind she became very quiet and thoughtful, which William took to mean she had capitulated, and would now do what he said. The fact was Etta Mae realized that she had been a pawn of Lena Meinschein all along. The domineering and vindictive woman had won for now, but she was not going to take this deceit lightly. Etta Mae should have known something was terribly wrong when she whispered the words in her ear just before they had set sail for New Orleans. What did she really mean when she had whispered, "Have your fun now, because you will earn it later."

They arrived at the farm just before dark and Etta Mae had admired all the land and crops that William pointed out, as belonging to him and his family. One field was full of milk cows, forty or fifty of them. Then just ahead as they passed over a large hill, she saw the house. Her heart sank even further. The house looked just like the barn, big and plain, with no porch or window shutters, just a door in the middle and three long narrow windows on either side of it. It was a two story house and on the second floor six more long narrow windows appeared which now reflected the evening sun. A cold shiver coursed down her spine as she looked at the huge barn and house. William was explaining to her that the building closest to the house was where they stored the milk from the cows until it was picked up and taken to the city for disbursement. Etta heard William, but she could not answer, her mind had already begun to think of ways she could escape this dreadful place.

They were met by William's two brothers and Etta Mae's heart sank even farther as the brothers leered at her disgustingly, as they unloaded the valises from the carriage. The three men stopped several times and whispered to each other and then they would all laugh and laugh.

"Maw said to send Etta in as soon as you got here. She said she wanted to welcome her, herself." Alfred Meinschein, the oldest brother, jeered at her. "Here Etta Mae, take this valise and go inside!"

"No! I won't go without William. You take me in William, please." Etta Mae pleaded with her husband.

"Oh, ho, ho, a real firecracker. So uppity for an Indian gal, don't you think, brother Henry?" Alfred spoke with amusement as he eyed Etta in her defiance.

"William did you hear me?" Etta Mae's temper was commencing to get the better of her. She was now standing with her hands on her hips and a foot on one of her trunks.

"Yes, I heard you Etta Mae, but I think my mother wants to see you alone. She must have something special to tell you." William had taken her by the arm, picked up the valise, walked her to the door and practically shoved her inside. Etta Mae tried to grab hold of him but he was much stronger. He pulled away from her and rejoined his brother. Etta Mae was so surprised by William's actions she just stood inside the door not moving for a long time. She looked about the huge room which was barely lit by one coal oil lamp. Shadows danced on the walls from the fireplace and Etta Mae felt afraid in the huge poorly lit room.

"Well don't just stand there girl, come over here and let me look at you closer." The voice was demanding and cold. Etta Mae looked closer now in the direction the voice had come from. She saw Lena sitting in a tall straight back chair by the fireplace. She moved toward Lena, shaking internally with fear.

Lena Meinschein knew Etta was frightened of her, for she was the matriarch in this house.

"You should be in the family way by now if you did right by my son. Did you let him have his way with you, when he wanted it?"

Etta gasped. She was horrified. How dare this woman ask such a question? Lena, however, was not to be deterred but pressed on.

"You may as well answer my questions now because you will not be going upstairs until I finish with you. Do you understand?"

Etta Mae was shaking all over now and felt she might faint, but she did not. She might as well tell this old witch what she wanted to hear.

"Yes. William was satisfied several times a day." Etta Mae blushed a bright red, "I don't know if I'm pregnant though." Lena made a disapproval grunt of "Hum-m-p."

"You will obey. You will continue to let him have his way as much as he wants until you have your days, or you don't. Then you will lay with each of my sons, whenever and however often they want it. You understand me? We own you now, and you will do whatever is asked of you! Don't look so shocked. What did you expect? You are just an Injun gal. I'll unpack your chest and take all those fancy waistcoats and dainty things out of it. You won't be needing them here!" Lena was curt and totally enjoying herself. Etta Mae stood frozen in disbelief at the words that had come out of her mother-in-law's mouth. Surely she had heard wrong. Finally, she found her voice and turned to leave. But before she could speak Lena's hand reached out and yanked her back, almost making her fall. Panic overcame Etta Mae and she began to scream.

"William! William! I'll get William, he won't allow this!"

"Don't trouble yourself with William. We've had this agreement all along. He just got to have his pleasure because you picked him to marry. This shouldn't trouble you so much, being an Injun. I'm sure you are used to this sharing of your bed. They tell me you women are just like them nigger women, they'll sleep with anyone." Lena screeched these horrible words at Etta Mae as she pushed her toward the stairs. Etta Mae's anger was boiling now, and she wanted to reach out and slap this beady-eyed old hag across the mouth for what she had just said to her. How dare her! Papa would take care of her. But how could she get word to her Papa? She wondered. She was trapped! Lena was still holding her tightly, so she was trapped for now in an unbelievable nightmare. She was so frightened that she barely heard Lena's next words.

"Your room is the first one on the right up these stairs. You can go to your room now, but, you will get up at five and fix breakfast for us, and dinner and supper. The food is on the stove in those kettles. Don't just stand there with your mouth open, get busy. Your days of leisure are over. Do you hear me?" Lena's eyes had grown harder with each word, and her face had taken on the contempt she felt for this girl; she didn't care if she was her son's wife, for she was the boss in this house. Etta Mae could barely walk to the kitchen. It was a dark and dreary place with the lamp turned down so low she could hardly find it. Once she found it she turned up the light and took a look in the iron kettles on the stove. There was a pot of beans and a pot with some boiled meat and potatoes. A half pan of biscuits sat in the warming oven at the top of the wood stove. She tested the food and found it without seasoning. She looked around for something to bring up more flavor. There was nothing anywhere but salt and pepper. She was afraid of that old woman in the other room, and equally afraid of the sons. In her dazed state she just couldn't believe William agreed with what his mother had said. She was lying, surely. At just that moment William entered the kitchen from the outside door and Etta Mae jumped in fear, because she thought his brothers were with him, but thankfully, he was alone.

Etta Mae could not look William in the face and busied herself filling a plate so that he could eat. She did not look up or even flinch when he came behind her and placed a hand on each of her breasts. She was repulsed by his touch now, but tried to let on like nothing was wrong. Maybe, just maybe, he didn't know what his mother's intentions for her were, but quickly changed her mind as he reached under her skirt and pressed his other hand between her legs. She trembled with rage and humiliation remembering what his mother had said about Indian women.

"Stop it, William!" She turned and slapped him with the big spoon she held in her hand. "I said stop it! Take your hand away, and sit down at the table and eat!"

"Don't get sassy with me. I can do anything I like to you, whenever, and wherever I want to. Didn't Maw make that clear to you?"

Etta Mae could control herself no longer. Tears streaked down her cheeks as she placed the food on the table. Suddenly she felt very strange and light headed. That was the last she remembered as she floated away into some dark place. She awoke to find herself in a strange bed. William was sitting beside her.

"Where am I? What happened?" she asked wistfully.

"You fainted in the kitchen last night so I brought you upstairs to our room. Etta, Maw said it was nothing to worry about. She said I'd probably got you in the family way." William boasted.

"No! No! No!" Etta screamed at him, "I can't' be in the family way. It's too soon."

"Sure you can. We've been doing it two and three times a day and again at night. Just talking about it makes me want it now. Take off your clothes!"

"No, I won't. I still feel sick," Etta grabbed hold of her clothing and held them tightly against herself, but William forced her hands away and tore her clothes off until she was totally naked.

"Don't ever tell me no. That just makes me want it more." He climbed on top of her and took her again and again. Etta Mae was sobbing now and clawing at him but he fought her off. Finally, he rolled off her, spent, and went fast asleep. Etta Mae was almost hysterical as she sobbed into her pillow. She had just been raped by her own husband. He took her two more times that night in the same rutting manner. She did not sleep that night. Somehow, she had to get away from these people. Just how, she couldn't fathom. She had noticed that there were no close neighbors on the road as they came in. Maybe on the other side there might be. She would look out of the far window at the end of the hall to see if there was a house in sight, at sunrise.

Etta Mae rose from the bed at the break of first light, and tiptoed down the hall and searched the horizon for some sign of a house, or anything that moved. She saw nothing. She had thrown on a wrapper over her gown and suddenly realized it was way past five o'clock. That old woman would skin her alive if she didn't get breakfast ready and fast. She also realized now that her private area was raw from William's rutting last night, but there was no time for her to take care of herself. She flew down the stairs, made biscuits, fried some ham and eggs, sliced the leftover potatoes and fried them. The coffee was done and everything ws ready. She rushed now to set the table before anyone came down the stairs. In her frantic effort to get the breakfast done she had not noticed Alfred, the oldest brother, standing just inside the side door. She jumped in fear as he addressed her.

"Well, missy you're going to have to do better than this. We've already milked the cows. You should have had breakfast ready an hour ago. Maw said to let it go this time since William probable was having fun this morning with you." As Alfred walked past Etta he slung his arm around her waist and kissed her hard on the lips. She gagged and tried to get away from him, but he was too strong. She pounded him with her fists, but to no avail.

"That's it! Fight me! I like women wild, not like you were with my brother last night. Just you wait until it's my turn. I'll show you what a man really is." He laughed boisterously, and then shoved her away from himself. Etta Mae screamed at him now horrified.

"Oh my God! You watched William and me? My God, My God! You people are all insane. What kind of family have I married into?" Etta Mae was so incensed she screamed at the top of her voice at Alfred.

"Get out of my kitchen, and never come back in here again. I hate you, all of you!" Alfred just laughed at her frustration and joined his brother who was now sitting at the table. Lena entered with William just as Etta Mae brought in the platters of food. Her hands trembled as she served each one of the family, and she did not look at William at all. She sat down at the place she had reserved for herself and pretended that nothing at all was wrong. Lena however, had more instructions for her.

"After this, you will not sit at this table with us. You can find something for yourself in the kitchen before or after we eat, but never sit at this table with us to eat. You are here to work and to pleasure my boys, have babies and nothing else! I thought I made that clear last night!" Lena looked at William now but he was not returning her gaze. Instead he was sitting with his eyes lowered and did not raise them or acknowledge that he had even heard his mother. Etta Mae said nothing, but rose from the table and took her plate back into the kitchen. She was not hungry and Lena's words kept ringing in her ears. She was to be a virtual slave in this house. She had to escape, somehow. She grabbed a biscuit and a small piece of ham, and ran out of the kitchen door. She ran to the little knoll a short distance from the house. She strained and strained her eyes in every direction and finally saw what looked like a house down a small back road. That was it. She would run down there when Lena and her boys went to milk at sundown. Now she knew she had to get back to the kitchen before she was missed. She would write a letter to her Papa and get the people to mail it for her.

Lena was standing in the kitchen glaring at her as she opened the door to let herself in. Her heart sank and she almost panicked but she knew now that she had to keep her head, in order to outsmart this horrible woman.

"What were you doing outside?" Lena barked at Etta Mae.

"Your work is here in the house. Don't ever leave the kitchen when we are eating for we might want you for something! See to it! Make sure you get the entire house cleaned and have dinner ready promptly at 12:00. Supper will be at 6:00. I will write down what we want for our meals every day. I suppose you can read and really know how to fix a good meal." Lena turned away trying not to let Etta Mae see her mocking smile, for she knew that her new daughter-in-law was scared to death of her. Etta Mae sank down into one of the straight backed chairs when Lena left and tried to gather her thoughts as to how she would get to the neighbors. How would she give them a letter to her Papa and get back without anyone seeing her. She prayed hard that the Creator would come to her aide. She could not find paper anywhere, so she ripped off a piece from a large sugar sack that was sitting in the little pantry off the kitchen. Then she remembered that she had stuck some paper and an envelope in her hand valise from the hotel in New Orleans. She ran up the stairs to get it as soon as the boys and their mother left the dining room table. Back down the stairs she flew for time was of the essence now. She must make every minute count. Write the letter, address it, clean the house, fix the meals and be ready to run down the back lane just as soon as everyone went to do the milking.

Etta Mae had never moved so fast in all her life. She virtually flew through the housework, hating everything she saw as she cleaned. She was now glad that the rooms were sparsely furnished. The living room was the best furnished and the only room, except the one downstairs bedroom, that had any kind of window covering on the one window. There was a horse-hair stuffed sofa and two overstuffed chairs, a large oak library table and several golden oak stand tables in this room. On the floor in front of the fireplace and the chairs, was a huge woven rug. It was the only floor covering in the entire house. She had never been in the downstairs bedroom before, but now found that Lena must have unlocked the door so she could clean it. Cautiously, she turned the knob on the door for fear that someone was in the room. Etta Mae could hardly believe her eyes. It was like entering another world. The room had two long narrow windows that were draped as was the walnut canopied bed. There was a large robe closet to match, and a huge chest on chest. Next to the fireplace sat a beautiful winged chair covered in a lighter shade of wine, almost pink. Beside the chair was a matching drop-leaf table on which sat a lamp. The globe of the lamp ws richly painted with pink roses, and gold and green leaves. A truly beautiful room,

Etta Mae thought, but somehow she felt there was some kind of mystery about this room. Was it just a guest room or was there some other reason that Lena kept it locked all the time?

As Etta Mae rushed through the house she noticed some very strange things; it seemed only one of the rooms upstairs, besides hers and Williams had been slept in. Where had the boys slept? Here with each other? Why had the other two rooms not been slept in? Where had Lena slept last night? She wondered. The room downstairs had not been used either, unless Lena had gotten up and made the bed before she had come downstairs. She thought not, for Lena wanted her to have to do as much cleaning as possible. Puzzled Etta Mae thought on this development, but soon decided that she did not have the time to figure it out. She worked faster and faster and soon was finished with the upstairs. Now, she realized she had just barely enough time to get the dinner on the table.

Now finished with the dinner which had been simple for her to fix, she took out the paper and envelope and wrote a short letter to her Papa and Mama. She begged them to come and get her as soon as possible. Something sinister was going on with Lena and the boys, and that Lena had made a slave out of her. She wrote that Lena had told her that if she did not become in the family way this month that the brothers would have to help. Etta Mae did not know just how to tell her parents just what that all really meant, and she did not have time or paper to try and explain it. She knew her Papa and Mama would know what she meant.

Just as she was finishing the letter in her room she heard a door open downstairs. She shoved the letter in her apron pocket and crept down the stairs to see who it was. No one seemed to be anywhere in the living, kitchen or dining room. Strange, she thought. Then she heard a noise coming from the downstairs bedroom. She tried to turn the knob on the door but it was firmly locked. Lena must have come in from the outside. She was about to turn away when strange grunting noises came from the room. Curious now, Etta Mae put her ear to the door and she could hear Lena and the voice of a man, but she could not make out the voice. A thought hit her; maybe she could see who it was through the keyhole, so she stooped down and put her eye to the keyhole, and just as abruptly lost her balance and fell on the floor, shocked. She was aghast at what she had just seen. Lena and Alfred were sitting on the canopied bed naked from the shoulders down and Alfred was nursing on his mother's breast. Lena in the meantime, was taking off Alfred's trousers.

Stunned at what she had just seen Etta Mae could not get to her feet. She finally just crawled away from the room's door and threw up. Then she realized that the two boys and Lena had slept in the same bed all night. The evil of what was happening on the other side of the door was more than Etta Mae could bear. She had heard whispers about this kind of thing but never with a woman and her sons. She hastened to clean up her vomit, and went into the kitchen. The clock said it was a little after three. She mustered up the courage and got the evening meal ready, set the table and tried not to think about what she had seen earlier. Did William know about this? Surely not; he had seemed so much a gentleman while they were on their honeymoon, but then she thought of how he had let his mother take over without one word of defense for her. Had William slept with his mother too? Oh God, please help me get through this horrible mess I have made of my life. How I wish I had not gotten so angry with George. I know that he is a real gentleman and that he really does love me. I've been so foolish Lord, please forgive me, and help me to get out of this awful marriage. Etta Mae prayed and prayed. Over and over she cried in silence for God to come to her aide, all the time remembering how she had seen Lena and Alfred coupling together like two wild animals. She could hardly work when she realized that Lena had decided to nap after her sexual encounter with her son. She wondered if this sort of thing was against the law. She knew it was against God's law. What would

Papa do when he got her letter? Finally she saw Lena come out of the bedroom and pick up the milk pails and head for the barn.

Etta Mae ran from the house the minute Lena was out of sight taking a small valise with her. She held the letter to Papa in her hand and continued to run as fast as she could, stopping only to catch her breath now and then. She stopped within sight of the little garden gate that led to the front of the house. It was a quaint little cottage with a bed of flowers on each side of a flagstone walk. The beauty Etta now saw did not deter her in her mission. She banged loudly on the front door once, twice and three times. Nothing! She waited and was about to bang on the door again when the door slowly opened. A little woman in a deep brimmed dust bonnet appeared. The woman seemed to be about sixty years of age, with white hair peeping out from under the bonnet. She seemed almost frightened.

"Who are you and what do you want?" The little woman asked in a heavy accent of German in her English. Etta Mae could hardly speak, but breathlessly did so.

"I'm Etta Mae Dickerson and I need your help. Please help me! Please." Just at that moment another little woman appeared at the door.

"What is it, child?" What on earth is the matter?" This woman was a bit younger than the other and seemed genuinely concerned.

"Come in, come in. Tell us, what is the matter? I'm Annie Brandt and this is my sister, Bernadette." Etta Mae caught her breath and tried to explain.

"I need to get this letter to my parents so they will come for me. Can you help me please? And I need a place to stay until they come. I'm in danger."

"Danger?" Annie Brandt asked curiously.

"Yes, I married William Meinschein, your neighbor, but I didn't know what awful trouble I was getting into. They are awful people. The mother and the brothers are vile creatures, and my husband William is letting them work me to death, not to mention all the other horrible things that are taking place over there." Annie Brandt frowned now but looked at Etta Mae with great concern.

"I'm sorry, but you cannot stay here. Those people will find you and make us pay for helping you. We can and will mail your letter to your parents though."

"Oh, what am I to do?" Etta Mae cried for she was more frightened than ever. If Lena and the boys missed her, God only knew what they would do to her. Annie could see how frightened this young girl was and wished she could do more for her, but knew she must not. She had her own run-in with that horrible Meinschein woman.

"You must go home quickly, before they find you gone. I'll take your letter and mail it first thing in the morning. That's all I can do." She had taken Etta Mae back to the door.

"Before you go, just one more thing; Lock yourself in your room and don't come out. That's what I would do. Take some food with you and conveniences and don't come out until your folks come for you. I've heard what goes on in that house!" With this bit of advice she let Etta Mae out and closed the door. Etta Mae hesitated but a moment and then ran all the way back to the house, crying as she ran. Hopefully, she thought, she had not been missed. What if she had? Oh, God help me now, she prayed. She flew into the back door of the kitchen and found that no one was in the house. Relief overcame her for a moment and then she began to fly around the kitchen to get the food ready for the evening meal.

Milking was over and Etta saw the boys and their mother coming in to eat. She shivered from the thought of having to look at any of them and decided that she would not. She was glad that she was not allowed to eat at the table with them. She could not have stood it. William came into the kitchen and forced her to kiss him. She decided that she would go along with him for now and get through the night. Maybe she could make it through another night without the boys touching her. She had to bide her time, for it would take a couple of days for the letter to get to her folks. And then it happened. She started her monthly menses. She thanked God that she was not in the family way, and begged him to let her period last the usual six or seven days. Surely Papa would get there by then.

Six days passed and still no Papa. Etta thought her time had indeed run out. Her period was over and she knew that anytime the brothers would come into their room and commit their indecent act upon her. What could she do? William would not help her for his mother had made him promise that he would share his wife's body with his brothers, or she would cut him out of her will and he would get nothing when she died. Then she remembered. "Lock yourself in your room. That's what I would do." I'll take a big piece of ham, a couple of apples and a couple of biscuits tomorrow. Surely, Papa would be here by then. Etta Mae was talking to herself and making preparations to hide some food in her and William's room. I'll carry this stuff up with a stack of the linens that I washed and William won't be any wiser of what I'm doing. Also, I will be as sweet as I possibly can muster up toward William tonight and maybe he will not let his brothers in our room.

Etta Mae slipped her free hand around William's waist as they ascended the stairs, preparing to go to bed. She had promised him a night of "pure heaven", she had said to him. William thought he knew what she meant and he could not wait to go to bed. He was even very loving toward Etta Mae, but all of Etta Mae's plans vanished into the night when they found that Alfred and Henry were already in their room. They had plans of their own for the little Miss Etta Mae. Their mother had told them that they were free to bed their sister-in-law down anytime they saw fit. "She still is not in the family way and you boys have to help your brother get me a grandchild."

William and Etta Mae stood frozen for a minute knowing what the brothers were about to do. Etta Mae's heart skipped a couple of beats and then she bolted out of the room and ran down the hall and locked herself in. Trembling all over she wondered, could she hold them off? Would they knock the door down or break the lock somehow? She quickly moved the trunk and chest of drawers up against the door just in case and threw herself down on the bed and sobbed herself to sleep.

Lena had heard the boys cussing and banging on the door of the room demanding Etta Mae to come out, so she climbed the stairs to see what all of the commotion was about. The noise had subsided somewhat when she reached the room. There on the bed she found her three sons half naked in their underwear swigging on the bottle of some home brew. They had far too much by this time and were pretty tipsy. They looked at their mother and invited her into the room.

"Where is your wife, William?" Lena was somewhat perplexed with them.

"She flew the coop. The three of us frightened her and she went down the hall and locked herself in." Henry burped as he slurred out the words. Alfred laughed loudly and beckoned his mother to the bed but she was all business now.

Etta Mae was awakened by the loud banging on the door. It was William and he was very angry as his mother had demanded he make his wife come out and make breakfast for all of them. The fact be known; he did not want his brothers having any part of his wife, but his mother was relentless.

"Etta Mae, let me in. I'm your husband. Unlock this door now!" William waited a few seconds and when she did not answer he banged on the door harder.

"I said, let me in. I have rights, you know. All I want is for you to come down and fix breakfast. Maw is on a real rampage." Etta breathed a long sigh and then answered.

"No, I won't unlock this door, and I won't come out, never, ever again. You are all beasts. I never want to see any of you again. Let your mother fix her own breakfast. I am not your slave. Go away." She began to cry again and William softened his plea, he did not know just what his mother would do to him is he didn't get Etta downstairs.

"Come on, unlock the door. I won't let my brothers touch you. You have to get breakfast ready. Maw is in a fit of temper but breakfast might help calm her down." William was remembering how his mother had whipped him with a buggy whip once for not minding her, and he knew that she would not hesitate in whipping him and Etta Mae as well.

"Etta Mae come on out and fix our breakfast. I'll take the boys to the barn as soon as they eat so as not to bother you. Maw will break the door down if you don't, and horsewhip you with the buggy whip."

"William, I will come down on one condition. All of you have to go to the barn and milk the cows while I fix breakfast. I will watch for you all to go to the barn and then I will come down, but, if anyone comes back toward the house, I will lock myself back in." Etta Mae grabbed her clothes as she waited for William's answer.

"Okay," he said sullenly "I'll see if I can get Maw to do it this way. She is mad as a hornet about last night, but I'll try." Etta waited and then she heard his footsteps getting lighter and lighter, then she ran to the window to see if all of them really were going to the barn. William told his mother what Etta Mae said and he thought for a minute she was going to explode, but she didn't. She calmed down and said, "We'll do it, but just you wait until after we eat. I'm going to whip that little Injun until she can't ever walk again. She won't be able to run away again." With those words, she grabbed her hat and led the boys out to the barn.

Etta Mae flew down the stairs and around the kitchen; baking biscuits, frying meat and eggs, setting the table and eating bits and pieces as she worked. She looked out of the window often making sure that none of the boys, or Lena, were coming back up to the house. Just as she started to fix herself a plate she saw Lena coming toward the house, carrying a large leather whip.

She poured herself a cup of coffee and bounded up the stairs and locked herself back in the room. Breathless, she leaned against the door terrified to think she had to stay in this house another day. Where was Papa? Maybe he didn't get her letter. What in the name of God was she going to do? William said Lena would break the door down and horsewhip her. She prayed and prayed to the Creator to help her and then wrapped herself in a heap of bed clothing. She vowed to herself that she would never give up no matter what Lena did. She would rather die first.

She waited for William or Lena to come and break the door down but she heard nothing. Several hours passed and then she heard loud banging beneath her window. She looked out and saw the brothers raising a huge ladder just below the window to her room. She knew now their plan was to climb in the window and hurt her. She was doomed, she thought. She ventured a peep out of the window and saw Lena standing at the bottom of the ladder and saw the boys mounting the steps. William was outside her door pleading with her now.

"Etta Mae, please come out of the room. I won't let them hurt you. Really, I was just kidding about Maw whipping you. She ain't mad at you anymore since you fixed breakfast, so come on out and we will spend the day in our room together."

"Never, never will I come out and if your brothers try to come through my window I'll hit them in the head with the big water pitcher and the wash bowl! I will try to kill them! Get away from my door! I hate you! You are all evil!" Etta Mae was screaming at the top of her voice and she meant every word she uttered. She now took the pitcher and the washbowl over to the window and waited to hit the boys one at a time when they raised the window. Hopefully, if she hit them hard enough they would fall off the ladder.

Etta Mae placed herself just to the side of the window and got ready to swing the pitcher. As she looked out the window to see how far up the ladder the boys had come she saw a wonderful sight. She saw a big black carriage flying into the yard with three men holding shotguns. It was Papa, Uncle Kip and Uncle Greyfox. They had come just in time to save her. Etta Mae sank to the floor nearly fainting.

Ben and the two Uncles jumped out of the carriage and aimed their guns at Lena and the two brothers on the ladder.

"Don't any of you move, or we'll blow your brains out! Where are my daughter and William? Where is your other son, Lena?" Ben walked closer to Lena as he spoke sharply to her. "You two up there come down off that ladder and don't try anything funny. We got a gun on each of you and we'll use it. Right boys?"

William had not seen or heard the carriage arrive and was still standing outside Etta Mae's door, begging her to unlock it. She was not hearing him now, but pulling the dresser and trunk away from the door to let her Papa in or at least so she could get out. William had given up and was making his way down the stairs where he opened the door and saw the three men holding shotguns on his mother and brothers. He attempted to close the door and hide, but Greyfox was too quick for him. He grabbed William by the shoulder and dragged him out of the house screaming in a loud voice to Ben.

"I got this no good William, Ben! Then shaking William back and forth like a rag doll, he marched him over to stand by his mother.

"Where is Etta Mae?" Ben now demanded as he shoved the gun a little closer to Lena's face. "You no good cow, you had better answer me!" Ben's face was livid with rage as he looked back and forth from Lena to William.

"I said- where is my daughter?" William stuttered with fright as Ben turned the gun on him.

"She, she's upstairs locked in a room. We were only trying to get her out!" Greyfox backed both Lena and William over to stand against the house, and then withdrew a knife with a long sharp blade out of his pants. He let it flash in the sun before he spoke.

"I've got these bastards covered, Ben. Go upstairs and find Etta Mae, I'll take care of these varmints. Keep them ornery critters right there on the ladder for now, Kip, but shoot to kill if they make one move." Ben took the stairs two at a time calling Etta Mae's name all the while. Etta Mae rushed out of the room and into her father's arms, sobbing and trying to talk all at the same time.

"They took most of my clothes and put them somewhere. That old witch hid them. She said I would never need them again. Oh Papa, I was so afraid you wouldn't get here in time. These people here are all evil. They wanted me to do horrible things, just like they've been doing!"

"Hush, daughter, it's all over now. Your Uncles and me came to take you home as soon as we got your letter. You are safe now. Come downstairs with me, we will get your things. Ben was stroking Etta Mae's hair and hugging her fiercely to reassure her.

"Come daughter, Papa will walk you downstairs. I'll see to it you get all your things and all the things that woman took from you."

Ben walked Etta Mae out the back door past Lena and William to the carriage. Once seated in the carriage he walked back to Lena, took her by the arm and marched her into the house.

"You no good cow! You get all of my daughter's things together and be quick about it Make sure you get the trunk and the things in it that you took away from her. Move!" Ben shoved the shotgun right into Lena's ribs as he urged her back up the stairs.

Greyfox marched William over beside Kip and ordered the boys on the ladder to come down, slowly. Once down, Greyfox and Kip tied each one of the boys to a separate tree. They were all too scared to resist or utter a word. This done, they checked on Etta Mae, then entered the house to help Ben. The two men helped tie up Lena and stuffed some rags in her mouth to stop her screaming. She tried to kick the men but was of little use as they had complete control over her. Etta's valises were carried downstairs, and Kip and Greyfox loaded them into the carriage. Ben turned his attention to Lena and later to the boys, especially William.

"Don't ever let me see anyone of your faces again. If you ever come near my home or Etta Mae, I will hunt you down and skin you like the pigs you are. You William, I gave you credit for being better than your Mother, but I see you are weak and just as evil as she is. I will go to a lawyer tomorrow and have this marriage annulled, just like it never happened. If I ever hear of you mentioning that you were married to Etta Mae you will regret it the rest of your life. It never happened! Do you understand me?" William was trembling all over. He had never seen anyone so angry, except maybe when his mother had whipped him with the horsewhip. Knowing that this man was Indian, he knew that Ben meant every word he said. Stuttering, he answered Ben.

"Yes, yes sir! I, I will never tell a soul. Neither will my mother or brothers. Did, did, you tell my mother about the annulment?" William was now shaking uncontrollable.

"Yes I did. I told her the same as I told you, and I will do as I said!" With these words, Ben turned and leaped into the carriage beside Etta Mae. Greyfox whirled the carriage around and took off down the lane to the main road, never to set eyes on any of the Meinscheins again.

NR

CHAPTER THIRTEEN

HOPE FOR ETTA MAE'S MATURITY

Etta Mae was so traumatized and humiliated by her ill fated marriage to William Meinschein, she refused to talk to anyone except her parents, and her sister Rose. She stayed in her room for days on end, eating very little, and crying most of the time. Whenever her Papa made her come to the table to eat, she would sit with her face downcast and toyed with her food. Grandma Jane would try to talk to her but she would just get up from the table, run to her room and cry hysterically. Dovie was so busy taking care of the small children she did not go after her or try to console her. She knew her humiliation, for she had suffered the same when J.P. had left her when Rosie was but a tiny baby.

After several days of this behavior, Morning Star (Grandma Jane), decided she must speak with Etta's parents about the situation. The children had gone to bed so Morning Star asked Ben and Dovie to come to the great fireplace to hold council.

"We must talk about Etta Mae, my daughter, and son. As her parents you cannot allow her to sulk in her room any longer. It has been long enough, Ben, for her to face up to her actions and shoulder the consequences. She must get on with her life. She is making everyone's life miserable, especially the younger children. They don't understand at all what is wrong with her. It is time for you to take Etta Mae to Henderson and get the marriage done away with, like it never happened." Morning Star was emphatic. Ben and Dovie shook their heads in agreement.

"You are right as always, Grandma Jane. I only hope Etta Mae has learned a lesson and stops being so head strong. I know it is really our fault we have pampered her too much." Ben rubbed his new growth of beard, rose and stood beside his mother-in-law, then took her hand in his.

Looking into her eyes beseechingly, he spoke again. "You are right. It is time to put an end to this. Dovie and I will take her to the justice tomorrow and we want you to come with us. We need your help."

"Yes Mama, you are so wise. Ben is right, we will go tomorrow." Dovie eyes glistened with tears as she spoke to her mother. She rose from her chair and put her arms around Morning Star, and then helped her climb the stairs. Ben also rose and placed an arm around her waist and acted as if he would bodily carry her up, but she would have none of it.

"Stop this, Ben; I only need your help. I need to keep moving so I don't get so stiff." Morning Star giggled, and then looked at her son-in-law and daughter totally embarrassed.

Ben and Dovie rose earlier than usual the next morning and scurried to finish their chores. Then they woke Etta Mae and Rosie and told them to dress for a trip to Henderson. Etta Mae tried to protest but Ben would hear none of it. When she started crying and saying she didn't want to go anywhere, Ben stood his ground.

"Etta Mae, I don't want to hear anymore. Get up and get dressed. You are going with me and your mother. We have very important business to attend to. Wipe your tears away, this is a new day." With these words Ben left both girls wondering what their father meant.

Etta Mae tried to plead with Rosie but Rosie said she didn't want to hear anymore about her shame of having married William. Etta kept babbling about her disgrace but reluctantly started her toiletries. Her Papa had spoken rather sharply to her, she thought. This was indeed a very rare thing. He may have done this once or twice before, so she had best do as he said.

Grandma Jane had also risen earlier than usual and was making breakfast as the girls came downstairs fully dressed in their white batiste waistcoats and ankle length dark blue skirts. Rosie was all smiles, but Etta Mae was sulking a bit with her head down, refusing to look at anyone. Dovie had gone to her room to finish dressing for town, so Ben felt it necessary to explain the trip before them.

"Come girls, sit down with me. I want to talk to you for a minute. Grandma you come her and sit with us."

"I'm not hungry, Papa." Etta whined.

"It doesn't matter, my dear, you will put some food in your stomach. The trip we are about to make will take all day I'm sure, maybe longer." Etta Mae looked at Ben now for her interest had been peaked.

"Whatever is so important that it might take more than a day?" Rosie queried, and Etta Mae looked from her sister to her father and then to Rosie for an answer.

"Your mother and grandmother, and I as well, feel we have waited long enough to take care of canceling your marriage." Etta Mae gasped, and tried to speak, but Ben cautioned her to silence. "If it is not done now we nay not be able to get it annulled as they say. You have been through much but it is time to let it go, daughter." Ben's voice was soft and compelling and brought tears and sobs from Etta, but it did not deter him from his purpose. "I also know that you are embarrassed about the choice you made. That of course will take some time to get over. We all believe though that getting the annulment will help you to be able to heal your wounded soul."

"Oh, Papa, I'm so ashamed! I'm ruined for life. No man will want to marry me now!" Etta Mae sobbed.

Morning Star now rose and came to Etta's side. Taking her chin in her hand she raised Etta's face so she could look into her eyes as she spoke.

"My darling child, and this is what you are. You only made a mistake. Not just you, but all of us. We all wanted you to have whatever you wanted, and did not take the time to look into these horrible people's existence. It is not all your fault, we must bare some of the burden of guilt," Morning Star hesitated and kissed Etta on the cheek and then continued.

"Your Papa and Mama, as always, want what is best for you. So today you will dry your eyes, get the annulment and never look back, only forward to the rest of your life. As to your not every getting married, it is not so. You are a beautiful girl and you will have many offers. This time you must be certain of your feelings within your heart, not the wishes of your mind. I have talked with White Feather of this. Now eat, and think no more of shame, for it is not for you to bear, but for your offenders." Morning Star patted Etta Mae to comfort her, gave Rosie a hug and sat back down and finished her breakfast.

Etta Mae stared at her grandmother for a ling time and wondered at the relief she felt. The fault was not all hers. She began to eat with an appetite she had not felt for weeks. As she ate she thought - Grandma spoke to Grandpa White Feather about me. Then it must be so, the fault was not hers alone.

Dovie and Ben smiled at each other as they watched Etta Mae reach for another biscuit and butter.

Everyone sat nervously listening to the proceedings presented to Judge Miller. The Judge listened patiently as barrister Fine stated the case for annulment. He studied the charges, and then studied Etta Mae. She was shaking and on the verge of tears again. Ben and Dovie kept patting her to comfort her. Rosie also hastened to try and comfort her sister, but she could not keep back her own emotions, and voiced her opinion to the Judge.

"And, just who are you young lady?" Judge Miller spoke with much impatience for the interruption to his thoughts. Rosie had not meant to speak out and now stood red faced as she answered.

"I'm Rosie Dickerson. Etta Mae's older sister. We share a room, and I know how hard all of this is for her." Rosie blushed even deeper.

"Perhaps I should talk to you. I believe there is more to this than the papers say. Come with me Rosie, where we can have a private talk." The Judge rose and motioned her to follow him.

Etta Mae collapsed into her chair and covered her mouth with her hand. She knew Rosie would tell the Judge all the sordid details that she had told her. Ben and Dovie were too stunned to speak but sat holding each other's hands, in silence.

Rosabelle, never lost for words, now spewed out all the details that Etta had told her about those evil Meinscheins. Such a delicate subject was hard to approach, but she did. As soon as she mentioned the mother had said Etta had to lay with all her sons, and that she, the mother, was lying with her older son and sleeping in the same bed with the younger one, the Judge held up his hand to silence Rosie.

"Say no more, young lady, the motion is granted. You can be assured I will have this looked into. Go back to your parents while I finish signing these papers.

The annulment was granted that day and true to his words, Judge Miller had the family brought in on charges. Soon after that, William and Henry joined the Army. The older brother threatened to leave the farm too. Gossip had it that Lena had a nervous breakdown and was placed in a hospital somewhere, to undergo treatment. The rumor was that the hospital was for the insane.

"Lest your sins will find you out."

The little family arrived back at the Star Farm to be greeted by all it's inhabitants. Grandma Jane (Morning Star) had gathered the families together to make a celebration for Etta Mae's deliverance. It was a happy gathering and Etta gave all the credit to Rosie, for the speedy annulment. Rosie said, "All I did was tell the real truth to the Judge. No fancy legal words, just the horrible things those people were doing."

Etta Mae, still embarrassed at her actions managed to get through the day, but it was noticeable that she no longer demanded that her every wish be fulfilled. She had grown somewhat a little closer to maturity.

WALKING ON

Etta Mae and Rosie followed their grandmother up the stairs helping her as she struggled to make each step. The pain was so great now for Morning Star that she had taken to smoking a pipe several times a day to get relief from the rheumatism. Ben would hunt out the best cured leaves from his tobacco fields for the nicotine. He even encouraged her to start dipping a little snuff between smokes. She had even concocted an ointment of goose grease and peyote buttons, but still the pain grew even worse. As she struggled up the stairs she decided that Dovie was right, it was time to move her bed downstairs.

Some nights she would sit up all night, because to lay her head down caused her great pain in her spine and much dizziness. Still she didn't complain but beseeched the Creator for relief. She found that the children she loved so much were just too much for her to deal with. She could not help them, and she could not hold them on her lap because of the soreness in her bones. This caused her much agitation and then she would fret.

Dovie and Ben begged her to go to Henderson to a doctor, but she refused. Always she would say that she could doctor herself as well as any doctor. This fact was known, so Dovie and Ben sought out the fresh sage she said might help her. She made a very strong tea which was soothing for a short while, but the disease continued to progress until she could no longer walk. She was so exasperated at the condition she began keeping more and more to herself, meditating. One could hear her calls to White Feather and the Creator most anytime they would be near her room. Ben and Greyfox built onto the back of the house enlarging the room off the kitchen to accommodate her needs. The family all took note that Grandma Jane needed them all to take care of her. She worried about Etta Mae and Rosie's future.

Had she taught them all of the Blackfoot ways, she wondered, so more and more she would hold counsel with all of the children on the farm. She would glean as much information about their lives, loves, their aspirations, then give them the best of her vast knowledge. As the days became months she would need more and more help just to get by in every day life.

Etta Mae and Rosie were assigned the duty of looking after every need Grandma Jane had. She in turn grew more and more impatient with the nagging ever present arthritis. If the girls were not prompt with whatever she needed she would take her wooden cane and bang furiously on the floor for the needed attention. The girls would just laugh for they truly loved their Grandma, as well as all of the members on the farm. Sometimes they felt a little afraid of the revelations she got from the Creator. They were even more in awe of the things she revealed that she said come from their long dead Grandfather, White Feather. Many times they would find their Grandma in a trance-like state, and knew to leave her alone.

Late in Autumn of 1913 Morning Star (Grandma Jane) would call all of her family together to celebrate their wonderful harvest, and to relate a very important message to them. She would tell them after their feast that she had asked the Creator to let her go so she could find White Feather. She said he was waiting for her to come to him, for her work here in Kentucky was nearly done. A great silence filled the room a she spoke, but Dovie and Greyfox knew what her words really meant. Tears filled both of their eyes, as did Ben's. Dovie's lips trembled and her voice cracked as she knelt down by her mother's chair.

"Mama, don't talk this way. You cant' go away yet, we all need you here. We do know you suffer much pain but we are selfish. We wish so to keep you with us a little longer." Dovie ended her plea with a sob that shook all the adults in the room. Morning Star, however, was not deterred.

"Calm yourself, my daughter. It is the way of our Creator. He has spoken his desire, and His words will be honored when it is time. Do not fret but promise to keep the Blackfoot ways and teachings. Remember always who you are for it is an honorable heritage. Let there be news of new life and loves at my passing, for I'm only crossing over to another life. Now let me return to my room to rest for it has been a good and happy day." Morning Star seemed spent, so Greyfox hastened to help his mother to her room, with Ben and Dovie close behind.

Early the next morning, Morning Star sent for Etta Mae to come to her room. What on earth could Grandma want of her? she wondered, but heeded her wishes. Etta Mae tried to be cheerful but her Grandmother's speech last night had shaken her as well as the other members of the family. Hesitantly, she greeted Morning Star.

"Good morning, Grandma Jane. How are you feeling this morning? Better I hope." Etta Mae hesitated for her Grandmother's answer.

"I am fine, young lady. Come here close to me for I have to say something to you." Etta indulged her Grandmother, and placed herself close to Morning Star's face.

"Listen to me, my child, you must stop fretting about your mistake and get on with your life. Etta Mae you must marry George. He has the heart of an Indian, he is a good man. You must not tax him unduly. Have your Papa and Mama make the announcement right away. You have waited long enough to know your own mind, and I can tell you not to make him wait any longer. A year for the engagement is a long time for a man. Speak of this today. Let your parents tell George for he will be so happy at this news. You must be married soon; it is my last wish for you, and for our family. Go now and tell your mother, it is my last wish." Somewhat stunned at her Grandmother's words, Etta bent and kissed Morning Star and quietly left her room.

Etta Mae entered the kitchen where her mother was drying dishes and repeated the words her Grandmother had just said. Dovie dropped the dish she was drying and grabbed Etta Mae and practically pushed her out of the door with urgency as she spoke.

"Go to the barn and fetch your father. Tell him to stop whatever he is doing and come to the house. Run Etta Mae!" Etta could not conceive why such urgency was needed, but Dovie again urgently repeated her words.

"Go, run Etta Mae, get your father. I must go to my mother now, hurry child!" Etta Mae was breathless as she conveyed the words of her mother to Ben. Ben seeing the alarm on Etta Mae's face, he grabbed her by the hand and ran to the house.

As Ben and Etta Mae entered Morning Star's room she held up her arm and beckoned them to her bedside. Dovie was already there with Rosie. They now stood on either side of the bed.

"Come in Ben," Morning Star uttered in a whisper. "Come here to me one last time. I want you to know that you have been our salvation, here on this earth, and I want to thank you for it. PEACE is mine now. I leave my family to you now for their safe keeping. Remember to keep our Blackfoot ways and teach all of the little ones what is the right path for them to take." With this her last whisper, Morning Star closed her eyes and went to sleep for the last time in Kentucky.

Grandmother Morning Star was laid to rest in the little cemetery on the farm with a head marker that read:

Here lies Morning Star Little Dog White Feather
1850-1915
An undaunted spirit and an Unconquered Blackfoot Heart

Grief stricken, the entire farm turned out for her Indian burial, as well as most of the neighbors from miles around. Little White Dove Flying, Benjamin Dickerson, Grey Fox, Golden Eagle, Bull Bear, and Kip Mackenzie wrapped her body in the Blackfoot burial winding cloth and laid it to rest on the bosom of Mother Earth. Then as was the custom, Many Waters danced and chanted the mournful burial song. Dovie and Grey Fox would follow their tradition and visit their mother's grave every day and pray for their mother's safe journey to the great Creator. Sadly they would return to their homes each day but this was about to change.

A few weeks passed and on a bright Sunday morning a fancy carriage, carrying one lone passenger, arrived at the farm. It did not stop at the main house, as was the custom for most visitors, but continued down the hill and stopped at Grey Fox's.

NEW HOPE

THE CARRIAGE WAS DRIVEN BY A MAN DRESSED IN A DARK SUIT AND A TALL BLACK HAT, AND SEEMED TO KNOW JUST WHERE HE WAS GOING. DOVIE AND BEN WERE OVERWHELMED WITH CURIOSITY. SO WERE ETTA MAE AND ROSIE. WHO COULD IT BE, AND WHY DIDN'T THE CARRIAGE STOP AT THEIR HOUSE? THEY WONDERED. PRESSURED BY HIS WOMEN FOLKS, BEN DONNED HIS HAT AND SET OFF FOR GREY FOX'S CABIN. AS HE APPROACHED THE CABIN HE SAW THE CARRIAGE AGAIN, AND KNEW THAT HE HAD NEVER SEEN IT AT THE FARM BEFORE. GREY FOX HAD SEEN BEN COMING TO THE HOUSE AND NOW STOOD IN THE DOORWAY.

"Come in, brother, come in." Ben stepped inside, and to his surprise, there sat George Henry Hutchinson, hat in hand, smiling. George hastened to his feet and offered his hand to Ben. Grey Fox could not contain a grin of pleasure.

"Well, howdy, George. What a surprise to see you. Why didn't you stop at the house?" Ben asked.

"Sir, I thought it not appropriate. I wanted to talk to Grey Fox to verify what I had heard was really true about those awful people in St. Phillips." George turned bright red now as he thought about what Etta Mae had been through. "I didn't know if Etta Mae was really back home, and if she is free." George had difficulty uttering the last few words. His face now matched his curly red hair.

"Well like they say, bad news travels fast. Etta Mae is home and we have had the marriage annulled. She had been through Hell, but she is doing much better now. I'm sure she would want to see you, but honestly George, I think it is a bit too soon." Ben tried to not show his true feelings of utter delight in seeing George was still interested in Etta Mae.

"Well sir, you know best." George hesitated and then he said that which he should have said long ago. "Sir," George stammered a bit, "Sir, I love Etta Mae, and I've been a fool not to talk to you long ago. I wish to marry her is she will still have me. I realize it's too soon to speak to her of this matter, but I do want your answer."

"I'm glad George, that you have finally spoken your mind. I wondered if you were serious and like Etta Mae, I'm afraid I thought you weren't." Grey Fox said sincerely.

"I know, sir, and you have every right to feel that way. In my stupid way I thought I needed to make myself more worthy of Etta, so I was over in Indiana building our house. Before I asked to marry her I wanted everything just right, and I lost her. I don't want that to happen again." George finished on a very nervous note and Grey Fox stepped in to ease the conversation a bit.

"You must need a cup of coffee George, to settle your nerves. It's not easy to admit one's mistakes. Etta Mae had finally admitted hers by seeking the annulment." Grey Fox handed George a steaming cup of coffee from the old granite pot that always sat on the stove.

"Thank you Grey Fox. I really do need this!" George tried to laugh but he laughter never came. He was grateful that Rose Marie had now entered the room smiling and bidding him a fond hello.

"My, my, what is going on in here?" George, ever the gentleman, rose from his chair and greeted her.

"It is my pleasure to see you again, Miss Rose Marie. You are looking well. How are the children, fine I hope?

"Yes, we are all just fine. How about you? I'm hoping you are here to see Etta Mae." Rose Marie could sometimes be as forward as her mother, Annie Lee.

"In a way you are right, but mainly I'm here to ask Mr. Dickerson if I can marry Etta Mae." George blurted out the words which were coming easier now for him to say.

"I appreciate what you have been saying, George, but I still think Etta Mae is not ready to think of marriage again." Ben had to stop and clear his throat, for he really thought that this was just what she needed.

"Ben I, I think this is just what she needs right now. She needs to know that George has asked you for her hand. You know she feels terrible about her mistakes." Rose Marie was convincing and George flashed her a smile of gratitude.

"I guess I'm out numbered. We must form a plan George. I think you should let me tell her that you asked to see her again. I want to tell her you have asked if you could marry her sometime in the future. I know that she needs a lot of time before that day. It could take a year.

"Whatever you think, sir, I'm ready to do. I will come back in a couple of weeks to get her answer. If she agrees, I will start the formal courting. Here, let me show you the ring I bought for her. When the time comes we can be engaged. You will know when she is ready." George blushed again as he fished the ring box out of his pocket.

"My, you are serious! Take a look everyone, it's a beauty." Ben handed the box to Etta's Uncle Grey Fox who let out a shrill whistle.

"She will just love it, George. It's her birthstone isn't it?" Rose Marie exclaimed.

"Yes, I believe it is." George felt pride in himself as Ben gazed at the ring.

"Mr. Dickerson, I do not want an engagement party. I just want to see Etta about once or twice a month at first, if that is fine with you and her mother. When the time comes, we can have a marriage celebration.'

"That will be just fine and I think Etta Mae and her mother will agree. Her mother will probably insist on an Indian Ceremony too. Grey Fox and Rose Marie are good at planning this, so beware." Ben chuckled now relieved that this jolly Irishman still wanted to marry his darling Etta Mae.

"I best be going back to the house before the women come after me. Have a good trip home, George. I'm pleased that you have come here and stated your feelings. Come back when you feel ready." Ben clasped George's hand, gave Grey Fox and Rose Marie a hug and made his way back to the main house, whistling as he went. Morning Star is right as always, the Creator will take care of everything that he thinks is best.

Curiosity was about to overcome Dovie and Myrtle as Ben entered the back door. They practically pulled him inside the kitchen door and began quizzing him immediately.

"Who was in that carriage Ben?" Dovie asked first. "Why didn't they stop here first, as most people do?" Ben could not help but be amused by the questioning.

"Hold on, ladies. I'll tell you something incredible. Where are Etta Mae and Rosie?"

"Upstairs looking after the baby and playing with the little Boss. Why do you ask? I can see that you are excited about something. What is it, Ben?" Dovie and Myrtle looked at each other puzzled.

"Well, you are not going to believe what I'm about to tell you. Come into the parlor where we can talk without the girls hearing us." Ben moved as he spoke, with both ladies following him like two curious cats.

"Okay Ben, what is this unbelievable news?" Dovie asked impatiently. "Yes Papa, why are you being so secretive?" Myrtle was now frowning at Ben.

"The visitor to Grey Fox's was none other than George Hutchinson." Ben said.

"What! Oh, what did he want?" Dovie cried in shock. "Did he have to come here now? I hope Etta doesn't find out, she will be mortified to death!" Dovie was exasperated.

"Shush, Mother, let Papa tell us what he knows," Myrtle cautioned.

"Dovie, George came here to find out from Grey Fox if the rumors were true that he had heard from the storekeeper, Gerber. Wait is it good news," Ben could see the frustration mounting in Dovie's eyes. "When I went down there he was down right pleased because he didn't want to come here until he knew everything was as it is. He said he had been stupid for not asking for Etta Mae, and now he had come to do so." Dovie clasped her hand across her chest and uttered softly;

"Oh my God. My God, so soon." Ben hastened to cajole Dovie.

"I told him it was too soon and he agreed. He said he wants to court Etta, and marry her if she will consent. I told him we would talk to her and that it might take a year." Dovie was nodding now in agreement.

"You are wise Ben, she must take her time. No more rushing into anything. I'm glad the man has not let his imagination blind him to what it is he really wants." Dovie looked upward and muttered her thanks to the Creator for his welcomed news.

"All the time he spent not coming to see Etta, he was making himself more suitable for marriage to her. He was and is building a house for the two of them. He said that it is near Mt. Vernon on land that he owns."

"That is good, but when does he plan on coming back to see Etta Mae himself?" Dovie asked with a bit of impatience.

"In a couple of Sunday's. Whenever he feels he is ready to start the courting. Anyway, it is to see if she has any feelings for him. We must sit Etta down tonight and tell her of this. Oh, by the way, he has bought her a beautiful ring that is her birthstone, to show his intentions. You know, she threw the one William gave her, away. Out the upstairs window she said, she flung it." Ben's voice was now mixed with chuckles.

"Yes, she said she couldn't stand to look at it." Dovie answered.

"Couldn't' look at what, Mama?" Etta Mae carrying Lela had come down the stairs and heard only the end of her mother's statement. "She couldn't stand what? Who are you talking about?" Etta did not wait for an answer before continuing. "Papa, who was in the handsome carriage that went to Uncle Grey Fox's cabin?" Ben sat motionless for a long moment, gathering his thoughts as to how to tell her the news. He had hoped she had not seen who was in the carriage, and now he wished she had. Best he thought, to just spit it out.

"Never mind what you mother just said. We do have something to discuss with you, so come and sit down with your mother and me." Ben took little Lela from Etta's arms and handed her to Dovie. Etta Mae frowning slightly seated herself beside her mother. Sensing something of great importance was about to be spoken, Etta waited for her father to speak. Ben cleared his throat, looked first at Dovie and then Etta Mae.

"This visitor at your Uncle Grey Fox's was of great importance to all of us, but especially for you daughter." Etta Mae sat up straight in her chair now and looked from her mother to her father. A look of anticipation crossed her brow, but she dared not to interrupt. "You see our visitor was none other than George Hutchinson!" Etta Mae gasped and started to rise from her seat, but her mother placed a hand on her shoulder to stop her. Etta Mae was visibly shaken and could no longer contain her outburst.

"What did he want? I knew he would never want to see me again. He must hate me for he didn't even stop at our door to see you and Mama." Tears were now dripping down Etta's cheeks.

"Dry your tears, daughter, for you are wrong. George came to your Uncle to see if you were really back home and free to see him again." Etta Mae looked astounded at her father.

"He, he did? He asked about me?" Disbelief now resonated in her voice.

"Yes he did. It seems he did a little investigation into the Meinscheins with Jake Gerber. He told him about our going after you and bringing you home."

"Oh, Papa, I'm so ashamed. Everyone knows about," Ben interrupted.

"Hush girl. Be thankful we got you out of there!"

"Yes, Etta Mae, let your Papa finish." Dovie scolded as she placed her free arm around Etta Mae.

"Now, to continue; Please don't say anything until I have finished. What I have to tell you deals with the rest of your life. George is a decent and honorable man, and what you thought, and I too thought was indecision on his part, and lack of feelings for you, was all wrong. You see Etta he was gone all that time because he was building a house in Point Township near his brother Ed."

"Oh!" Etta Mae uttered in amazement.

"Yes, I was surprised at that myself. He said he wanted to make himself more presentable for you. He also asked if he might start calling on you again. He will be coming back in a couple of weeks from now for your answer." Ben watched his daughter's face change from amazement to excitement. "Etta Mae, this is your decision alone, so take your time and be sure of what you are doing this time. Don't play games with George, for he has asked for your hand in marriage." Etta Mae's face now registered disbelief at her father's last words, and started to speak. But Ben held his hand up for her to wait until he was finished.

"I gave consent, but I also said it was too soon for you to answer. I also told him that if you choose to see him again, that it might take a year before we feel you could be ready to be sure about marriage again. Your mother and I agree you are not ready to make but one decision now. Do you want George to start courting you again seriously?"

Etta Mae could hardly answer she was so choked up with feelings of elation at the knowledge George still wanted her. She was also overwhelmed with disgust for having not believed his words that he loved her. She knew that she had done something that he really should not forgive her for, but she was ever so grateful that he still wanted her to be his wife. What a true gentleman George is, she thought. He does not consider me damaged goods like some people might. The love she felt for him now welled up in her heart but she knew Papa was right; she was not ready for marriage. Etta Mae sat in silence for what seemed like an eternity to Dovie and Ben. They were pleased that Etta did not rush her decision and breathed a sigh of relief when she finally spoke.

"Mama, Papa, you are right. I'm not ready to step into marriage. I've put all of my family and George through so much misery. My own selfishness caused the entire problem and I can't begin to say how sorry I am for my past behavior. Please forgive me. I will see George for he is truly the one I've always loved. He must understand I cannot consent to marriage just yet. Papa, you must tell him how I feel because of all the horrible things that happened in that hateful house in St. Phillips. I can't' really speak of it to anyone but Rosie, not now anyway." Etta Mae's voice quivered and had turned to a plea to her parents. Silently Dovie had listened to Etta Mae and realized the importance of the conversation. She had heard her daughter humble herself and admit her mistake. Dovie knew she must speak to reassure her daughter.

"You're a Blackfoot woman who has the right to an honorable husband. One who will care for you and defend your honor. I believe George to be right for you, but learn your lesson well. Never play with a man's feelings again. Be steadfast in your duties as a wife but first you must be his sits-beside-me-wife, or he will stray from your tepee. Forgive me Ben, Father White Feather has spoken to me. He said I must speak as I did to you, Etta Mae, for it is my duty to make sure you understand the ways of a Blackfoot wife, as told to me by your grandmother. So be it, I have spoken."

Etta Mae did not like to be reminded that she was an Indian, but she nodded her head in the affirmative at her mother's words. As Dovie turned to leave the room, Etta Mae stood and embraced her mother and whispered to her.

"Thank you Mama, and thanks to Grandmother and Grandfather White Feather; I will remember your ways and teach them to my children. I love you all, and I will keep your words in my heart always." Etta Mae hugged her mother fiercely, and asked for her blessing. Dovie took Etta Mae's hand in hers and raised the other one toward the sky as she spoke with reverence.

"May the Great Spirit give you the strength and knowledge that you will need for the rest of your life. May it be blessed in many ways; Give this child much happiness and bless her with your love, give her healthy children and grandchildren." Silently, as was her custom, Little White Dove lowered her hand and placed it on her daughter's head. Then looking deep into her daughters eyes she continued. "Go now my child with the honor our Creator will restore in you. Let there never be any reference to your mistake ever again, for as your Grandmother said, 'The fault was not yours alone.' All will be well with you again." Little did anyone guess that this might be the one bit of advice that Etta Mae would hold on to and take strength from, as many changes were about to take place in her life.

Etta Mae would repeat the words her mother had spoken at her marriage to Ben, and her grandmother had spoken when she married White Feather. Etta Mae spoke these words with reverence as her Uncle Grey Fox performed the Sacred Eagle Ceremony. This however, would be the last time she would acknowledge her Indian heritage, publicly.

CHAPTER FOURTEEN

SUDDEN SORROW AND SACRIFICE

A FEW MONTHS AFTER MORNING STAR'S PASSING, DOVIE DELIVERED HER NINTH CHILD, BENJAMIN BANKS DICKERSON. HE WOULD ALWAYS BE KNOWN AS BANKS BY HIS FAMILY AND FRIENDS, ALL OF HIS LIFE.

Ben and Dovie showered all of their children with love and affection, but Morning Star's death left a large hole in their hearts. Dovie and Grey Fox made daily trips to their mother's grave as was the custom of the Blackfoot. Neither of them could let go. They talked endlessly about their mother and their life with their father, White Feather, but their loss was so deep, they each felt very alone in the world. Dovie told Ben over and over that she felt so alone, and that she had no one to guide her. Ben too felt Morning Star's passing but knew that he had to stay strong for Dovie and his children. His answer was to take Dovie across the river to visit with Etta Mae and Rose, but this too proved to be very hard. There was so much work to be done in the tobacco fields tending the livestock and especially the horses. Corn fields had to be planted and tended, and help was short now on the Star Farm, for many of the children had grown, married and left the farm for their own lives. Many of the parents now older had moved with them.

Rosie had married Samuel Farmer, and Ethel threatened to run away if Papa and Mama didn't let her marry Harry, Sam's brother. They tried to tell her that she was much too young to get married but she cried day and night until they relented. This left Myrtle, Lela, Boss and little Banks to care for, and only the help of Many Waters and Golden Eagle to work the horses. Grey Fox was limited to what he could still do because he had inherited his mother's infernal rheumatism, limiting him with his duties.

Nothing seemed to bring Dovie out of her depressed state over her mother's death until little Agnes Marie Hutchinson arrived May 30, 1918. Dovie was there with Etta Mae with the birthing tea that her mother had taught her to use at these times. Marie as she would be called, all of her life, was a beautiful child. Rosy pink and plump, she would steal the hearts of all who saw her. She had her mother's sky blue eyes, light brown hair and a sweet natured disposition. Dovie and Ben were completely captivated by their first grandchild. It was the perfect medicine to bring Dovie back to her own sweet self.

Etta Mae and George were blissfully happy with their precious little girl. Etta Mae took to going to all of the functions where George and his brothers played their music, just to show her darling little girl off to their neighbors. On many of these occasions, George's sisters Ella, Nora, and Audibelle would join them. On one of the nights, Ella and her husband Artie told everyone that they were moving to Arkansas. They said that the place they were going to was just across the river from Malden, Missouri where some of the Van Bibbers lived, including Clarence and Gertie Van Bibber, Etta Mae's brother. They said that they were ready to move just as soon as they finished the paper work for the sale of their farm. They also said they had made the decision because the last flood had nearly wiped them out.

Parts of Kentucky and Indiana were still flooded and it was said that the waters hadn't even reached its crest. Artie also told everyone that he had had it with farming and wanted to find another line of work. He also told everyone that there were good jobs to be had; plenty for everyone who wanted to work in Arkansas and Missouri. Audibelle who had only been married a few months tried to persuade George and Etta Mae to join her and Ella. George and Etta Mae listened to these stories which sounded very interesting to Etta Mae. Their little farm had also suffered a lot of damage from the backwaters, but George had not even considered giving up to the Wabash and the Ohio Rivers. Etta Mae however, began thinking a great deal about Ella and Audibelle's stories. It all sounded like a great adventure to her, and a soon to be tragedy would make it seem even better.

Little Marie was only six months old when a letter from Papa Ben brought sad news, Little White Dove had fallen ill. She had the German measles, and now a cold had come on her that she didn't seem to be able to shake. The doctor said that he was afraid that it would turn into pneumonia. Come home, for your mother is pinning to see you, and your family, and to please tell Rosie. Etta Mae was devastated. Between her sobs she said that they needed to go now, maybe she and Rosie could help out with the younger children, and with their mother.

George and Etta Mae met Rosie and Sam at the ferry in Mt. Vernon, but were told the ferry could not cross for there was too much high water for it to reach land on the Kentucky side. After much consulting, the Captain said he would take them as far as he could; then they would have to go the rest of the way in a skiff. Rosie and Etta were frantic about their mother's health and insisted they make the trip any way they could.

Sam helped George, Rosie and little Marie into the skiff, but decided his weight would nearly sink it, so he returned with the ferry to Mt. Vernon.

George and Rosie took to the oars and paddled the little skiff through the turbulent waters as far as Uniontown. Exhausted from their struggle across the swirling waters they had to stop outside Uniontown. George knew most of the people in this little town, and finally found a friend who took them to The Star Farm and Schoolhouse in Smith Mills.

Ben was thankful that the girls had made the trip arriving just before dark. He cautioned them that their mother was even worse than he had said in his letter. He warned that all was being done for her that the doctor could do. The girls hugged their father and cried softly as they entered their mother's room. Neither girl was prepared for the sight that was now before them.

Dovie was draped in a make shift tent with some foul smelling fumes coming from it. She seemed almost lifeless but recognized her daughters with relief. She had been afraid they would not arrive in time for her to speak to them one last time. All of the children had gathered at their mother's bedside, some with their spouses, some without. Myrtle and Lela had little Banks in control for all he wanted to do was get in bed by his Mama. He tried to break loose every chance he got. Boss and Mae were working in the kitchen and the rest of the farm was trying to keep all the work caught up. Only old Doctor Cronk was in the room when they entered. Torn and tried from their ordeal of crossing the flood waters, Etta and Rosie cried in unison to their mother.

"Mama, Mama, we didn't know you were so sick. Forgive us for not coming sooner." Ben tried to console his daughters but was unable to say a word. Dovie could only whisper her concerns for her family.

"Help your father with the children." They nodded in agreement and looked at the doctor for answers. He motioned for them to follow him into the next room to continue their conversation.

"I'm afraid there is little more I can do. Your mother just can't shake the fever and the inflammation in her lungs. To complicate her condition she now had the infernal influenza. Maybe you didn't know but most of Kentucky is down with it. All any of us can do now is to pray." The doctor shook his head and offered his sympathy as he returned to the sick room.

Etta Mae and Rosie burst into tears again and tried to comfort each other. How could such a thing be happening to their beautiful mother? Neither one could begin to acknowledge that she was so near death. Seeking solace the girls found their siblings who were hiding in an upstairs bedroom. Rosie always the strong one, knew she had to take hold of the situation.

"Come Myrtle; bring Banks and Lela downstairs with us. We will fix you something to eat." The two older girls picked up Banks and Lela and Myrtle followed. The ever practical Rosie busied herself making some chicken soup, vegetables, biscuits and butter and fixed her mother a bowl of soup for Etta to take to her. "Etta, tell Papa to come to the kitchen and eat. I'll bet he hasn't eaten in days."

Etta Mae did as she was told and sat down by her mother and spoon fed her a little of the soup at a time. Dovie could hardly swallow, but she did manage to eat a little. The effort though was almost too much. Her color did seem to brighten a bit as she fell asleep, exhausted from the effort.

Etta and Rosie took turns bathing their mother's brow but the fever raged on. Dovie would awaken and call for Ben to come to her even though he was by her side most of the time. For three days she would sleep intermittently before she slipped into complete delirium. She would call for her mother, and occasionally recognize her children. On the fourth day she rallied for a few minutes recognizing everyone long enough to beg their forgiveness for leaving them, but said she had to go. Then softly and silently she slipped away forever. She was 49 years old and was laid to rest in what is now known as the Smith Mills Cemetery, along side of one of her babies.

Ben was crushed beyond words, as were all of the children. To them all, she had always seemed so invincible. She was never ill nor did she ever complain of any pains even thought she had begun to suffer form the hated arthritis. The older girls wondered what on earth their Papa would do with their little brother and sisters. How could he manage the farm without Dovie and Grey

Fox? Grey Fox was so overwhelmed at his sister's passing, and his mother's death, he and Rose Marie left their cabin and moved to their son's house in Point Township. They knew that Ben would have to find another place to live according to the Blackfoot customs.

Little by little each family that was left, saddened by Dovie's death moved to other places in Kentucky, and Indiana. Ben sold the farm to two different people and bought a small farm just across the river from Mt. Vernon, Indiana. "There," he said he would be closer to Etta Mae and Rosie. Also, after much consultation with all of his children he knew he had to find help to raise the remaining children. Etta Mae and Rosie took turns staying with him but he knew this was not fair to them and their families. The very idea of looking at another woman to take Dovie's place was unthinkable, but he knew he had to do something, especially for the little Banks.

After searching the local papers, and asking everyone he knew if they knew of any lady who might be interested in helping him, it would come quite by accident.

Ben had taken his children shopping for new clothes at the local dry goods store called Rosenbaums. He noticed two ladies in the store and by chance he over heard them say that one of them had to find a job. Ben cautioned his children to mind their manners as he approached the two women.

"Excuse me ladies, but I couldn't help but overhear your words just now about needing a job. My name is Benjamin Dickerson. I'm from just across the Ohio River in Kentucky and I have something you might be interested in." Ben, not used to approaching strange women, now felt slightly embarrassed at his forwardness. The older woman immediately stepped forward somewhat taken aback.

"And sir, just what kind of job do you mean?" Her voice was shrill and defensive. The younger woman recoiled to stand behind the older woman's back, but she was most interested in what the man's answer might be. Ben hurried to explain himself when he realized what he had said might be taken, perhaps, the wrong way.

"Forgive me ladies for the misunderstanding I may have given you. Let me explain. I lost my wife, my children's mother, sometime back and I'm looking for a lady to help me look after them and the house." Ben put emphasis on the word ladies, for he did want someone who could rear his children in a proper manner.

"I see," the older woman exclaimed thoughtfully and then added, "just how many children do you have at home, and what kind of wages are you willing to pay?" She finished in a bit of an indignant tone.

"Five; counting my older daughters who are old enough to help out. The smallest is the little fellow over there. His name is Banks and he misses his mother so much. His sisters look after him now but when they are in school I have to take him with me to do the farm work in the fields. You can understand that that is not too good. I break and raise horses which can sometimes be dangerous for little ones." Ben took a deep breath as he sized up the younger woman, and then added what he could pay.

"I could pay twelve dollars a month and room and board for one woman. Of course children can be a handful, so the job would require a younger woman." Ben felt awkward now and began to stroke his short beard as he looked toward his children who were now patiently watching. What was their father saying to these strange women, they all wondered.

"Of course, Mr. Dickerson, the job we are looking for would be for my daughter, if we should be interested and found the job suitable. I would eventually return to Galveston." Mary Howard's voice had taken on a haughtiness that Ben found repugnant.

"Of course, ma'am, I don't' believe you gave me your name, or the name of your daughter, and I would like the name of your relations you are staying with. Perhaps I know them." As always Ben was straight to the point.

"I'm Mary Howard and this is my daughter, Molly. We are visiting my brother's wife Catherine, who is a school teacher in Mt. Vernon. Do you know them?"

"No, I can't say that I do." Ben was pleased, however, at this bit of news. Molly now moved from behind her mother and addressed Ben.

"I would be interested in the job with your children, Mr. Dickerson. I've had schooling through the eighth grade and two years at Miss Patty's school for girls, in Galveston. I can keep a clean house and cook, but I've had little experience with children. I think I could learn though. Your children seem well behaved." Molly blushed at her own brashness, but she found this man very interesting. She felt he had to be a good person to be indulging his children to shop with him. Too, she sorely needed this job to get out from under her mother's strong grasp.

"Molly!" Mary Howard's voice cautioned her daughter.

"I will make the judgment as to whether this job is suitable for you, or not!" Mary was not accustomed to this forwardness from Molly, and wished to retain the upper hand.

Ben smiled now at Molly realizing that her mother was trying for the best deal she could wrangle out of him. Molly smiled back at him, easing the tension in her face. She relaxed her slender body a bit as she continued to smile at Ben.

Molly Howard was no real beauty. And one could easily tell that she had passed her prime for marriage. Her face was thin like her body; her nose was very slender and a bit long for a girl. Her hair was dark blond, mingled with brown. Her eyes were rather small, but their color was intense gray-green when she smiled, which tended to light up her otherwise drab features. Molly wore her hair straight back from her thin face, just like her mother's, knotted in a small tight bun at the back of her neck. Mary Howard was more hawkish, very tall and thin with slightly graying hair. She wore tiny eye glasses that rested on a slight hump in the middle of her nose. Ben had become accustomed to the ways of the Blackfoot and their trust in people, so he was somewhat taken aback at Mary's next words.

"You must understand Mr. Dickerson that my daughter could not work in your home without me there, or without marriage. Her name would be blemished living in the house with an unmarried man, alone." It was Ben's turn to become a little indignant now.

"Begging your pardon, ma'am, I'm not looking for a wife! I'm looking for a housekeeper! I don't believe her name would be ruined in Kentucky, and she is of an age that she can make up her own mind. I understand you would want to live with us to make sure everything is as I say, and that would be just fine, for awhile. Perhaps we should think on this matter and if you are interested at all, I will come back to town next week to get your answer. Where do your folks live in Mt. Vernon?" To himself Ben thought- "My God, who does this woman think I am, some whoremonger?" Mary Howard's face now felt the sting of almost losing what could be her daughter's salvation so she answered as sweetly as she possibly could.

"My brother's house is 2 blocks west of Main Street between Fourth and Fifth Streets. You can't miss it, for it's the largest house on the block. Three o'clock would be a good time to call." Mary took Molly by the arm now and quickly led her to the front of the store, and disappeared.

Ben was glad to see them leave, but still had the dilemma of trying to get help for his children, and thus far the search had been fruitless. The Howard's were the only possible solution he had found and he wasn't sure about them. He didn't like that Mary Howard, for he could easily see that she dominated Molly, and with no affection.

Ben paid for the merchandise that he and the children had settled on and returned to their buggy. They drove a couple of miles out of town to Rosie and Sam's where they planned to spend the night. Etta Mae and George had written to Ben that they all wanted to get together at Rosie's for Sunday dinner. She had said that they had been missing their family and wanted to spend some time with him and their siblings.

Dinner at Rosie's was always a treat for everyone. She had baked and cooked everything that she knew each one loved. After dinner Ben had the littlest children leave the room while he cautiously told his daughter's of his intentions of hiring someone to look after the children. Both girls seemed surprised, but understood that he needed help. He then told them about his offer to Miss Molly and her mother. Rosie said that she knew of the Howard's and that they were pretty well to do, but she did not know this Molly and Mary.

Etta Mae sat silently for a few minutes. She had been very despondent since her mother's death, and she was very restless. Nothing seemed to please her and she was having a lot of trouble being alone most of the time. There had always been a lot of people around their house in Smith Mills, and she had yet to adjust to the new house across the river. She had even suggested to her father that surely he didn't have to keep the Blackfoot tradition and sell their home. Ben had told her yes, he did have to keep their ways for they were Blackfoot and nothing could change that. He also said that she would remember her promise to Grandma that she should keep their ways, too. Etta had said no more at that time, but she had to speak her mind now.

"Papa you aren't going to hire the two women are you? Is this Miss Molly an Indian? Is she Mama's age? The house is pretty small. How would you make arrangement for two women to live there with you?

"No, I don't plan to hire both ladies. The mother would just stay until she was satisfied that Molly would indeed be safe from me." Ben chuckled, "I know the house is small but I will just sleep upstairs with the children, and no, she is not an Indian, and no, I didn't make mention that we are." Rosie looked at Etta Mae now and did not take her eyes away until she finished speaking to her father.

"Papa we know how hard it has been for you since Mama passed. We both know that no one can take Mama's place in your heart or ours. But we also know that you and Myrtle need help with the younger children. So we say that you are doing the right thing in getting help, and not separating the family. Etta Mae and I could continue taking turns with the two younger children but I know you don't want that, and Mama would not like that arrangement either. You have my blessing. What about you Etta?"

Etta's face now broke into a frown of concern, and her eyes were moist with tears. "Rosie is right as always, Papa. You must do what is right for you and our brother and sisters. Why, oh why, did Mama have to leave us all?" George was quick to comfort Etta Mae and Sam looked on a bit disgruntled. He hated any display of emotion.

Myrtle and Lela protested even the thought of a strange woman in their house, but only to their sisters. By this time both girls were dating and Myrtle was serious about John Johnson. She, more than any of the other children knew her father needed help. Being the oldest left at home, she had to take on the responsibility of the house and the care of her younger siblings. After much consideration she decided Papa had a good idea and agreed to meet with Miss Molly. Etta Mae and Rosie also agreed to accompany their father to meet with her and her mother.

Ben was very nervous as he tapped the knocker on the door of the Howard's house. His stomach felt like jelly and the palms of his hands were wet with perspiration. Was this a mistake, he wondered? He knew he had to have help, but what was Molly's mother going to require of him? As he waited patiently at the door he remembered Banks' cries throughout last night and the many nights before, and sucked in his breath vowing to himself to make the best of it.

The door was finally opened by an elegantly dressed woman of about 60 years of age. As Ben greeted her he searched her face for signs of relationship to Molly and Mary. He found none, and then remembered it was her husband to whom they were related.

Catherine Howard had been a real beauty in her younger years, and still one could readily see she still possessed good looks. She was tall and very slender with very smooth skin and a very warm smile, which she now exhibited as she greeted her visitors.

"Come in, Mr. Dickerson, we have been expecting you."

"Thank you Mrs. Howard. I hope you don't mind that I have brought my three oldest daughters with me. And oh, this is Myrtle who does most of the housework and takes care of little Banks right now. They all want to meet Miss Molly." Ben turned now and touching each girl as he continued.

"This is Rosie Farmer and Etta Mae Hutchinson, and Myrtle." Mrs. Howard smiled at each girl as they in turn half curtsied at the mention of their names.

"It is such a pleasure to meet you and your father. Follow me, Molly and her mother are waiting in our parlor. I will leave you all to get acquainted, and bring in some tea later."

Molly and her mother rose from the rose colored sofa on which they had been seated as Ben began the introduction again.

Rosie and Etta Mae stared at Miss Molly and her mother. Molly was not at all what they had expected. In their minds they had decided that she would look more like their mother, but were now relieved that she did not. She was actually homely they thought, and certainly their Papa was not at all interested in her as a woman. But just as they drew in their breath in relief, Molly smiled at them with kindly eyes. The girls smiled back and politely greeted her mother and then took seats on either side of their Papa. Miss Molly was relieved that here were three girls that were pretty polite. As she looked them over she made a note of their shining black hair, their brown skin, but then she noticed that Etta Mae was not dark, and had big beautiful blue eyes like her father. She rallied from her thoughts as the girls began asking questions.

"Do you have other family besides your mother, Miss Molly?" Rose quizzed.

"No girls. It's just me and mother, and of course the Howard's here."

"Have you ever been married?" Etta meekly asked.

"No, Etta Mae. I have not and of course I have no children, but I like them a lot. I think your brother and sisters are very nice children. I'm sure I can take good care of them. I am educated in my letters, as they say in the South, so I can help the little ones to read and write." Molly felt the need to offer what skills she had. Mary Howard had been silent until now. She felt that Molly was no competition for these two adult girls and Ben, so she thought it time to bring the interview to an end.

"Mr. Dickerson, girls, I believe it is of utmost importance that Molly and I should see your home before we can come to any terms of agreement. Would you not agree to that, Molly?" Molly a little frustrated with her mother only nodded her head in assent.

"That can be arranged. I can take you both across the river today if you wish. There would be room for you valises should you choose to take them. Rosie and Etta won't be going with us."

"Then let it be done. I'm sure Catherine will be grateful to have us out of her house, at least for a little while. Right, Catherine?" Catherine Howard had just entered the room carrying a tray with tiny little cups of tea and some sugar biscuits. She smiled at everyone, but did not answer Mary.

Ben looked at Mary and thought she seemed a little too eager, but again he remembered Bank's cries in the night. He needed a woman to take care of him. Rosie, Etta and Myrtle looked at each other with a bit of concern. Molly seemed alright but they did not like her mother. She was too bossy.

Ben and the two women arrived at Ben's farm just as the sun was setting behind the big horse barn. As the carriage came to a stop beside the big front gate, Ben's smaller children ran to meet him. They all stopped short on seeing two strange women seated in their father's carriage, and then ran to fall into their sister Myrtle's arms.

Mary Howard was disappointed as she surveyed Ben's little bungalow. It was a typical house in these parts where the Ohio River flooded most every year in the spring and sometimes in the fall. The little house set high off the ground approximately four feet to keep the flood waters out of the house. The space underneath the house was used as a storage area for toys, hoes, racks and other needed garden implements. The house itself had three small rooms and a large kitchen downstairs with two bedrooms upstairs. The bedrooms upstairs were very large and accommodated the children very well. There were no toilet facilities inside, except for a pump at the kitchen sink. Everyone in that area called it a 'Bottoms House'. The soil was rich and the crops were better than in non-flooding areas from the silt the flood waters left behind. Mary uttered a sound of distress, accompanied by a voice full of indignation.

"Well now, Mr. Dickerson, you did not tell us that your house was so small. Just where are we to sleep?"

"Mother, don't be so judgmental! You haven't even seen inside, and just look at those lovely children. They have such sweet faces."

Molly frowned at her mother but smiled sweetly at Ben. She liked this man. He was genuinely concerned for his children and she liked that a lot. Ben took Miss Molly's arm and helped her out of the carriage. He found himself praying she would take the job. He liked her for standing up to her mother, but he felt nothing more. Introductions were made and Ben picked up little Banks and carried him inside. Lela and Frances stopped their dinner preparation and came to greet their father and his guests. They had not expected to see the two strange women who now stood inside their parlor.

"Hello ladies, sit down and make yourselves comfortable." Ben ushered the women to a small leather upholstered love sear, and then addressed his two daughters.

"Come in girls and meet Miss Molly and her mother, Mary Howard. Miss Molly is the lady I spoke to you about." Ben now placed Banks down on the floor, on his own two feet.

Baby Banks looked first at Mary and then at Molly, he hesitated for a moment and then ran straight to Molly and held his little arms up to be taken by her. She lifted him to her lap, he turned, looked straight into her eyes and said one word.

"Mama?" A hush fell upon the occupants of the room for indeed it was a total surprise to each and everyone there. Molly's decision was made right then. She would take this job no matter what her mother said. She looked at Ben, smiled and said sweetly.

"Mr. Dickerson, I would like the job of helping you raise this sweet child, if you will have me." Ben's heart leaped in gratitude.

"Girls, set two extra plates for our guests, and I will fetch in your valises, ladies."

Mary Howard could not believe her ears. Her daughter was all too anxious and she was going to let her know that she was much too impulsive.

"Molly, you can not mean what you just said. How can you make up your mind just like that?"

"Mother, I want this job. I have no children and this little one seems to have taken to me. Never you mind, I know what I'm doing, and I'm going to do it despite what you think." Molly was firm in her response.

Mary Howard started to retort her answer for Molly's words, but at that moment Benjamin came in loaded down with all of their valises, smiling broadly.

"I'll put these in the bedroom downstairs. The girls will be glad to freshen up the room with clean sheets and towels for you ladies. Now I expect you would like to see your room before we eat, so follow me."

Myrtle set up the room with linens that she knew were needed. She did not like what was happening, however. The bed had been her mother's and the beautiful rose on ivory bowl and pitcher had also been hers. Now Papa was using it for these two strange women, who she didn't like very much. The fact was she did not like Mary Howard at all. She would talk to Papa for she did not believe she could ever take to Miss Molly the way he did last night. She entered the room just as she heard Molly exclaim her intentions.

"I can be a good mother to little Banks, I know I can." Molly's grey-green eyes now shone with warmth none of them had seen before. Myrtle watched her father now as he spoke.

"You know I believe you can." Ben looked away from Molly as his feelings reached deep within his heart. His mind said he must do this but his heart said no. Myrtle returned to the bedroom with the clean linens while Mary Howard sat and watched as she went about making up the bed. Myrtle said nothing and continued to make the bed as she had been taught by her mother. Mary Howard saw that she was not being heard, so she left the bedroom and returned to where Ben and Molly were discussing the children. She hesitated as she heard Ben mention her.

"Molly, I know your mother will not let you stay here alone. I also know that the three of us could not get along for long. I expect the only thing to do is to look after the children for awhile and if you still want to stay on, we will have to make other arrangements. I expect the only thing we could do then would be to consider marriage, to placate your mother. What do you say to that?" Ben hesitated, then added, "Don't say anything now, for this is all very sudden." Ben finished his words with a dry mouth and throat. He felt as if he had swallowed a large piece of cotton. These were words he thought he would never utter again, but he knew he had to have help, especially for little Banks. Mary now stepped into the room with a sly look on her face as she spoke.

"That's right! Don't say anything right now. You cannot stay here in this house. It would ruin your reputation." Mary was a bit too quick, and too caustic, which brought a quick retort from Molly.

"Be damned my reputation. I'm an old maid and not much can ruin my reputation. Yes, Ben, I will stay, and on your terms. I will do my best to take care of you and your children."

"No you won't stay! Molly, don't be stupid!" Mary was horrified at Molly's newfound independence.

"I'm not being stupid. If I'm acceptable to Ben, we will be married and you can go back to Galveston, or MT. Vernon, wherever you want. I'm staying here!" Molly's voice was firm and unrelenting.

"Ladies, ladies, please don't argue. Let's all just get better acquainted so we can all get a good night's sleep. Things may seem a bit different in the morning."

Ben retired with his children in tow to the bedrooms upstairs. He was tired and still not sure that Mary Howard would not talk Molly into leaving. He had heard the ladies conversation become a bit heated, but could not understand their words. As he carried little Banks, now sound asleep, he marveled at how he had taken to Miss Molly.

The early morning crowing of the old rooster had awakened Molly. She slipped out of bed, dressed, and quietly went to the kitchen and started breakfast. Ben had already gone to the barns and taken care of the horses and other livestock. As he entered the kitchen door, the aroma of the coffee perking taunted his senses. His mind now wandered to another time in his life with Little White Dove. It seemed like it had been forever since he had enjoyed this early morning salute to the day with fresh coffee. It really had only been a little over a year, but it seemed like forever. Tears stung his eyelids as he remembered their happy life together. He shook himself back to the reality of now, and what he must do now for his little ones. As he stepped into the kitchen he saw a plate of ham and eggs and Miss Molly taking a pan of biscuits out of the oven. She smiled at him as she poured two cups of coffee, and he smiled back.

"Good Morning, Mr. Dickerson." Molly said shyly.

"Good Morning to you, ma'am."

"How do you like your eggs sir?" Ben blushed as he answered "Over easy will do it. Thanks for making breakfast."

"You are welcome. I decided that if I am going to take this job, I should get at it," Molly looked at Ben, hesitated and then finished her sentence.

"Mr. Dickerson, I have made up my mind to stay if you will have me on your terms."

"Does your mother agree?"

"I didn't ask her. Little Banks made the decision. No child has ever taken to me like he did."

A few months later, Ben and Miss Molly stood before the Justice of Peace and were married. Molly held Banks in her arms as she said her vows. Mary Howard smiled broadly as she fingered the $500.00 in her pocketbook that Benn had given her for Molly.

The marriage was strictly a business proposition. Ben continued to sleep upstairs and Banks bed was put in Molly's room downstairs.

CHAPTER FIFTEEN

ALONE WITH A KILL – HOME AGAIN

Etta Mae was not at all enthused at her father's marriage to Miss Molly. She resented any woman who might take anything away that she thought belonged to her mother. She did realize though that it was the best thing to do for her father's sake, and she was glad when Myrtle told her and Rosie, that Papa did not sleep with Miss Molly.

Etta had taken George's sisters plea for them to come to Arkansas and Missouri to work, seriously. The flood waters had taken its toll on their little farm, and they had lost their crops this past spring. Finally, George began to consider Etta Mae's pleas to listen to his sisters, Ella and Audibelle. Maybe, he began thinking, we could go there and save enough to come back and start all over in Indiana.

George had also seen Etta Mae's grieving more and more after her mother's death, and determined a change of scenery would maybe help her get over her loss. He would talk to Ed, his brother, and see if he would take over their little farm. Ed and Emmy were delighted to take over the farm, and promised to give it back to them if they decided they wanted it back. So George hurried home to tell Etta Mae the good news, knowing she would be overjoyed to hear that they were going to move with his sisters.

Etta Mae was thrilled to learn that George had made it possible for them to join his sisters in the adventure of moving to a new land. She was, however, a little doubtful about leaving her Papa. But then she remembered that he now had Miss Molly to help him with the younger children. That would be good, but what about leaving Mama out there in the cold, cold ground? And what about leaving her beloved sister Rosie? Etta pondered these questions over and over in her mind.

The train ride was both exciting and enjoyable. Etta Mae had all of George's attention and he was so in love with her that he was sure this move would be a good one. Little Marie was a happy baby and delighted to have both of her parents undivided attention. Then too, the women passengers made over her and coddled her and she would coo and smile at them. Even the conductor had to take his turn in holding her. Etta Mae was thrilled that everyone was making over her darling baby girl.

The landscape flew by, some of it beautiful and lots of it nothing but woods and lots of rocks. Some of the farmland that they did see looked more like a rock pile instead of land to be tilled. The closer the train got to Missouri, the more they realized how much wilderness made up this country. Etta Mae's excitement now turned to a sick foreboding in the pit of her stomach. Even George felt much apprehension at what this adventure might bring to them but he said nothing.

Upon their arrival at the little Arkansas train station, Ella and Audibelle were waiting for them. After much hugging and kissing the two sisters took their brother and family to the boarding place for the men who were working at the logging camp. Etta Mae was disappointed to say the least, for it was nothing but a rough hewn, long, log building consisting of three huge rooms. One room was the kitchen; one was a huge dining room with rough tables and no cloths on them. The other huge room was filled with cot after cot, lining both sides of each wall. A few people had made makeshift dividers of blankets and sheets to partition off their own little space. The occupants were mostly couples, but there were a few who had children. Etta Mae and George now looked at his sister in dismay. This living situation was terrible and shocking to them.

"This can't be where we are going to be living, surely!" Etta Mae exclaimed in disbelief.

"Yes Etta Mae. It's not so bad once you get used to it. You know the men work in shifts, so the room is half empty most of the time."

"But Ella, there is no privacy. We can't stay here for a minute." Etta looked at George for reassurance, but he was as shocked as Etta Mae at these living quarters.

"You both must understand that you will have to live here for awhile until the Company feels you are a good hand. Then they will make you permanent and you can go elsewhere if you wish." Audibelle tried to soften their disappointment as much as she could.

"Surely there must be other quarters since we have a baby." George just couldn't believe what his sister had said.

"I'm afraid not, George. Ella and I felt the same way when we arrived, but like I said the Company demands it for at least thirty days. Then if they think you are a good employee to hire permanently, you can live away from the camp. Really, it is not so bad. The food is good and free, you know it is part of your salary. Come with us and we will show you the spaces that they have assigned to you." George and Etta Mae followed his sisters to the far end of the room.

"Here we are. You can put your valises on the shelf there and you do have a table and some chairs to sit on. We made sure that there would be enough space for little Marie to have her own bed." George was the first to respond as he saw that Etta was near tears.

"Thanks girls, for your help. We will just have to make the best of it. I guess if you can tolerate it, so can we for a little while.

By the way, where are your quarters?" Audibelle was quick to respond.

"Just a few feet from here, see, over there by the window there is a green satin curtain. That's our place and Ella's is just next to us. It's the one with the plaid blankets for privacy. When we heard you were coming, we went to the company store and bought you all some things too. We got little Marie a little bed and you a set of sheets and blankets for your little space. Come, see what they are." Audibelle now felt very glad that she and Ella had these things ready. They could readily see Etta Mae was still horrified at the lack of privacy.

The first week of their stay in the logging camp was pure Hell, for both George and Etta. Little Marie did not like her new home either. Her parents took turns walking her in the night to keep her from crying. George's muscles screamed at him from the alien exercise they were getting from all of the hard work. He slept very little. Etta fretted and complained most of the time, until she had no one to complain to. Then a sudden blessing came to take her mind off the unpleasantness. Ella and Audibelle brought the news to her.

"Etta Mae, the cook here is looking for someone to work in the kitchen to do some of the baking. We told him we knew a woman that could bake pies and biscuits that melted in your mouth. The pay is good too. Also, you can move up near the kitchen where you will have more room, and better accommodations. Audie and I will take care of little Marie for you. What do you say to that, Etta?" Etta was very flattered. She didn't know that her sister-in-laws thought that about her cooking.

"Whatever George says, I will do. What do you think, George? Should I take the job, we could really use the money."

"Yes, it might be a good thing. It would give you something else to keep you busy, and the girls are right, you make the best biscuits I ever put in my mouth." George could see that Etta Mae was truly interested in the job, and he would have agreed to anything to help to soothe Etta's pride.

Etta Mae relished in the attention and praise she received for the baking. She delighted in cooking, and baking pies was her very favorite thing to cook. At first George liked what she was doing, but as time wore on, he began to feel as if he was not getting enough attention from his wife. Also, he hated leaving little Marie with her Aunts every day. When he mentioned this to Etta she would just laugh at him, and tease that he was only jealous of all the compliments she was getting from the men. The truth was she was right.

A few months after their arrival in Missouri, Etta Mae found herself pregnant again. At first thought she was very happy about a new baby coming, but then she thought it really was too soon. She worried about having a baby in this God forsaken place. This was the way she referred to the State of Missouri. She did not tell George right away for fear he would make her quit her baking job. Four months into her pregnancy, her boss came to her one day and said what he had suspected for a couple of weeks. His helper was pregnant.

"Mrs. Hutchinson, I'm afraid that I am going to have to let you go. Not because I don't need you, and certainly not because your baking isn't wonderful, but it is the Company's policy. They can't allow a woman in the family-way to work in the kitchen. I'm really sorry for I will miss you greatly." Etta Mae was stunned. She thought that she had kept her condition well hidden. Even George had just begun to question her about the weight she had gained.

George Henry III was born a bit earlier than he was supposed to be, and was really a seven months baby, and weighed 5 pounds and 6 ounces. However, he was strong and wiry and everyone fell in love with him at first sight. It was October and the weather had turned very cold. Etta Mae worried constantly that the baby would catch cold from all the drafts of cold air that came from the workers' comings and goings. One of the older women whose living quarters was nearby brought a brick to Etta and said that it was to keep the tiny baby warm. She also said that cook said she could bring the brick to the kitchen and he would heat it up several times a day. This lady, Audibelle and Ella, helped Etta with the brick, and little Georgie stayed warm and cozy, and did not catch a cold that winter.

Etta's days now were filled with the care of her children and taking care of her husband. The first few months after little George arrived Etta was content, but soon she began missing her job making pies for the logging camp. She still couldn't believe her Mama was gone, and oh, she would say, "How I miss my Papa, and my brothers and sisters, especially, Rosie." Etta was fond of her sisters-in-law but they were not Rosie. She could tell Rosie anything and everything, and she always understood. She also could keep her secrets to herself. Etta wanted to go home she said to George. You know just for a visit, but George being a practical man would try to tell her they just couldn't up and quit this job. When she said that maybe just she could go, George said they just couldn't afford it right now.

"Try and be patient, Etta Mae. We have saved very little money and we had to spend most of that for the baby's birth. Where would we go if we went back there now? You know that jobs are very scarce in Indiana and Kentucky." Etta would sob from her homesickness and George would hold her in his arms and tell her how much he loved her, how lucky they were to have two beautiful children, a job, and plenty to eat.

Winter in Missouri the year of 1919 was a fierce one. The inhabitants of the logging camp were very glad that they had a nice warm place to live, even though they were a bit crowded. The women spent their time making quilts, comforters, crocheting and embroidering. The children were only too glad to play games inside, while the winds laced with snow blew in gale force much of the time.

The winter months passed none too quickly for Etta and George. The little town nearby the camp was almost inaccessible with their muddy streets and sometimes fallen trees across the road. However, on one visit to the local supply store, George asked the storekeeper if there was a cabin or house for rent in town.

"Well yes sir, Mr. Hutchinson, I happen to know of a little house down by the railroad tracks. It's further out, but it's a nice little place. It belongs to my Aunt who passed on a few months back. Her children meant to rent it, and I'd be pleased to mention your name when one of them comes into the store. They live over in Malden, and only come over once in awhile. I 'spect they will be in this week, or the next and I'll get back with you then."

George was glad he had said something to Mr. Hawkins about a house, and he knew Etta would be ecstatic to be able to have her own place again.

"Thank you, sir, I would appreciate that."

George left feeling very good about finding a new home. "Here sire, take these and have them hold the house for me. I'm a carpenter by trade and could keep the place fixed up real nice." George handed a couple of silver dollars to Mr. Hawkins. George's eyes now twinkled as he looked at the storekeeper and gave him his best smile.

"Yes sir, I'll do just that. I don't know just how much rent they want, but my guess is that this will probably cover it. By the way, where is that pretty wife of yours?"

"Oh, she had to stay at home; the baby's got a bad cold. I sure hope this is the last of this cold weather. I'll be back in next weekend, maybe you can take us out to the house."

George reached across the counter and shook the storekeeper's hand. "Oh, and before I go, I'll have Mrs. Hutchinson and the children with me next week."

George grinned at the storekeeper and picked up the sack of groceries that he had purchased for Etta and the children.

Etta Mae was thrilled beyond words at the prospect of having her own little house again. She couldn't wait to tell Audie and Ella the good news, so she hastened to find them.

The house sat up on a little hill looking quite forlorn, but Etta Mae did not think about that. All she could do was exclaim over, and over, "I can't believe my eyes. It is fully furnished with beds and linens and everything we need. Oh, George, you are the best husband in the whole world. How did you find this place? Can we move in right away? We can have company and I can cook them dinners, and the children can have their own rooms, and oh, my, my, I feel like I've been let out of jail."

George laughed at Etta Mae, picked her up and swung her around and around in the nice little parlor that they could now call theirs.

"Guess what, Etta? I can make my music too, and we can have friends over for a party."

And party and entertain they did. There was never a weekend that went by that the little house did not brim over with guests. Their little home felt like a bit of paradise after living in the cramped quarters at the logging camp.

Spring arrived bringing the birds singing in the trees, the occasional croton and then the daffodils that lined the path to the front of the house. Bushes of spirea bloomed all around the little front porch, and then soon bushes of peonies burst forth with their buds of pink and white. Etta Mae was ecstatic to have her own little place for a garden, and began the planting soon after they moved in.

She also found that there were many rabbits scampering back and forth in the garden, eating her lettuce and the tops of some of the other plants. George took his gun down from its safety place on the wall and said he would make sure that they had rabbit for dinner for many days. Etta Mae loved rabbit to eat and commented to him that maybe the lettuce was not lost after all.

Missouri in 1919 and 1920 was still very heavily wooded and dense with thickets of briars and brambles. There were very few cleared areas and most of them were filled with crops. There were many patches of wild berries just for the picking, and blackberry season came a bit earlier that usual that year. Etta Mae and

Audibelle donned their long sleeves and wide brimmed bonnets, wrapped up the babies and set off for the briar patches.

The young women found many patches of luscious berries with fruit as large as a lady's thumb nail. This did not happen though, without them having to climb through the brambles and bushes to find them.

They encountered little animals of every kind, and lots of snakes, lizards, toads, spiders, some of which were huge. These things did not bother them much, but the howls of panthers, wildcats and wolves did.

On these days, the women would gather up the children, their buckets, and make hasted from the briar patches. Etta Mae spoke to George many times about all the wild animals that they had heard and said how frightened she was for the children. George said he didn't think she should worry because he had fenced the entire yard at their house, but what Etta Mae could only think of now, was going home to see Papa and Rosie.

Etta was constantly begging George to take her and the children home to Kentucky, or even to Southern Indiana. He tried to remind her that jobs were mighty scarce back home and that they just didn't have the money to leave at this time.

"Try and be patient with me, I will take us back as soon as I can make sure that we have enough to start over at home. Don't take the children back to the berry patches and I'm sure you will be safe here in the house."

"But George, the berry season is just getting started and I need to can some for our use next winter." Etta Mae was not defiant. She desperately wanted to do as she pleased, but said nothing more.

George arrived home a few days after to find Etta in tears.

"What on earth is the matter, Etta Mae? You look like you have seen a ghost!" George consoled. "Surely nothing can be as bad as all of these tears."

"Yes it is! Audie came over today and we went out to the patches, just a little past the barn. You know down the road a piece where there were those huge berries we saw getting ripe last week, and, oh, George, I just can't stay in this wild country any longer." Etta started crying all over again.

"Tell me, sweetheart, what happened!" George was now alarmed because he could see Etta was almost near hysterics.

"Audibelle and I went down to the road to pick those big berries, and we just put Marie and Georgie down on a pallet in a bare spot near the road. We were just a few feet away when Marie screamed. We both jumped out of the patch and right there, just a few feet away from us, was the biggest black panther you can imagine. He was about to pick up little Georgie, but our sudden jump at him frightened him for a moment. He snarled at us just daring us to get close to the children, but Audie was too fast for him. She threw her big bucket at him and he finally ran away, snarling. He didn't go very far, but we grabbed the children and fled to the house. We didn't realized that the panther followed us, but, but, when we glanced out the window, we heard a strange noise and there he was, right in the yard. Oh, George, I was so frightened I didn't know what to do, but Audie did. She grabbed your gun off the wall and ran out and shot at the panther. Twice she shot at him before he moved. She didn't hit him, but on the third shot he jumped the fence and ran away. George, I can't stat in this wild country another day, I tell you, I'm going home. I'm taking the children and going home to Papa's."

Etta Mae was now sobbing uncontrollably.

George held his wife in his arms. Caressed her beautiful black hair and kissed her over and over, trying to console her. He didn't want her to go off even down the road for fear that she would see one of the big cats nearby. He wanted to go home too, but he also knew that they had not been able to save enough money to be able to get their own place.

He laid awake most of the night knowing not what to do. He knew Etta Mae was head strong and she was very homesick. He pondered the situation over and over and decided that he would work longer hours for at least a month, and then he would have the money they needed to make the trip back home.

At breakfast the next morning, George laid out his plans to do extra work at the camp, and that he was going to take that job of playing harmonica and violin for the little bar down the street at the edge of town. Etta Mae just looked at him as she fried him some eggs and side meat. She plunked down the freshly made biscuits with some butter and jelly that she had made from the blackberries she had picked. She stood now beside his chair and blurted out her intentions.

"George, I love you so very much, but I can't live in this place another day. I'm going home, with, or without you." She bent down and kissed him on the lips and with tears in her big blue eyes; she sat down at her place at the table, and choked down a few bites of food. She knew she needed to eat for little Georgie's sake. She had to have milk for he was still breast feeding. George looked at his wife and said to her as he prepared to leave for work.

"Etta Mae, you know that you and children are my life. I love you better than anything in the world, but we just can't leave right now. I will be working more hours from now on so that we can get the money we need. Stay close to the house and don't leave the children alone, not even for a minute. The big cat knows where you are and he will possibly be back, lurking nearby. I'll go past and tell Audibelle to come over and stay with you."

Etta Mae, looking forlorn, now only nodded at his words and then with pouted lips kissed him goodbye, warned him again.

"George, I mean it, I'm going home."

"I know honey, We are going home soon."

"No George, I mean I am going home. I'm too scared to stay here, even with Audibelle with me." George tried to be patient as he tried to explain his intentions.

"I know dear, you are very scared, but please just be a little patient. I'm making arrangements to get us the money to leave on, today." With those words, George bent and kissed Etta one more time, and saw the tears in her beautiful eyes. He knew he had to leave now or he would not be able to if he waited much longer. He kissed little Marie who was now toddling out of the bedroom in her nightgown. Baby George lay snuggled up to his mother's breast, sleeping peacefully.

Etta Mae sat at the little table for a long time. Then put baby George down in his bed, then fed Marie her breakfast. As she helped her little daughter eat, she contemplated over and over how serious was the jeopardy that she and the children were in; out here amidst the woods, the tall grasses and thickets, where all sorts of animals could hide.

She knew George meant well, and that in his own time he would keep his word that he would take them all back home. But could she afford to wait? Her heart ached at the thought of leaving her sweet, wonderful husband, but she knew that her children's safety came first. She was still sitting at the table mulling over what to do when Audie arrived, frightened out of her wits.

Audibelle drove a small buggy with one horse to wherever she wanted to go. She had been glad to say that she would go over and stay with Etta and the children when her brother had stopped by on his way to work. Just as she turned to go into Etta's house, she saw something move out from behind the barn. At first, she could not make out what it was and then as she got closer she saw the big black panther. He had one of Etta's big hens in his mouth and was dragging it off to eat. Audie shuddered, and cold chills ran up and down her spine. She thought, 'I am going to have to carry a gun with me when I come out here in the future.'

She would have to warn George that the panther was stalking the house. Audie drew up the buggy as close to the front gate as she could, tied the reins to the post and ran into the house. Flushed now with the fear she felt, she entered the house breathlessly.

"What is it, Audie?" Etta questioned. "What on earth is the matter?"

"I just saw that big black panther, he had one of your laying hens in his mouth. You mustn't go outside Etta Mae. It's too dangerous. I'm going to get a gun for myself, and I will shoot that damn thing!"

"Here, sit down Audie. You have made my decision. I'm going back home. I tried to tell George that I am leaving and taking the children where we will be safe. You have got to help me."

"You talked to George about leaving?"

"Yes, but he just doesn't think I mean it. I DO mean it, and I want you to help me get our things together and take us to the train. I'm going today! I cannot spend another day or night being scared out of my wits."

Audie, still frightened, just nodded, took a deep breath, and sat down at the table to drink the cup of coffee that Etta Mae had poured for her.

Tired and weary from his long day at work, George arrived home after dark. He unharnessed his horses and then by the light of his lantern, he made his way to the house. It was then that he saw the white and red feathers scattered all over the chicken yard. Cautiously, he checked out the hen house and saw that many of his hens were missing. He knew in an instance what had happened, so he ran to the darkened house, trembling with fear. Where was Etta Mae? Then he remembered that Audie was going over to stay with her, so perhaps she had taken Etta and the children home with her. He felt relief thinking that his wife and children were safe with his sister. He lit the coal oil lamp in the parlor, and sank down in one of the two upholstered chairs. He thought, 'I'm just too tired to go over there right now', and that was the last thing he knew until he was suddenly awakened by his sister and brother-in-law.

"George, wake up!" George shook himself awake.

"What is it, Audie? Where is Etta Mae! Is she over at Ella's!" He could see that Etta Mae was not with his sister.

"No, George, she is not at Ella's. When I came over this morning, she said I had helped her make up her mind. The big black panther was out at the chicken house and was dragging off your hens. When I said she could not go outside, she said that she knew it was too dangerous for her to stay here any longer and that she was going home."

"Yes, I know about the hens. I guess he had gotten a lot more than one or two. Feathers were everywhere, but where is Etta Mae, if she is not with Ella?"

"I'm trying to tell you. What on earth happened, did you two get into a big argument? What happened? She was crying and crying and insisted she had to go home. She asked me to help her get their clothes together so she could leave. And, she asked me to loan her the money to take the train since she had very little money of her own. She said that you would give it back to me."

"What! Did you give her money?" George could not believe his ears. He knew that Audibelle did not have that much money either.

"Yes I did. What ever happened out here? She was crying and crying, and insisted that she had to get away from this wild country. Ella and I tried to talk her out of going, but she said it was no use, and that she would get there with or without our help. I've never seen her like that before. Whatever happened between you two?"

Audie now had thoughts that something other than the big panther's presence was behind Etta Mae's insistence that she had to go, and right now.

George was in a state of shock. What had he done? He now began to realize just how frightened his wife had been, living out here in the wilds by herself. Why didn't he heed her warnings? How can she take care of herself, let alone the babies? Head in hands, now George bemoaned.

"My God, Audie. She said this morning she was leaving, but of course I didn't take her seriously. What can I do? I just can't up and quit my job, but I can't live without her and the children, way off down here. What to do?" George kept asking over and over as he went from room to room as if expecting to find his family.

Audibelle tried to console her brother, but he was inconsolable.

"George, George, get a hold of yourself. Stop this ranting and raving. It's true she did leave of the train, but not before she sent a telegram to her Papa. She will be just fine. After she sees her father and her sister Rosie, maybe she will come back."

Audie knew her words were falling on deaf ears.

"Come home with me George and stay the night. You will be able to think more clearly in the morning."

"No, no! I have to stay here. Maybe she will come back. Maybe she will bring the babies back home to me." George had commenced to pull his curly red hair, and pace the floor, back and forth with big tears rolling down his cheeks. Audibelle was becoming very worried now for she had never seen her brother so upset. He always seemed to take all things rather lightly, but this was something to be concerned over. What might he do? She wondered.

Precisely at that moment, a knock came at the door. George sprang to his feet certain that Etta Mae had come home. He quickly opened the door only to see Artie there looking for Audibelle and Ella. George collapsed nearly falling to the floor. Artie fixed George a stiff drink and tried to console him, but he could not. Audie held him in her arms telling him over and over that everything will be all right. George finally succumbed to the drink and fell asleep in his sister's arms.

Nervously, and with ticket in hand, Etta Mae boarded the train for Springfield, Missouri. With the conductor's help, she found a comfortable seat for herself and the two children. George III was unconcerned about everything for he had his food, and his Mama was taking good care of him. Little Marie, however, was fretful. She wanted her Daddy. Just a little over two, she was curious about the train, which to Etta's relief, helped keep her quiet. People tried to coax her to come and see them, but Marie was very shy and stayed close to her mother. The conductor and some of the women on the train kept telling her just how pretty she was and admiring her very blond beauty. She only turned her head away from her would be admirers.

"Where is my Daddy, Mama?" Whey isn't he here?" she asked over and over until Etta Mae could stand it no more. After many of these questions, she finally broke and gave into the pent up tears of anger and loneliness. She vowed to herself though that George deserved her leaving him. She had to protect her children. Deep down, she prayed that George would soon follow them.

Twenty hours later, and covered with soot from the train, she began to wonder what she would do when she reached Kentucky or Indiana. She would just let Papa think that she had come for a visit until she could figure out what to do. Her Papa would be able and willing to help her.

The train gave a sudden jolt and finally lurched to a stop. The conductor called out that they were in Springfield and telegrams could be sent. Etta quickly decided she should let her Papa know just where to meet her, so she sent a new 'gram' off to him:

'PAPA MEET ME AT THE MT. VERNON TRAIN STATION SATURDAY.'

Her first telegram had read only,

'PAPA I'M COMING HOME WITH THE CHILDREN. ETTA MAE.'

The ferryboat Captain rode his mount as fast as he could to Ben Dickerson's house. He now had two telegrams for him. One telegram was very important in those days, but two in the same day, well, that was even more so.

Ben couldn't imagine who the horseman would be, and whey he bounded off his horse as if some demon was after him. Something must be wrong, Ben thought. Ben jumped from his chair and ran to meet his unexpected guest.

"Hello! What do you want?" Ben yelled at the man.

"I'm John Roberts, from the ferry boat."

"Oh, hello John, I didn't recognize you. What is it?"

"I have a couple of telegrams for you. Must be danged important." John said with curiosity as he handed the envelopes to Ben. Ben puzzled, ripped open the envelopes both at the same time, and grinned as he read them.

"It is good news John, my daughter Etta Mae is coming for a visit. I'm to meet her today at the train station. I guess I'd better get a move on, so I can cross over with you."

"That is good news. I was afraid it wasn't. It's not often I get to deliver good news."

"Come on in the house John. Miss Molly must have a bite to eat and some coffee."

"No, Ben. I best get back to the ferry, but we will wait for you, to take you over."

Ben handed the telegrams to Molly. She was pleased to hear Etta Mae was coming home. She had not wanted her to go to Missouri in the first place.

"Well Ben I guess I had better get this house cleaned up and fresh bed clothes on the bed for her and the children, for you know how particular she is." Ben just laughed at Molly.

"Yes, you had better get everything in order. Etta Mae is a bit fussy. Go out and tell her sisters and brother that she is coming, so they can help you. I got to get going so I can meet the train."

Ben donned his best hat and jacket, hitched up his surrey and made his way toward the ferry crossing. His heart was light and filled with anticipation. He was meeting his beloved daughter and grandchildren.

George Henry Hutchison was utterly devastated over Etta Mae's leaving so abruptly without as much as a kiss goodbye. Well maybe that kiss she gave him was her goodbye, but it didn't seem like that to him at the time. He knew his wife was headstrong but never would he have believed she would up and leave with the children. Still he had to admit it was his fault for not putting a better plan forward so that they could go home together. AS he mulled over his situation, he knew he had to follow her. His job now was not so important without her. The only thing to do was for him to find his way to join her and the children.

First things first. He would have to tell the logging camp manager of his intentions to quit, and beg for as many hours as he could manage for the next week or so. He would sell what little furniture they had bought for the little house, he would also have to sell their carriage and horse. He knew just where he could sell the cow and the chickens that were left. He shuddered now, realizing just how determined the panther was in robbing them of everything he could get his claws on. This done he would have enough money to pay Audie back, a train ticket and a little left over. As George thought about how frightened Etta Mae was, he heard scratching on the front porch. He got up from the little table where he had been planning, grabbed his lantern, and cautiously opened the door for a look. There, bigger than life, crouched the big panther with his green eyes flashing in the lantern light. George slammed the door shut, shivered for a moment then grabbed his gun. He ran to the window and raised it just high enough to get the gun under, aimed and pumped two shots into the panther. There the panther sprawled across the porch floor, lifeless. George sank to the floor in shock. He could not move for a long time, but finally he slowly rose and looked out the window to make sure that the panther was really dead. In its eerie silence, the huge animal did not seem so fierce, but George now knew that his wife had every reason to be afraid to stay in the house. Then he realized that the huge animal had fallen against the door making it impossible for him to leave by that entrance. He would have to get help to drag it off the porch. He sat back down at the little table shaken, but now more determined than ever to join

Etta Mae. His heart began to loose some of the heaviness he had felt earlier. He was determined that nothing was worth the loss of his family. He would surprise Etta Mae and assure her his love for her was what was paramount to him. Maybe he would send a 'gram', or maybe he would just surprise her and the children. Slowly and methodically, George undressed and fell into the little matrimonial bed and slept, peacefully, with dreams of his reunion with his precious wife and children.

Morning arrived bringing with it several of the local farmers. They had heard the shots the night before and had come to see what had happened. On seeing the large cat lying lifeless up against the front door, they all began shouting exclamations of delight, and as George emerged from the rear of the house, they hoisted him up and congratulated him on his kill.

"I've been trying to get that cat for over six months. He had nearly robbed me blind!" Homer Harris exclaimed as he helped the other men hoist George onto his shoulders.

"Yawh, I've took many shots at him too. He has carried off several of my piglets, and I wanted him bad, but he always seemed to get away. Tell us Hutch, how did you manage to get him?" Elmer Davis asked.

George a bit embarrassed at all the fuss the men were making, turned bright red as he spoke to the men.

"I couldn't help but get him; he was trying to get into the house."

"Well, I'll be gol darn, Hutch. He came to you, did he? Wal he won't be botherin' us anymore. By the way, where is your wife and kids?"

George stuttered for a moment. He did not want the men to know that Etta Mae had left him, so he decided to tell a little white lie.

"I sent her and the babies back home. She had seen the panther several times in the briar patch and was afraid to stay here in the house. You know it just wasn't safe her for her and two small children." George smarted as he took credit for Etta Mae's safety.

"Well you sure did us all a favor, and we want to treat you to a drink down at Jake's after work. Come on boys, we best get goin' or we'll be late for work. See you Hutch, don't forget."

"I won't forget. Thanks, for coming over. Give me a hand and help me drag this cat off the porch."

"Better than that, boys, let's load this monster in our wagon and take him into town." George and the three men grunted and strained as they loaded the lifeless cat into the wagon, which was almost more than they could do, but finally they had him half in, and took a rope and pulled the rest of him onto the tailgate of the wagon.

George was glad to be rid of the big cat. Even in death, he was a formidable foe. He now realized that he could probably sell all his livestock and chickens to these very men. He couldn't wait until the time to join them at Jakes bar.

George boarded the train to St. Louis with a large sigh of relief. He had been a fool the second time with Etta Mae. This time he would learn that she meant what she said, when she said it. He vowed to never make that mistake again as he settled into his seat, dozed, and watched the countryside go by, intermittently.

Just outside St. Louis, George was suddenly awakened by the conductor who was going from car to car making his announcement. "Hear ya'all! Floodwaters are rising and there will be a delay of possibly two or more days before we can continue from St. Louis. Some accommodations are possible but only for women and children. All other passengers can remain on board, or they can spend this time in the rail station!" As the conductor shouted his message, he moved on. George decided to stay on the train for the time being, but changed his mind as some of the passengers moaned and cried as they passed by him. Seeing the struggle of the women with children, he decided he had to help any way he could. He gathered up several small children and helped them and their mothers off the train.

The St. Louis Rail Station was enormous and held no fascination for George. He was restless walking up and down the station with nothing to do but wait. Then, on second thought, he realized there was something he could do; he would send a telegram to Etta's father, Ben. He would surely know where she was, and could let her know that he was on his way home, just as soon as the train could cross the Wabash River. The Wabash and Ohio Rivers could be very treacherous and just as unpredictable in southern Indiana and Western Kentucky. After pacing the floor in the train station for several hours, George decided he would get back on board, take a good book with him and spend his waiting time reading. The seats on the train were quiet and comfortable so George read until he drifted off to sleep awakening to another announcements from the conductor. It seemed that they were not going to be delayed as long as had been predicted, but would be able to resume their journey later in the next day. It seemed that the water had receded from some of the tracks out of St. Louis and they felt that they would be down far enough for them to cross the Wabash into Indiana.

BACK HOME AGAIN

Etta Mae had pretended the first few days of her visit that it was just a visit, but then feeling guilty and remorseful, she knew she had to tell her father what had really happened in Missouri.

Admitting she had done something as bad as leaving George in Missouri, was almost more than she could admit, but she knew her father had to be told. What the consequences would be she had no clue, but she gathered her thoughts together and told her father what she had really done. She knew that this time her father was going to be very angry with her. Even she knew now that she had acted hastily.

Ben could hardly believe what Etta Mae had just told him. He just sat staring at her for a few minutes, then trying to control his own temper he spoke sharply to his daughter.

"What on earth are you saying? What have you done? Etta Mae, it is about time that you grow up and act like a responsible wife and mother! You just can't continue to do as you please! George is a good, kind, and decent man who loves you very much. Why, why would you put him through this? You know you love George, but a man has his dignity too. You just can't continue to do as you please. You should have talked this out! You have great responsibilities now with two small children, and if I guess right, another one on the way. I God, girl, I can't keep fixing things for you. You must take responsibility for your actions." Ben was horrified at his daughter's willfulness.

"Papa, Papa, don't be mad at me! I know I shouldn't have just left, but I was too afraid to stay there with all those wild animals close to our house! I was afraid they would get into the house and carry off one of my babies. Please Papa, I tried to tell George but he was only interested in his job!" Etta now sobbed, and sobbed.

"He will probably never forgive me for leaving. Oh Papa, what am I to do?"

Ben could never stand to see his daughter cry, so he took her in his arms and rocked her back and forth, as if she was a little baby.

"There, there daughter don't' take on so. I 'm sure George would have made arrangements to leave if you would have just waited until he could get the job done. Didn't you talk this over at all?"

"Yes, Papa, but he kept saying we didn't have the money to leave, and…," Ben interrupted, "Etta Mae you just cant' take matter in your own hands. George is your husband and you were wrong to up and leave him. When are you going to understand you and George must make decisions together?"

"Please, Papa, don't be mad at me. I can't stand that. What am I to do now? Tell me what to do. Can I still stay here for a while? I can't go back to that horrible place, it's nothing but wilderness."

"No, you can't go back. We will cross the river and send George a telegram that you and the babies are with me and that you are alright. Fair enough?" Ben hugged his daughter again, took little George from her, and carried him outside. It was day 7 of his daughter's visit.

Marie and Grandma Molly followed Ben, and close behind was brother Banks, leaving Etta Mae to nurse her wounded pride alone.

Ben, Etta Mae, and baby George arrived at the ferry just as it was about to dock. The Captain waved to them. He was glad he wouldn't have to make the mad rush to Ben's farm to deliver another telegram. He would just give it to Ben when he got everyone on board.

Ben pulled the 'gram' from its envelope with a sigh of great relief at what he had just read. He decided to say nothing to Etta Mae about its contents. Let her be surprised, he thought. The streets in Mt. Vernon were very busy with the usual Saturday shoppers. The farmers, their families, and a number of young couples were sauntering up and down the main street between the park and the courthouse. Ben and Etta Mae waved to some of the shoppers as their carriage carried them through the little town. When they had almost reached the station, Ben suddenly stopped the carriage in front of a little café directly across the street.

"Come daughter, you must be hungry. Let's get a bite or two, and then we will go over to the station and send a telegram to George." Ben was hoping George's train would arrive by them for he had said he should be in by 3:00. It was getting close to 2:00 now. Ben and Etta Mae had ordered their meal and were almost finished eating when Ben heard the first whistle from the trains' arrival. Ben pretended not to hear it. A few minutes later, the sound of the locomotive could be heard coming into the station. Still, Ben said nothing. Baby George was tired and fighting sleep. He wanted his dinner too. Ben took the moment to say he would just run over and send the 'gram' while little George nursed.

"I shouldn't be very long." Ben jumped into his carriage and drove over to the train yard, hitched his horse to a post and walked as fast as he could into the station. The passengers were just beginning to enter the lobby and file past Ben. Many couples, women and children filed past him. Just as he thought the last of the people has left the station, he spied George and all of his luggage.

George walked slowly toward the exit. Properly dressed as always, with a tall black silk hat, popular to the day, gave George height and character to his small demeanor. His red curly hair escaping from under his hat, however, gave him a rakish look. Ben laughed to himself at the joy he felt as seeing his son-in-law as he now walked closer. George was unaware that anyone he knew was anywhere near, as he struggled with all of the boxes and valises he was trying to carry.

"Let me help you with your luggage, man." George looked up and saw Ben. He dropped the valises he had been holding and gave Ben a warm bear hug. George then looked around for his family, but frowned deeply when he did not see them.

"Etta Mae, where is she, Ben? Is she alright?"

"Yes, George, she is fine as well as the children. I just got your message this morning. We were on our way over, she thinks, to send you a message. We were, or I should say, I am over here on a pretense to send you a 'gram' to say she and the children are just fine. She and baby George are in the café over there across the street."

With the valises and boxes packed snugly in the carriage Ben turned to George and addressed what he was sure was on George's mind.

"Before we go to the café, I must tell you I do not condone what she has done, and she knows it," George grimaced at Ben's statement.

"Sir, that is all my fault. I didn't take her serious when she said she was leaving. I realize now that she always means what she says. Thank you for taking care of her and the children. I'm not sure just what we will do, but I assure you I will find work and take care of her. I really did not know just how unsafe she was until just a day or so ago. I had to kill the panther she was so afraid of, right outside our front door. The chickens were not enough for him I guess."

"Say no more, George. I believe you, but now let's go give her your big smile for a surprise."

As the door to the café opened, Etta looked up and nearly dropped baby George. She screamed as she rose from her seat where she had placed the baby.

"George is that really you? Oh, thank God it is you!" Etta Mae threw herself in George's arms and planted kisses all over his face. George felt such elation at the welcome he was getting he could not even be embarrassed, as he normally would have, in such a public place.

"Oh how I've missed you. I will never, never leave you again. Papa is right; I've been a very selfish woman thinking only of myself. Please, please forgive me. I will do whatever you want; I must have been crazy out of mind, to do what I did." George could only pat and hug Etta, for he knew that some of the blame lay with him.

"Whoa, whoa, now that you two lovers are back together let's all go down to Dagger's Bar, and say hello to my friend before we cross back over the river. He might have some information about jobs. You know he knows everything that goes on, in and around Mt. Vernon." As predicted, the bartender gave George a handshake, and gave him some news about a new Dam being built down river on the Ohio.

John Roberts, Captain of the ferryboat, was George's brother-in-law. He had married George's sister Sophia. He was delighted to see George again, and said he might be able to help him find work on the new Dam and he did.

After a couple of days at Ben's house with Miss Molly and his children, George moved his family to his sister Sophia's house in Uniontown, Kentucky. They remained there for about a month.

Sudden pains gripped Etta one day and she lost the baby she was carrying. He was a perfect miniature baby, but a stillborn. They named him Johnny and gave him a burial in Sophia's backyard, where his tiny bones remained forever. Etta Mae was remorseful feeling she had caused the stillborn birth. She felt that she was being punished for her actions. No one could convince her otherwise. A year later, she would rejoice to find she would give birth to another baby boy whom she and George would name Rudolph Houston Hutchison.

By this time, the little family had moved just across the river again to a little place called Hovey Lake, in Point Township. There, George was more accessible to his job on Dam 49. Etta Mae raised a wonderful garden, canned fruits and vegetables, and bather her little family in the love she felt for them all. George and Etta were madly in love and felt that nothing could ever destroy their love, or even task it, but they were wrong.

Summer had come and southern Indiana was muggy and very hot. Etta would take her children outside and place them on a palette to get any breeze that might come their way. It was on one of these days while waiting for George to come home from work that it happened. Marie, George, and little Rudolph were running and playing on the front porch when Rudolph, only two, slipped, stumbled and fell off the porch. He landed on a large rock striking his head just above his ear. Etta Mae was almost there in time to catch him, but not quite. She rushed him into the house and tried everything she could think of to stop the bleeding and the pain, but the baby continued to scream. George arrived home soon after the fall and tried everything he could think of to help, but nothing seemed to quiet him. Out of desperation, Etta Mae gave him a drop of paregoric in a little water and sugar, and he was finally able to sleep. The next morning Etta and one of her neighbors took little Rudolph in to see Dr. Doerr. The baby was feverish and a large knot had risen above his ear. The doctor gave Etta some medicine for the fever and instructed her to keep giving him baths to help keep the fever down. The neighbor women came in and helped Etta Mae with the baby and the other children, but nothing it seemed would make the fever go away. Four days later Rudolph became delirious from an infection that had set in his ear. All the bathing and special herb teas did not work and little Rudolph died from the fall. Etta Mae nearly succumbed herself she was so grief stricken. Nothing or no one was able to help her through her grief. For months, she walked like a ghost in her own house, blaming herself for his death. She tried to pray to the Creator for forgiveness for all that she had done wrong, as she sat looking out at the Ohio River, and the many boats that traveled its waters. She sat as if in a trance, when a voice came from out of nowhere. At first, she was frightened, and then she recognized the voice was that of her Grandmother, Morning Star. How could that be? She wondered and listened.

"None of this is your fault Etta Mae, but you have failed to keep the ways of our people and the Creator. This must change for you to have peace, and the courage you need. You must honor all that has been given to you in such abundance. You must rise early in the morning and give thanks for the day, for the gifts you have been given, and the love that has been bestowed upon you. Never, never, must you forget who you really are, and you must rear your children in the Blackfoot ways, and in the Creator's name. Remember I am with you always, but need this warning, for you will need our Creator's strength if you are to survive. Go now child and love that which you have."

Etta Mae woke with a start. Had she been dreaming? No, she said to herself, no, I saw Grandma just as if she was here as real as she could be. She shivered now at the thought that Grandma cam with a warning. She must change her ways. She must call on the Creator for guidance, and praise him for what she had. She sat for a few moments in deep thought and then raised her arms toward the heavens as she had seen her mother and grandmother do so many times, and praised the Creator's name. From that day forward, Etta Mae never forgot her Grandmother's words, and most of all, she was so thankful that her Grandmother Morning Star was with her and looked down on her with her blessings.

True to the Blackfoot tradition after a death in the house, Etta and George moved their little family to another little house on the river. On July 23, 1925, they were blessed with a baby girl. George named the baby Ruby, for the month of July and Jewell to honor his mother and her Cherokee family. The midwife who helped deliver her said that this was a special baby for she was born with a veil that covered her face. Her parents knew she was special even without the veil.

Life was good for Etta Mae and George. The felt extremely blessed with little Marie, George Henry and now baby Ruby Jewell.

They told everyone that times were hard but they had all they needed. They had love, a family, a job and they had George's beautiful music.

CHAPTER SIXTEEN

BIG HAPPINESS, BIG SORROW, MANY CHANGES

The little girl sat in a clump of grass on the highest part of the little hill waiting, and watching. From time to time, she would partially cover her eyes with her tiny hand and peer intently on the bend in the road, just below the hill. She sat cross-legged, Indian style, in the tall grass. She wiggled often and sighed, but never moved from where she had plumped down her little bottom.

Suddenly, she bounded to her feet, and with the swiftness of a scared deer, she ran toward the figure of a man barely in sight, coming around the bend in the road. Down the little dirt lane she ran as fast as her little legs would carry her with her long curly strawberry-blond curls, flying and bouncing in the wind.

The small red-haired man smiled as he watched his smallest child bounding toward him, as she did each day. The man carried a small lunch bucket in his one hand, and a toolbox in the other, for he was coming from his job on Dam 49. George Henry Hutchison II was very tired but happy to be working. It was June of 1927, and jobs were very scarce, especially around Mt.

Vernon, Indiana. George Henry was a small, but muscular man, proud of his Irish and Indian ancestry - honest and very pleased with himself, for he had a very good job working on the Dam, which paid him well above most other jobs, if they had been available. He was proud of his little family, which consisted of three lovely children and the only woman he had ever loved. Etta Mae Van Bibber – Dickerson. George was chuckling to himself now as he watched the apple of his eye running toward him with outstretched arms to greet him. His laughter brought a wonderful twinkle in his sky blue eyes, and his heart filled with love for this little one. She was a true reflection of him, both in spirit and in looks. His other two children, George III and Marie, were much older than Ruby his smallest child and a disposition like their mother, shy and quieter in spirit. George Henry II was now 47 years of age and his children were very precious to him as an older father, and he treated his children as if they were precious jewels. His heart now swelled in pride as he watched his youngest child approaching him full of excitement at seeing him.

"Daddy, Daddy," I gasped, breathless as I neared my father, "I thought you would never come home today." My father placed his toolbox and dinner pail on the ground and lifted me high above his head, and teased me, as he did every day, and kissed away my fears.

"I am a little late today honey; I had to work a little later today. And my precious little one, I didn't get to get your sack of candy." I looked at my father with apprehension and then giggled.

"Oh, Daddy, it's not true, you say that every day." I hugged my father tightly for he represented everything good in the world, then pouted my lips and frowned at him hard; just to let him know I was on to his tricks. My father then laughed loudly, smacked my bottom and set me down on the dirt road. He then reached for his dinner pail, opened it, and sure enough, there was the little bag of goodies he brought me every day. With a big sigh of relief, I hugged him around the legs, and then his neck as he bent over to hand me the sack. My world that day was again complete.

"Now remember, Ruby Jewell, you must take it all home and then share it with Georgie and Marie."

"Yes daddy, I will share it with them, just like I do every day." I answered him patiently, for now I felt safe that he was home, and he had not forgotten to bring the sack of goodies. My father took my hand and led me back to the house, singing an Irish tune as we walked.

As we neared the house the smell of supper met my nose, and I ran into the house to show my mother the sack of goodies. My brother and sister, smiled at me as they saw I was carrying the little brown paper sack, and then gave Daddy a big hug, welcoming him home. The ritual never changed. Mother would then place the little bag on the counter and then turn to my father for her greeting of hugs and kisses from him.

Our little house sat amongst two large oak trees, a few maples and a big garden that my mother tended to, in the rich soil of southern Indiana. The house was very close to the Ohio River and at that point, where the Wabash River met the Ohio. It was a very simple little house consisting of four rooms, all in a square with a porch across the front of the house. My father and mother had talked many times, of how they needed a larger house now that I was no longer a baby and George Jr. needed his own room away from my sister.

Mama had our supper of cornbread, navy beans, corn on the cob, sliced tomatoes and boiled potatoes, ready and waiting. I was starving and anxious to eat, but Daddy was still hugging and kissing my mother on the lips, which made her giggle. Finally, she pushed my father away, giggling, but quickly gained her composure.

"Everyone make sure your hands are clean, so you can eat." Mama was a stickler about cleanliness, so I washed up with Daddy, and then we all sat down to eat, after my father had sat down.

I was starving as usual but dared not touch anything until the 'blessing' was said. Sometimes my Mama referred to it as "Oppie". I didn't ever quite know exactly what that word meant, except it was to thank God our Creator, for our food. Most of the time, Mama said the 'blessing' but as I grew older we three children had to say it together.

This night Mama had made blackberry cobbler for dessert, from the many jars of blackberries we had canned from the last year's picking. She would take us three children with her to the briar patches. This was not much fun for me, since I spent most of my time sitting in the little red wagon that was brought into the patch. George and Marie climbed through the briars picking the berries along with Mama. Sometimes I was allowed to play in the grass, if there was a nearby clearing, where my mother could keep a close eye on me. Always I would come home just as full of chiggers as everyone else. Chiggers meant a soda bath, and some kind of horrible smelling ointment made with coal oil, and lard of goose grease all mixed together. Exactly what else was in this mixture I never knew, but it didn't' seem to matter, when I had a mouthful of delicious berry cobbler and sweet cream in my mouth.

Our meals were usually spent listening to my parent's conversation, since us children had to remain quiet, unless spoken directly to. Most evenings after our meal was over, Daddy played games or music with us. He was a gifted musician, and played many instruments. He would sing Irish songs and dance Irish dances. On summer nights, we were allowed to stay up late and chase fireflies, play jump frog or hide-and-seek until dark. Then Mama would send us all off to bed. Going to bed was something that I did not like much. I would fuss about it until Daddy would either read or tell me a story. Sometimes he would sing an Irish lullaby until I would drift off to slumber land.

Mama was always sewing. After the kitchen was cleaned, she would get out her basket of sewing or embroidery and would still be at it when we kids went to bed. She made all of our clothes, so she would be making a new dress, a shirt, or coat, or putting on a patch on our clothing. She was meticulous in her patching, and none of us ever minded wearing something she had patched for it could barely be detected. Kids in those days badgered you or teased you about wearing patched clothing.

This night would be different. My father called my mother to come and sit with him on the porch. He said that he had some news she was going to want to hear. Of course, we three kids were very interested in what Daddy was going to tell Mama, so we sat down on the porch floor and listened.

"Etta Mae I've finally found it! A house we can rent that is grand compared to this little house we live in now. It isn't too far from here and closer to the schoolhouse. It has an upstairs and the rooms are large. I know you will love it. We won't be able to see the river, but it has a wonderful garden spot and lots of outbuildings." Mama threw her sewing aside.

"Really, George, you mean you actually were able to find us a bigger house? When will we move? Oh, my garden is doing so well; I hate to have to leave it." Mama's voice was full of anticipation, but she wore that frown that meant she was not completely happy. My father just smiled at her and gave her a big hug.

"Now, Etta Mae, my sweet, you won't have to leave your garden, we won't be moving until most of the vegetables will be picked. Mr. Hargrove is doing some repairs, and it won't be ready until then. We can come back to pick the last tomatoes, after we move. In fact, Georgie and I can to that, can't we son?" Georgie was prompt to answer.

"Yes, Daddy, we'll do that and Mama and Marie can put them in cans for the winter."

My brother then hid his face for he was so bashful.

"I can help too," I said, not wanting to be left out.

"Of course you can help, my little Jewell." Daddy said to me soothingly, but Georgie just laughed at me, and proceeded to tickle me in the ribs. This was something that I just hated and would try everything to keep my brother and sister from doing it to me.

We three kids adored our father and mother, and were always ready to please them as much as we possibly could. I sat listening to my parents' conversation and tried to be as patient as possible which a chore it was indeed, for me. As I listened, a strange sadness crept into my very being, at the thought of leaving the river. The river was always so important to me. I felt that it was the most beautiful thing and so close to our house. I just couldn't envision why my mother was so excited about leaving it. Always alert to us children and our feelings, my father now saw the frown on my face.

"Why are you frowning so, my little one?" My father had reached over and taken my face in his hands tilted upwards to his.

"Why do you look so sad? What are you so sad about?" My father then hastened to explain more about the house we could be moving to.

"Ruby Jewell, you will just love the new house. It is really big, with many nut and fruit trees, a nice barn, and lots of clear land all around it". I made a face at him and was close to tears, and then it was as if he read my mind.

"We can come back to the river as often as you wish. We will never leave the river behind for it is as much a part of our lives as can be. What you say, I take you all over to look the house over, tomorrow?" Daddy rose suddenly, lifted Mama out of her chair, and danced her all around, carried her into the parlor, where they fell on the little black love sear, laughing and hugging each other. We three kids then ran into the house and piled on top of our parents, happy because they were happy.

The next day was a Sunday, and after we left the little church house where we went every Sunday, Daddy drove our buggy to the new house. We didn't take many excursions, so this was indeed a treat for all of us. Mama and Daddy had on their best church-going clothes; Georgie wore his best knickers and cap.

Marie and I had on little flowered lawn dresses that Mama had made for us for Easter that we could only wear to church. Mama had tied pink bows in mine and Marie's hair, which I thought made us look especially grand, but Mama and Daddy I thought, looked the most wonderful of all.

My mother's long, silky black hair coiled into two large round rolls, and placed behind her ears, accentuating her beautiful blue eyes. Her dress was a cornflower blue with white organza cuffs and collar, and a large ruffle of the same material at the bottom of her dress. She looked like an angel to me. My father wore his best black suit and white shirt, set off by his shiny black hat from which his red curls kept escaping, taking away the soberness of his clothes. His sky blue eyes danced with joy and a bit of mischief this day. As soon as we were away from the church house, my father began to sing and insisted we all join in as we made our way merrily down the graveled road.

After what seemed like an eternity to me, we were passing the Lawrence Schoolhouse. This was a revelation for I had never seen where my brother and sister went off to school each day. As we passed by, I clambered for an explanation as to what they did there and wanted to get out and go inside the building. My parents just laughed, and explained that I would have to wait until after we moved and school started again. Then I could go inside. I had to think about this and was surprised as I felt my father's hand on my shoulder, with the announcement for us all to look ahead.

"See that house in the distance, the yellow one? That's going to be our new home." We all peered ahead and after a few minutes, we could better see the house. Mama gasped and placed her hand over her mouth, and I could see that she was surprised by what she saw. A short distance ahead we could all see a beautiful, large, two story house, painted a soft buttery yellow, with shutters trimmed in white. It looked like a grand castle to me. It was so large.

Georgie and Marie were out of the buggy as soon as it stopped. They ran ahead excited with the new adventure of a new home, but I felt a little overcome with the houses' size, so I clung to my mother and father's hands.

The house had a front and back porch with a swing on the front one, which was a real curiosity to me, but a wonderful delight for my mother. She said how wonderful it was to sit and swing, and that she had not been able to do that since she had left her parents home in Kentucky. Mama was also thrilled with the huge kitchen that had sinks to drain water from and a pump that brought water into the house. This was a real miracle for I had never seen anything like this before. Water that came in by itself, how could that be, I wondered. There were four huge rooms downstairs. "One" my mother said, "would be her and Daddy's bedroom, and that the large room at the front of the house would be our sitting room because it had a fireplace". Something else I had never seen before. Mama began to fuss and was wondering how on earth, she would be able to furnish all these rooms for we had very little furniture. Daddy said for her not to worry for he had a good job and they could buy what they needed, a little at a time, or pay for it a little at a time at the Allises' furniture store. I had never seen my father so happy. He swung my mother up in the air, and then proceeded to dance his wonderful Irish jig with her. Laughing all the time until all of us laughed with him.

I followed Georgie and Marie up the stairs as best as my little legs could carry me to explore the rest of the house with them. Mama and Daddy in the meantime, went out to try out the front porch swing. The upstairs consisted of three very large rooms. We checked out all the windows and their views of our new neighbors. Georgie pointed out the different houses and told me who lived in each house. Directly south of the house was my Uncle Ed and Aunt Emmy's house, my Daddy's brother. They had two sons, Darryl and George Edward whom I adored. To the west was the house where the Phillip Schneider family lived. I would soon become acquainted with this family and their daughter, Mary Ruth. She would become my very best friend. To the north lived a family named Curtis, and they had three children, none of which anyone seemed to know except for the youngest, named David, who was in a class ahead of my sister. To the east of us were two families living almost across from each other, named Schmitzer and the Hargrove family. All of these people would become and integral part of our lives.

All of our new neighbors were farmers, who owned their own farms and were growing mostly corn and wheat, a few cattle, pigs and chickens. The largest of these farms were the Schneider's, who not only had lots of acres of wheat and corn but a large herd of cows, and they had ELECTRIC LIGHTS. What a phenomenon that was to all of us. Mrs. Mary Jane Schneider would become my mother's best friend. Many years later, I would find out that she was like my mother, an Indian.

As we were investigating as to who lived where, we were suddenly brought back to the present as our Daddy hollered up the stairs at us.

"George, you and Marie bring Ruby Jewell downstairs for we must be going home." I had never climbed so many stairs by myself before, certainly not gone down by myself, so Georgie and Marie held my hands, and helped me down into my father's arms.

Sundays were always special in our home, but this had been an extra special one, Daddy had said. Even so, we would follow our regular routine; first, changing our church clothes for simpler ones and eating our lunch that Mama had prepared the day before. Then Daddy would play his 'fiddle' as he called it, sometimes he would also play his banjo, or guitar, or he might play all of these instruments, while teaching my brother the 'Jews harp' which seemed to fascinate him. When Georgie played music, Daddy would take turns dancing with Mama and Marie, but best of all he would dance me around in his arms, then put me down and teach me all his wonderful dances. Early on, he had found that I would imitate him and it delighted him to show me everything he knew. Along with the dances, he taught me little songs and took delight in having me sing them for anyone who would listen.

Much to my mothers' chagrin, he delighted in showing me off at his best friend's bar, and was just as anxious to hear every new song and dance I could perform. Mama hated that Daddy had me doing these things because of the alcohol served there. Daddy would hug and kiss my Mama when she would complain to him about it, and then she would relent, and say that it was all right, but just when she was shopping with Georgie and Marie. Daddy loved to shoot pool and did so on most of the occasions when we would go there. He would have me do my little songs and dances on the bar, and the men would pay me with ice cream and suckers to get to do 'just one more song and dance'. I am sure this reward for work made an indelible mark on my future life.

My mother seemed sad most of the time when Daddy was not at home. I was to learn years later, that I had had two brothers born before me. One, born two years after Georgie, named Rudolph, who died from a severe ear infection, which had resulted from a fall off our front porch. Then two years before Mama had a stillborn, which she named Johnny. This birth happened at my Aunt Sophia's house in Uniontown, Kentucky and there is where he was buried. Mama would never talk to us much about these deaths but our Aunt Emmy would tell us the story. She said that these deaths affected Mama so much, that for four months after each of the deaths, Mama would take her daily trip to the little church (which was more than a mile away through the fields) to say prayers for any sin she may have committed to cause these deaths. She also told us that when Mama became pregnant with me, she made daily trips to the church to pray that her baby be born healthy and to let it live to be grown. She promised God in those trips that she would always be faithful to the Creator, and always keep His word. Aunt Emmy told us that when Mama became very heavy and had trouble walking, my Uncle Ed or one of their boys would come to our house and take her to the little church to pray and that she would pray too for a healthy baby.

Healthy I was. I was the largest baby my mother had, weighing in at eight pounds and eight ounces. I was also born with what people of that day referred to as a 'veil/ over my face which was a spiritual sign that I was a SPECIAL, gifted baby. My hair was red like my father's, long and curly, and hung in my face. While my mother was still confined to bed, Daddy had to cut my hair leaving me with 'bangs' which curled up off my face. One of my first memories was of my sister Marie and Mama wrapping my hair into long finger curls, for which I had little patience. I always wanted to be doing something, swinging in the little swing Daddy made for us, or begging from someone to read me a story. I couldn't understand why I couldn't read, so I desperately wanted to learn how. My mother would say over and over to me, "Well maybe I should have named her 'Curious'." They would laugh and laugh, leaving me to wonder what on earth was so funny. Actually, my father named me Ruby, for the month I was born in, and Jewell, his mother's maiden name.

That summer my father started teaching me my a, b, c's by singing the little song that I would repeat after him. He would draw pictures for us to color the next day to be graded. He took great pains in showing me how to stay within the lines and to always keep my strokes in the same direction. Once we learned that, we got to draw our own pictures. This was a true delight for me for I would express myself in a way I had never been able to before. Neither my sister nor brother cared about drawing, but preferred needlework or building things, which interested my brother. Mama was always busy with her gardening, which we kids had to help with, and later we had to help with the canning of the vegetables, and fruits, which we had grown. We did not have much time for play for we were always busy with some kind of work, except for Sundays. If we did anything like sewing on Sunday, my Mama would tell us that we were not to work on the Creator's Day and if we did, we would have to pick out the stitches with our nose when we went to Heaven. I could never understand just what or how this could be managed with my nose, so I would ask question after question until she would give me that stern look; I knew that it was time to let it go. "No more questions!" Mama would say.

July the 4th was my father's birthday. It was this same summer that I have my first memory of the park down by the river, in Mt. Vernon, Indiana. It was also the first summer I remembered that my Grandfather Dickerson lived just across the river from Mt Vernon. Grandpa came to visit us every week but I just didn't know how he got there.

He just showed up and he always brought us things to eat or wear. As I got older, he would always give me and my sibling's money for our own use. It was the July 4th, we were going to the park, and Grandpa would be there. We would have a picnic in that wonderful place. We would be allowed to go down "the slicky-slide" as we called it, and Mama said that I could swing in the swings all by myself. I was very intrigued by the little water fountains and the little house where we could spread out our picnic goodies that Mama had fixed for us to eat. There was always a big birthday cake for Daddy, a freezer of ice cream, fried chicken, potato salad, and fry bread. Mama would make this bread for us often and we were allowed to put honey or powdered sugar on it, for it looked somewhat like today's pizza. Sometimes she would have us wrap it around a piece of meat or place a slice of yummy cheese on it when it was hot. Best of all though, I had come to celebrate my father's birthday. He knew everyone who was there. At this early age, I did not know that July 4th was a holiday; it was just my father's birthday because he was an important man. The day was always wonderful, with many other children to play with, ponies to ride, and of course the usual firecrackers. Mama was like a different person on those days. She would be laughing with Daddy and Grandpa, and hugging and kissing us kids, but always with the ever-watchful eye.

I don't know exactly when it happened, but sometime after my 3rd birthday in July, my Daddy was brought home early one day in an automobile, a Model-T, it was. Two men carried Daddy in the house and placed him on the bed in the front room. My Mama was crying and crying, almost hysterically, with Marie and Georgie crying too and holding onto Mama. The two men took Georgie aside with me clinging to him, trying to explain what had happened to Daddy. They said that Daddy had been hurt bad at the Dam 49 where he worked and that he would have to rest for a long time. They also told us that the doctor would be out to see him later on in the day, for he had been hurt very bad. I remember screaming at the top of my lungs, "No, No, my Daddy can't be hurt! Let me go see my Daddy!" and bolted away from my brother's grasp, running into my parents bedroom. I stopped short when I saw my father's upper body bandaged up tightly, and his arm in a white sling. Mama was sitting on the bed with her arms around Daddy, sobbing. She slid off the bed the minute she saw me, grabbed me in her arms and whisked me out of the room, then turning me over to Georgie and Marie. Sometime later, Mama came into the parlor where we had been waiting for someone to tell us what the Doctor had said.

"Your father had been hurt bad, but the doctor has given him some medicine to make him sleep. Marie, you and Ruby will have to finish up supper; Georgie you must do your and your Daddy's chores." Mama wiped away the tears that had been streaming down her face, and continued in a calmer voice, while we three kids stood in awe at seeing our mother cry.

"We must all be as quiet as we can, so go along now, and do as I say while I tend to your father!" Mama turned around, went back into the bedroom and closed the door, leaving us kids frightened beyond words. None of us had ever heard such anger form our Mother, nor had we ever seen our Mother crying as we had just seen. All of the joy we had seen in our mother since we had moved into the big yellow house was now gone, and our father was lying helpless and we couldn't even be with him. We had all loved the big yellow house but now I felt lost in all the space it had so wonderfully provided us. Most of all, I could not understand why I was cut off from my parents. Even with the loving care my sister and brother tried to give me that night, I felt abandoned and cried myself to sleep. My sister and brother tried to comfort me but in their own suffering, they could only join me and cried along with me.

Many people came to see my father and after what seemed like ages, he was able to get out of bed and sit on the porch swing with me, while Mama took Georgie and Marie to school each day. I could not understand why Mama left each day until sometime later. Daddy tried to explain that Mama had taken the janitorial job at the school. Why did she do this? I asked over and over. Finally, with tears in his eyes, Daddy explained it to me.

"Ruby Jewell, please understand that I can't go to work right now until I get better, and that leave me with no money for our food and rent. Your mother is a brave woman and will do anything to take care of us all. She cleans the school, banks the fires in the morning and banks them every night. That is why she goes away twice a day. You must be a good girl for you are to look after me and help me when I need it. You can do that, can't you?" My father tousled my hair and gave me a big hug and kiss, and made me feel needed.

"Yes Daddy, I will look after you." I was thrilled to think I might be able to help my father get well.

My father and I would sit in the swing in the sun, he would read stories to me, and as the weather got colder, we would sit on the little black leather love seat he had made for Mama. Soon I learned every word by heart for we did not have many books. My father would draw pictures and then tell me to draw the same. I would try hard to duplicate them, but soon was ready to try my own hand at what I wanted to draw. Of course, he admired them all and coaxed me to draw more. I loved to color my drawings and he and I would draw together. To teach me words, we would draw a cat or dog and then he would write the word for that animal or house etc., and instruct me to do the same. Soon I had learned enough words to start putting them together in sentences. Daddy was so proud of me, and would say, "Ruby Jewell you are going to be a real artist someday." Of course, if Daddy said it, it must be true.

Mama would only smile when Daddy would show her what I had done during the day. Somehow, I could detect a strange sadness come over my mother but she never complained. Every time my father would cough, I could see my mother cringe. Georgie was so busy at night doing all the outside chores that we didn't get to play together. Marie was always busy in the kitchen or helping Mama in some way with the washing and ironing or cleaning. I tried to help, but of course was too little and just got in the way. Sometimes, Mama would say, "Shoosh, Ruby go sit with your father, or go see if your father needs anything. Empty his spit can." I would run to my father to see if I could help, but usually he had fallen asleep. As the days passed, Daddy slept more and more and coughed harder and harder. Mama tore up bed sheets and made them into little handkerchiefs for my father to use. It was my job to keep him supplied with these little cloths because, in those days, there was no Kleenex especially in our house. The Doctor was coming more often now to see my father, and would examine me every time he came. He would then talk to my father in low tones while he sent me out to fetch something or the other; I was to learn later that he felt it was a given that I would surely come down with my father's sickness, tuberculosis.

One day when Mama and my siblings came home after school, Daddy told Mama that he wanted her to get his shotgun and bring Georgie in to talk to him, before he went out to do his chores. Mama shook her head, leaned over Daddy and tried to whisper, but I heard what he said to her anyway.

"Etta Mae send Georgie to me, I must teach him how to use my gun while I still can. I know he is small but he can be a help to us. He is such a good boy he will be careful and do as I tell him." Mama's eyes filled with tears she tried not to cry, but

I could tell she did not want to do what Daddy had said, so I volunteered to go get my brother and ran out before Mama could stop me. I repeated the words that I had heard my father say. Georgie's eyes got real big, but all he could say was, "are you sure that is what Daddy said?"

"Yes," I answered, "so come now, and see what Daddy wants." I tugged at his sleeve and he walked to the bedroom with me holding onto his arm.

"Ruby said you wanted me to come in, Daddy.' Georgie was a very shy little boy, the direct opposite of me.

"Yes son. Go fetch my shotgun off the wall and bring it to me." Georgie looked at Daddy in disbelief, as I did, for we were forbidden to ever touch Daddy's gun. Georgie never hesitated, but went into the room by the kitchen and got the gun down after several tries.

"Thank you son, it seems that I am a little sicker than what everyone thought at first, and I can not get out to do any hunting this season. Your mother could use a rabbit or squirrel for our dinner, so I am going to teach you how to use his gun. Okay?" Georgie stood there in disbelief at what our father had said.

"Georgie, did you hear me?" Daddy waited, but Georgie did not answer right away.

"Yes Daddy I heard you," he finally said, "but I don't know how to shoot a gun."

Daddy just laughed and said, "I know that, but you can learn. You have gone on many trips with me to hunt so you know how it is done. Now all you have to do is learn to handle the gun and do it safely. Beginning right now, I will teach you. You see Georgie; you are the man of the house now that I cannot get out to do much. So, you are just learning some more of what has to be done around here." My father took the gun, checked it out to see if it was loaded, put it up to my brother's shoulder and grimaced from the pain it caused him. Daddy then caught a glimpse of my face and spoke to Mama, who was watching nearby.

"Etta Mae, take Ruby out with you and have Marie help the two of you carry in the wood that Georgie usually brings in." My father was firm in his orders, but a little smile moved his lips and his blue eyes lit up in a twinkle. Mama smiled back at him and led me from the room.

This scene would continue every night for sometime, until Daddy informed us he had sent Georgie out to kill a rabbit. Mama was horrified.

"George, my God, he might shoot himself. He is so little. The gun is as big as he is! I thought you were kidding about him going hunting now, so soon. I'm going with him!" Mama started to leave but Daddy stopped her.

"No, Etta, no!" Daddy's words shocked her for he had never said 'no' to her before. She always had her way.

"Georgie has learned very well how to use the gun. He will be fine. He may not find a rabbit this night, but he will go out every night until he does. You will need him to help you more and more, as you know I can't do it anymore. Maybe never." Mama flung her arms around Daddy and began to weep so hard that Daddy's pajama top was wet from her tears.

"Don't cry little darling. Everything will be all right. Don't fret so." With these words, Daddy began coughing quite hard, and I ran to take him a little white handkerchief, to spit in. I didn't' understand what had just happened, and it would be a long time before I would. It would have been much better if I had, at least for me.

A few days after this incident, my father decided that he and I would cross the field to go to my Uncle Ed's house. Winter had set in and I had overheard my parents talking about money, and "how in the world", Mama had said, "Are we going to make it through the cold months?" Daddy had said that he was going to talk to his brother Ed and Emmy. I was very excited to be going to my Uncle's house for I loved his family, dearly. They all treated me as if I was something special. Even at my very young age, I knew that they pampered me for they would play with me from the time I arrived until I left, they would get me anything I asked for.

Uncle Ed and his two boys who all played some kind of string instrument, and Aunt Emmy played the organ that sat in the parlor. Best of all, she would help me try to play too. Many times Daddy and all of Uncle Ed's family would join in and make the most wonderful music you would ever want to hear. This visit however, was very different.

By the time we had walked the mile through the fields, Daddy was very pale and coughing very hard. Uncle Ed met us and helped Daddy into the house. Aunt Emmy also ran out to meet us and gathered me up in her arms and took me into the kitchen where my two boy cousins sere sitting at a big table. Aunt Emmy handed me over to my cousin, George Edward, who was the younger of the two boys and gave them orders to fill.

"You boys look after Ruby while I help your Dad with Uncle George."

"Okay Mama, we will take care of our little cousin," George Edward answered obediently and took me from my Aunt's arms.

Much later, Uncle Ed took Daddy and me home in his little buggy because his Model-T had a flat tire. The road from Uncle Ed's house went past the school, so as we were about to pass the school, Mama ran to meet us. She climbed into the buggy to ride home with us. Daddy was coughing and coughing all the way home. Mama took one look at him and began to cry as she hugged him tightly. All I knew to do was to cling to the both of them.

"Etta, Etta, I'll be alright. Don't cry. Everything will be fine. Ed and Emmy are going to help us out until I can get back to work." Daddy was stroking my mother's beautiful black hair as he tried to comfort her between coughs.

"That's right, Etta Mae, I'm going to butcher a hog for you so you all will have meat for the winter and me and the boys will cut wood for your fires. I got a new saw I need to get some more work out of."

Uncle Ed spoke with a gentle voice but he did not feel as self-assured as he sounded. He winked at me and patted my head and I hugged him, I then began to feel that everything would be just fine again.

Mama put Daddy to bed when we returned home and that is where he stayed all winter. I stayed with him and ran little errands for him, as best I could. I really was in seventh heaven spending all my time with my father; reading, coloring and learning everything he could teach me. I was far too young to realize just how sick he really was.

A man by the name of Clarence Todd started visiting our house often and I was to learn later that he was the Trustee of Point Township. He always brought us milk and other things, like flour, sugar and sometimes fruit. During one of these visits, I heard him mention a very strange word beginning with a "T" during this conversation with Daddy and he kept referring to something called "T.B.". I later asked Daddy what that meant and he said that it referred to the "terrible big" cough he had. This explanation appeased me for I wouldn't have understood much of any other explanation about the dreaded tuberculosis.

That winter was both happy and sad for me. It seemed I couldn't learn fast enough for either my father or for myself. I wanted to know how everything worked, and my father never seemed to tire of teaching me. Mama was so busy with all the work at the house and her job at school, she had very little time to be with me. Her time with Daddy came at night after she had put me to bed, sometimes a very hard chore for her, I'm sure, for I never wanted to leave my father's side or go to sleep.

One day in early March, my father had us three children and mother come into his room and told us an astonishing wish. "I called you all in here to make my wishes known to all of you. Son, you are the man of the house. I think that you know that all too well. You really are almost a man in size too, and between us men, your mother and sisters will always be taken care of. Right? Well, if things ever get so bad that we can't make it anymore, then I tell all of you that you have a way to do it. Talk a good look in my mouth; can you see all the gold in there? It is worth a lot of money, so we can just sell it to take care of us." Daddy laughed in his infectious way and continued.

"Etta Mae, my darling girl, never be afraid to take this gold out of my mouth. It will take care of you for a long time. Don't let it go in the ground." Mama gasped, covered her mouth and fled from the room. For a few minutes we three kids just stood and looked at each other and then at Daddy. Always being the curious one, I had to take a better look in his mouth. I had to see the 'gold' for myself.

Indeed his mouth was full of gold. Every tooth seemed to be capped in or covered with the gleaming yellow stuff. I looked at my father curiously for I was just too young to grasp his meaning, but Georgie and Marie began to cry. Daddy said nothing but hugged them into himself and cried with them.

Soon after this, my cousin, Louise Roberts came to stay with us to help Mama and Marie with all the chores around the house and garden. She also helped Daddy and me while Mama was at work. Louise was Daddy's sister, Sophia's daughter, who lived directly across the river from us. Her father was the Captain on the ferry that took people across the Ohio River to Uniontown, Kentucky. He would later lose his life on that boat's paddle wheels where he was entangled.

My father was now coughing up lots of blood and his bed had to be changed often. Also, school would be out soon and Mama said she would have to find another job until school started again in the fall. I simply came to adore Louise. She was a saint, doing all the work that she could do and taking care of Daddy now that he was so very sick.

April came, bringing with it the green grass, dogwood, tulips and yellow daffodils and hope for a new beginning. It left taking my father with it, leaving a sorrow so intense that only one can know who has suffered the loss of a devoted parent. My father died holding my hand but I was told he was only asleep. I was taken out of the house and carried to my Uncle Ed's house, crying and screaming all the way that I did not wish to leave my father. Something was terrible wrong, I knew for I was always able to wake my Daddy by kissing him, but now he would not wake up, no matter what I did. Mama said I had to go with Uncle Ed and that I would be spending the next few days with them. Everyone was crying and I fought hard to keep from leaving, but to no avail. The next few days turned into weeks under the ever-watchful eyes of Aunt Emmy. I kept trying to run off and go home, but I never got any further than the edge of their backyard.

Finally, after what seemed forever, my mother came for me. Georgie and Marie were with her and they ran to meet me. I can still remember their red eyes and swollen faces and I wondered just what had happened to my father. Mama would not speak to me for she was sobbing, so my Aunt Emmy tried to console her and told Marie to take me outside and try to explain.

"Explain what?" I asked, innocently. "What is wrong with Mama?" Marie began crying, so I cried with her. Finally, she dried her eyes and began the task of telling me that Daddy was "gone to sleep forever". She said that he had gone to join the angels in Heaven. I knew a little bit about Heaven, so I knew this was serious, but all I could do was scream and scream.

"No, no, no! I don't believe you. Daddy would not leave us here alone. You are lying to me!" I pulled away from Marie and pounded my little fists against her chest. She tried to stop me, but I could not let her touch me. My two boy cousins came out of the house to help Marie console me, but I had already began running as fast as I could, across the field in the direction of our house. My cousin, Darryl, finally caught me, but I kicked, screamed, and tried to bite him so he would let me go. I finally managed to scratch and claw my way loose from his strong arms but to no avail, for by this time and all of the adults had also joined in to try to control me. It was of little use until my mother grabbed me by the arms and commanded me to stop screaming and fighting. Mama shook me and her angry voice was not to be ignored. She had gotten control of her own grief and started talking to me in a very soft voice, which had a calming effect on me, long enough for her to try to tell me the truth.

"Ruby, you have to stop this screaming and fighting. Nothing you or anyone of us can do, or say, will bring your father back to us. He is gone, Ruby, he is dead. Dead like your little white kitten. God took him because he was so sick and hurting so much." Mama reached down and shook me again by the shoulders, and then asked, "Do you understand? Your Daddy has gone to be with God?"

"No, no, no!" I yelled at the top of my lungs. "I hate God if he took my Daddy away. I know Daddy is at home just like always." I sobbed at her defiantly. "Daddy would never leave me." Tears were now streaming down my face, but I could see the shocked expression on my mother's face at my disbelief of her words. Her shock quickly turned to anger, but Georgie came to my rescue, shielding me from Mama. She had never struck us kids, but it seemed to him that she was about to hit me.

"Mother, Ruby just don't understand, anymore than I do, why Daddy had to die." Both my brother and sister were now shielding me and trying to comfort me in my agony.

"Mother," Marie said pleadingly to Mama, "we have known a long time how sick Daddy really was, but Ruby was just too young to understand. Let me and Georgie take her home and explain some more, please." Marie's soft voice and gentle ways always seemed to settle Mama when she was upset, so Mama nodded her consent. Georgie and Marie took turns carrying me across the field, while I sobbed in disbelief.

The house was empty and almost dark. My heart pounded furiously in my chest. It must be true, I thought, Daddy would never be in the dark. The last few days I had spent with him, he had complained to Mama that he couldn't see her very well and to light the coal oil lamp that set by his bed. He had even told me my hair looked much darker, and as if in after-though, he had me find the scissors. He said that he wanted to cut a lock of his curly hair and then said to me, "See, my little jewel, I just can't' see very well, but our hair is the same color."

He held the hair against mine and then added, "little precious girl, keep this lock of my hair and I will be with you always." He had then lapsed into a violent coughing and choking spasm. All I could do was to hand him a cloth to wipe his mouth and hold the little pan for him to spit into. Mama had rushed in and held him up until the spasm was gone, but he was so weak that he had fallen asleep almost immediately. I still have the lock of his hair, and so indeed, he is still with me.

Marie and Georgie led me into Daddy's room and I could see it was empty. Where was Daddy? Why wasn't he in his bed if he was asleep? I asked those questions over and over, and my sister tried to explain as the tears rolled down her cheeks in her own sorrow.

"Ruby, Daddy has been laid to rest in the little cemetery by the river. You know, where all the big trees and stones are down by the Greathouse school building."

"No!" I cried, "No, Mama wouldn't put him in the ground. I've got to see him. I don't' believe you!" I did believe her somewhat, but it was just too much for me to comprehend. I broke loose from my sister arms and ran from room to room, calling out 'Daddy, Daddy where are you?' and finally threw myself on his bed. It was sometime before I could look at, or answer the many pleas for me to eat or drink. I finally cried myself to sleep that night, and for many nights, thereafter.

The following days were passed in a dream like state for me. I wanted to die too, so I could be with my daddy. Nothing or anyone could control my rage at having been left out of seeing what had happened, and where my father had been taken. I remember having this huge pain in my throat and chest as if something was trying to squeeze the very breath out of me. I couldn't' eat, and I couldn't' look at my mother. If she tried to console me or talk to me, I would run and hide; only my brother George could coax me to come out of hiding. I feel badly now, as I write this, for I know now how much my mother suffered, and I was making it worse for her. But, all I can say is, I was just too young to see how much she suffered in her loss of my father.

Many days passed before we had any company, when finally Mr. Todd, the Trustee came to visit. I didn't care any more to see if he had brought us good things to eat, I didn't' care that it was impolite if I didn't' come to greet him. Mama, however, did, and sent my brother to fetch me and cautioned me to be polite to Mr. Todd.

"Well hello there, Ruby. My, my, don't you look pretty." Mr. Todd was always complimentary but I didn't care. I could not answer and kept my eyes lowered and twisted my foot back and forth on the floor. This was something my mother hated for me to do. Georgie whispered to me to be polite to Mr. Todd, for he was a nice man. I finally found my voice and in almost a whisper, I did what I knew that I must do.

"Thank you, sir. Pleased to see you too, sir." I did like this man and felt better having spoken a few words to him, but he was not my daddy and that was all I could think about.

"Come here Ruby. Mr. Todd has comet o take us all for a ride in his new car." Mama pulled me to her, smoothed my hair and adjusted the ribbon that was tied around my long curls. "I know you would like to ride in his new car, wouldn't you?" I looked at Mama and saw that she was not going to allow any funny business from me, so I whispered 'yes'.

"My goodness, where is that happy little girl who always runs out to meet me?" Mr. Todd asked cautiously. I looked at him for a moment and the next thing I knew a tirade of words came out of my mouth. Even I was astonished.

"My Daddy left me and I didn't' even get to say goodbye, and I don't' know where he is. Mama says his is in Heaven, but Marie says he's in the ground in the cemetery by the river. I don't know where my Daddy is, Mr. Todd" The tears streamed down my face as I bolted from the room. As I ran from Mama's arms, I heard Mr. Todd say to my mother in a low voice, "It is time, Mrs. Hutchison, it's time she can see the truth for herself. Come let's show her where he is. Maybe then, she can heal." Mama did not reply. Georgie ran after me and persuaded me to go back to the room, so I could go for the ride that Mr. Todd had promised us.

We three children sat in the back seat with me in the middle, of course, holding on to my sister and brother for dear life. I sensed this was not just any ole ride in a new car. We passed Lawrence Schoolhouse where my siblings attended, and then took the road toward the river. I remember feeling like we had entered a secret place as we entered a small dirt road that looked like it would lead us to the riverbank. At this moment, everyone in the care stopped talking and I had risen up, leaning on the front seat so I could see the river more clearly through the many trees. Just at that moment, the car stopped moving and Mama said that we were to get out of the car. Her voice shook and her lips trembled as she helped me out of the back seat. Georgie had already gotten out of the car but Marie hesitated, and in a very soft voice, almost a whisper, she pleaded with Mama to let her stay in the car.

"No, Mama, I can't, please don't make me." She leaned back in the seat and hid her face. Mama just looked off in a distance for a moment and then took me by the hand. Mr. Todd took my other hand and they led me out of the clearing farther into the secret place. I saw little crosses stuck in the ground, and big rocks all around us. We finally stopped beside a small stone where the dirt was mounded up and dried flowers lay on top of it. My mother leaned over me, tilted my face up to hers, and softly spoke to me as her eyes filled with tears.

"Ruby Jewell, this is where your Daddy's body lies, deep in the earth. His spirit though, has gone to the Creator. Some day we will all go there to be with him again, and he will no longer be sick. The Creator will heal him of all his sickness.

"No, no, Mama it can't be true!" I cried wanting to scream but the pain in my chest wouldn't let me. "No, it can't' be true, no, no, no!" Mama tried to hold on to my hand, but I shook loose somehow, and flung my little body across the dead flowers, sobbing and sobbing. My mother made no effort to pick me up, but let me remain there for some time. I don't know how long she let me stay there, or when I got home, but I remember waking up to find my mother rocking me and singing words I did not understand. (I know now that she sung me an Indian lullaby). My sister and brother rocked me, trying to console me. Everyone who came tried to console me, but I was inconsolable. My brother, Georgie, was finally the one that said the magic words – words that my daddy had said to him just before he died.

"George Henry, you are now the man of the house. You must always look after your sisters and take care of your mother. You must make sure that Ruby understands that I cannot help but go to our Creator, for this is what he wants, but I will always be with all of you, for you have been the most important thing in my life. When I'm gone from this earth this is your job son, to always take care of your mother and sisters." Georgie never forgot our father's dying words. All of my life he was there for me. He was the only person I could always turn to for anything, no matter what it was. He tried to treat me the way he knew that Daddy would have wanted him to.

One month later, on May 30, it was Marie's twelfth birthday. Somehow, Mama had managed to buy her two beautiful tortoise shell combs for her hair and Georgie had made her two new hoops for her embroidery work. I felt ashamed that she was having a birthday and I had nothing to give her. My sister was like an angel to me. She was so gentle and soft-spoken. She took a handkerchief out of her apron and wiped away my tears and exclaimed.

"Little sister, you have the most important thing of all to give. You can give us the songs and dances Daddy gave to you, can't you?" I looked at my sister in total surprise for I hadn't ever thought about giving away songs and dances. I smiled at her, at my brother, and then at my mother for her approval. She smiled at me and gave me her consent and I began to sing, "When Molly Was a Lady." I went through all of the motions that Daddy had taught me, and did the little dance I always did at the end. I couldn't believe how much better I felt after singing that song, and from then on, when I thought I was going to cry or my chest started hurting, I would sing a song that Daddy taught me, or dance one of the many Irish dances he also taught me.

In the fall and winter in Point Township (and probably other areas close by) it was customary to hold 'pitch-ins', which were suppers and usually a dance. Everyone would gather at different houses each week. The women would bring their favorite dish and everyone would eat and dance to my father and his brother's music. That did not happen for us that winter because we were in mourning and it was not acceptable for us to join in at these affairs. My mother also cut off a lot of her beautiful black hair. She then cut Marie's and Georgie's as I watched, horrified. Next, she picked me up, sat me on a stool in one of the big chairs and proceeded to cut my hair much shorter. I started to cry, but she took a deep breath, and explained to me that this was a necessary thing for us to do, for it showed our respect for Daddy's passing. She also told us that our family had been doing this custom for many, many years. I tried to object but she just said to me, "It is the Creator's way, and we will save your hair along with the piece of hair that your Daddy gave to you." That satisfied me, for I knew when the Creator said to do something, one must do it. That same night she also told us that we would have to move from the big yellow house as soon as Mr. Todd could find us a place to move to. She also said that was the way of her own family and that we had to abide by it, for another reason, we could not afford to stay there any longer. I had never heard this word before, so I asked, what that word 'afford' meant. My mother, Georgie and Marie all burst into laughter at my question, but soon my mother tried to explain it to me.

"Ruby, it means we don't have enough money to pay the rent for this house, and it is going to be hard for Mr. Todd to find us a place that we can afford. School is out now, you know, and I don't' have a job to earn money. But you are not to worry, for I have dresses to make for several of the ladies here in the neighborhood and I am to make several dresses for the little Schneider girl. You know what, I'll just take you with me this time and you can get to know little Mary Ruth. She is just about your age." Mama sat me on her lap and hugged me tight and hummed a little song as she rocked me back and forth.

The very next day, Mama and Marie took me over to the Schneider's and I met Mary Ruth and her six brothers. Mary Ruth showed me the 'electric lights', the orchard, the grape harbor and the big, big barn. The world took on a different color for me that day for I had never seen all these things before. I was a little frightened by all the cows, horses and chickens, but I pretended that I wasn't. Mrs. Schneider was a very pretty woman, taller than my mother, very slender with a sweet face and jolly laugh. When she spoke, her dark eyes sparkled. Her hair was the same color as my mother's and she wore it loose about her face. She would become my mother's very best friend as well as mine. Mary Ruth and I liked each other from the very beginning and she and I were best of friends, until she married and moved away.

All that long winter after my father's death, we stayed at home most of the time. Mama was always busy working at something. During the hot months, she had worked with the wheat thrasher ring; cooking for the workers and Georgie took on the job of the water boy. The jugs he had to carry to the men for them to drink water were almost as big as he was. Mama also shocked wheat, worked at the local mortuary dressing the dead, and when fall came, she went back to her job at the Schoolhouse. During the day while she was not at the Schoolhouse, she shucked and gleaned corn for the local farmers. At night, she kept us, three kids busy making quilts, rugs for our floors, and teaching us to embroider and quilt. Most of our neighbors had bare floors, but Mama could not stand our floors bare, so we crocheted or braided old clothes into rugs. These rugs were sorely needed in the house that we finally moved into, for it was a far cry from the big yellow house with its porches and swings.

It was a hard and mostly solemn winter that year, with all the work Mama did. We had our vegetable garden and the berries we picked and we never went hungry.

Mr. Todd came at least once a month and brought us milk and other things like sugar and flour. Occasionally, he would bring us some bananas; something that I thought was absolutely wonderful to eat. On many of his visits, he would sit and talk with my mother about things I had no understanding of. I knew what ever they were talking about upset my mother, and sometimes she would seem to be arguing with Mr. Todd. At these times, she would send me form the room and of course, she never told my siblings or me what their conversation was about. We all knew though, that whatever he had said to her made her angry and she would talk to herself a lot. I heard her on more than one occasion, saying words or phrases about not letting them do it. Or, 'it can't happen, what ever can I do? I'll just have to find another job'. When we would ask her what she meant, she would just set her mouth in a tight thin line and say, "it is nothing for you to worry about, I don't want you children to worry about anything, and we are just fine."

CHAPTER SEVENTEEN

STRANGER IN THE HOUSE

1931 – 1934

UNCLE ED, AUNT EMMY AND THEIR SONS, GEORGE EDWARD AND DARRELL, ARRIVED AT OUR HOUSE IN A TRUCK TO HELP US MOVE TO THE NEW HOUSE, WHICH WAS CLOSER TO THE SCHOOL, MAMA HAD TOLD US. SHE HAD ALSO SAID THAT WE WERE NOT TO EXPECT MUCH, BUT MAYBE IN A FEW MONTHS WE COULD FIND SOMETHING BETTER. IT'S MUCH SMALLER, BUT WE CAN MAKE DO WITH IT.

When we arrived at the new house, I was very disappointed. It didn't' even have a porch and it was unpainted. Mama said that it had been whitewashed but it needed to be done again to make it livable. Mama was a stickler for cleanliness and somehow he had always managed to buy paint to repaint our kitchen chairs and table every spring. Now this house was not painted, but too dirty to put our things in until she cleaned it. So, we all set about scrubbing the floors, walls and windows while the men set our things off the truck an went back to the big yellow house to get the rest of our belongings.

The house was what Mama called 'a shotgun house', meaning the three rooms downstairs were all in a row. The upstairs had one large room which Mama curtained off making a room for Georgie and one for Marie and me. There, of course, was no insulation in the walls so the house was never really warm except when you were close to the potbellied stove. I hated the house at first look, and hated it even more after we had moved in, even if it was closer to school. Our next-door neighbors were very close by, actually just across the fence that enclosed their yard. They were the 'Weatherfords' and their kids were all big kids to me, so I was left playing by myself or tagging after Georgie and Marie. When anyone of us kids complained, Mama would always say that the house didn't matter as long as we were all together. My heart would hurt me when she said this, because we were not all together, Daddy was gone. We did not talk much about Daddy, for none of us could stand the thought of his being gone.

Fall came again and school started once, again, but now everything was much different. Mama would get us all up every morning and the four of us would traipse to the little red brick schoolhouse. Marie and Georgie would help Mama light the fires and make sure everything was ready for the teacher, and the students, when they arrived. Mama would make sure that I sat at one of the little desks while she made things ready. It didn't take much persuasion, because I wanted to know everything about going to school. I wished I could stay with the other kids, but as soon as the teacher arrived, Mama would take me home in the little red wagon that she had brought me in.

The rains came, sometimes sleet and snow and with it brought me sickness. One night after Mama and I had walked home in the rain I became very hot and could hardly get my breath. Mama put smelly Vicks salve on my chest, which helped me breathe a little better, but she could not make me cooler. Frantically, she went to the Weatherford's and asked them if they would go get the doctor for me. Mrs. Weatherford also said that she would stay with me while Mama went to the school to do her job. By the time the doctor got to our house, I was too sick to know of his arrival, but he stayed with me for a long time until I finally rallied. I did not want to eat or drink, my chest hurt too bad, but the doctor kept giving me some kind of liquid along with some white pills and helped my mother make a sort of tent over my head. I also heard him say to Mama that I had double something or other. I didn't' care much, I felt so bad. Mama cried and cried, but I didn't for it hurt my chest too much. Georgie and Marie stayed home from school for many days with me, and Mama went to the schoolhouse by herself. Mr. Weatherford and his boys took over Mama's job for her while I was so sick, so that she could stay at home with me. It was a long time before I was feeling better and a big, big surprise to the doctor when he made his next visit. Doctor Doerr was an older man, older than my mother, with a mustache and a very sharp voice. He scared me, but I was so glad to hear him say that I was a hundred percent better, which he couldn't even begin to believe because most children with double pneumonia died. Then too, "I wasn't sure that she didn't' have her father's disease, that awful T.B." Well, I can tell you that remark didn't' set very well with my mother. She gave the old doctor a piece of her mind for talking that way in front of me. The doctor just laughed at her and said he was sure that I didn't understand what he had said. Mama just glared at him and I was really glad when he left, for he gave me the very first shot I had ever had, and I didn't' like it a bit.

One very cold morning when we arrived at the school Miss Stallings, the teacher of the lower four grades, helped Mama get the fires going. She also rubbed my hands and feet to get them warmed up for they were nearly frozen. Mama was so worried that I was going to get sick again, she started talking to Miss Stallings about dragging me out on such cold days.

One day Miss Stallings said to Mama, "Why don't you let Ruby just stay here at the school with me. I could just put her in a seat and let her participate with the first graders, if she wants to?" Miss Stallings looked at me and then at my mother and continued, "I've seen her coloring and I know she can write her name and numbers, so I think she would enjoy herself. I can see, too, she has a zest for learning." Miss Stallings's words sounded like music to my ears, for I desperately wanted to be able to read books like my brother and sister.

"Please, Mama let me stay today. I promise to do everything Miss Stallings says for me to do. Please, Mama," I begged.

"Well, maybe since it is so bad outside, maybe that would be alright, but only once in awhile. I guess she can stay today. I have work to do in the work room downstairs, so she can stay up here today." I fully understood that my Mother was saying this is only a temporary thing, so don't expect it every day. Later I was to learn that even though Mama was reluctant for me to stay, she was also relieved. Miss Stallings seemed excited that I was going to stay. She was so excited that she picked me up and placed me in one of the empty seats in the first grade row. She then went to her desk, tapped on the desk a couple times and class began.

"Good Morning class." Miss Stallings said beaming at all of us kids.

"Good Morning Miss Stallings." The class answered, and I joined in.

"As you can see, we have a guest with us today. This is Ruby Jewell Hutchison. She is going to be coming in to visit every once in awhile, and if I can talk her mother into it, maybe every day. Okay class let's begin. We will all pledge allegiance to our flag." I watched all of the other children and imitated everything they did, the best I could. The words were all alien to me, but I tried to repeat what the other children were saying. I was left handed at the time and had a very hard time putting my hand over my heart, only to be laughed at. I finally realized that it was my right hand to use, not the hand that I wrote with.

My first day staying at school proved only to whet my appetite to learn more. I pleaded with Mama every day to let me stay at the school, but she didn't' let me stay very often, only on the very worst days of winter.

Christmas seemed very far off to me but seemed to arrive much sooner that I expected. Mr. Todd came a few days before and brought us a big sack of groceries. There were oranges, juicy red apples, nuts, and candies. We kids had not seen many oranges and very little candy from the store. This sack was a real marvel to my siblings and me. Mama was elated as she took the many different things from the big sack. She was so thrilled that she began making cookies and other good things for us to eat. Mr. Todd was smiling a big smile as he went out to his car and brought in a huge box with four big packages in it. He also said that he was playing Santa Claus, but we could not open our gifts until Christmas morning. He also said that Georgie was to come out to the car for he had one more package for us, so that we could have a Christmas tree. We were to take our sled out and find a tree and cut it down, bring it home and Mama would help us decorate it. Then he said we could put our presents under it until Christmas morning. That was the first time I remember having a Christmas tree. Mama popped corn and we kids strung it and placed it around the tree. In the one box that Mr. Todd had given to Georgie, was several more boxes filled with the most beautiful balls I had ever seen and candles with little clips on them to attach to the tree. Of course, I wanted to light the candles right away, but Mama said no, not until Christmas Eve. On Christmas Eve before we went to the little Methodist Church, Mama told us a story about our Creator and the baby Jesus' birth. The church presented a little pageant about the baby Jesus' birth and had a nice Nativity scene set up on the altar. After the services were over, the minister and several helpers handed out little brown sacks of fruit and candy to all the children. I was so thrilled for I loved candy of any kind, just like my Mama.

When we got home, we lit the candles on the tree and we sang every song that we all knew, and Mama made us all hot chocolate and gave us some cookies she had baked. Later she let us open our gifts from Mr. Todd. I don't remember much else except the wonder of the porcelain baby doll that was in my package. She was so beautiful in her lovely pink dress and bonnet to match, and of all things, she had little patent leather shoes to wear. I was so happy I could hardly believe it was all true. It was just the thing that was needed, to help ease some of the sorrow of my father's death.

Our little house was very cold that winter. There was no heat upstairs so Mama madc us beds downstairs and heated bricks to keep us warm. Sometimes, when it snowed and the wind was blowing, snow would drift in under the eaves of the house and around the windows. Sometimes when we would wake up in the morning, snow would be stacked up inside our front door. Mama would stuff more rags under the door and around the windows, trying to keep out as much of the cold as she could. No matter how hard she had to work or what she had to do to keep us warm and fed, Mama did it and she never complained. February came and with it a mass vaccination at the Lawrence School for all the children and some adults, for Smallpox, Diphtheria Fever and Scarlet Fever. I didn't' want to get this vaccination, but Mama said that I had to for it was a health law for all the children that lived in Point Township, so of course that meant me too. I had an extreme reaction to the vaccination and my arm swelled double in size and I had a bad fever for several days. Again, Mrs. Weatherford came to the house and stayed with me while Mama went to the school. My cousin Louise and her family came over to visit and Louise decided to stay over so she could help Mama with me while she was working. Only a few days later another trauma took place. Mama was washing the windows at the school and getting ready to do what she called 'spring cleaning', when she fell off the stepladder onto one of the little desk tops. She landed in such a way that she ruptured herself, and had to be taken to the hospital from the school. I was frantic when Mrs. Weatherford came over and told us the news, for I had no idea what it was all about, except Mama was hurt and was not coming home. Georgie and Marie came home from school that day in tears and much fear about what had happened. Marie was such a comfort for me, for she took over all the duties that Mama did around the house with Louise's help. After about a week Mr. Todd came and took us to the hospital to see Mama. I felt better after seeing her and that she was looking alright. She reassured us that she would be home soon, as good as ever, and that everything would be just fine again. This, however, was not to be exactly true.

A few days after Mama came home form the hospital, Mr. Todd brought us a big pail of sweet milk and some butter. Mama had to lay in bed a lot to rest and excused herself saying that she was very tired. Mr. Todd and we three kids helped Mama to bed, but Mr. Todd did not leave right away saying that he needed to talk to our mother about some business. Georgie and Marie took me out to the kitchen where Louise was cooking our dinner. I was so happy to have Mama back home; I didn't suspect that there was a much bigger problem that I or my brother or sister could ever have dreamed of. I got out my coloring book and went back into the sitting room to color and heard some of my mother's and Mr. Todd's conversation.

"I just don't know what I can do, Mrs. Hutchison. The officers have already questioned me as to how you were going to be able to take care of the children now," Mr. Todd sounded very worried, "I can only hold them off for a little while longer, until you are able to get around better." I peeked around the corner and saw my mother sit up in the bed at this remark. She had a look on her face that I had never seen before as she retorted loudly to Mr. Todd.

"I won't let them or anybody take my children away from me. Never!" Mama shook her fists at some unseen thing as Mr. Todd continued to speak.

"But Mrs. Hutchison, knowing who you are and your background, it's the law. You know that is why your sister's children were sent to an orphanage in Illinois." Mama shook her fists again and her face flinched with anger at Mr. Todd's words.

"Don't ever talk to me about those people taking my children away from me, I'm their mother! They are not going to any orphanage! I've seen what orphanages are! I'll do anything to keep my children, to keep my children together! I will work at anything! I will fight whoever comes to take them from me!" What on earth were they talking about that made my mother so angry? I had never seen her so angry before and neither had Mr. Todd. Who wanted to take us away? I wondered. I felt very frightened now, but I continued to listen to their conversation for Mama said pleadingly.

"Please, Mr. Todd, there must be a way, a way to save my children." Mama's face was still flushed, but she had stopped speaking so angrily. She was pleading now, for some kind of answer from Mr. Todd. For a few minutes, Mr. Todd said nothing. Then he took a deep breath and said words I never ever wanted to hear.

"Yes, Mrs. Hutchison, there is a way but I know that you are not able or willing to do what must be done. The answer is for you to get married again. It would have to be with someone who has the means to support the entire family. You would have to be able to stay home with your children and not have to work outside the home." My Mama gasped, then clinched her mouth into a very thin line and started to cry.

"There, there, don't cry. I will do everything I possible can to ward off the officers for now. You need time to heal a little longer from your fall. You probably have about two months to figure out what you are going to do. I will be bringing you out some more groceries next week. In the meantime, get your rest and your strength back." Mr. Todd hesitated for a moment, and then turned back to Mama to ask her a strange question.

"Oh, by the way, the gentleman you introduced me to at the hospital, what was his name again?" Mr. Todd had asked the question as if in afterthought.

"Ozro Castle" my Mother replied but seemed puzzled as she spoke the name. "He was the brother of my roommate. Remember, her name was Elsie Carey. Why do you ask?"

"No reason, really. Just thought he seemed like a nice fellow. Single man, wasn't he?" Mr. Todd laughed now, and seemed a little embarrassed. Mama just looked at him for a long moment.

"Well, I must be on my way. Say goodbye to the children for me." I quickly hid behind the door for I knew it wasn't very nice to listen in on people's conversation, especially when I had been sent out of the room so I couldn't hear the conversation they were going to have.

Mama sat in her rocking chair a long time after Mr. Todd left. She was rocking and thinking. Even I, a nearly five year old, could see that. I wanted to tell her that I heard Mr. Todd talking about some men who were going to take us kids away from her, but I didn't dare. Finally, I could stand it no longer and went into Mama's room and asked her what was wrong. She looked at me for a long moment before she spoke again.

"You were listening to my talk with Mr. Todd, weren't you?" I knew better than to say no, for that was a lie, and Mama would not stand for anyone lying to her.

"I just heard part of your conversation about some men taking us away from our home." I varnished the truth a little, as Mama shook her head and answered almost in a whisper.

"You are just too young to understand. Don't you worry though, I will figure out something to keep our family together. Don't you go and tell Georgie and Marie any of what you heard. I will tell them and I tell you now, no one will ever take you from me! I would kill them first!" Mama put her arms around me and gave me a big hug and smacked my buttocks a bit hard.

"Leave my room now. I'm going to lie back down and take a nap." With these words, she gave me a little shove and closed her bedroom door. I knew only too well that she meant, 'don't disturb me'. So I ran to the kitchen where Georgie and Marie were and started pressuring them to play with me. They said they were finishing up our supper so Mama could rest, so I gloomily found my crayons and began to draw and color. What I had overheard slipped away from my mind for Mama said that everything would be alright, and if she said it, it was true. Still, I thought that Mr. Todd was pretty worried. I just would color and conquer the demon that came into my little life and it would go away. I kept thinking over and over, this demon's name was something called 'Orphanage'.

Several weeks passed with no mention of Mr. Todd's visit and I forgot all about it. Then one day a big fat letter came in our mailbox. This was very exciting for me for we did not get very much mail. We all asked Mama who it was from, and what it said, but Mama did not appease our curiosity right away. She took the letter into her room and said that it was very serious and she needed to be alone to read it. This was very strange for Mama to do for she was not a secretive person. We all waited and waited. Finally, Mama came out of her room after what seemed like forever to me. She waved the letter in the air with a big smile on her face.

"We are going to have company this weekend. My letter was from the lady whom you met at the hospital. You remember, Mrs. Carey, the lady who was in the bed next to me?"

"Yes," we all said in unison, "when is she coming, Saturday?" Georgie asked.

"No, she is not coming Saturday, but her brother is coming to see all of you." Mama took a deep breath and continued. "His name is Mr. Castle, and maybe he can help us all stay together." My sister Marie was going on thirteen and she was really smart, Mama always said, so she wanted more information and I detected something was upsetting her. I immediately chimed in with my own doubts as to how a Mr. Castle could help us. Suddenly, I remembered Mr. Todd had asked my mother about this man. With deep furrows in my brow, I asked Mama just what could a Mr. Castle to do help us. Mama was very impatient with our questioning and answered before she thought.

"Ruby, you are too young to understand. Marie and Georgie, this man is coming to see me. He, he has a personal interest in me and would like to be part of our family." Mama blushed a bright red, stuttered some, and then continued. "He thinks I am beautiful and this would be a visit to meet my children." Mama sighed as if she were in pain. She was right; I couldn't comprehend the meaning of all of these words.

"How could he be part of our family?" Georgie asked seriously. "When will he be here, what time?"

"It will probably be around 12:00 before he can get here. You see, he lives in Tell City and it will take him three to four hours to drive that distance." Mama hesitated for a second before she continued.

"Mr. Castle will be spending the night since it is such a long drive home." Mama gave each of us that 'don't ask anymore questions' look, but I was not at all satisfied yet.

"Where is this Mr. Castle going to sleep?" I asked innocently. Mama looked a bit shocked, but tried to remain calm at this questioning.

"Well, I will have to sleep upstairs with you and Marie for you kids know that the guest always gets the best we have. Now run along, and don't' ask so many questions." With this Mama left us standing looking at each other trying to figure out just why was this man coming to see us. We had never had a man visitor before, especially one that was 'interested' in Mama. I didn't like the sound of it at all, and I was to find out later neither did my sister or brother.

Saturday came and Mama was all askew. She was very nervous; she scrubbed me down until I thought she was going to take my skin off. She washed my hair and wrapped it in little sausage curls and dressed me in my best Sunday dress. I also was given strict orders not to go outside and get myself dirty. Mama then directed Georgie and Marie to clean themselves up and put on their Sunday clothes. Mama took her beautiful black hair down from behind her ears, and brushed it until it gleamed. She then powdered her face, rouged her cheeks and put on her pretty flowered dress. She had not done this since my father's passing and it made me feel very uncomfortable. My mother was a very beautiful woman. The word unique would have fit her, but at that time, I didn't know what that meant. Her skin was fair, her eyes were cornflower blue and her hair was as black as a piece of shiny coal. I had heard a couple of my Uncles exclaim at her beauty to her sisters about just how beautiful Etta Mae was. This day to me she looked extra beautiful, with her eyes shining in anticipation for this strange man's visit.

Mama had put on our very best tablecloth, which she had crocheted herself, and had cooked a special meal for this visitor, who finally arrived in the biggest truck that I had ever seen. We all ran out to greet our guest with Mama instructing us to be on our very best behavior. To speak only when spoken to. A very hard job it was for me.

The man was rather tall and a little on the heavy side. He wore eye glasses and walked with a limp. He took my mother's hand and held it for a moment and then placed his other hand on her shoulder. Mama stepped back at this gesture and then laughed in a shrill sounding giggle. We three kids looked at each other for we had never heard Mama laugh like that before. She then motioned for us kids to come to her side and we were introduced to Mr. Castle.

"These are my children, Mr. Castle. This is Agnes Marie, the oldest; George Henry, Jr. and Ruby Jewell." Mr. Castle just looked us over for a moment, and then turned his attention back to Mama and she quickly invited us to all go into the house.

"Come, let's all go into the house, for I'm sure you are hungry. I have dinner ready, but first I'm sure you would like to wash up." Mama, always a stickler for cleanliness, was not about to let a stranger sit at her table without first washing. Georgie and I snickered at this, but a look from Mama cautioned us to be quiet. Still holding Mr. Castle's hand, Mama led him through the kitchen door. The aromas floated out to greet us all, and I was pleased when Mr. Castle made a note of the delicious food Mama and Marie had prepared.

Not much conversation was had at the table except to ask Mr. Castle how his trip was and did he have any problems finding our house. We three kids just sat and listened to the conversation. I had been instructed by Mama not to start asking questions, but to sit and be quiet. This was still indeed a struggle for me, for I had a million things I wanted to ask this man, but Mama had her ever watchful eye on me and somehow I managed to remain quiet, but attentive.

After our dinner was over Mama gave us three children the chores of washing the dishes, cleaning the floor and general tidying up, while she entertained our guest in the parlor. I didn't like what was happening and loudly voiced my opinion to my sister and brother.

"Georgie, why is our Mama sitting on our love seat with that Mr. Castle? Daddy made that for Mama and I don't like him sitting in it." I couldn't begin to understand what was happening. My ever protective brother didn't know what to say to appease me, so he turned to my sister for the answer.

"Marie, tell Ruby why Mama is sitting so close to that man." George was very shy and having made this statement, turned red and ducked his head. He then picked up the dish towel and continued wiping the dishes. Marie gave Georgie a sharp glare, wiped her hands and ushered me to one of the chairs that sat in our kitchen.

"Sit down beside me, Ruby. I will try to explain." My sister was always patient with me as well as everyone else she came in contact. She now wore a strange look on her face, almost as if she was going to cry, so I quickly obeyed her.

"I don't exactly know how to begin, but I believe Mama is being what adults call it, 'courted'. I believe too that Mama is going to marry Mr. Castle."

"Oh, no, no, Marie, she mustn't do that. I don't like this man!" I started to cry and Georgie stopped drying the dish he held and looked at my sister dumbfounded, as he spoke.

"Mama surely won't do that! Tell us she won't Marie. We don't know this man." Georgie pleaded, but Marie just calmly answered.

"Yes, I think she will. She told me she had to get married because Mr. Todd said it was the only way out."

"Her only way out of what?" Georgie asked.

"She would not explain what she meant, but that she had to do it. We are not to question our mother. She knows what is best. Now Ruby, try to understand. He won't ever take Daddy's place, so try to understand." I could not even begin to fathom why on earth Mama would want to bring this strange man into our home.

"I won't do it! I won't understand! I don't like him I hate him and Mama. I won't understand for I don't want her to marry him." I was full of anger now and my chest felt as if it was going to explode. I couldn't keep back the sobs, for it seemed like the end of the world to me. A six year old just couldn't understand this kind of situation. The thought of a stepfather was just too painful. I jumped from my chair and bolted out of the room before my sister could catch me. I ran straight to the parlor for my mother to comfort me.

"What is it, Ruby? Why are you crying?" Mama took me by the shoulders as she questioned me.

"You can't do it! Please Mama, don't' do it!" I cried.

"I can't do what, Ruby?" I sobbed into her chest as she held me.

"Tell me, what are you talking about?"

"Getting married! Please Mama, please say it isn't so," I sobbed. Mama looked at me for a few minutes then hugged me quite fiercely and told me to go to my room.

"Go upstairs and play. You must have something to color. Dry your eyes and tell Mr. Castle you are sorry for interrupting our conversation!" I couldn't believe my mother was scolding me in front of this strange man. I looked first at Mama and then at this stranger and felt totally crushed to think I was to apologize. This man had invaded our secure little home. Defiance and fear gripped me but the hurt was just too deep to let it go.

"No, I won't apologize Mama, I haven't done anything wrong." I couldn't' believe I had spoken these words, and then I saw my mother straighten her back and set her lips in a tight thin line. I knew then that I had overstepped her authority, but I didn't care. I quickly ran from the room and up the stairs sobbing as I went. This was the first time my mother had scolded me in front of a stranger; it would not be the last.

I cried and cried until my brother and sister joined me. It seemed they too realized our world was about to change, and not for the better. I never really understood why our mother did not just explain to us why it was the only way she could keep us together. Why it was her only way to keep us from being sent to an orphanage, because she was an Indian woman. Of course in those days women did not have many rights, and Indian women had none. They were not declared citizens until 1934.

A few months passed with Mr. Castle visiting several more times. Each time he came, we three kids would have to go somewhere to visit. He, in turn, always brought us good things to eat. Usually fruit or candy. It helped a little, but we kids did not ever feel he really liked us very much.

After a few of these visits, Mama informed us that they were getting married the coming weekend. She also said we were to call him Dad or Daddy after they were married to show respect. I screamed at her and so did my brother and sister.

"I won't call him Daddy!" I remember saying, "he is not my Daddy. How can you ask us to call him that Mama?" Mama relented somewhat and it was obvious, even to me, she didn't' really care what we called him, so she dropped the subject. Then, after a long moment she dropped the dreaded words on us, almost if it was very painful for her to say them.

"Next Saturday after we are married, there will be a get together of our friends and neighbors. This is called a shiverie, and Uncle Ed, Uncle James and probably George Edward will make music for dancing. We must make lots of food for everyone to eat. Mr. Castle gave me money to buy the extra things we will need to make a celebration. It will have to be just like the one your Grandmother and Grandfather gave me when I married your father. First things first, we must clean the house so it is spic and span." And so, it was a very fine party the likes of which I had never seen before.

Mr. Castle was very nice to us, but we three kids just couldn't accept him as a father. We all called him Dad to his face to placate Mama, but he was always Mr. Castle when we spoke of him otherwise. Even Mama called him Mr. Castle except when she was irritated or angry with him then she would call him Ozro, as if she had a bad taste in her mouth.

Nine and a half months passed with 'Dad' treating us kids just great. He would bring home treats for us sometimes and on Christmas he took us all in his big ton and a half truck to visit his brother, Benjamin Castle, and his family. We kids immediately fell in love with Uncle Benji and Aunt Esther.

They also had three girls, Agnes Geneve, Margaret Ada and Lois. Lois and I were about the same age and became great friends. I remember the first Christmas with them as being very special. They had lots of fruit, nuts, candy and many presents. I was fascinated by all these different things, especially a set of pickup sticks and a kaleidoscope that Lois had received as one of her gifts.

Their house was much larger than ours was and nicely furnished. In their parlor sat a wonderful piano and Margaret or Agnes would play it for us. Everyone would sing lots of songs together which was a lot of fun for me, for I loved to sing. My favorites from their song book were, "The Bear Came Over The Mountain", "The Old Grey Mare Ain't What She Used To Be", and best of all, “The Big Rock Candy Mountain”. It was the very best Christmas that I had had as a little girl.

Mr. Castle was not happy in our little shotgun house, so he moved us to the Morlock place on the corner of school road and the main road to Mt. Vernon. Much to my surprise and pleasure, it also was very close to the river where Georgie and I could go fishing every day if we got our chores done on time. It was also the house where I found my brother, now 13, smoking grape leaves with a couple of his little buddies. Another big surprise was my sister had a beau and he came calling when she was almost 15. His name was David Curtis and he was almost 18. These two things gave me the leverage I needed to get my siblings to take me along wherever they went. All I would have to say was, “I’ll just have to tell Mama you were smoking!” or “I saw you kiss David.” They would then just take me with them wherever they were going. Years later, my brother said he and Marie didn’t really mind having me along with them. My brother and I went fishing in the Ohio River several times a week. Mama showed us how to make dough balls and bake or fry them for our bait. Somehow, we managed to catch a good amount of fish even though I had a hard time being still.

I became bored just sitting and waiting for the fish to bite. I would end up playing in the water and singing. Georgie would scold me a little and tell me to be quiet, but I couldn’t last very long doing nothing but holding a pole in the water.

November 1932 came in with the snow and ice, making it very hard on us to walk to school. At the time, we didn’t think too much about it because everyone in our school had to walk a long way. There were no buses from any direction for the Lawrence Schoolhouse.

Thanksgiving came and my Aunt Rose and her family came for dinner. She had two boys, one my age named Donald, and his younger brother, Sammie. I remember it was also one of the few times their father came with them. He never liked Mr. Castle very much and would always make some excuse not to come with the family.

In those days, Thanksgiving was a week earlier than it is now. It was on this day that I first noticed that my Mama was wearing a different kind of dress than she usually wore. It was a kind of apron and I thought that it made her look fat, but she just laughed when I made mention of it. A week and a half later on November 28, we three kids came home from school to find a strange girl in our kitchen. She said her name was Claudia, and that she would be doing the housework and cooking while Mama was sick. She also told us that the strange car belonged to the doctor. Mama was never sick, so I was very alarmed and ran past the doctor into my mother's room. Panic overcame me when I saw her lying in the bed and looking very pale. My mind asked right away, "is she going to die too and leave me?" I tried to climb up on the bed but Dad (Mr. Castle) grabbed me before I could do so. Then I heard an unfamiliar noise, a baby's cry. Mama was all prepared for this moment.

"Come look, Ruby, the doctor brought you a little brother." Mama coaxed, but Dad intervened.

"No, Etta, she might hurt the baby!" Dad answered as he held me from the bed. He, however, could not keep me from talking.

"A baby? You have a baby? How did it get here?" I was most impressed, but still curious.

"The doctor brought him while you were in school." My mother added. She was filled with pride and I could feel it, and I did not like it one bit. I was being replaced. I wrenched myself out of Dad's hands and leaned over the bed to see a tiny little infant all wrapped in a soft little blue blanket. He was not much larger than my doll that Mr. Todd had given me. Mama showed me his little hands, I was enthralled and I wanted to touch him, but Dad would not let me. He became very abrupt and possessive and said I should leave the room. Mama quickly said no.

"No, Ozro, she needs to see the baby." At that moment the doctor, Marie and Georgie came in the room to look at their new brother. The doctor let us stay a few minutes and then ushered me out. Something very strange came over my stepfather at my little brother's birth. He would never be the same toward us three kids again. He had his own!

At that day and time, women were ordered to stay in bed for nine days after the birth of their child. That is, white women. As all the people in Point Township, we had a smoke house where our meat was cured and kept. The first thing Dad did was to tell Claudia she was cooking too much meat for us kids. She, however, kept on cooking what she thought was right until Mama's eight-day confinement. I remember well, the look on her face as she told Mama that Dad had locked up the smokehouse and told her not to fix any more meat for us kids.

"What am I to do, Mrs. Castle? What should I fix for them to eat? Mr. Castle has left in his truck and I don't know what to do." Claudia's voice sounded strange and cold to me as I watched my mothers face take on many different changes. First, I thought that she was going to cry, and then it changed to utter rage. I watched as she threw off the bed clothing and heaved herself out of the bed, picked up little David and handed him over to Claudia, as she shouted.

"Here Claudia, take the baby! I'll just go and see just how locked up the smokehouse is. No one is going to deny my children food that they need!" With these words, my mother set her mouth in that tight thin line and walked barefooted out to the smokehouse. She stopped momentarily at the woodpile and picked up our axe, and proceeded on. We three kids were following close behind. What on earth, we all wondered, was Mama up to? Barefooted and in her nightgown Mama raised the axe up and hacked and hacked at the lock on the smokehouse door. We couldn't believe our eyes as Mama hacked and hacked in rage. Horrified, Marie ran close to Mama and tried to pull her away, but Mama screamed at her and told her to go back into the house.

"Back away, Marie. I'm fine, and I am chopping this lock off the door. No one, you all hear me, no one is going to lock my children out of their food. Do you hear me?" Furiously she struck the lock over and over until it finally sprung open.

At that precise moment, Dad drove his truck into the yard. He jumped out of the truck and tried to take the axe away from Mama, but she held on to it. She had a tight grip on the handle and furiously held on.

"Get away from me!" She screamed as she struck the lock one more time knocking it completely off the door. Breathless, she dropped the axe on the ground and placed her bare foot on it.

"Ozro Castle, you have done a terrible deed today! You will never again lock food away from my children. Do you hear me? I said do you hear me! Never, ever, do such a thing again or you will pay the highest price of your life!" With these ominous words, Mama stood defiantly but trembling in the cold November evening.

Not long after this episode, Dad moved us to a beautiful house near St. Phillips, called the "Wedeking Place". Mama was thrilled with this house for it had beautiful hardwood floors and a lovely sunroom. I was also very pleased with the house for we all had our very own room, a dining room and a huge kitchen. We also had about ten acres for a large garden, peach, plum, pear, apple and walnut trees. Another surprise, we had a separate room that was heated for a washroom.

David was just beginning to toddle around getting into everything he could, and was prone to running off down the hill if we didn't' watch his every move. We had to do the washing on a scrub board; it was my job to wash David's little clothing and to keep an eye on him. Also, he loved nothing better that to grab the washing powders and spread it all over the ground. Of course, I would have to clean up all his messes, but he was such a cute little boy in his striped rompers, that I couldn't stay angry with him very long. Whatever he did wrong always turned out to be my fault, according to Dad. It is a wonder I didn't' grow to dislike little David, but I didn't. I cannot say the same for my stepfather.

He always found fault with everything I did. He tried to insist that my mother whip me for just about everything, but she would ignore his wishes. I remember several times I might be a few minutes late getting home from school and he thought she should give me a whipping for something that I could not help. Our school was many miles from our home with no transportation, so to cut down on the mileage; I crossed the fields for a two-mile shortcut. This meant that I had to cross fields of snow, climb fences and take a little dirt lane through the woods.

When Dad would admonish me about being late, or whatever, Mama would look him hard in the eye for several minutes, set her mouth in that tight thin line, as if to challenge him. It always seemed to work and he would stalk off, cursing to himself.

By now, Marie was in the eighth grade and Georgie was in the seventh. In the summertime, Mama would send my sister to my Aunt Rose's house, so that she could help her. Marie was a very beautiful girl and wanted some freedom from our stepfather too. Aunt Rose lived on a dairy farm, which sold milk to the nearby market. Grandma Molly had finally sold Grandpa's farm. She had no family except Grandpa's, so Aunt Rose encouraged her to move to a small little house that was located on the dairy farm. So each summer Marie would not only help Aunt Rose, but she also helped Grandma Molly too.

It also became evident that boys found Marie very attractive, but my stepfather did not like this at all. Many times, I would hear my parents arguing about Marie. I could never understand just what they were arguing about, I just knew that it had something to do with her. Something else I didn't understand for a long time was also happening.

Money was always an issue in our house and the depression only made it worse. My stepfather had been receiving a pension from the government, because of the loss of this leg in the service. Every month as soon as he received it, he could be gone for days at a time. He would come home smelling very sour to me and Mama would be furious. They would argue and argue. I soon came to know he had been off drinking, and heaven knows what else.

On one of these occasions, he came home with a can of malt, yeast and bottles. He told my mother he was going to make homebrew, whether she liked it or not. He said also, that I was to help stir the malt to keep it from burning. Mama flew into a rage when he kept insisting I help him make his "devil's brew". Making it did not stop his taking off each and every month. On one of these occasions, he was gone for a very long time. Since he had left without giving Mama any money, it left us not only with no food, but no way to get to a store to buy groceries. Mama fretted around for a few days and when Dad did not come home, she sent me to our neighbors with a sealed note. As soon as Mr. Wedeking read the note, he spoke to his wife and then drove me home in his Model T Ford.

When we got to the house, Mama had already gone down to the cellar and brought up bottles of homebrew and several jugs of blackberry wine. I watched Mr. Wedeking load the bottles and jugs into his car and then hand Mama several bills of money. She thanked him and laughed heartily as he drove away. Minutes later, Mama sent Georgie on his horse off to St. Phillips to buy what she needed.

When Dad finally arrived home, he was furious at my mother for selling his homebrew. Mama just smirked at him set her mouth in that tight line and admonished him.

"I only did what I had to do! Don't question me. But, where have you been for so long this time?" Dad said nothing but left he house in a huff.

Soon after that episode, Dad moved us back to Mt. Vernon to my great Aunt's house on East Second Street. It was a huge house of nine rooms. Three porches and it sat on approximately a half acre of land, or more. Dad immediately set to turning the house into three apartments. On the back of the lot, he and Mama planted a large vegetable and flower garden. Mama took care of this garden mostly by herself, with a little help from me. I was nine years old by then, and in the fifth grade.

Mama and I would pick the vegetables and flowers and then we would take them to the Division Street Market. Mama would make me sit on the curb across the street from the market, while she sold the produce and flowers. Sometimes, Dad would insist that I go with him so that we would peddle the vegetables that were in excess of what Mama would be able to sell. I hated this job, but found that after a few times, I was very good at it. However, as much as we tried, we barely could keep our heads above water. The depression was in full swing and to make matters worse, Dad lost his pension!

Undaunted, Mama took in washings, ironings and any other work she could find. This did not satisfy Dad for very long, and his answer was to send Georgie off to work on a Dairy Farm in Loveland, Ohio. Georgie's leaving nearly crushed me and my mother could not speak his name without crying.

Finally, Dad found work on the W.P.A., but our life savior was Grandpa Dickerson. Grandpa came every week and he always came weighed down with food and gifts of clothing for me and gave me a quarter for my very own. I suspect that he gave Mama some money too, because Mama would have a special treat after Grandpa left us. Dad would always tell my mother that a quarter was too much money for me to have, but Mama would always say, "No it isn't".

"No Ozro, it is not. Papa gave it to her to spend or save as she sees fit. It also will help her to learn how to handle money when she is older. We can't give her any money, so she gets to keep all of it." I would always put a dime back so that I could to the movies, which cost nine cents. Of course, the extra penny went for candy, and in those days, you could get a lot for one cent.

Mama was busy all of the time, cooking, washing, ironing or sewing for several ladies. These ladies had Mama cut their hair too. They would ask Mama how she kept her long hair in such good condition and she would answer smugly.

"Ruby brushes my hair every day and we use nothing but rain water to wash our hair. Ruby can also fix hair. She can roll or finger-wave as well as the beauty parlor." These ladies would then ask me if I would do their hair if the paid me. Of course, I said yes. It was about this time that I learned that if I wanted any new clothes or any other thing I would have to work for them. It was also about this timc that I found out about mascara and lipstick. Helen Joest, who lived just behind us, gave me a little box of Maybeline mascara and showed me how to use it. I had very long, thick reddish-blonde eyelashes, and what a difference the mascara made to my eyes. Mama, however, would not let me wear the mascara or the lipstick to school.

It was also around this time my sister Marie married David Curtis and moved into one of the apartments in our house. She and David had been living in Point Township in a little house there, but David thought it best to move closer to the doctor, for she seemed to be having some kind of problem besides her acute asthma. It was also at this time that Georgie came home from Ohio, with Typhoid Fever. He was very ill for a long time, lost all his hair, but grew a new crop of very curly hair in its place. I was so thrilled to have my brother home and well, that I could not see what was coming. I guess Georgie did, and he never complained when he said that he had to join the CCC Camp in Winslow, Indiana. I begged him not to go but he said that he had to, but that he would write to me at least once a week, and he did. He also sent me money along with the few bills he sent to my mother to help out. The money he sent me, he said, was to buy my school books and supplies.

Not long after Georgie left for the CCC Camp, a strange official looking envelope arrived in our mailbox. Dad was off on one of his sojourns, so Mama opened the envelope when Dad did not come home that day. I thought the end of the world would surely come, for my mother never ever said bad words. But now she did, and she screamed, stomped and slammed things around the room. After about five minutes of this ranting, she fell onto our davenport and burst into tears. She would periodically beat her fists on the davenport and cry, over and over.

"Oh God, what can I do now?" then much to my curiosity she began talking to Dad as if he was in the room.

"So, that is where you've been going. You damned bastard, I'm going to kill you when you come home!" I was so frightened I ran upstairs to Marie's apartment. My sister, at the time, was very pregnant and did not feel well a great deal of the time, but she was all I had to turn to now. Ever the sweet person, she tried to console me with her soft sweet voice.

"Surely Mama isn't all that mad, Ruby." I shook my head in the affirmative and answered. "Yes, she is! Just come see for yourself."

"Oh, goodness, are you sure?" she asked again.

"Yes! She cursed Marie, and said that she was going to kill Dad," I answered fearfully for cursing was just the worst thing one could do.

Marie was having trouble walking now, so I helped her down the stairs. As soon as Mama saw Marie, she calmed down a bit, then handed her the unsealed envelope. Mama then gave a note to me to take it to our cousin, Noble Ford. Noble had a barbershop just a block from our house. Noble read the note from Mama and said I was to tell her that he would be down to talk to her in about twenty-five minutes. Mama had calmed down some by the time I got back from Noble's shop. As I entered the living room, Marie was going back upstairs and asked me to come up to her apartment as soon as I gave Mama my news. I lingered around with Mama until Noble arrived and Mama sent me upstairs. I was so curious about what was going on and what my mother was so angry about, I decided to linger just outside the door in the hallway. Mother greeted Noble and then closed the living room door. I listened with my ear pressed up against the door and could hear almost all of the talk.

"Come in Noble. Thanks for coming right over. I don't know what to do; I guess we will need a lawyer, won't we?" Mama's voice trembled as she spoke to Noble.

"Yes, Etta, it sounds like it to me. Let me see the letter." I heard rustling of papers so I knew that Mama had given him the letter. After what seemed a long silence, I heard a long whistle.

"Yea, Gods, Etta. I see what you mean. You know I never trusted that man. Rose told me he was always as sweet as pie when he was around her, but she said that she knew he was not like that at home. Where is he, by the way?" Noble asked salaciously.

"I don't know! He has been taking off a few days a month for a long time now. He never tells me where he has been most of the time. I'm afraid he will lose his job, and then we will be in a harder place than now, without his salary. I'm so ashamed, what if other people find out?"

"Shush, Etta, you have no fault in this, just the opposite. You really do need a lawyer to answer this letter. There is one in my building, and he will be discrete. I will talk to him for you. Don't think that Ozro can get away with this any longer." As I peeped through the keyhole I saw Noble stand up and put his arms around Mama, and I knew he was about to leave, so I scampered upstairs, undetected. As soon as I entered Marie's door, she took one look at me and made a face and 'tsk, tsk' sound before she spoke to me.

"Ruby, you stopped and listened to Noble and Mama's conversation, didn't you?" I turned bright red as I was caught. Lying was out of the question.

"Yes, I did. What is wrong? What has Dad done that is upsetting Mama so much? And why does she need a lawyer?" I asked innocently. My sister shook her head, shrugged her shoulders and tried to change the subject.

"I don't' really know. It's nothing for you to worry about." She replied.

"But you read the letter. Why is Mama so upset that she would curse?" Marie just looked at me for a moment, and then calmly answered thoughtfully.

"Yes, Ruby, I read the letter but it didn't make much sense to me. It is nothing for you to worry about its Mama's business. Mama is angry because they will have to pay a lot of money to hire a lawyer. I don't' know where the money will come from." My sister then pressed her hand on her tummy and smiled at me.

"Here Ruby, put your hand here." She patted her round tummy, and I did as she said, quickly pulling my hand away as I felt the movement inside.

"What is that in your stomach?" I asked, bewildered.

"It's my baby! It moves all around now. I pray that it's healthy. Didn't you know you're going to be an aunt?" My eyes grew large as I tried to understand what she had just said.

"No, I didn't know that. How did you get the baby in there?" My sister laughed again and pulled me closer to her, as if to tell me a secret.

"It's about time you understand about babies and marriage. Someday you will need to know, so I'm going to tell you a little. Lets' see, you are nine now, aren't you?"

"Yes, I am."

"Well, in a couple of years you will become a woman and boys will be attracted to you. Mama will fill you in at that time. Boys will begin to want to take you out, and you will have to be careful and not let them touch you. You know, in your private area, or you could get a baby. Mama will explain all of this when the time comes. Aunt Rose told me all about it before I married David."

I was not impressed about getting married or having babies.

"I don't want any babies. I just want to go to school. If a boy tried to touch me there, I'd knock his block off!"

My sister laughed heartily now, and patted me on the shoulder.

"Good, little sister. I believe you. I don't' think you will have any trouble with boys. By the way, do you have a boyfriend?"

"No! I don't want a boy friend, I don't' have time for boys. They are only good to play ball with!" Marie nearly broke up with laughter at this remark, but I couldn't see anything funny about it. I really liked her husband, David, but I was sure that I would never want a husband. My sister was only 17, and about to become a mother.

Dad came home that night, all-apologetic, for having been gone for so many days. I heard him say he had gone to Chandler to visit his brother, Benji. That excuse was all my mother needed to jump all over him. She didn't even bother to send me out of the room.

"Chandler, or Tell City? What did you tell her? Does she know you are married?" Mama had raised her voice to almost a scream and her face was all red and sweaty.

"What on earth are you raving about?" Dad tried to remain nonchalant, but it only made Mama angrier.

"This! Take a look at this! Just what are you going to do about this?' Mama flung the letter at Dad, and then placed her hands on her hips, looking much like she was going to hit him.

"What the hell is this? Just what are you doing opening my mail? It's addressed to me. Whey did you open it?" Dad was yelling back at Mama now, but she stood her ground.

"Don't you accuse me of anything. I thought it very important, and didn't know when you'd be home! It's a good thing I opened it, for I'm sure you would never have let me see it! Now I know where you've been off to for the past couple of years. Well, I got news for you! You will go to a lawyer first thing in the morning. You will settle with her and pay what you owe. You will not let that child suffer. Do you hear me?"

"This is none of your business, Etta. I'll take care of this my way. Besides, she is lying, I tell you, and it's not mine!"

"Oh yes it is, Ozro! You will do the right thing, or I will leave you and take David with me. I will not live one more day with you. I know the child is yours, or she would not have gone to a lawyer. I've already spoken to a lawyer, so you can settle this matter once and for all!" Mama was breathing very hard, and had set her mouth in that tight thin line of determination. I knew, and I think my stepfather knew, he had lost the battle for he seemed to shrink in size.

"We don't have money for a lawyer." Dad said slyly.

"Yes, we will have the money. Noble will loan me the money, and I will do what ever it takes to pay him back. This child is three years old and you will not do what my father, J.P. Van Bibber did to my mother!" Dad looked at my mother for a long second and slyly said the worse thing he could have said.

"You don't have anywhere to go. You can't threaten me, or leave me, or take David either. I won't let you! This is none of your business, and certainly none of Noble's." Dad's voice had become very sharp and loud and very threatening. I grew very frightened. If Mama left, where would I go, what would I do?

"You just try me! I'll go to the Van Bibbers in Missouri, or to Papa Dickerson! You had better hope I don't' tell him about your filth. He will cut your heart out! As far as Ruby, well, Rosie will be glad to look after her. Make up your mind, and don't come to our bed tonight! You are half drunk, I can smell it!" Mama stomped out of the room, slamming the door behind her.

Dad sat in his chair for a long, long time. He drank from a bottle that he had pulled out of his pocket and mumbled between sips. I could not understand him and Dad didn't even realize I was still in the room. I soon became very frightened of him and tiptoed to my room, taking little David with me.

True to her words, Mama was up early the next morning packing my clothes and David's into a cardboard box. When I asked her why she was doing this, she just said she had business to take care of, and David and I were going to Aunt Rosie's place. Always happy to visit my Aunt Rose and my cousins, I offered no objection. With the packing finished, Mama quietly slipped us out of the house and into Noble's waiting car. As she kissed us goodbye, she gave me final instructions.

"Ruby, you are to take care of David as much as you can. Your Aunt Rose has lots of work to do, so try to do everything you can to help her. Here is a note to give to your Aunt, so she understands what has happened here. Do you understand? Don't you worry, I'll come for you in a couple of days."

I nodded my head in the affirmative, for I was only too glad to leave whatever "business" was at hand.

I only missed one day of school, for on Monday the following week, Mama and Dad arrived in his big truck to take us home. Whatever happened during our absence, Mama never ever mentioned this incident to me or to David. I had almost forgotten about the letter until I cam across it when I had to clean out fifty years of collected paperwork in Mama's attic. There was an old weathered box tied with a red ribbon. The letter lay on top in its envelope from a group of attorneys; I still have the letter somewhere. I later spoke to my Aunt Rose about it and she told me that Mama made Dad pay for his child and acknowledge that the child was his. She believed that the little girl did go by the last name of Castle, and that she lived just outside of Tell City.

Further inspection of the old box gave up another letter that tore at my heart. It was a letter from Grandma Alice to Mama; Mama was about twenty-three years of age at the time. Grandma spoke of how much she loved my mother and that she was going to be a wonderful mother someday. She was right!

As I searched through the box, I found pictures of Mama and Daddy holding little Georgie, with Marie standing beside them. The pictures were taken in Missouri. There were embroidered handkerchiefs given to Mama from Daddy and some from her father, Grandpa Dickerson. Also, still wrapped in its original paper container, was a bible sent to her from J.P. Van Bibber, as a birthday gift. The very best thing I found, was some of my father's clothing and a little collapsible cup that I had carried drinks of water to him when he was so very sick. I still have this cup tuck away as my own keepsake.

CHAPTER EIGHTEEN

A REAL JOB AND SUDDEN HEARTACHE

The new knowledge I had learned from Marie about babies was not something I could keep to myself. I felt so knowledgeable I just had to tell my cousin, Donald. He was not very impressed with my news because he said he already knew about that. This made me more curious than ever, for I wanted to know what he knew, but he wouldn't discuss it with me. He said his mother, Aunt Rose, said he wasn't to talk about this, especially with girls. I had to be satisfied with what I already knew. The Creator sent babies to people he thought would give them a good home.

Three months passed and my sister Marie was now very large with child, and unable to walk very far. Mama fretted over her condition most of the time. It was much too hard for her to climb stairs so David, her husband, moved them two houses down into a first floor apartment. The move nearly did her in, and for the next month she was unable to do anything but rest.

I overheard the adults talking with my mother about Dr. Raines and why he thought my sister had grown so large. He told my mother he thought that Marie might have grown a tumor, but nothing could be done until she gave birth. I tried to ask Mama what was meant by giving birth, but she said I was too young to understand.

I was at school when the ambulance came and took my sister to the Deaconess Hospital, in Evansville. Mama came home that night very late. I was awake for I had not been able to go to sleep, for I was very worried about my sister. Mama was shocked to see that I was up, and questioned me thoroughly. "What on earth are you doing up at this hour, Ruby Jewell?"

"I just couldn't sleep. Is Marie alright? Does she have her baby now?" This was all such a mystery to me as to what was happening. My mother broke down, sobbing as if her heart would break. I ended up trying to console her. Dad also got up but on hearing Mama crying, turned on his heel and went back to bed without a word of consoling.

"What is wrong, Mama? What is the matter? Is something wrong with Marie?" I innocently asked her.

Mama really broke down then and she sobbed and sobbed. I had no idea what to do or say, so I just sat beside her and patted her shoulder. Finally, she wiped away her tears and tried to explain her fears.

"Ruby, Marie asked for you to come to see her tomorrow. The doctor did find a tumor, but she has lost a lot of blood and the doctor has not found a match as yet. They want to test you. I'm afraid for her life. She has a very high fever but she insists on seeing you."

Mama was totally exhausted so she just lay down on my bed and held me in her arms. All I could think of were her words that my sweet sister might die. All I could do was to ask the Creator not to take my sister away from us too.

When I entered my sister's hospital room, I could not believe how pale she was. She did not let this keep her from talking and talking about her baby. She wanted to know if I had seen it, and of course I had to say no, for children were not allowed anywhere near the nursery. Marie was wearing the old bracelet that Mama had given her when she married David.

It was the bracelet that Daddy had given to Mama, and it had her name engraved on it.

Now it seemed, Marie wanted me to have it. She took it off her arm, kissed it, and then asked to kiss me. I didn't realize at that time it was a goodbye kiss, and I'm glad I didn't, for my memory of my sister was that last kiss and smile, and her touch of putting the bracelet on my arm.

The nurse came in then and said I had to leave the room. She insisted Mama and me go with her. She escorted us into a little room, where she proceeded to take blood out my arm. It hurt me really bad and I cried and cried until the nurse told me it was to help save my sister's life. I wiped away the tears and waited with my mother for the results.

At least an hour went past before the nurse returned to the little room where we were waiting.

"I'm sorry Mrs. Castle, but we can't use Ruby's blood. It is a match, but she is very anemic. We will have to find it somewhere else, and very quickly. Your daughter's husband is having all of his family tested. Maybe we will find the blood somewhere!"

Mama just stared at the nurse, set her mouth in that tight, thin line, and took me home.

A few days later they found a match for Marie, but it was too late. She had died of peritonitis before they could get the women's blood to her.

Mama collapsed when she was pronounced dead and remained completely detached from everyone but her infant grandchild. David and the baby came home from the hospital with Mama, and remained with us until after Marie's funeral. She died just before she reached the age of 18 – in the moon of her birth – May.

This time was such a painful one for me. I knew my mother was suffering far more than I was. For two weeks Mama carried little Charles around almost constantly and tried to help David deal with the loss of his beloved wife. My brother David became my total responsibility except when I was in school. He was a real challenge for my mother and for me. It seemed he was always running away, and could not be let out of our sight.

One day while Mama was doing the washing he unlatched the screen door and ran out into the street where he narrowly missed being run over. Dad was furious with me and Mama. He said it was our fault for we were not watching David. A few days later Mama bought a halter and leash for him. After what, wherever he went, David went on a leash. Dad hated this but Mama stood her ground again and said it was to keep him safe and the leash would stay. Dad took his wrath out on baby Charles and his father David.

I had just come in from school to hear him yelling at Mama.

"I don't care what you want," he yelled, "this is my house and I say he has to go! Let his parents take care of his baby!" Mama gasped at this and covered her face with her hands. I stood immobilized in the hall.

"You can't do this Ozro! You can't take the only thing I have left of Marie! Have you no mercy in your body? David can hardly go to work every day he is in such a state over Marie's death!" Mama fell into one of the chairs in our parlor and began sobbing.

"Stop your sniveling, for I've made up my mind! If you don't tell him, I will!" The front door slammed, but Mama and Dad took no notice of it. It was David now who stood just inside the parlor door holding his dinner bucket.

"What is wrong, Mom? What was Mr. Castle saying to you that has you so upset?"

David was always very gentle and kind toward my mother, and so grateful for her help with baby Charles. Mama couldn't even answer David she was sobbing so hard, but Dad did.

"You came at a good time. I was just telling Etta that you needed to move back with your parents with the baby. Your mother and sister would like that, I'm sure." Dad acted very nonchalant, as if he hadn't been yelling and demanding David's departure. David looked as if he had been hit with a sledgehammer. He could hardly comprehend what was happening to him. He stood perfectly still for several minutes trying to digest what Dad had said, then spoke very slowly his answer.

"Sir, Mr. Castle, I can pay more money for Mom to care for the baby if that is what you want."

Dad only shook his head no.

David frowned now and took a deep breath before pleading his case. Even I could see that he was dumbfounded by the request to mover farther away from his job.

"How on earth will I get to my job? My parent live over fifteen miles from Mt. Vernon. My old car just will not make that distance every day."

"No, I don't want your money, and I'm sure you will figure out something. I just want you to leave and take the baby with you. Etta spends all of her time looking after it now, and I want some peace and quiet around here again!"

Dad walked out of the room and sat down on the swing on the front porch. He had delivered the ultimatum and left Mama to deal with David. Mama was just horrified at what Dad had said and pleaded with David.

"I can't let this happen. I don't want you to leave, David. I can't give up the baby, too." Mama had just crumbled down on the sofa now crying over and over, "I can't let him do this."

David sat down beside her and tried to console her, but she didn't even seem to hear him.

"Mom, I can't stay here, now. You heard what he said. I can't stay where I'm not wanted. He is right, too, about the baby. My parents will take good care of him. Ruby, come in here with your mother and me. I want to talk to you a little bit."

I was still sitting on the stairs in the hall and David's call jolted me back to reality, for I was feeling very sad that my stepfather wanted the baby to be gone with his father. My sister's death was still paramount in my mind, but like Mama, Marie's baby had sort of taken her place and eased some of the pain we felt.

"Come here Ruby, and sit beside me," he hesitated in thought, "I wanted to stay here, so little Charles could get to know his grandmother and you, his Aunt. I'm afraid when I take him home, my folks will not allow him to come here very often. I had no idea Mr. Castle disliked me and the baby so much." David hesitated, dropped his head and the tears rolled down his cheeks, unchecked.

"Mom, I appreciate all you have done for me and I want you to know you will always be in my heart and that I will never love anyone else like I loved Marie. She can never be replaced."

David now rose and he and Mama slowly began to get his and baby Charles's things together so that they could leave. Our next door neighbor, Mr. Bass, took David and little Charles and their belongings to his parent's house. Just as David suspected, David's parents and old maid sister, Dorothy, took over the entire chore of raising little Charles. We would have little chance to see Charles except when we would happen upon them on the streets in Mt. Vernon. Even David was not allowed to be a true father to him. However, as Charles grew into a teenager he wanted to see his mother's people, so he packed his clothes and went to see Mama, and later came to my house. He stayed with me and my family for several months before enlisting in the Army. He told me it was so important for him to know me, for he was sure that I was like his mother. He retired from the Army and had a lovely family, consisting of a wife and four children. Three girls and one boy.

With David and little Charles gone, Mama had to work ever harder to keep enough money coming in for all our expenses. Mama never really got over Marie's death, and then to lose the care of her baby was not easily forgotten, or to forgive.

This episode had a bad effect on me as well. I just could not understand why my step dad was so hateful, and why he made David take his baby and leave. I totally understood that my mother's anger at him was just smoldering underneath. I also wanted to have new clothes and shoes, which my step dad forbade her to buy for me. He said they couldn't afford it. This gave me the knowledge that I really wanted anything I would have to get a job.

It was summer just before my 10th birthday that I decided to ask all our neighbors if they had any work that I could do. Mrs. Markham, who lived across the street from us, asked my Mama if I could rally wash dishes and scrub floors. I had offered to do this for a quarter a week. Mama said, "Yes, of course she can."

Every night after I got our dishes washed and put away, I would go over and wash, dry and put away Mrs. Markham's dishes. Then on Saturday morning early, I would scrub her kitchen floor and wax it. My mother made her own wax, so of course I had to buff the floor down with a padded brick that my mother had made for me to do our floors. This buffing would give the floor a soft, soft gloss.

I never understood this, but as soon as I finished Mrs. Markham's floor, she would cover the entire floor with newspapers. I never knew if she left them on all week, but when I would arrive on Saturday, the floor would still be covered with the newspaper.

The money I earned bought yard goods so Mama could make me new dresses and buy me a pair of shoes ever so often. She would; however, let me have enough so that I could go to the movies and have a few pennies for candy.

Much of the time that summer my step dad complained about his job and the loss of his pension. I became very aware that this was really totally unfair for him to lose his pension, since he was disabled. I thought about this a lot and concluded that if he got his pension back, maybe he would not be so hateful towards Mama and me. Maybe there is something I can do if I can get some help, I thought.

September came and school started again. I was in the world I liked most, and decided that I would write a letter to the

President and ask him if there was not something he could do to get Dad's pension back. I told the President that it was very unfair to take away the pension since he had served in the Calvary and lost his leg doing so. After all, I said, I believed he had earned it, and there were not many jobs that he could do now that he only had one leg. I also said that if he wore his artificial leg too long, it became really sore and then he couldn't walk on it at all. I also said that my brother had to go to the CCC Camp, and my Mama had to take in washings and ironings just to help feed the four of us. I also said I wanted my brother to come home, for he was like my real father and that I missed him very much. Then, I added that my Daddy died just before I was four years old.

My teacher, Mrs. Ruminer, helped me address the envelope and mailed it off for me. I don't know for sure whether the letter had any effect or not, but Dad's pension was restored about three months after I mailed the letter.

I was afraid to tell Dad what I had done, but of course I told my mother. Her reaction was, "Ruby that was a good thing for you to do, but you must also ask our Creator to have mercy on us and to let the letter be read. It's up to Him to set things right." Mama always gave me credit after that for the pension being re-instated.

Soon after the pension was restored, Dad moved us to a place out in the country, which had a house and a barn, set on about 10 acres.

I loved that place with its large pastures that allowed us to have out own cow and calf, and a huge, huge garden. The very best thing though, it was only about five miles from Aunt Rose. It was also the house where my brother George came home from the CCC Camp. This was also a wonderful gift for Mama, for she had missed my brother so very much.

Georgie's presence at home even for the short time that he was there, brought Mama out of the depression she was suffering, from Marie's death. Georgie had saved some money while away and bought himself a Model A coupe with a rumble seat. He would take Mama wherever she wanted to go, and he would beg her to let me go places with him. He also began to have girl friends and they didn't seem to mind that he took me along with them on their dates.

My step dad did not like this very much and reprimanded Mama, and penalized me for having a good time. Georgie though, would laugh it all off and go on about his business. Everything seemed to be going much better at our house and my mother seemed so much happier with Georgie around. My brother David started school and this suddenly changed everything again.

We had not seen Grandpa Dickerson very often after moving from Mr. Vernon and I would beg to go visit him and Grandma Molly. It had always been our custom for me to spend several weeks with Grandpa each summer, so when cousin Wanda Lee came to visit that summer, we spent most of our time with Grandpa. Uncle Banks was twenty now and still working with his dad in the corn and tobacco fields. He also was looking for a girl friend at night.

He was very good to us girls and gave us a lot of his time, taking us frog gigging, and teaching us to ride the horses. I had a great time but Wanda was a little frightened, especially at the frogs jumping around in the sack we had to hold so Uncle Banks could put those huge frogs in it.

One Saturday night, Grandpa and Uncle Banks took us to a new place down on the Ohio River. He said he wanted to know, "what in tarnation was down there that was so gall darn fascinating to Banks."

Well, it turned out to be a Dine and Dance Club that served alcoholic drinks. Grandpa laughed and told us girls that he was going to be in a pack of trouble with Etta Mae because she didn't hold to drinking of alcohol. She didn't consider wine an alcoholic drink since it was made from natural berries. Grandpa cautioned us not to mention that he had brought us to that place, 'if you can help it.'

Of course, that is the first thing we told Mama because we thought it was so grownup to go to a dance club.

We told her we only went there so that Grandpa could check it out because Uncle Banks had been going there a lot. Mama laughed at this and said, "Well, I guess you two are none the worse off for it.

Summer ended too quickly and Wanda Lee had to go back home to Indianapolis. I entered the seventh grade at Thompson School House, and met one of the teachers who would make a big impression on me, and my life.

His name was Carl Curtis, and I was learn much later that he was a relative of my Grandmother's teacher who had been severely beaten for teaching Indian children in Kentucky. Of course, I had no knowledge of this at the time.

My Uncle Banks grew up loving the horses on Grandpa's farm, and was interested in horse breeding. Miss Molly; however, was always afraid that he was going to get hurt. She then took to shielding him much as one would shield a girl in those days. Banks loved Miss Molly, as he called her, but he resented that she never wanted him out of her sight. Finally, Ben put a stop to her nagging Banks about going out to places without her. He said it was only natural that he did not wish to be tied to her apron strings.

Banks took to tasting his father's brandy toddy without his father's knowledge. Grandpa Ben suffered a little of the infernal arthritis, and a shot of brandy, lemon and honey helped to ease his stiffness. He was unaware that for some time Banks was embedding, but when he found out about it he tried to put a stop to it. Banks; however, did not heed his father's warning and sought other places to get his drink. He also like to dance, and with his father by his side, he became a regular at the local dance hall close to the ferry. This would ultimately lead him into trouble.

Molly spoiled Banks continuously. It was as if he really was hers. No matter what he did, it was either grand or he is just too little to know what he is doing. Myrtle soon felt the added work load of having and extra person in the house. Miss Molly would get up and fix the breakfast and then tend to her toiletries. By the time this was finished, Banks and the other little children would be up and wanting their breakfast. Molly would help out, but the burden of the cooking and cleaning fell on Myrtle's shoulders. Lela and Boss helped out as much as they could, but they were too little to do much of the washing, ironing and cleaning. Let alone the cooking. It seemed that Miss Molly did not know how to do much cooking past the breakfast table, except for cooking beans and making cornbread. Her cornbread was fantastic, but as Myrtle said to her boyfriend, John Johnson, "one can't live on cornbread."

Time passed none too quickly for Myrtle, Frances and Lela. After some discussion about all the work, Myrtle decided that papa would have to get along without her. She was going to marry John Johnson, and they were married in a very simple ceremony in the little chapel in Morganfield. They made arrangements to take their honeymoon in Indianapolis, where John would be going to work with Myrtle's brothers, Otto and Walter. Ben gave her his blessings, and also enough money to rent a little house and buy some furniture. A year and a half later, Lela followed her sister and married Jenks Hunt and also moved to Indianapolis.

1936

The dark, velvety warm night under the stars in Kentucky seduced the young people into a state of amenity. The music was great for dancing and most all of the young people were gathered at the outdoor dance pavilion by the Ohio River. Banks Dickerson was one of them. He was almost 21 and was madly infatuated with a local girl named Janie.

Janie was a real beauty, and all the young men wanted to be the one she sought out, but she had decided that Banks was the one she wanted. She made no effort to hide her feelings, for she loved to dance, and Banks was a wonderful dancer. He also treated her very special, and never tried to take liberties with her, as some of the other boys did.

This particular night started out much like most every other night at this dance club. Soon after their arrival at the club, on of the young ruffians began taunting Banks with slurs. Every time he and Janie got up to dance, he would try to cut in. Banks was known to have a very bad temper, and when he got a little to drink, he was even easier to make angry. Finally, after a few cut-ins, Banks lost it.

"Get the hell away from us. Janie doesn't want to dance with you!" he yelled at the would-be intruder. The young man doing the taunting and jeering was named Dick Buckman. He laughed and laughed at Banks for losing his temper and became even more disgusting with his remarks, some of them directed at Janie.

As the night wore on, and a few more drinks were under Bank's and Dick's belts, they became more boisterous, and the slurs became worse, then they erupted into to pushing and shoving. The last straw for Banks was when Dick came over to where they were seated, grabbed Janie up and pulled her to the dance floor. Janie was protesting all the time and trying to break away from Dick, but he held fast. Banks tried to interfere but Dick swung Janie away and bellowed out loud with laughter and more insults above the sound of the music.

"You get away from Janie, she is my girl. She couldn't possibly want to dance with someone like you. Everyone knows that you are just a dumb-assed Indian, who thinks he's Jesus."

That was the last straw. Banks threatened to punch Dick in the mouth for insulting his parents. Dick then shoved Janie away, grabbed Banks and tried to stab him with a knife, but Banks was too fast and too strong. He grabbed his own knife and stabbed Dick in the chest several times. Dick fell to the floor, bleeding profusely. Girls and guys alike started screaming and struggling to escape. Janie fainted and Banks stood alone in the melee. Shocked at his own action, he stood holding the bloody knife, alone now on the dance floor. Bank's father Ben was called to the scene by someone, possibly by the management, and was by his son's side when the local sheriff arrived. He was still holding the dripping bloody knife. Dick had been picked up and taken to the hospital in Henderson, where he later died.

The sheriff knew Ben and his family very well, and knew that it had not been all of Banks fault, but they arrested Banks anyway and took him and his father to the local jail. Banks was released into Ben's recognizance until a court hearing could be held to sort out all the facts from witnesses.

Grandpa Dickerson (Ben) never liked riding in cars, but would if absolutely necessary. The trips with Banks to the Henderson court house were some of these times. He did not own a car, so his long time friend, John Dekemper, took him and Banks back and forth to the court hearings. On the day of the trial Banks was scared for his life, but Grandpa told him everything was going to be alright, and reminded him that he should ask the Creator for a fair trial. Banks tried to do this, but having very little education in the ways of his Grandmother Morning Star, he was feeble to say the least.

Witness after witness came forth and testified that Banks did not start the fight, neither did he draw his knife until Dick came after him with his. It took the jury less than an hour to acquit him.

Benjamin Dickerson was more relieved it seemed than his son Banks. He suggested that they should all have a drink to celebrate. He had his usual toddy, brandy, lemon and honey. They laughed and joked for a short time and then made their way toward home. About half way to Smith Mills, a large telephone truck attempting to pass a car in front of them slammed head-on into the car Grandpa and Banks were riding in, killing Grandpa and grossly injuring Banks and DeKemper. The telephone pole atop the truck had crushed my Grandpa, who was riding in the back seat, barely missing DeKemper. Banks was hospitalized for sometime. He had to have a plate placed in his jaw and he had many other head injuries. DeKemper suffered the same. It was 1936 and I was eleven years of age, and unable to believe my precious Grand Papa was dead.

The sad news of her father's sudden death completely devastated Etta Mae, as it did all of his children. The funeral was the saddest thing that I had ever been to. I loved my Grandpa with all my heart for he was someone in my life as a child that I could depend on. Each and every Saturday, he would cross the Ohio River to visit with Mama and us kids.

Banks did not recover in time to attend his father's funeral, but all of his other children, grandchildren and friends did. It was a huge procession of mourners to the local cemetery, and all I could do was to cry and try to comfort my mother. She could not stop crying for a minute. Our hearts were so heavy that I could not play with my cousins, who had come from Indianapolis, Missouri and Arkansas.

Grandma Molly sat in a big chair after the funeral, saying nothing. She did not have an inkling as to what to do. Mama and Aunt Rose brought her home with them, taking turns in trying to help her decide what she had to do. My Aunt Myrtle took Banks home with her and took care of him until he was able to go back to the farm. Banks never really ever got over his father's death, blaming himself for getting into trouble and causing his father's death. Everyone tried to convince him it was not his fault, but he never bought it.

Grandma Molly finally sold the farm and lived for some time in a little house on the farm where Aunt Rose lived, until Aunt Rose left the Mt. Vernon area and moved to Indianapolis. Grandma Molly, then would move to mothers and live there until she passed on.

We kids always asked Grandma Molly just how old was she and from the time, I can remember she would say she was 77. I can remember asking her how come you stay the same age Grandma, and she just answered, "You don't have to take on age if you don't want to."

Banks would later join the Army during WWII. After he came home, he too moved to Indianapolis, married, and had one child whom he named Ruby Jean. He always told me he named her after me.

CHAPTER NINETEEN

EDUCATION MUST BE FINISHED

My grandfather's death was a terrible blow to all of us, but to my mother it seemed as if the world had come to an end. She could not eat or sleep, and many nights I would hear her walk the floor, chanting over and over, "What on earth will I do without my Papa? I have no one to turn to, no one who really cares if I have food to eat, or my children have clothes to wear." I would try to console her, but I too was totally devastated that my wonderful grandpa was gone to Heaven.

My stepfather seemed unaware of my mother's true feelings of loss. His answer was to move us to a house in a little village named Bufkin. I didn't mind the move because we were going to live within a few miles of my Aunt Rose.

The Marin house had a nice upstairs with two rooms for my brother George and me. It also had a big barn and a huge garden space. Once again, I would enter a new school.

My brother David also started school at the Thompson school. It was a two room school house with the lower four grades taught by a Miss Bottomly, and the four higher grades by Carl Curtis.

Mr. Curtis was always very encouraging, and under his tutelage, I finished the eighth grade at the age of twelve. I was so excited that I would be going to high school in the fall. Mr. Curtis said I was a bit young but he was sure that I would do just fine. He cautioned my mother that it might prove hard for me for I would be much younger than most of my class. Mama was so proud of me that she cried when Mr. Curtis said I was so very young and said that the Creator must have his reason for my getting through school so young. She said the Creator would see me through. I was very embarrassed at all of the commotion and fuss.

My stepfather's answer to all this was to move us farther out into the country to a little place called Caborn.

Caborn was only a wide place in the road with just a couple of houses, but it did have a school bus which would take me to Mt. Vernon and to high school.

A whole new world opened up for me and I soon learned the school had its own library; and best of all, someone had recommended me to take the art class under a Mrs. Beaver.

To this day, I don't know who it was, but I was so thrilled with this class, I practically lived for it each day. Mama had always insisted on my studying and thought that if I didn't have homework I wasn't doing my very best. Mama encouraged me in my interest in art, as long as I brought home really good grades in everything else, meaning only A's and B's.

Aunt Rose was also interested in my ability to draw and encouraged me. I spent many, many days with her, especially in the summer after our garden had been planted. One of my art projects was to draw her vase that had lovely roses painted on it, and Aunt Rose said that it was an antique. She kept this piece for years and years, but when she sold her house furnishings and moved to Indianapolis, the piece was purchased by someone.

As I became older, I began to realize that my stepfather resented me more and more. I never understood this, but he treated me as if I was only good for working. He would tell my mother that girls didn't need an education, and forbade my mother to buy me any new clothing. Mama of course, paid little attention to his demands. There were times though, I could not understand why everyone would get something from the Sears catalog but me. My brother George did understand and came to my aide and took the sting out of being left out.

My only birthday party, George arranged for me. It was for my thirteenth birthday, and he bought me a beautiful organza dress and a pair of white patent slippers, with heels! I felt like a real princess, for that is what my brother called me as a little girl. That same year at Easter, my mother bought me my first store bought dress and a white straw hat. She took me into Rosenbaum's and let me pick out the dress I liked. There were two dressed made just alike; one was green and the other was red. Of course, I picked out the red one. Mama immediately told me that the green dress would look best with my red hair and coloring. I was a bit disappointed, but of course my mother was right, so I got the green one.

To make me feel better, Mama said I could wear the hat home. I still remember how I felt and how the ribbons tied on the back with a big bow, floated down upon my back and onto my long curly hair.

I also remember my new dress and hat caused a big fight with my stepfather. He ranted and raved that I didn't need such fine clothing, but Mama stood her ground. I remember her admonishment all too well.

"Ozro, don't tell me what I can spend my hard earned money on. None of the money was from your check, and besides, you are too hard on Ruby. She is becoming a young woman and needs to be treated as such. She works hard for us, makes good grades in school, and does what ever we ask of her! You should be ashamed of yourself! You have hurt her feelings so many times by leaving her out, I don't ever want you to do it again! I know you resent her because she looks like her father with red hair, and coloring, but you shouldn't do that. She can't help how she looks, and besides, she is proud that she looks like her father." My step dad glared at my mother, and looked at me with hatred in his eyes, then grumbling, walked outdoors, cursing.

My mother turned to me and uttered a phrase I would hear many time over the next years. She said, "Ruby, what I just said to Mr. Castle is true. You are becoming a young woman, but I must remind you that at times you are a bit sassy. I want you to mind your tongue for we must "KEEP PEACE IN THE FAMILY!"

A few weeks after this, mother became very ill. It started out with her vomiting everything she ate, then her left arm swelled twice its normal size and her temperature rose to a dangerous 104 degrees. At first, my step dad refused to believe she was really sick. I was frantic to see her suffering so, and knew she needed help. I ran across the road to my friend's house that had a telephone and called the doctor. By the time the doctor arrived mother was incoherent. She was diagnosed with have streptococcus, and would have to have her arm lanced. I was assigned the job of helping the doctor. I nearly fainted as the puss oozed from the lanced places. Somehow I held on just long enough to hear the doctor say, "Ruby, you did a good job, and I couldn't have done this without you." Then I fainted.

Mama seemed to begin to get better right away, but the doctor cautioned us not to let her stay out of bed except for toilet necessities. Aunt Rose finally arrived and the doctor told her what to do as far as dressing Mama's arm and her medicine. She fixed dinner for us, but then had to go home to her husband and boys.

Mama was ill for many weeks, leaving me to take care of the house, meals, milking the cow [twice a day] and getting myself and my brother David, off to school each morning. Aunt Rose took over the laundry and came several times a week to help me with the cooking. My step dad seemed oblivious to the fact I needed him to help me with all the chores. He constantly complained that I had to quit school. I said, "No, I can't. I won't. Mama said I had to finish."

And I did.

My little brother David, would always take up for me and tell his dad that I couldn't quit school because I had to help him. This was not really true, for David was always a very good student in school, actually, a near genius.

Later that spring, a few weeks after Mama was back on her feet, I came down with a severe case of tonsillitis. My throat swelled shut and I had a high fever. A visit to our Dr. Challman resulted in his saying I had to have my tonsils and adenoids taken out. I missed several weeks of school that spring, but my teachers were just wonderful and gave me make-up lesions so I could pass my year-end test.

One of my teachers took a big interest in me and in my second year of high school. She gave me extra projects to do in our English / Literature class. It seemed that I was always giving a book report to our class, and in later years, I would be remembered for all these reports. I dearly loved this teacher who did so much to encourage my writing. Her name was Jane Alexander. My history teacher soon came to know that I had a passion for history, and he too, gave me extra projects to do to gain extra credits. His name was John Nelson. Even with all this interest from my teachers, my favorite classes were still Art and Literature.

Mrs. Beaver had traveled Europe and studied with some of the very best teachers. She not only wanted to share her talent with her students, she did so with much joy.

My mother was so very proud that I was getting a good education, but she also learned a lot from my books. She worked extra jobs, sewing, ironing, washing, etc., just so she could buy my books and school supplies. My step dad complained all the time that I would never amount to anything, drawing and reading my life away. Most of all, he hated that if I wasn't drawing, I was writing everything I could think of down, like my father had said I should do, so I would not forget them.

My Aunt Rose told me lots of stories about our family and how they came from Montana, but she cautiously never mentioned that they were Indian.

Later, I learned that my mother had made all her brothers and sisters swear that they would never tell us children she was Indian.

I matured very fast and was always as mature as anyone in my classes, even though I was much younger than most of them. I had had a few little crushes on an eighth grade boy, and then on one of my teachers, but they never knew about it from me. I was fourteen and a sophomore before I realized that boys seemed interested in me. I was pretty shy at that time, but my best girl friend started going "steady" with one of the boys who sat directly in front of me in home room. Secretly, I thought he was good looking, but off limits to me. One day he asked me if I wouldn't like to go out with him and Doris and his buddy. I told him I would have to ask my mother. He went on to say that we would go to the movies and to the drive-in for cokes or sodas, and that they would take me home early, or whatever time my mother said.

The word "movies" peaked my interest, for I had not been able to go to the movies since we had moved out to the country three years before. My mother gave her consent, but that I had to be home by 10:00, and that I could only go on Friday or Saturday.

We had a wonderful time. The boys bought us a coke and some peanuts. I was very shy, being out with a strange boy, but had been well prepared about how to act and what not to do with any boy. After eating and drinking, the boys took me home first so I would be home on time. On the way, I began to have terrible cramps.

By the time I was home for just a little while, the cramps became unbearable. Mama gave me some kind of tea, and the pain subsided so that I could sleep. The next day at school, on the way downstairs, the pain hit me again and I fell down the steps. The next thing I remember, I was in an ambulance and on my way to the Deaconess Hospital, in Evansville.

The doctor had said that he was afraid that my appendix would burst and it did. I was out of school for two months, but again, my teachers gave me make-up lessons at home, and I passed my year-end tests with flying colors.

My step dad said that this appendicitis was the last straw. I couldn't go back to school!

I was devastated, for school was my life. Mama, on the other hand told me that I must finish school. That we must pray to the Creator to help us find a way. This seemed somewhat hopeless to me, but every night Mama would come upstairs to my room and we would kneel beside my bed and pray together.

After a few nights of our prayers, I suddenly remembered that our Dean of Girls had offered to help me if I ever needed it.

That was the answer! I would go to her and ask her for help. I had no idea what she could do, but I hopefully told Mama my idea. She agreed this could be a solution, and that I should write my brother George to come and take me to see Mrs. Howard.

Mrs. Howard was only too glad to try and help me. Also, Mr. Hodges, our principle, said that he had been contacted by a few families who were looking for girls who could stay with them and work in exchange for food and shelter, and still be able to continue school. They assured me that they would find me a nice place to stay.

I could hardly wait to tell Mama. My step dad didn't want to hear any of this and still said I should stay at home and help with all the work. I heard Mama arguing with my step dad several times, Mama always saying I had to stay in school.

On one occasion, she was very agitated and exclaimed loudly to my step dad, "Ozro, I let you send George off to Ohio to work on that dairy farm, and then you insisted that he join the CCC Camp. I let you force me to give up my grandchild, but I will NOT let you ruin Ruby's life. She is good in school and determined to get an education, and the Creator has given her a way. She is like my grandmother, who found a way to educate little children in Kentucky. We WILL continue to pray to help Ruby finish school. Now THAT IS THAT!"

I rode the bus for several days to school that August, getting my list of books that I was going to be needing, and found that I did not have near enough money to pay for all of the books and my other school supplies.

I was near tears, for I knew that Mama did not have anymore money for me. I had entered study hall and was about to take my seat when Mrs. Howard came in and was talking to our study hall teacher. I instantly knew they were talking about me, even before they called me to the front desk. Mrs. Howard smiled at me and enthusiastically began telling me the good news.

"Ruby, come with me to my office. I have a very nice lady there that wishes to speak to you about living with her, her husband and their little three year old daughter. They are well to do and very nice people by the name of Spellman. Come, let's don't keep her waiting any longer."

My heart leaped in my chest I was so excited. Then I began to pray that they would like me, for this was an answer to our prayers. I decided right then and there, as I followed Mrs. Howard to her office, that no matter what they wanted me to do, I would take the job.

Bertha Spellman smiled as we entered the office and I smiled back at her. I could feel she was a very kind person. She reached out and took my hand before she spoke to me.

"Ruby, I hear many good things about you from Mrs. Howard and Mr. Pence. They all say that you are an excellent student and well behaved young lady. I can see they are right. What we are looking for is someone who will take walks with our little girl, Carol Sue, do her laundry and help me with the housework. In return, we will pay for your books and give you a small allowance each week for your personal needs. You will be sharing a room with Carol Sue, but you will have your own bed and closet space.

We want someone who can become like a big sister to Carol Sue."

I listened quietly, but inside, I trembled. I must have heard wrong. This was just too good to be true. I finally blurted our the one thing that had made the most impression on me.

"You know Mr. Pence? He is my very favorite teacher."

"Yes, Ruby, we are friends with Mr. Pence and his family. We would like for you to bring enough clothes to start staying with us tomorrow after school. Carol Sue and I will come and get you after school, then on the weekend we will drive you out to pick up the rest of your things."

Mrs. Spellman smiled at me again before addressing Mrs. Howard. "Do you agree with our offer to Ruby, Mrs. Howard?"

"Yes, I think you will all be compatible because I know that Ruby loves little children. She substitutes in the First and Second grades when we can't find a regular teacher to do so. The children always ask for her to be their teacher." Mrs. Howard put her arm around me and she asked the most important questions I had yet to be asked.

"What do you think, Ruby? Does this job seem like something you want to do?" I hardly waited for her to finish her question before I spoke.

"Yes, yes! I will really do anything you ask of me. I can cook too, and I will take really good care of your little girl. I will bring my things in tomorrow; and thank you, thank you! My mother will be so happy I can finish school!"

Tears of joy had formed in my eyes and try as I did, I could not blink them back. Mrs. Spellman took her handkerchief and wiped them away, sealing what would become a steadfast friendship and admiration on my part and hers. I was almost fifteen years old.

I fell in love with their little girl, and she in turn, wanted me to do everything for her, which I did. I learned many things in the Spellman's house. I ate new things that I didn't even know existed; like grapefruit and fresh vegetables in the winter. They introduced me to many of the finer things in life, such as the opera, and were instrumental in getting me tickets to see several stars when they gave a performance in Evansville. For the first time since my Grandfather had been killed, I now had $2.00 a week to spend any way I wished. They bought me clothing and made me feel as if I truly was one of their family.

All good things must come to an end my mother said when I had to leave the Spellman's when I came down with the mumps. I had to go home.

I was devastated when I found out later that Mr. Spellman had been transferred to some place in Ohio, as a District Manager, for the food chain he worked for. I was truly devastated to lose my wonderful new family. Once again, Mrs. Howard found me another family to work for and go to school.

The Eichoff's were a much younger couple with a brand new baby to care for. They also had two other children, Kathryn, or Kotsie, as we all called her. Her older brother Donnie, was four, and would later serve as ring bearer at my marriage to Albert Happel.

I would meet Albert in my senior year of school. I was sixteen; he was almost twenty-one. I knew the first time I saw him he was the one for me. He was very tall with broad shoulders, very dark brown hair, olive skin, and the most beautiful blue eyes I had seen on a man since my Grandfather. He also had that cock-of-the-world attitude, and I was told that he dated many girls, none seriously.

We were married soon after the outbreak of World War II. My mother was very leery of Albert at first, because he was from a German family, but she soon came to love him like a son. My mother and father-in-law were wonderful people. They treated me like their own daughter. When my husband had to go into the service, they insisted my little daughter and I stay living with them. They knew that my step dad had forbidden my mother to allow us to come live with them.

CHAPTER TWENTY

1942 – 1944

SCHOCK AND AWE

ON OCTOBER 14, 1942, MY FIRST CHILD WAS BORN. I HAD PONDERED OVER WHAT THE BABY'S NAME WOULD BE IF IT WAS A GIRL, AND DECIDED TO HONOR HER GRANDMOTHER'S NAME AND NAMED HER PEGGIETTA; PEGGY FOR HER GRANDMOTHER HAPPEL, AND ETTA FOR MY MOTHER. I COMBINED IT FOR FEAR ONE OR BOTH WOULD BECOME JEALOUS OF THE OTHER.

At her birth, I was shocked when the nurse brought her into me. She had black, black hair, and very dark skin; but Mama was ecstatic.

I now realize that Mama could see her own self in my baby. Since I did not know of my Indian ancestry, I surmised that she had just taken after my husband. Everyone kept telling me that she would lose her first hair, but she didn't, until she was much older.

Mama was very proud of here ever increasing family. She now had three grandchildren. My brother George and his wife, Reba, had two and now I had one.

However, before my brother left for the wilds of New Guinea, he would have three sons.

During the war years I worked for the shipyards, Servel, Inc., Seeger-Sunbeam and after, at the Office of Price Administration and Rationing Board. It was at this position that I would receive a desperate telephone call from my cousin, Aileen Nelson.

As soon as I heard Aileen's voice, I immediately knew something awful had happened. Her voice trembled and sounded if she was crying. I could not begin to conceive as to what could be wrong. So I had to ask.

"Aileen, is that really you?" I asked knowing full well it was.

"Yes, Ruby, it's really me, and I ..." Her voice broke now before she could go on. My mind raced as to what might have happened. Was something wrong with one of her children or her husband? Fear, in the form of a chill, raced up my spine, dreading to hear what the call was all about. Choking back her sobs, Aileen finally spoke, almost in a whisper.

"Ruby, you need to come home as soon as possible. Your mother and David need you." My first thought was for my mother.

"What is it, Aileen? Is Mama all right? What is the matter?" My chest tightened as fear flooded throughout my body. "What is it, Aileen? What has happened?" I managed to ask, again.

"Your mother is alright, but pretty shaken up as well as little David. He ... found his dad in the coal shed. He shot himself."

"Oh my God! Mother! Aileen, are you sure she is alright?"

"Yes, Aunt Etta is shook up pretty bad though." Aileen was now starting to cry.

"David is shook up too. He finally has stopped screaming! Aunt Etta said you are to come as soon as you can to help her make the arrangements. The coroner is here now, and the sheriff. Ruby, Mr. Castle is dead!"

Aileen's voice now broke up with sobs. I was too stunned to answer right away, but finally I got control and answered as comfortably as I could.

"Tell Mama I will be there just as soon as it takes me to pick up Peggietta and a few clothes and drive down there. You are sure Mama is going to be alright?"

"Yes, and I will tell her what you just said. I will be here at the house with her and David, but hurry, Ruby. I need you too."

I set the phone back in its cradle, too stunned to say anything to anybody for a few minutes. How could such a thing happen, and how did it really happen, I wondered. Why was the Sheriff still there?

After a few words to the girls in my department, I picked up my coat and stepped into my boss's office. Ruth McCutchan looked up as I began to explain my presence there.

"What is it, Ruby? You look pale as a ghost. Are you ill?"

"No ma'am, but I have to go to my mother now. My stepfather has shot himself. He is dead!"

My words tumbled out and it seemed that someone else had spoken them. I was dazed and my thoughts kept going back to the scene that Aileen had described. My God, I thought, what a thing for David to see! Dazed as I was at this picture, I managed to control my emotion until Ruth asked.

"How will you get there, Ruby? Don't you ride in a carpool?"

"Yes I do. I don't know just how, but I have to get home and pick up my baby."

Bewildered at this new problem, I just sank into one of the chairs nearby Ruth's desk.

"I guess I don't have a way to get home, do I?"

"Yes, Ruby, you do. I'll take you. I don't live far from you. Come, I know you need to go now. I'll just have Betty or Louise sit in my office.

I do not remember much after that except that Grandma and Grandpa Happel took me to mother's. We decided on the way there it would be best if Peggietta, now two years old, go back home with her grandparents. It was not a situation where a little 2 year old was needed.

Mother and David had calmed down somewhat by the time I arrived, but still in a state of shock. The coroner and sheriff had left, which took some of the panic off my mother's shoulders. How did this all happen, I wanted to know. Mother tried to tell me the best way she could.

"We were getting ready to go to Mt. Vernon to shop, but first David's dad sent him out to check his traps. I had cleaned and dressed my usual amount of chickens for customers. With the help of Mr. Castle (as she called him), we shook rugs and cleaned up the house. I thought his helping was strange, because it was the first time he had ever done so. I dressed myself and laid out clean clothes for the men. David returned to the house and I sent him out to find his dad to tell him that we were ready to leave for town. That is when he found him."

Mama began to wail again and looked as if she was going to faint. Over and over she cried, "It shouldn't have been him who had to find him. What are we going to do?"

Their house was a large one, with a summer house with three rooms attached to the back of the kitchen. One for washing one for the wood shed and the third and last room was the coal shed.

That is where Ozro Castle was found, in the coal shed. He had rigged up his shotgun with wire and a stand on which he had placed the gun, aimed at himself. When he pulled on the wire, which was attached to the trigger, the gun fired straight into his chest, blowing it completely away.

David screamed and screamed, but mother could not hear him right away in the house. Wondering what was keeping them, she ran into the washroom and that is when she heard the screams.

Panic overcame both of them, not knowing what to do. Mama grabbed the shotgun, then laid it back down, nearly fainting as she did so. David did pass out and Mama had to half carry him, half drag him, back into the house, where she then called the Sheriff's Office. She then called my cousin who lived closer to her than I did. Come quickly, she said, there has been an accident. Together they called my Aunt Rose and me.

By the time I arrived, David was still near hysteria. I did everything I could to quiet him. I held him in my arms until he finally slept. Then I laid him down on the bed which I was to sleep on. None of us got much sleep that night. Mama needed to talk.

She told me and Aileen that my step dad had been acting strangely ever since he had been diagnosed with diabetes. That his already amputated leg was going to have to have more surgery, due to the sores and infections he had been wrestling with. She also said that just a few days prior, he had taken his revolver our of his trunk and had moved the gun all around as if to shoot all of us, and himself too.

She said he said, "Maybe I'll just shoot all of us, then you won't have to worry anymore."

Thankfully, he was not able, for some reason or other, to get the revolver to fire. It had been in his trunk for years, so that alone was probably the reason.

Dave was twelve years old. I believe that he never ever was able to overcome the event of his father's death.

Three days after the shooting, we buried Ozro Castle in the little Chandler Cemetery. Shortly after the funeral, Mother asked me if I could help her somehow because she had to move out of their house. I understood that she did not want to stay there with the horrible memory, but I did not know then that it was our tradition to move out of our dwelling when a family member dies in it. All she said was it is a tradition I have to keep.

"Grandma made me promise when I was a young girl." She also told me that she had very little insurance left after the burial fees. I asked her what did she want me to do, and her answer amazed me.

"I want to move to Evansville. You are the smart one, and the only one I can depend on. Georgie is in New Guinea and Reba has all she can do to keep their family together. Find me a house where you and Peggietta can come live with me. I can take care of her while you work. We can live together until Albert comes home, and he can live with us too, if he would want to."

I was amazed that Mother had thought this all out in just a few days, so I knew I had to do what I could to help her.

I had been saving all the money the government sent for Peggietta and me to live on, a mere $60.00 a month, and had been putting it in Postal Savings. I chose the Postal Savings because I had found out that they paid better interest than any of the banks. This money was for us to have a place to live, furniture and anything else we would need when Albert returned home. I had saved a good sum, but now my mother was in need, and I would have to take whatever was needed and help my mother find a place in Evansville to live.

Everything at the War Price and Rationing Board was decided by its board members. This board was made up of doctors, lawyers, bankers and real estate men. Since I participated as an advocate for the public with the board members, I knew them quite well. I too, knew that they would give me good advice. The banker from the Union Federal Savings and Loan Company told me to find a house that I thought Mother and I could afford, and the Savings and Loan would grant me a loan since I would be living with my mother and brother.

I searched and searched in the cold and rainy weather for a house, and just as I had begun to think that there wasn't anything we could afford, I found one listing in the paper that sounded too good to be true.

"Large, two story, with basement, recently reduced to $3900.00."

I called the real estate person and made an appointment to see the house. She told me the house was in a fairly new neighborhood, created by the war. I asked her why had it been reduced and why was it so cheap, what was wrong with it, etc.

She laughed at me and said that actually there was nothing wrong with it, but it was an older house that had been moved to this new neighborhood on the north side of Evansville. She said that it was on Evans Avenue, in a middle-classed neighborhood, and had originally been a farmhouse. I knew that neighborhood, since my sister-in-law, Edna, and her husband, lived a few streets farther north.

Much to my surprise, the house was nestled on a small city lot, had a garage and two porches, which I knew my mother would love. The house was in need of a few repairs, but livable. It had four large bedrooms and a bath and large basement. I knew that with a little work, we could fix it up and have a nice place to live. I went straight to the Post Office the next day, withdrew $500.00 to place with Mother's $300.00, and called Mr. Burnett at the Union Federal Savings and Loan.

The next day I took mother to see the house and then to our appointment with Mr. Barnett to sign the final papers. Our payment was $39.00 per month. Mother was so elated at the thought of moving to Evansville, that she could hardly wait to go home and pack.

On the other hand, I was leery of telling Mom and Dad Happel, that Peggietta and I would be moving to Mother's. You would have thought that I was moving to China or some other foreign country. After much explanation and a promise to bring Peggietta out every week-end to see them, they finally felt a little bit better about our moving. I also explained that it would be a lot easier for me to go to my job because I could catch the city bus just a block away.

We were only gone from their house for nine months. Albert came home from the Army and we moved back so he could help his father with his farm. The relief his parents felt at our moving back was like their three children who had been lost, were back home.

Mother and David were so happy with the house on Evans Avenue and mother lived there for over 40 years, maintaining it inside and out until she was up in her eighties. She received a small V.A. pension from Ozro's time in the Army, but not nearly enough to take care of herself and David. I paid her to look after Peggietta and she in turn took in another little boy to look after named Cookie. That was his nickname because his mother put a bobby-pin curl in his hair to keep it out of his eyes. He and Peggietta would become great little playmates.

My mother would also take in washings and ironings for several families to supplement her income. Later, she would also hold political parties and elections in her living room. She would remove all of the furniture to make space for the voting machines and cook meals for the workers of the polls. Sometimes friends and neighbors would eat there after voting. They would donate to the expense of the food because she couldn't charge for the meals. It was a lot of work, but she was paid handsomely for it.

The house on Evans was also perfect in another way. It was only three blocks from the Mechanical Arts Schools where David would later attend, and graduate with high honors.

His love of the new industry, television, would land him his first and primary job with Sears and Roebuck, in their television department. Etta Mae paid off that house, never once being late, or missing a payment, while making repairs, beautifying the yard and planting a full size garden.

She would become a faithful member of the Concordia Lutheran Church, never missing a Sunday service as long as she was able to walk there. She took David with her (and later his children), until he became older, and would sometimes refuse to go.

She kept her word to call on the Creator to help her find the peace she needed in her life. She worked hard for the church, and a member of the ladies societies, serving, cooking and doing anything else they would ask her to do. She was well contented with her life and home until an unexpected visitor paid her a call.

CHAPTER TWENTY-ONE

THE STRENGTH OF A WOMAN

THE DAY STARED LIKE ALL OTHER DAYS.

First, breakfast, then she made her bed, tidied up the house and then worked in the garden. She had finished the weeding in the garden, had a bite to eat and was bout to go back outside when out of the blue, a knock came at her front door.

Not expecting anyone, Etta, feeling a little afraid, and as she always did when something unexpected happened, peered out her front door at a strange man on her porch. She opened the door slightly to see the man better as he addressed her.

"Is this where Etta Mae Van Bibber lives?" he inquired.

"Yes it is, and who are you?"

The man seemed familiar, but Etta Mae decided she did not know him. He now laughed at her reticent answer and removed his hat from his head.

"I'm Charles Jarrells, from Kentucky. Remember, you and I went to the same school when we were very little."

Etta's face took on a frown, then a studied look, as she peered at the jolly looking man standing just on the other side of the front door.

"No, I don't remember you. What do you want?" Etta Mae's lips were now clasped together in a tight thin line.

"I came to see you, Etta. I'd like to get reacquainted. Your lady friend, Mrs. Corbett, gave me your address. I hope that is alright." Charlie Jarrells questioned now.

It had been a lifetime ago, but even now he could see the pretty little girl he once knew. Etta Mae, very untrusting, stood silently for a few moments, still peering intently at the man. Finally she opened the door and joined him on the front porch.

"We can sit here on the glider for now," she said, still frowning.

"Okay, that is fine. I guess it was presumptuous of me to think I could just barge over here and you'd welcome me with open arms." Charlie now spoke apologetically, then he laughed heartily. Etta now smiled at Charlie because she did remember that little red headed boy; but she was not going to let him know.

"No, it's alright, if you really know Mrs. Corbett. She lived here with me for a long time. I rented her a couple of rooms." Etta's face now had the start of a bigger smile.

"Yes, that is what she said." Charlie cleared his throat with the relief he felt, but before he could continue, Etta Mae interrupted.

"Are you married?"

"No! I was, but I lost my wife several years ago. I have two sons and a daughter. How many children do you have, Etta Mae? I lost track of you after you moved away from Kentucky."

"You kept track of me? Whatever for?" Etta's curiosity was now peaked as she stared at this jolly looking man sitting beside her. He now seemed embarrassed.

"I always thought you were the prettiest girl I ever knew. I guess you could say I had a school boy's crush." Charlie looked away now, and watched the children next door as they roller skated down the sidewalk. Etta Mae's face now began to turn pink.

"Oh my goodness, what a thing to say! I'm afraid I don't remember you at all. I didn't go to that school very long. My grandmother taught me my letters at home."

"Yes, I knew that. Think a moment, Etta Mae, remember the little kid that knocked another boy down who called you a dirty injun kid. A scrawny red headed kid with freckles. That was me."

Etta Mae gasped as she recalled the incident and all the insults she had suffered were still engrained in her mind. She turned to Charlie now, fearful that he remembered the word 'injun'.

"But I'm not an injun," Charlie interrupted her knowingly.

"I know Etta Mae, and your secret is safe with me."

Etta Mae had not been reminded of her ancestry for many years, and now she was growing very fearful that Charlie knew.

Just how many other people really knew, she wondered.

"I think you had better go now." Etta was now on her feet, and motioned for Charlie to rise. "I expect my son anytime. By the way, what kind of work do you do?" she quizzed.

"I'm a carpenter, always have been. I have a farm near Madisonville too. Etta, can I come back to see you again?"

"Maybe." Etta abruptly opened the door, chuckled to herself, and disappeared inside.

Charlie shook his head with frustration. Then seeing Etta peering out of the glass front door, smiled back at her, tipped his hat, and walked down the sidewalk to the his car, chuckling to himself.

'Just as independent as ever,' he thought.

Well, I will just come back again next week.

And he did.

'Next week' turned into many months of courtship and happiness for Etta Mae and Charlie. They married in the next year and lived happily together in Etta's house for two years. They took trips to Florida, to Charlie's farm in Madisonville, Kentucky, to his children's house and to our little farm in German Township, off Denzer Road. Here is where Etta Mae would come to my aide, after my fourth child, Krisann, was born.

Six weeks after the birth, I began hemorrhaging and had to be rushed to the hospital. I nearly lost my life.

Once back home I was weak and could not look after my family because I was still suffering from the shock of so much blood loss. I guess my mother knew that I really needed help, because she and Charlie showed up one day with a girl to help me. I was not too interested in anyone spending nights with us because our house was little and barely housed everyone. Mama persisted; so that was that.

1954 arrived in Evansville, Indiana with a cold, blustery wind and ice storm on the horizon. Etta Mae and Charlie weren't worried for they were snug in their house on Evans Avenue. They had even begun to talk about plans to go back to work as soon as the weather broke a little. By the last of March, the weather had cleared a bit, the snow and ice were gone, and the little robins had started their nest in the trees.

Etta Mae and Charlie were able to plant a garden in the back yard in April. The peonies were in full bloom and the two were planning another trip to Florida to visit one of Charlie's sons and Etta Mae's sister, Rosie. Rosie had married Orville Baker and moved to St. Petersburg. Life was great and they didn't have a worry in the world.

But tragedy was to strike Etta Mae once more.

Charlie had gone to work as usual and Etta Mae did her household chores. Etta was finishing up with dinner when Charlie drove in the driveway. Happily, Etta turned off her stove and ran to meet her husband after a hard day's work. Just as she opened the front door, she saw Charlie stagger to one of the maple trees, grab hold, then fall to the ground.

Horrified, Etta ran to his side thinking she could help him, but it was too late.

Charlie was dead. Etta fell on his body and tried to wake him, but it was of little use. He never moved.

A nearby neighbor had seen what had happened and ran across the street to help her. When he was able to pull Etta off of Charlie, he saw he was gone; so he pulled Etta to her feet and helped her to the house. He told me later that Mother kept mumbling over and over, "why, oh why, God? Why did you have to take him too? I've kept my word with you. Why do you have to take everything I love away from me?"

The neighbor made all the calls to David, me and the Browning Funeral Home. He stayed until someone came to help her. Mother was too dumbfounded to do these chores herself. In fact, she did not seem to be able to do much of anything. All of her brothers and sisters and her children came to the funeral, but nothing seemed to register with her, except that Charlie was gone too.

Finally, Aunt Rosie came to her aide. She advised us all that she was taking Etta home with her and Orville.

Etta said that she did not want to go anywhere ever again, but Rosie insisted and it was the best thing that could have happened.

In the new surroundings, Etta could think of what she had to do now. She was restless and after a few weeks, decided she needed to go home to her empty house. She said that she would just have to start again and that she was grateful for Rosie's help, but she had to go home.

She said that she had to get back to her church and than the Creator for giving her two happy years that she had with Charlie. She told Rosie that she had not done all the things that Grandma Jane had said for her to do, and she had to change that.

"What in the world are you talking about?" Rosie asked.

Etta's only reply was, "I must pray to our Creator and ask for him to help me do whatever he wants, not what I want. I've been too selfish in many ways during my life."

Etta Mae had had several bouts with Deaconess Hospital and met a nurse there with whom she became friends. Bertha was also a close neighbor, but Etta was so enthralled with Charlie, that she had not been in touch with Bertha for several years. That was also about to change.

One day while sitting on her front porch trying to sort out her life, Bertha came hobbling up the front walk. At first, Etta hardly recognized her old friend. She had not come to Charlie's funeral, and now said how sorry she was, but that she had been confined to her house because of her recent knee surgery. Bertha was still on crutches and Etta was immediately sympathetic for her because she too, had began to suffer from arthritis in her hands, knees and hips.

The two old friends spent the remainder of the day chatting about everything that had happened in their lives. They then fixed themselves a little supper and continued to discuss the situations in their lives. It was during this discussion that Bertha would suggest to Etta that she should rent out part of her house again for the income she would now need.

Bertha finally left for home, leaving Etta pondering on her suggestion. Yes, she thought, that could be one of the answers she needed right now. The next morning she called the man who had helped her and Charlie do some repairs on the house. When he left, he assured Etta that he would fix the two rooms and bath downstairs so she could rent them out. He also suggested that he might know a gentleman who might be interested in renting them, and he did.

A whole new spectrum had now opened for Etta and she threw herself into cleaning and getting the rooms ready to rent. She now had a new purpose in life. She now would be able to put back a little money in a savings account.

Mother was a stickler for routine. On the first of the month after her checks from the V.A. and the Social Security would come, she would take the bus downtown, go to the Old National Bank, and make a deposit, cross the street to the Union Federal Savings and Loan and make a deposit into her savings account. This routine never varied until she no longer could walk because of her ever increasing arthritis and a stroke.

Etta would travel to Indianapolis to visit her sisters, Mrytle and Lela, and her brothers, Banks, Walter and Otto. She also would make trips to visit me and Albert in Indianapolis, and later in Florida.

Her last long bus ride was to our house on Merritt Islands, Florida, at the age of 78. She mentioned to me at that visit that her arthritis was getting pretty bad. It had crippled her fingers, and her hips were causing her a lot of pain. But, she said, she wouldn't give into it.

It was no wonder that she had so much arthritis, because she had worked so hard, she had just worn out the cartilage and joints.

Etta sought help with old Dr. Laubscher, but it was of little use. He told her to take aspirin when she needed it. This, she did for a few years, getting little relief. But she never complained to me about the pain.

During the years mother lost most of her hearing and telephone calls were almost of no use except to let her know I was thinking of her. I could never make her understand what I wanted to tell her, so a letter was the only way we communicated. She would answer, but again, she never complained.

She did tell me that my brother's daughter, Donna Jean, was living with her, but she was working and not a lot of help around the house.

Dorothy, David's wife, had become Mother's standby for almost everything. She helped her with her groceries and other household chores.

I was so thankful to know about my sister-in-law's help, and I was totally shocked when I received a letter from Mama begging me to come home to Evansville because she needed my help. She said that she was down and unable to walk and couldn't get off the couch except to crawl. She said the pain in her hip was so agonizing that she just couldn't take it anymore, so she pleaded, "Please come home right away."

I knew that if my mother said she needed my help, she had to be in a very bad way. So, I took the first flight out the next day. When I arrived, I found my mother just as she had said – on the couch in the living room. It was only a few steps from the kitchen and the bathroom, but she had to hop or crawl to reach either one. She just could not stand on her leg.

The next day, I took her to Dr. Laubscher's office and was absolutely infuriated at her attitude. He said without much concern, "Well, after all, it's to be expected at your mother's age."

I let him know in no uncertain language that I expected more from him, like x-rays, to find out what was really causing her such agonizing pain.

Aspirin was certainly not the only answer.

My mother was not one to complain; so for her to say that she "can't stand the pain", I knew the pain must be horrendous.

I was so irritated at his not caring and not offering he some help that I could hardly keep from giving him a big piece of my mind, which I would not have been very pleasant.

In the car, mother turned to me with tears in her eyes and asked pitifully, "Ruby, what on earth can we do?" I was quick to answer her because I already had formed a plan in my mind.

"Don't fret Mama, I'm going to take you home with me and get you a good doctor in Florida. We will find out what is causing you so much pain."

She blinked back her tears before she asked her next question.

"How are we going to Florida, Ruby?"

"Mama, there is only one way. We will fly back, just you and me." Mama looked even more afraid, so I continued. "Mother, you will just love flying. You will feel just like a bird on wings, and it won't take very long at all to get there. I promise."

"I don't know," she said, "I'm scared. I've never been on an airplane," she said, with doubt.

I had to smile and reassure her with words.

"I'm sure you will just love it like I do. Just you wait and see."

I took Mama to a specialist that I knew who took x-rays and found her hip ball and socket was almost completely gone. She would have to have surgery if she was to get any relief. The doctor tried to get us scheduled in at St. Petersburg, but they were booked until a year later. Not many places were available in the East or South for this kind of surgery in 1977.

After many calls, the doctor finally got us an appointment at Durham, North Carolina, at the Duke University Medical Center. We were to see a Dr. McLaughlin for the surgery. The next question was how could we get Mama all the way to Durham.

My sister-in-law, Reba, and brother George, finally decided that we needed to rent an RV so that Mother could lie down all the way.

My brother could not take off from work for a very long time, so Reba and I rented a Winnebago from a man I knew on Cocoa Beach, and set off for Durham, North Carolina.

Neither of us had ever driven such a large vehicle (the RV was a 28 foot behemoth) but we were determined that we could do it.

We arrived in Durham without any problems, found a parking place just outside of town and took Mama to her appointment the next day.

Duke University Medical Center is a huge, imposing structure outside, and just as imposing on the inside, with its many corridors; and Dr. McLaughlin was a very imposing man himself.

Extremely pleasant and thorough, but he was hesitant to do the surgery on Mama.

He told us she had only a 50 / 50 chance of surviving the surgery. I told him my mother was a very strong woman, but that I couldn't say to go ahead without him telling her what her chances were. He said that part of her problem was her weight.

She was much too overweight and that made her risks even higher.

I also told him again that my mother had an iron will and she needed to make the decision herself if she wanted to take the risk.

He agreed to tell her the facts. As he summoned the nurse to bring mother back into the room, I smiled to myself, thinking that he didn't have any idea just what he was in for.

"Mrs. Jarrells, your first name is Etta Mae, correct?"

"Yes sir, my name is Etta Mae. You are the one that is going to fix my hip, aren't you?" Mother was always direct. No fussy words.

"Well, yes, but I need to tell you what might happen. You see, you are very overweight, which can cause a big problem with your heart during the surgery." He hesitated, but before he could say more, mother interrupted.

"And just what is wrong with my heart? I've got a good heart!" she blurted indignantly.

At 154 pounds and just 5 feet tall, the doctor's concern was warranted. "I can lose some weight once I get fixed, doctor." Mother insisted.

"But that is the problem now, Etta Mae. You must lose the weight first, because to do the surgery now, you have only a 50 / 50 chance of surviving the surgery. Your heart is a bit weak, also due to the weight."

Dr. McLaughlin was speaking to mother with great concern, but Mama was not taking to his words.

I saw it coming, but the doctor had no clue. She had set her mouth in the tight, thin line before she spoke to him again.

"You listen to me, young man! I've left my home in Indiana, went to Florida, and now I'm here in Durham, North Carolina, sitting in your hospital. I came here to have this surgery and I can tell you I'm not going to die. And furthermore, I'll eat nothing but lettuce after the surgery. I'll lose the weight if that's what I must do, but get this straight, I'm not going home, or anywhere else for that matter, until I get the surgery. Do you understand? I can't take this constant pain any longer!"

Dr. McLaughlin grew pale and looked to Reba and me in exasperation. I had to speak up, and looked to Reba to back me up.

"Dr. McLaughlin," I said cautiously, "please understand our mother is her own person, and if this is what she wants, I assure you we agree with her. It is her choice."

"That's right, doctor, I speak for her son George, my husband. She has the right to choose."

Reba put her arm around Mama's shoulder and said to her, "Mom, Ruby and I agree with you. If this is your choice, we stand behind you. We will call George and David and tell them what the doctor has said and your decision."

Mama looked at me; I nodded my head, then at Reba, and then to the doctor.

"Can we get it done tomorrow, doctor?" Mama asked condescendingly. Dr. McLaughlin hesitated for a moment before he spoke again with much concern.

"Yes, I can schedule you for admittance for tomorrow. But first, you must also know that after the surgery you will have to spend approximately four weeks in rehabilitation. You will be moved to that building as soon as you can tolerate the pressure of standing on your hip. Because of your weight and age, that will probably be a week."

It was evident that Mama's mind was racing a mile a minute and she refused to believe she wasn't going to be able to walk in a few days. I could see her mind was made up and nothing was going to keep her from walking.

"I don't think I will be needing rehabilitation for a month! Whatever I have to do, you can just tell me and I'll do it. I'll talk it over with the Creator and he will see me through. I'm ready right now."

Dr. McLaughlin was not exactly sure as to how to continue, so he beckoned his nurse to take Mama from the room and see if there was a bed available for her. After she left the room, the doctor took a very deep breath, and then said to us with a little irritation.

"I see your mother does have a mind of her own. I'm sure she thinks she won't need physical therapy, but she will. We have never had a patient who did not, but I will start the therapy as soon as she leaves surgery."

I thanked the doctor, but I could not help but let him know that my mother was not just being cantankerous.

"Doctor, we thank you for your patience, and do try to understand, our mother is a very strong woman. She has been through much in her life and has never given into adversity. You may be surprised at her ability to conquer all odds."

The doctor just smiled at me and Reba.

"Well, let's hope for the best, but again, I must warn you, it is a very difficult surgery. Many younger people have a very hard time adjusting. You must also be prepared should she not make it through."

I only nodded my head that I understood, never, ever, for a moment did I believe she would not make it.

The day of the surgery was a long, long day. The surgery was taking longer than expected, but I did not feel anxious about it. I knew everything was going to be alright. Finally, the doctor appeared wearing his green ops clothing, and a big smile on his face.

"Your mother is just fine. She did just wonderful in the surgery, even though I had to replace the ball and socket and the bone that attaches to the spine. We have placed her leg in a sling and I told her in the recover room she needed to keep it moving back and forth when she got back to her room. I don't know if she will remember that, but you can see that she does this. It could be a little painful, but it will help her walk sooner."

The doctor turned to leave, hesitated, turned around and with a very quizzical look on his face said, "Oh yes. I have to tell you what your mother said to me before surgery. She said, 'Doctor, you don't have to be afraid because I have asked the Creator to let you do a good job on me, and to not let you have shaky hands.' Can you believe that?" I just shook my head and smiled.

At that moment, a gurney bearing Mama came into the room where we were waiting. True to the doctor's words, Mama's leg was in a sling and she was swinging it back and forth. On seeing this, the doctor's mouth flew open in surprise.

"Just look at you, Etta Mae. You did remember what I told you." Mama just smiled sweetly at him, then said to Reba and me.

"It doesn't hurt anymore. Not even swinging it; doesn't make it hurt."

I thought to myself, 'that's because you're sedated.'

A few days later we went home. I had to get back to work at Cape Kennedy, and Reba had a job that she had to get back to, also. When we left Mama at the hospital she was still swinging her leg. The doctor came in before we left and said that she was amazing, and he had hopes for a short stay in rehab because she was doing so well.

One week later I got a call from doctor McLaughlin.

"Ruby,' he said, "your mother is the most amazing woman I've ever seen. She has completely fooled everyone in the hospital."

"What it is, doctor?" How is she 'really' doing?' I asked tongue in cheek, for now I envisioned all sorts of things.

"Unbelievable! Your mother has been walking with only a walker, up and down the halls of the hospital for the last three days." He laughed. "She is about to drive us all to drink. She is so anxious to come home."

"She is walking on her own? Is she in rehab?"

"No, she is here in the hospital. We can't believe her ability to walk like she does. She does not need to go to rehab. You can come get her as soon as you can."

"Okay, I will come and get her." I too, was a little amazed.

Mother stayed with me and sometimes with George and Reba for the next three months. She became so restless that we had to finally agree to let her go home. I took her as far as Atlanta, transferred her to another plane and had David meet her in Evansville. She left with the doctor's instructions that she should not climb stairs for some time. She needed to sleep downstairs.

Of course, Mama being Mama, she did not move her bedroom downstairs, but continued to climb the stairs, assuring everyone she would not fall, and she did not.

She did not change anything about her life except to do as she said she would. She ate lots of lettuce and lost twenty-five pounds, which helped her new hip and heart.

Six pain free years passed for Etta Mae after her hip surgery. It seemed even the arthritis in her hands and feet were even better. She continued to take care of her house and herself with a lot of help from my brother David's wife, Dorothy, and his three children. During this time, I was working for a large motel chain as a Relief Manager. This position kept me moving about the country. While in Louisville, Kentucky (90 miles from Evansville), I decided to take a few days off work and go visit my mother.

I arrived at her door about noon and after knocking many times with no answer, I let myself in with the key that Mother had given me, years prior. I was worried that perhaps she was not able to come to the door.

I searched through the house downstairs and saw no sign of her. I was about to go upstairs when out of the corner of my eyes I noticed the expansion ladder positioned directly in front of the back kitchen window. I froze because I knew that could only mean one thing: Mother had climbed the ladder to the upstairs.

I cautiously walked around the house, and sure enough, there on the ladder was my 86 year old mother, cleaning out the gutter on the 3rd story of her house. I was suspended into a state of utter fear. What to do, I thought. If I call her name suddenly, she might lose her balance and fall. I stood beneath the ladder quietly and finally she turned and saw me standing below her. All she said to me was, "what are you doing here?"

I had to smile at her indignation.

"I came to visit with you, Mama." I answered, shaking in my shoes. "Can you come down, please?"

I held my breath as she slowly started descending the ladder. Once she reached the ground, she turned to me and matter-of-factly stated, "I was done anyway. Looks like I spoiled a few birds and their nesting place. They just seem to love my gutters. Every year they try again, and every year I have to clean out their nests. They just never learn."

Mama ended with a big laugh, as I gave her a big hug and received one back with a kiss.

"I guess those birds are like some people I know; they just keep trying." I had to laugh now, happy to know she was once again safe.

"Mother, why didn't you just get someone to clean your gutters? It's much too dangerous for you to climb that ladder. A fall would put you in a wheelchair, or worse."

"Yes, I know that!" I had irritated her. "I called Mr. Radar and he said he would do it, but he just kept putting me off. The rainy season is coming and I just couldn't wait any longer, so I did it myself. Besides, I'm not going to fall. You worry too much."

Mama laughed heartily at me and my fears and walked to the back porch steps, where she climbed five more stairs, and promptly plumped herself down on the back porch swing.

My company transferred me soon after that to several places in Texas and then to Las Vegas, Nevada. During this time of two years, Mama had her first stroke, which left her in a wheelchair, and partially paralyzed.

I got a call from my niece that Mother needed my help. I took a leave of absence, graciously given to me by my Regional Manager, and took off again for Evansville.

I found my mother disgusted with her handicap, but pleased to see me. I told her I was going to be with until she was better. This seemed to help her determination to overcome her disability. In the next several months she would experience many little TIAS and then another stroke.

Fortunately, we were at her doctor's office directly across the street from the Welborn Hospital, where she got immediate attention. She would later undergo strenuous rehabilitation, and was ablc to walk with a walker and I was allowed to take her home.

The doctor did warn me that she really should go to a nursing home, but I just couldn't fathom doing that to her because her house, home and freedom meant so much to her.

It was during this time that my Aunt Rose came to live with my mother. She had lost most of her eyesight by this time and could no longer live in the retirement home in Mt. Vernon, Indiana.

CHAPTER TWENTY-TWO

1982 – 1987

THE CROSSING

WHEN I ARRIVED AT MOTHER'S IN 1982, I FOUND ETTA MAE'S HOUSE NEEDING A LOT OF REPAIRS AND REDECORATING. WITH MOTHER'S CONSENT AND APPROVAL OF NECESSARY CHANGES, WE MANAGE TO PUT THE HOUSE BACK IN GOOD CONDITION. HER HOUSE WAS NOW BEAUTIFUL AGAIN AND SHE WAS REALLY PLEASED WITH WHAT WE HAD BEEN ABLE TO DO, BUT SHE WAS GROWING MORE AND MORE DEPENDENT FOR PHYSICAL HELP.

She resented the fact that she had to have helped to take a bath, getting in and out of bed and any other chores she attempted.

This dependency began to change her disposition from one of pleasantry to hostile and combative.

The doctor had warned me again and again that I had to put her in a nursing home, that she was not safe and neither was anyone in the house with her.

"She really is not responsible for her actions because she does not remember what she says or does for any longer than a minute."

It finally became evident that I had to adhere to the doctor and his warnings.

In the following years, my mother would be in and out of the hospital many times, following them into a new nursing facility after each stay. She would reside in five different nursing homes before her death in 1987.

Throughout these five years she would maintain her dignity and the will to overcome her disabilities so she could go home. Never once did she give in, but fought to recover each and every day.

In the last six months of my mother's life, she began to call me Alice, her mother's name. I tried to make her understand that I was her daughter, but she would just smile and point to my picture and say, "no, that's my daughter, there in that picture."

I finally gave in and took to answering her when she would ask me, "where is Papa, and what is he doing," to being my grandmother Alice to satisfy her.

On one of these many visits, mother motioned for me to lean over her bed because she wanted to tell me something important. So I humored her.

She spoke confidently, but clandestinely, "I'm getting so tired of all this life as it is now. You must be strong like the sun and never let up. You must pass your strength onto your children, like our Grandmother did for me. Never forget where you came from, the ways of our people, for they are good. Everyday you must honor our Creator and He will always see you through the hard times. Then you will be blessed."

On the night of her passing she told her nurse at the eight o'clock bed check that "tonight's the night."

Her nurse later told me she had no idea what Etta Mae meant, but at the ten o'clock bed check, she found Etta Mae with arms crossed, Indian style, in a deep sleep, but on further checking, she found that Etta Mae had passed over with dignity.

Each and every night I hear her words, knowing that they were from Grandmother Morning Star, "for this is my heritage … this is my strength … this is my honor."

Etta Mae, 1987

EPILOGUE

I CANNOT FINISH THIS BOOK WITHOUT ADDRESSING THE SO-CALLED TRIBAL-CARD, THAT IS TO PROVE ONE IS OF INDIAN BLOOD.

It is one of the most hurtful pieces of paper that the Government of the United States initiated. It is horrendous and a virtual yoke around our necks, but many would be thrilled to have one.

However, it seems the card is very elusive for those Indians whose ancestors were not listed on the original roles of their tribes.

There are millions of us, around every corner, down every street and road, unidentified, lost in a world of confusion.

Who are we you might ask? We really don't know, for scattered throughout the world we have no power, no card, no real ties, only our souls crying out to be recognized. We have NO CARD telling us we belong to a certain group. What we do know is that we are an intelligent, multi-talented people, the mixed bloods – the French call us METIS'.

Many of our grandparents and great-grandparents lived outside the RESERVATION, some out of fear, some out of necessity and some because of being born wherever our mother was at the time of our birth. Most of our parents were afraid of being recognized, passing as white, because they did not "LOOK LIKE AN INDIAN."

The Federal Government forced this ethnic cleansing upon we mixed bloods.

Many mixed bloods don't fit the movie stereotype with our sometimes fair complexions, our light brown, blond or red hair; but the truth is we know our hearts, we are of the land, the Mother Earth. We are the Creator's people!

We are not pagan and never have been. We have always known of the GREAT MYSTERY, the CREATOR of the world.

Another appalling fact is that a great majority of the white world still see us as lazy, drunks, uneducated or living off the government. Or, to the other extreme, the government takes care of us. Many people believe that all Indians receive thousands of dollars to live on the reservation; or, that we get money from the gaming world.

While it is true that gaming has been the road for many of the tribes to have better schools, gainful employment and good housing, it is just a drop in the bucket. There are hundreds of tribes that are not in the gaming business and cannot get a contract to do so.

Most Reservations are poverty stricken with no jobs and with hundreds of children and elders without food. They have poor housing, many with dirt floors, no heat, and no water or toilet facilities. It is an abomination that we, the richest country in the world, cannot address this problem better.

Our government is willing to spend money to fight a war and refurbish a foreign nation to the tune of billions of dollars, but it allows it own people to struggle in abject poverty.

This is a true travesty of justice.

The BLOOD QUANTUM forced on every tribe by the Federal Government means nothing to a "REAL INDIAN." He or she know who or what they are; people with love for their families, people with integrity, people loyal to their ancestry, loyal to the Creator and to this land from whence we came.

Too many of we mixed bloods are still hiding and it is time we stand up and be counted. There is power in numbers. We must be proud of our heritage and not be afraid to change our voices from saying "those people" to "our people", then we can truly say … THIS IS OUR NATIVE LAND!

BIBLIOGRAPHY

Debo, Angie. "A History of the Indians of the United States", Norman University of Oklahoma, 1970.

Josephy, Alvin M., Jr. ed. "The American Heritage Book of Indians", New York, American Heritage Publishing Co., 1060.

Coit, Margaret L., "Andrew Jackson", Boston, Mass. Houghton Muffin, 1965.

Tuner, Katherine C., "Red Men Calling on the Great White Father", Norman University, Oklahoma.

Blackbird, Andrew J., "Ypsilanti", Ypsilanti Job Printing House, 1887.

Lumpkin, Wilson, "The Removal of the Cherokee Indians from Georgia", New York, Dood Mead, 1907.

Kloplenstein, Carl Grover, "Westward Ho; Removal of the Ohio Shawnees, 1832 – 33", Bulletin of the Historical and Philosophical Society of Ohio, vol. 15 (1957).

Kellog, Louise P., "The Removal of the Winnebego", (1984).

Creek Nation East of the Mississippi, Inc., "The Creek Nation East of the Mississippi", Poarch – Switch, Ala. 1972.

Foreman, Grant, Indian Removal, Norman University of Oklahoma, 1953, -- "Indian and Pioneers", 1936.

McKee, Irving, ed. "The Trail of Death", Letters of Benjamin Marie Petit, Indianapolis, Indiana Historical Society, 1941.

American State paper (Gales and Seaton), Washington, D.C., 1832 – 1800, "Military Affairs", vol. 7.

Gabriel, Ralph Henry, Elias Boudinot, "Cherokee", Norman University of Oklahoma, 1941.

Prucha, Francis Paul, "Indian Removal and the Great American Desert", Indian Magazine of History, vol. 59.

Ewers, John C., "The Blackfeet, Raiders on The Northwestern Plains", University of Oklahoma Press, Norman Publishing Div., 1958.

Reader's Digest, "Through Indian Eyes, The Untold Story of Native Americans", New York, (1955 Staff)

Van Bibber, Rosabelle, Farmer, Baker, "Personal Accounts of Life with Grandma Jane (Morning Star), Mother Alice Dean White, (Little White Dove Flying-Dovie) Uncle Greyfox, Papa Benjamin, Father J.P. Van Bibber and Brother Clarence Van Bibber and Houston Van Bibber and Family".

Aldredge, Louise, "Personal Accounts of Life with Aunt Etta and her Family".

Greenwell, Verna Rose, Uniontown, Ky., "Personal Account of Mother Ethel Dickerson and Family".

Myrtle, John and Annie Mae Johnson, Indianapolis, In., "Personal Accounts of Life on the Dickerson & Van Bibber Farms, The story of their trip from Montana," by Grandmother Morning Star.

Van Bibber, Dickerson, Hutchinson, Castle, Jarrells, Etta Mae: "Life Story as told to Author, Ruby H. Happel-Holtz".

Fry, Peter & Fiona, "History of Ireland", Barnes & Noble, 1988.

Dudley, Edward R., "Church and State in Tudor Ireland", Dublin, 1935.

Dudley and Williams, T.D., "The Great Famine", Dublin, 1956.

Hughes, K., "The Church in Early Irish Society", Cambridge, 1956.

Lechy, W.E.H., "A History of Ireland in the 18th Century", London, 1892.

Open, G.H., "Ireland Under the Normans", 4 vols., Oxford, 1911 – 1920.